An Introduction to Epistemology

JACK S. CRUMLEY II
University of San Diego

For my Mom and Dad

Library of Congress Cataloging-in-Publication Data
Crumley, Jack S.
  An introduction to epistemology / Jack S. Crumley II.
    p. cm.
  Includes bibliographical references and index.
  ISBN 0-7674-0008-9
  1. Knowledge, Theory of. I. Title.
BD161.C74 1998
121—dc21   98-3556
                                                                            CIP

Manufactured in the United States of America

10 9 8 7 6 5 4 3 2 1

Mayfield Publishing Company
1280 Villa Street
Mountain View, California 94041

Sponsoring editor, Ken King; *production editor,* Carla White Kirschenbaum; *maunscript editor,* Tom Briggs; *text and cover designer,* Donna Davis; *design manager,* Jean Mailander; *manufacturing manager,* Randy Hurst. The text was set in 10/13 Garamond by Archetype Book Composition and printed on 45# Highland Plus by Malloy Lithographing, Inc.

Cover image: Scala/Art Resource, NY.

♲ This book is printed on recycled paper

Contents

CHAPTER FIVE

Structure and Sources of Justification: Coherence Theory   121

Preface

I did not set out to write a textbook. My original intent was only to provide my students with some additional material that would make the textbooks we were using more accessible. Indeed, my students referred to that material as an extended handout. Once the idea of writing a textbook in epistemology did arise, I was guided by the same desires and aims that animated that original extended handout.

First, I wanted a text that did not presume a substantial philosophical background on the part of students, and I wanted to do something more than just gesture in this direction. My classes are typically a diverse lot— advanced majors, majors and minors who are just beginning their course-work, and a few students who have found their previous, brief exposure to philosophy intriguing. Thus, I have tried to remain aware of where new ideas or concepts arise in the text, regardless of whether it is the first or last chapter, and develop the material with sufficient patience. My aim in doing so was to have all students on an equal conceptual footing as they worked through the more challenging arguments of the chapters. As an aid to students, key concepts are listed at the end of each chapter and appear in the Glossary at the end of the book.

I have, perhaps, included more on the history of epistemology than some texts do. The chapters on skepticism, a priori knowledge, and perception use historically prominent positions to develop the main lines of argument. I am inclined to think that even the more contemporary issues in epistemology, such as internalism and externalism or the naturalization of epistemology, can make more sense to students if seen against the back-drop of historical positions.

At the same time, I wanted the students to see some of the subtlety, richness, and complexity of epistemology. Each chapter presents the more central, if more challenging, arguments. Although I wanted the students to be prepared to encounter these arguments, I thought it important that they see the main lines of argument in some depth. I have, however, tried to refrain from overburdening students. Arguments and counterarguments in epistemology can and do go on for a very long time, but I did not want students to lose sight of the central lines of dispute. This approach, of course, involved some selectivity on my part. My hope has been to produce a text that would enable interested students to turn to the original works, whether historical texts or recent books and journal articles, and genuinely benefit from reading those works. For those students wishing to pursue not only the arguments in the text in their original setting and finer detail, but also related issues, the end of each chapter provides a briefly annotated For Further Study section. The annotation indicates the relevance of the cited work to the chapter and in most cases the author's position.

The boxed material in each chapter subserves all of the above aims, as well as others. In some cases, the boxes explain certain terms in more detail without interrupting the flow of the text; they provide further information on positions that are only briefly covered in the text; they draw connections between the topic under discussion and other topics in the book; and on occasion, they serve to introduce topics in areas that fall outside the main lines of discussion in epistemology.

Finally, I hoped to produce a text that would be hospitable to instructors of differing philosophical persuasions and that would allow them to develop the course as they desired. This hope is reflected in two ways. I have tried to keep most of my own leanings in the background as much as possible, although it is doubtless inevitable that my choice of topics and the presentation of the material reflect some of my sympathies. (I must, however, have been at least partly successful; one of the reviewers thought my view on one of the principal dividing lines in epistemology was the opposite of what it in fact is!) Second, I have not tried to resolve or settle the major issues for the students, but rather provide them with the resources to come to their own understanding of the direction the argument should take. In any case, the text can be used in a class that emphasizes either a more historical or a contemporary approach to epistemology, or, of course, a course that links both approaches.

I suppose my real desire, however, was a text that students can read on their own and come away, not only with some understanding of the issues in epistemology, but also with an understanding of how and why those issues arose and the challenges that confront the principal positions in epistemology.

I first want to thank Ken King for even imagining that I might do this. I also want to thank the reviewers of this text: Tim McGrew, Western Michigan University; Frederick F. Schmitt, University of Illinois at Urbana Champaign; G. Randolph Mayes, California State University Sacramento; and Heather J. Gert, Texas A & M University. Their painstaking generosity made this a better text. My colleagues have endured me these past few months, and for that I am grateful. I am especially grateful to my colleague Linda Peterson who read early drafts of two chapters. I could not have managed without the patience and assistance of Leeanna Cummings, our department secretary. But mostly I want to thank my Dad and Mom, who made this possible, and my Mom for her encouragement, patience, and faith.

Introduction

In the late eighteenth century, a bit of a dispute was brewing. Many scientists, following Isaac Newton (1642–1727), had become convinced that the only appropriate method for arriving at knowledge about the world was to formulate generalizations based on observation and the results of experiments. This method forbade making hypotheses about unobserved properties or objects; it forbade the sort of scientific theorizing with which we are now so familiar. Although others had previously invoked unobservables as elements in explanations of various phenomena, beginning in the mid-eighteenth century, a handful of scientists began to dispute seriously that generalization from observation was the only appropriate method for acquiring knowledge about the world. In particular, these scientists thought that the cause of science could be advanced by postulating, or assuming, the existence of unobserved entities. According to this new method, a scientist would formulate hypotheses about unobserved entities—for example, that light is composed of waves. These unobserved entities would explain observed phenomena. To test these hypotheses, the scientist would deduce or draw certain conclusions from the hypotheses. The conclusions would then be tested by performing experiments. Successful experiments provided evidence or confirmation for the hypothesis, and thus evidence for the existence of the unobserved entities.

At issue during the latter half of the eighteenth and into the nineteenth century was whether this new hypothetical method was a legitimate method for obtaining knowledge. By the end of the nineteenth century, advocates of the hypothetical method had triumphed. The hypothetical method was thus recognized as a legitimate means of acquiring knowledge about the world.[1] This historical anecdote illustrates the type of dispute that is central to *epistemology*.

THE AIMS OF EPISTEMOLOGY

Epistemology is a *normative* discipline. Unlike psychology or sociology, which merely describe and explain how we acquire our beliefs, epistemology attempts to identify the principles for evaluation of our beliefs. The evaluative or normative task of epistemology is perhaps its most characteristic feature. But evaluation implies that we have some goal or aim in mind. We might, for example, evaluate a voice mail system as unsatisfactory because it fails to get messages to their intended recipients—and, of course, the goal of the system is to get messages to the right people.

Similarly, epistemology evaluates beliefs with respect to particular goals. Of the different ways of characterizing the aim of epistemology, two appear central in historical and contemporary epistemological discussions. One frequent characterization of an epistemological goal is the acquisition of true beliefs and the avoidance of false beliefs. In this view, then, a way to describe the aim of epistemology is the identification of principles for evaluation of beliefs, with respect to the goal of acquiring true beliefs and avoiding false ones. This description will not quite do, however. There is a long tradition in epistemology that focuses on the *reasons* for our beliefs. According to this view, it is not enough that we acquire true beliefs; we must also have adequate reasons for thinking that such beliefs are likely to be true. The assessment of the adequacy or soundness of our reasons for believing is an integral part of a very traditional view of epistemology. As we will see, these two views of the aim of epistemology can conflict and have been the source of many disputes. We would like a general characterization of epistemology that does not prejudge the issue. One way to think of this is that the aim of epistemology is to identify principles of evaluation of whether there is adequate reason to think that our beliefs are likely to be true. Notice that we leave open what counts as an adequate reason. Different interpretations of "adequate reason" lead to markedly different epistemological theories.

We can use this rather general characterization of epistemology to identify the particular *epistemic* concepts that are of special interest to epistemologists. These two concepts are knowledge and justified belief. Theories of knowledge and justification, the special province of epistemologists, provide analyses of these concepts. That is, epistemologists attempt to identify the characteristics or properties in virtue of which a person can be said to know or have a justified belief. Not all of our beliefs have these properties. Some beliefs are the result of wishful or confused thinking; some are the result of hunches or "intuition." We typically do not think that there is adequate reason for the likely truth of such beliefs; at best, they turn out to be true as a result of a set of happy coincidences. Beliefs that are justified, however, have certain characteristics by virtue of which they are epistemically legitimate. There is something about the belief—either the way in which it was acquired or the evidence or reasons for it—that explains why that belief is acceptable.

Now, you might wonder why epistemology is a discipline worthy of interest. The historical anecdote that began this section is fundamentally an epistemological debate. At the center of that debate was the issue of whether a certain method of inquiry adequately satisfied the standards necessary for knowledge. Whether this particular debate has previously engaged your attention, you undoubtedly have engaged in epistemological assessments. Think for a moment of the kinds of beliefs or claims that call for your evaluation on a daily basis: the belief that secondhand smoke is dangerous; the belief that repressed memories are reliable; your friend's belief that reservations at the restaurant won't be necessary; the claim of a supermarket or television tabloid that another celebrity marriage is in trouble; your belief that you have plenty of time to get to your chosen destination. We continually make differential assessments of our beliefs. We think that some of them are definitely true, some are likely to be true, and some are highly unlikely to be true. We think that some are based on good reasons and some are not. In a sense, we are involved with a bit of homespun epistemology every day. Epistemology attempts to articulate, clarify, systematize, and defend the principles of belief evaluation at work in our homespun epistemology. Of course, as a result of our epistemological theorizing, we may find that we change our evaluation of certain beliefs. We might also find that our theorizing is constrained by homespun assessments. But this is only the natural interplay of theory and practice. We might escape epistemology, but we cannot escape epistemological judgments.

Identification of the principles of belief evaluation tells us, among other things, the sources and conditions of knowledge and justified belief. It is worth noting the controversy over whether these principles are the sort of principles that can be employed by individuals in the revision of their beliefs. For example, if I accept the principle that honesty is the best policy, this policy guides my behavior. It shapes my decisions about what I will do and refrain from doing. It is a matter of some dispute whether epistemological principles, although evaluative in nature, are like the principle regarding honesty.

SOME IMPORTANT CONCEPTS

Our characterization of epistemology comes to this: Epistemology attempts to identify principles of evaluation for our beliefs, with respect to the adequacy of the reason for thinking that our beliefs are likely to be true. Such principles identify the properties in virtue of which a belief is justified or counts as knowledge. Another way of thinking of this identification of properties is as a kind of conceptual analysis.

Concepts refer to or pick out certain properties or objects. For example, my concept of a university refers to some things and not to others. The place where I teach is a university; the restaurant where I occasionally dine is not. Now, suppose I was given the task of explaining the concept of a university. What properties or characteristics should I cite? Having a library? Being accredited? Being expensive? Perhaps you get the idea. My task would be to explain the properties by virtue of which something is a university. If I completed this task successfully, my analysis of the concept of university would allow me to pick out all and only those things that are universities. If a restaurant counted as a university on my analysis, or if Stanford failed to count as one, then you would rightly be suspicious of my analysis.

The idea that an analysis of a concept provides the properties that pick out all and only things of a certain kind is sometimes characterized as providing **necessary and sufficient conditions** of a concept. Necessary conditions are like minimum requirements. A necessary condition of being president of the United States is being at least thirty-five years of age. Somewhat more technically, A is a necessary condition of B if and only if B cannot occur without the occurrence of A. But sufficient conditions are enough to bring about a particular event or property. That is, it is a sufficient condition of being president-elect of the United States that one gets a majority of the votes cast by the Electoral College. More technically, A is a sufficient condition of B if and only if whenever A occurs, B also occurs.

Epistemologists sometimes conceive their task as articulating the necessary and sufficient conditions of the concepts of knowledge and justified belief. In Chapter Two, we will be especially concerned with this type of analysis of the concept of knowledge. Often, however, we will confront positions that claim that a certain condition is or is not a necessary condition of the relevant concept. Note that it is controversial whether we can identify the necessary and sufficient conditions of the concept of knowledge. Our concept of knowledge, it is argued, is too imprecise to be analyzed in this way. There are too many borderline cases of knowledge, as well as too divergent a set of contexts in which we employ the term, to be able to single out any identifiable set of properties that uniquely characterize the concept of knowledge. Nevertheless, attempts at analyzing the concept bring out certain aspects of our concept that might otherwise go undetected.

We have already made extensive use of the concept of belief, and it will be worthwhile to say something about that notion. As we will use the concept, *beliefs* are mental states that have a particular content; this content represents some object as having some property or characteristic. Beliefs, then, are representational states by virtue of their having certain contents. Typically, the contents of the beliefs—what the beliefs are about—are described by means of propositions, and these propositions represent certain states of affairs or features of the world. Thus, for example, my belief that the coffee is cold represents the coffee as having a certain property, that of being cold. By virtue of their propositional content, beliefs can be either true or false. That is, they can represent things either correctly or incorrectly. If Sam believes that the ball is in the backyard, then his belief is either true or false, depending on whether the ball is actually in the backyard.

In the sense that we are using the term "belief," it probably comes close to the more common use of the term "opinion." But the present concept of belief should be distinguished from the notion of belief in which beliefs are opinions for which there is no evidence. That is, the concept of belief is sometimes used as a synonym for something like "accepting on faith." But there are certainly beliefs for which there is little or no evidence. Sara's belief that her ticket has the winning numbers for the lottery is a belief that has virtually no evidence for it. But this lack of evidence is not a necessary condition of belief. Indeed, all of us have beliefs for which we have a great deal of evidence. In fact, the present notion of belief also leaves open the possibility that some beliefs are instances of knowledge.

We have already mentioned the concept of justification or justified belief, but we need to say more about it, because this concept is central to much of the discussion in the text. Think for a moment of why we might call a certain action "justified." You lock your door at night because you believe it is safer. Locking the door is justified because you have good reason for thinking that it will help you achieve a certain goal—for example, having a restful and secure night's sleep. We can abstract from this simple example a schema for thinking of justified belief. A belief is justified if there is good reason to think that it is likely to achieve a certain goal. Now, recall that the acquisition of true beliefs is one characterization of our epistemic goal. Thus, a belief is justified if there is good or adequate reason to think that it is true or, at least, likely to be true. As we noted, there is some dispute about the nature of "good reasons." But at least historically, epistemologists thought that an individual or epistemic agent could cite the reasons for the belief. This historical view has been subject to recent criticism, as subsequent chapters will explain.

There is perhaps an intuitive connection between justified beliefs and rationality. In fact, some epistemologists hold that rationality is a necessary condition of justified belief. Roughly, a belief is rational if there are good reasons for it and those reasons are used in an appropriate way. This is, of course, a highly schematic account of rationality, but perhaps it provides the core features of the notion.

Although we have been focusing on introducing specific terms, we might take a moment to introduce two further concepts that identify two venerable traditions in epistemology, rationalism and empiricism. Each tradition has a general view of the nature of the epistemic legitimacy of our beliefs. **Empiricism** is the view that none of our beliefs about the world are instances of knowledge or justified belief unless those beliefs derive from information gained in sensory experience. Empiricists hold that our five senses—vision, hearing, smell, taste, and feel—are the door to knowledge. It is ultimately by means of the operations of the senses that we come to know that the coffee is cold or that the leaves have turned brown or that quarks are flavored. Thus, empiricism holds that all of our knowledge, if we have any, must arise from *sense* experience. **Rationalism** is the view that the epistemic legitimacy of some of our beliefs depends not on sense experience, but on the operation of reason. Rationalists often hold that some of our knowledge is *innate*, that everyone, regardless of their particular experiences, has such knowledge.

A related issue that sometimes divides empiricists from rationalists is the existence of a priori knowledge. Although Chapter Eight explores this topic in greater detail, the distinction will arise in other chapters, and it will be helpful to have an approximation of the concepts. *A posteriori knowledge* is, roughly, knowledge that depends on our sense experience. I could not know that the radio is on unless I had a certain sense experience—say, hearing the music or seeing an indicator light. *A priori knowledge* is knowledge that I could have independently of the senses. An uncontroversial example of a priori knowledge is that all bachelors are unmarried. A more contentious example is that all events have a cause. As might be expected, rationalists frequently claim that we do have a priori knowledge, while empiricists frequently doubt the existence of at least certain kinds of a priori knowledge.

This brief survey of various concepts provides an initial terminological background to begin our survey of various epistemological issues and theories. Like all good inquiring minds, you no doubt want to know what you might encounter in the subsequent pages. The next section gives a brief outline of what you will find.

LOOKING FORWARD

A Brief Outline

It might seem ironic that while epistemologists are concerned with identifying the conditions under which an agent might be said to know or have a justified belief, they have also been extremely concerned with showing that we do in fact have knowledge and justified beliefs. Often, the motivation of epistemologists is simply to defend this claim that we do have knowledge or justification. Doubts about whether we have knowledge or justified belief are referred to as skeptical doubts. In many ways, the issue of skepticism frames much epistemological debate. Skeptical worries and responses to those worries are the topic of Chapter One. An important feature of this chapter is that it provides us with an initial sense of certain conceptions of knowledge and justified belief.

Chapter Two takes up the more analytic task of explaining three contemporary theories of knowledge. The chapter begins with a particular analysis of the concept of knowledge and explains a type of objection to this analysis that leads to the development of the three theories.

In Chapter Three, our attention shifts to the topic of justification. We begin by explaining another contemporary and influential view of the nature of knowledge, reliabilism. But the bulk of the chapter is devoted to the reliabilist theory of justification.

Theories of justification are at the center of Chapters Four and Five, where we consider two prominent approaches to the theory of justified belief. Chapter Four examines foundationalist theories of justification, while Chapter Five examines two prominent coherentist theories of justified belief.

In Chapters Six and Seven, we take up more general theoretical issues concerning the types of conditions or factors that are relevant to our understanding of the nature of justification and knowledge. Along with the distinction between foundationalism and coherentism, the distinction between internalism and externalism is now seen as one of the central dividing lines in epistemology. In Chapter Six, we begin with two characterizations of internalism and then consider two attempts to reconcile internalist and externalist approaches to epistemology.

Closely connected to the internalism/externalism controversy is the recent attempt to naturalize epistemology, the view that epistemology is continuous with natural science. Chapter Seven considers the fundamental differences between traditional and naturalized epistemology and examines whether there is reason to prefer naturalized to traditional epistemology or whether some more conciliatory approach might be adopted.

In Chapters Eight and Nine, we return to consideration of two sources of knowledge and justified belief. In Chapter Eight, we examine theories of a priori knowledge. Chapter Nine considers various accounts of the epistemic legitimacy of our perceptual beliefs, beliefs that we acquire as a result of the operation of our senses.

Tradition and Revision

An issue that looms large in this text is the contrast between the approach of traditional epistemology and more revisionary contemporary approaches that seek to change our understanding of the epistemological enterprise. Although we will be developing these issues throughout, it will prove helpful to have an initial sense of this contrast.

Characterizations of traditional epistemology are a diverse lot, but it is not hard to find central themes, two in particular. First, traditional epistemology seeks to answer the question of whether we ever have good or adequate reason for thinking that our empirical beliefs, our beliefs about the world around us, are true. Second, supposing that we do have good reason for believing, the traditional epistemologist attempts to explain why the reasons are in fact good reasons.[2] The skeptic typically denies that we ever have good reason, and thus traditional epistemology is often thought to be motivated by the goal of disarming the skeptical challenge. The connection to skepticism is important because it is thought that in answering the question of whether we ever have good or adequate reasons, the traditional epistemologist can only rely on those methods or beliefs that are not disputed by the skeptic.

Perhaps no less important an aspect of traditional epistemology is that it is internalist, which is roughly the view that the factors relevant to justification or knowledge must in some way be reflected in the agent's beliefs or cognitive perspective. In Chapter Six, we will take up the issue of how this view might be elaborated, but for the moment, we can think of it as what reasons an agent might have or point to for thinking that a belief is true. In recent decades, some epistemologists have argued that the proper approach to epistemology is externalist. Again, roughly, externalism reflects the view that we look not to the agent's perspective, but to the factors that account for or explain the likely truth of an agent's beliefs. In the externalist view, the agent need have no "awareness" of such factors. Knowledge and/or justification are thus independent of the agent's perspective, and the aim of epistemology is to identify the appropriate factors. This departure from the traditional view of epistemology is dramatic and controversial, and for many, it constitutes a fundamental dividing line in the epistemological project. But before we look further at this issue, we had best begin at the traditional beginning—the challenge of skepticism.

Key Concepts

Empiricism

Necessary and sufficient conditions

Rationalism

Notes

1. This issue is discussed in more detail in Larry Laudan, *Science and Values* (Berkeley: University of California Press, 1984), pp. 55–58.

2. See Laurence BonJour, "Against Naturalized Epistemology," in Peter A. French et al., eds., *Midwest Studies in Philosophy*, Vol. XIX (Notre Dame, IN: University of Notre Dame Press, 1994), pp. 283–300, especially p. 284.

CHAPTER ONE

Skepticism

We are all familiar with the casual skeptical question. Doubts about particular claims to knowing something are part of our ordinary transactions with other human beings. You ask your roommate if she remembered to lock the door, and to her somewhat tentative "yes," you ask insistently, "Are you sure?" Or, as the two of you drive to school, you keep looking nervously at the gas gauge, noticing its proximity to the big red "E" and pleading that the car not run out of gas. When you arrive on campus, your roommate proudly announces, "I knew we'd make it," to which you can only shake your head and mutter, "You didn't *know*; you were just lucky."

Such skepticism is familiar and ordinary enough. But there is a more trenchant skepticism of the sort encountered in epistemology. This type of skepticism is characterized by the claim that all of our pretensions to knowledge in a particular area or a range of areas are merely that—pretensions. The skeptic denies that our claims to knowledge, or for that matter, justified belief, are legitimate. For example, we naturally suppose that we often acquire knowledge about the world around us. Such knowledge ranges from the mundane (my car is in the parking lot by the library) to the esoteric (energy equals mass times the speed of light squared). A skeptic about the external world would deny that we have any such knowledge. Notice that this is not simply the claim that we are sometimes mistaken in our judgments about the world. Rather, it is the much stronger claim that we are systematically mistaken about possessing such knowledge. In addition to having skeptical doubts about our knowledge of the world, we can be skeptical about our possession of, say, moral knowledge or religious knowledge. Skepticism can extend even to the justification or rationality of our beliefs.

Now, your initial temptation might be to dismiss such claims. You might insist that we obviously do know a great many things, and, moreover, that any competent person can say what they are. Indeed, it might very well seem that such skeptical claims can be of no more than academic interest. But this reaction would be unfortunate. Even if the skeptical challenge turns out to be wrong, investigating that challenge enables us to identify more clearly our conceptions of knowledge and justification. Perhaps as important, analyzing the skeptic's charge illuminates and deepens our conception of human beings as *rational* beings.

The aim of this chapter is to identify the motivation and reasons for the skeptical position. There are in fact various interpretations of skepticism,

the precise nature of the skeptic's challenge, and the legitimate responses
to skepticism. We cannot canvass all of these, but we can examine some of
the common issues raised concerning skepticism. To do this, we consider
the skeptical challenges posed by René Descartes and David Hume. We
then examine responses to the skeptic's view. This examination will serve
as the departure point for our investigation of the concepts of knowledge
and justification in the following chapters.

FIRST SKIRMISHES WITH SKEPTICISM

Modern epistemology's preoccupation with skepticism dates back to the
opening words in René Descartes's (1596–1650) *Meditations on First
Philosophy:*

> It is now some years since I detected how many were the false beliefs that I had
> from my earliest youth admitted as true, and how doubtful was everything I had
> since constructed on this basis; and from that time I was convinced that I must
> once for all seriously undertake to rid myself of all the opinions which I had for-
> merly accepted, and commence to build anew from the foundation, if I wanted
> to establish any firm and permanent structure in the sciences. . . .
>
> Now for this object it is not necessary that I should show that all of these
> [beliefs] are false—I shall perhaps never arrive at this end. But inasmuch as rea-
> son already persuades me that I ought no less carefully to withhold my assent
> from these matters which are not entirely certain and indubitable from those
> which appear to me manifestly to be false, if I am able to find in each some
> reason to doubt, this will suffice to justify my rejecting the whole . . . for owing
> to the fact that the destruction of the foundations of necessity brings with it the
> downfall of the rest of the edifice, I shall only in the first place attack those
> principles upon which all my former opinions rested.[1]

Descartes's avowed aim is to establish a permanent foundation for the
sciences. By this, he clearly means an *epistemic* foundation; that is, scientific beliefs must be based on beliefs that themselves are epistemically legitimate or justified. For Descartes, this sort of epistemic legitimacy consists
not merely in the truth of those beliefs, but in the certainty or indubitability
of such beliefs. To the extent that these fundamental beliefs are themselves
not epistemically legitimate, beliefs based on them are consequently also
epistemically suspect.

Descartes holds that we should refuse to count as knowledge any beliefs that are subject to doubt. The goal of our cognitive endeavors is indubitability or certainty, not mere likelihood or probable truth. A belief
qualifies as knowledge only if there are no grounds or reasons for doubting
that belief. Moreover, appropriate methods for arriving at our beliefs are
precisely those that lead us to indubitability. Thus, Descartes holds that the

construal of science as an empiricist and probabilistic enterprise is *methodologically* bankrupt. The *methods* that lead to putative knowledge claims are themselves suspect, because they lead to merely probable beliefs. Placing science on a *firm and lasting* foundation requires nothing less than getting rid of the methodologically bankrupt core of the science current in Descartes's day. And once the methodological basis is dispatched, *all* the beliefs held on that basis must be dispatched as well. Hence, Descartes accepts the need to dispense with all the beliefs he previously accepted.

In Descartes's view, indubitability is not merely a subjective matter of whether an agent thinks there are reasons to doubt. Rather **indubitable beliefs** involve the absence of *objective* reasons for doubting the truth of the belief. That is, there are no good reasons, independently of what the person believes or thinks, that could provide grounds for doubting. Thus, if the belief is indubitable, there is no *possible* doubt about the belief. We can compare the notion of indubitability with two other notions, infallibility and incorrigibility. **Infallible beliefs** are beliefs that cannot be mistaken or that cannot turn out to be false. **Incorrigible beliefs** are beliefs for which it is impossible to show that the person is mistaken.

These three notions—indubitability, infallibility, and incorrigibility—are independent of one another. For example, we might be unable to produce evidence showing that a person's belief is mistaken, but this need not imply that the belief *cannot* be mistaken. Whether Descartes actually thought that there was a connection between indubitability and infallibility is not our immediate concern. Contemporary responses to skepticism often consider infallibility to be the critical target.[2] In what follows, we will take Descartes to hold that a requirement for knowledge is infallibility. If the goal is infallibility, then we must find infallible methods, methods that yield infallible beliefs.

CARTESIAN SKEPTICISM

In our normal understanding, science provides us with knowledge—knowledge of the world and the nature of things, knowledge of the world's objects and their properties. The skeptic, however, wants to insist that we never have sufficient reason to think that any of our beliefs about the world are true. There is always room for doubt; we can always find some reason to suspect that the belief might in fact be false. And, says the skeptic, if there is room for doubt, not only are we not entitled to call that belief an instance of knowledge, but the belief is in fact not knowledge. An empiricist or probabilist will not be moved by such skeptical doubts. Merely because we can find *some* reason to doubt is no reason to cast aside a belief. But as we have already seen, Descartes thinks this is a mistake. Genuine knowledge cannot be had from so risky a practice, precisely because the results

Academic and Pyhrronian Skepticism

In the third and second centuries B.C.E., two schools of skepticism arose in Greece. *Academic skepticism* held that we know but one thing: that we have no knowledge. *Pyhrronian skepticism* denied that we have any knowledge whatsoever. Sextus Empiricus, the foremost exponent of Pyhrronian skepticism, held that we must content ourselves with appearances only, that we should suspend judgment about the truth of our beliefs. After all, for any belief, it was always possible to give equally compelling arguments for and against that belief. Interestingly, Sextus thought we would be happier if we learned to suspend judgment. The rise of modern skepticism, which culminated in Descartes, came about with the rediscovery of Greek Skepticism.

of such practices are open to the possibility of doubt. Thus, we have two contrasting standards: (a) the skeptical, which holds that knowledge consists only of those beliefs that are indubitable and certain, and (b) the fallibilist, which allows that our justified beliefs may turn out to be false.

The Dream Argument

Although Descartes himself is not a skeptic, he thinks that genuine instances of knowledge must be able to withstand the skeptical challenge. Thus, some of the beliefs that we normally count as knowledge are not in fact knowledge, simply because such beliefs are not infallible. Descartes holds that perceptual beliefs, or beliefs we form based on our five senses, are susceptible to skeptical attack. His argument against perceptual beliefs is typically called the **Dream Argument.**

There are, of course, times when our perceptual beliefs are inaccurate—we see something under bad lighting, or an object is far away, or our line of sight is not the best. But many of our perceptual beliefs seem not to be of this sort. That you are currently looking at a book page, that you have a pencil or pen in your hand, that other objects are close by—about these sorts of perceptual beliefs there is little room for dispute. Thus, even if our senses sometimes deceive us, some kinds of perceptual beliefs apparently are immune to doubt. Descartes recognizes this, but he reminds himself that he has on occasion been deceived by dreams. He remembers the times he thought he was sitting near the fire when in fact he was asleep in bed. Descartes claims that simply from the nature of the experience itself, from the content of his beliefs, he cannot tell *infallibly* whether he is dreaming or awake.

There are various versions of the Dream Argument, but our focus is on one given by Margaret Wilson. First, notice the sort of belief that Descartes wants to call into question: those perceptual beliefs that are formed under "optimal" conditions. Moreover, Descartes clearly intends to undermine our confidence in such beliefs by likening them to the "beliefs" we sometimes have in dreams. Now, if our "dream beliefs" do not reliably inform us of the nature of reality, then neither do our perceptual beliefs, insofar as they are like the beliefs formed in dreams. Descartes thus wants to suggest that we have reason to doubt that perception reveals to us the way the world actually is. Wilson urges that the real aim of the Dream Argument is to show that one cannot insist on the truthfulness of our waking or perceptual experience of physical objects. Her version of the Dream Argument goes this way:

1. I believe in the past I have dreamed that I was perceiving various physical objects at close range when it was false that I was really perceiving any such objects (when my experience was thoroughly delusory).

2. If I see no certain marks to distinguish waking experience of physical objects from dream experience when, I believe, I was deceived, I have reason to believe my waking experience, too, may be deceptive.

3. I see no such certain marks to distinguish waking experience from dreams.

4. Therefore, I have reason to suppose that waking experience, too, may be deceptive (thoroughly delusory).

5. But if I have reason to suppose my waking experience may be deceptive (thoroughly delusory), I have reason to doubt the existence of physical objects (for at present we are supposing this experience to be the best foundation for our belief in physical objects).[3]

The significant aspect of this interpretation of the argument is that Descartes cannot trust his inner experience, or the contents of his beliefs, to give him a reliable indication of the actual, causal source of his perceptual beliefs. From his internal perspective, from the nature of what he experiences, Descartes cannot be assured that these experiences or representations of the objects "match" the actual causes of his experience.

This clearly runs counter to our normal interpretation of our perceptual beliefs. For example, we think that if we have the experience of a blue book, we have that experience because the book is in fact blue. Our typical view is that our experience is a normally reliable indication or representation of the way things actually are in the world. But as Wilson suggests, Descartes is claiming that we have no certain *reason* to distinguish the delusory character of dreams from normal, waking perceptual experiences.

These experiences may get the nature of the external world wrong just as "dream experiences" get things wrong.

Frederick Schmitt suggests an importantly similar interpretation of Descartes's skepticism. Schmitt argues that Descartes holds that a subject must be able to tell *for certain* that a particular process produces true beliefs. But all that the agent can use in the attempt to guarantee the reliability or truth-productivity of the process is information available to him independently of the contested process.[4] We can perhaps put this in somewhat simpler terms. Descartes wants to know whether perception yields the sort of beliefs that qualify as knowledge. He wants to know whether we can trust perception. But we cannot use perception to verify perception. That is, if I think I see a blue book on the table, I cannot verify this belief by appealing to other perceptual beliefs, because it is perception that is in question.

Imagine, for example, that we are using a calculator to add sequences of numbers and then take the average of those numbers. Suppose that you suspect that the calculator is malfunctioning, perhaps due to a defective battery. You tell me that you doubt that the built-in averaging function is working properly, and I respond by using only this function to check our answers. You would resist the idea that this is a legitimate check on the reliability of the function; what you want is an *independent* check. You think that we should use something other than the suspect averaging function— perhaps old-fashioned pencil and paper. We can apply this example to Schmitt's interpretation of Descartes.

Descartes doubts the reliability of perception. He wants to be assured that perception really does tell us about the world around us. But just as we cannot use the suspect averaging function to check the averaging function, we cannot use perception to check perception. We need an independent check. Unlike the case of the calculator, however, we cannot turn to pencil and paper. Consequently, all that is available to an agent is the character or nature of her own experiences. An agent has the experience of blueness; she seems to be seeing something blue. But is this any guarantee that there is really something blue causing the experience? According to the Dream Argument, as interpreted by Wilson, the character of our experience alone cannot guarantee the reliability of our perceptual beliefs. Put simply, once we are confined to what is *inside,* to how things seem to us *in here,* there is no obvious way to guarantee the reliability of our senses. We cannot ensure that our senses are telling us what is going on *out there.* If this is so, Descartes argues, then we have reason to think that *perception does not reveal the essential nature of reality.*

It bears emphasizing why this is so in Descartes's view, because this will be important for what follows. The normal understanding of the formation of our perceptual beliefs is that there is a causal relation between objects in our environment and the resultant perceptual beliefs. Descartes is rejecting the idea that we can appeal to this causal relation as establishing the certainty of our perceptual beliefs. On the surface, the reason for this follows a standard skeptical pattern. If we know, according to the skeptic, then we can *show* that we know. This showing requires that we be able to rule out other possible explanations that, if true, would result in false beliefs. Descartes claims that because we cannot rule out the possibility that our perceptual beliefs are unreliable, just as our dream beliefs are unreliable, then perceptual beliefs are not infallible. Hence, perceptual beliefs are not genuine instances of knowledge.

This pattern is worth remarking in greater detail. Indeed, the pattern does not depend on the Cartesian requirement of infallibility for its skeptical bite. In our normal understanding of the connection between our beliefs and the world, we have a certain set of experiences that are caused by physical objects, which match or correspond to our experiences. Ordinarily, we take for granted that our experience of, say, a round blue patch is evidence for a blue ball. But the skeptic presents us with a competing hypothesis, an alternative scenario. With this scenario, we would have exactly the same experiences, exactly the same evidence. Thus, the skeptic urges, any evidence we have for the existence of the commonsense world would also count as evidence for the alternative scenario. Our experience does not provide us with adequate evidence for choosing between the "real-world" scenario and the skeptical scenario. We have, according to the skeptic, insufficient evidence for thinking that the cause of a round blue visual experience is a blue ball as opposed to a vivid dream—or, as we will see, an evil demon.[5]

We should also note that this alternative scenario exploits a conception of justification. In this conception, we are justified only if we have adequate reason for a belief. Now, the skeptic insists that this notion of adequate reason requires that an agent have evidence that would enable him or her to discriminate between the real-world scenario and the skeptical scenario. The skeptic further insists that there is no such evidence; hence, we are not justified in our beliefs about the world. In subsequent chapters, we will see that this conception of justification is the subject of dispute.

The Demon Argument

The Dream Argument specifically targets perceptual beliefs. Descartes has in mind, however, a far more powerful skeptical argument. Descartes recognizes that he may have beliefs that do not depend on the operation of his senses. Instead, these other beliefs might be taken to depend on his *reasoning* capacities. Descartes seems to have in mind mathematical propositions, such as that 2 plus 2 equals 4 or that a square has four sides, and other beliefs, which we might call rational truths, such as that bodies have shape. Descartes recognizes both that such propositions are psychologically irresistible and that the truth of such beliefs is independent of whether he is dreaming. Nonetheless, he suggests that they might be false. For all we know, some extremely powerful being, or demon, might cause us to believe such "truths" even though the propositions are in fact false.

According to the Demon Hypothesis or **Demon Argument,** our reasoning abilities alone cannot guarantee the truth of the beliefs in question. Reason alone cannot determine whether we have such beliefs because they are *in fact* true or because some demon has merely made it *seem* to us that they are true. That is, we are unable to find any reason for preferring our commonsense view to the alternative demon scenario. Our inability to rule out the alternative scenario means that we must admit the possibility that beliefs come from a deviant source. Now, the mere possibility that these beliefs come from a deviant source, a demon intent on deceiving us, is sufficient to show that these beliefs are fallible. We might be mistaken about the truth of these beliefs. And because we might be mistaken, we do not *know* that 2 plus 2 equals 4 or that anything that has color has a shape. Spelled out, the Demon Argument might run as follows:

1. I have some beliefs that are psychologically compelling.
2. It is possible that an evil demon, intent on deceiving me, could be the causal source of these beliefs.
3. If the origin of the beliefs is sufficiently deviant, then the beliefs are false.
4. I have insufficient evidence to rule out the evil demon scenario.
5. Hence, it is possible that the origin of the beliefs is sufficiently deviant.
6. Hence, it is possible that the beliefs are false.
7. Hence, I do not know.

Once again, the Cartesian skeptic argues that we cannot tell, merely from the contents of our beliefs, whether our beliefs have the sort of origin that we normally think they do. Suppose I believe that there is a green cup in front of me. Our normal, commonsense view is that I have this belief *because* there is a green cup in front of me. Or suppose I believe that the square root of 25 is 5. Again, our normal view is that I understand the square root function and that I understand 5 and 25. By virtue of this understanding, I *know* that the square root of 25 is 5. But the Demon Argument holds that if my beliefs come about in the wrong way—that is, if they derive from an unreliable source, namely, a demon whose sincere desire is my befuddlement—then my beliefs clearly will be false. Further, in the Demon Argument, my simply thinking about square roots and the numbers 5 and 25 cannot guarantee that the source of that belief is a reliable or truth-preserving source. I cannot tell from the *inside* whether I have locked on to some truth; my beliefs provide me with insufficient evidence to prefer one view to the other.

The Skeptic's Requirements

The Demon Argument leaves Descartes in a rather precarious position: He knows what he thinks, but he doesn't think he knows much else. He no longer thinks he *knows* whether he has hands or feet or even a body at all, or how many sides a triangle has; much less does he think he knows that there is green cup or a fire in front of him. Our aim, however, is not to rescue Descartes from his meditation, but to isolate two key assumptions the skeptic makes.

First, of course, the Cartesian skeptic holds that if we know, then we cannot be mistaken. If Sam knows that there is a green cup in front of him, then it is not possible that Sam is mistaken that there is a green cup in front of him. Closely connected to the infallibility requirement is the claim that if someone knows, then the person must be able to show that they know. We can take a moment to illustrate the sense of "showing" at issue.

Suppose I know that there is a green cup in front of me. This implies that I cannot be mistaken in this belief. Quite clearly, however, I would be mistaken if I were dreaming or an evil demon caused me to have this belief. So, it seems that if I know there is a green cup in front of me, I know something else, such as that I am not dreaming. Now, why do I have to know that I am not dreaming? Would it not be sufficient for me simply to believe this? Descartes's skeptical alter ego claims that it would not be sufficient. My simple belief that I am not dreaming might turn out to be false, and so my belief that there is a cup in front of me might also turn out to be false. The only way of "protecting" my knowledge that there is a cup in front of me is by knowing that I am not dreaming, by having evidence sufficient to rule out the possibility that I am dreaming.

In one sense, this is quite right. If you know that you are lying on your bed reading, then you also know some other propositions. You know that you are *not* sitting in the library reading; you know that you are *not* riding on your bicycle; you know that you are *not* at a friend's house watching television. And you know that you are *not* dreaming. If you know a certain proposition, then you know that "competitors" of that proposition are not true.

Neither the skeptic nor Descartes is satisfied with this, however. The skeptic makes the further claim that if you know, then you can show that you know, in the sense that you have sufficient evidence to rule out the possibility that you are dreaming or are being deceived by a demon. You must be able to rule out even the possibility that you are dreaming. In the

Cartesian view, knowledge of the world requires having enough evidence to rule out the possibility of mistake. Now, we typically accept that someone must have reasons for a belief if that belief is to count as an instance of knowledge. But it is quite another matter to suggest that a person must be able to provide reasons that are sufficient to demonstrate the impossibility of mistake. We will return to this issue in the section "Skepticism and the Defense of Our Cognitive Practices," in which we consider responses to skepticism.

Cartesian skepticism holds that the aim of our cognitive endeavors is infallibility or certainty. It suggests that our normal means of acquiring beliefs—perception and perhaps some uses of reason—are inadequate methods for acquiring infallible or certain beliefs. Reflection on the contents of our beliefs cannot assure us that our beliefs are sufficiently trustworthy. We might *think* that our beliefs are trustworthy, but this is no guarantee that they are trustworthy. As we noted previously, the skeptical problem can arise even if infallibility or the impossibility of mistake is not our cognitive goal. The skeptic can insist that at the very least, we must have evidence that would make it more reasonable to accept our normal interpretation of our experience rather than the skeptical interpretation.

HUME, SKEPTICISM, AND ENTITLEMENT

You are doubtless familiar with a common instruction on various tests: Show your work. You are enjoined not merely to provide an answer, but to demonstrate how you arrived at the answer. Indeed, the right answer with the wrong method may not be worth much more than a wrong answer. The reason is fairly simple, if not always stated: You are not "entitled" to that answer if you do not know the right way to get there. In the following sections, we will be concerned with entitlements of a different sort—epistemic entitlements.

Cartesian skepticism is motivated by the thought that our epistemic goal is certainty or indubitability. Epistemic methods are suspect to the extent that they are unable to produce indubitable beliefs. David Hume's (1711–1776) worry is somewhat different. Hume is willing to grant that we often get things right. Many of our beliefs about the world and its denizens are no doubt true, or at the very least are likely to be true.[6] Hume claims, however, that we are not entitled to think of such beliefs as instances of knowledge or even as rational beliefs. We are not entitled because the methods we use to acquire those beliefs do not provide us with adequate reasons for such beliefs. It is not enough, however, that our reasons are good reasons; we must have some reason for believing that our reasons are good reasons. If we think of the methods we use to acquire our beliefs as providing the reasons for our belief, then Hume requires that we have some reason for thinking that we are using the appropriate methods. But, Hume claims, our beliefs are rational or represent instances of knowledge only if we can show that we are using epistemically sound methods. When asked to show our work, to give our reasons, Hume argues, we can't. And he won't give partial credit.

Hume's emphasis is thus somewhat different from Descartes's. Hume is more concerned with our ability—or lack thereof—to justify the methods by which we arrive at those beliefs we consider epistemically praiseworthy. Indeed, Hume suggests, ours is a mere pretension to knowledge and rationality. In the end, we are possessed of a kind of animal habit, not some cognitive superiority that is grounded in our rational abilities.

Hume's Assumptions

When I leave the room and return a few minutes later to my computer, I *naturally* believe that it is the same computer I just left. I believe that the computer continues to exist independently of my being there to observe it. My belief in the constancy and continued existence is not anything that I rationally infer, according to Hume. In this I am no different from the rest of animal creation. Thus, Hume claims,

> It seems evident, that men are carried, by a natural instinct or prepossession, to repose faith in their senses; and that, without any reasoning, or even almost before the use of reason, we always suppose an external universe, which depends not on our perception, but would exist, though we and every sensible creature were absent or annihilated. Even the animal creation are governed by a like opinion, and preserve this belief of external objects, in all their thoughts, designs, and actions.[7]

But if Hume does not doubt that many of our beliefs are natural, he does doubt that we are *rationally entitled* to at least some of those beliefs. Hume thinks that we cannot explain how we could have rationally or justifiably arrived at certain kinds of belief. In particular, Hume doubts that we are rationally entitled to our beliefs about the nature of the external world and the nature of causality, and to beliefs arrived at by means of inductive inferences. Our focus here is Hume's worry about **induction.**

Barry Stroud suggests that Hume might be thinking along the following lines: We are inclined to think that a belief is justified only if there is some reason to think that the belief is true. But these justifying reasons cannot be arbitrary; we cannot simply conjure them out of the epistemic air. We need, then, some reason to think that the justifying reasons are adequate, that they are indeed *justifying* reasons. Or, as Stroud puts it, "It would seem that reasonable belief also requires that one see or take that something else [the justifying reason] *as* good reason to believe what one does."[8] Understood in this way, Hume argues that we can never be in this position, that we can never have reason to think our reasons are good reasons.

Hume is willing to allow us this much in the attempt to justify inductive inferences. Beliefs based on past or present experience are justified. For example, I am justified in believing that in the past, my turning the knob on the stove has brought about the boiling of the water. In general, beliefs about past experience, or what one has observed, are justified. Hume is also willing to allow that deductive reasoning can justify certain beliefs. Deductive arguments are characterized by the claim that the truth of the premises guarantees the truth of the conclusion. Unlike Descartes, Hume assumes that mathematical and logical truths are certain and demonstrable. The notion of a four-sided triangle is, for Hume, inherently contradictory. Hume thinks, however, that these types of belief are inadequate to justify our inductive inferences.

The Rationality of Our Inductive Inferences

Human beings credit themselves with rationality. This view manifests itself in one of the most basic features of human actions, that of deliberating about the appropriate means to a given end. We want to attain or bring about a certain state of affairs, a particular end, and we think about the best ways to achieve that goal state. We consider some options as ineffective or too time consuming, and others as appropriate and efficient ways of bringing about the desired end. It is difficult to conceive what kind of beings we would be if we didn't make plans and have *reasonable* expectations about the likely outcome of those plans.

Lurking not too far below the surface of this way of thinking is a certain pattern of inference. It is not quite an inference like modus ponens or hypothetical syllogism, but it is an inference nonetheless. It is a slightly more precarious inference, one that is typically characterized as a type of inductive inference.

In the 1960s television series "The Beverly Hillbillies" the character Jethro never quite mastered the concept of doorbell. He did, however, come to believe the conclusion of a particular inductive inference. Jethro noticed that a rather elegant-sounding chime wafting through the mansion was invariably followed by visitors at the front door. Upon hearing the sound, he would eventually go to the front door, open it, and find someone standing there. Jethro's experience was of a constant conjunction between these two events, the sound of the chime and the subsequent discovery of someone standing at the front door. Jethro consequently and, according to

Types of Induction

Inductive inferences purport to show that their conclusions are probable. Hume focuses on a particular type of induction, generally known as *enumerative induction*. Enumerative inductions proceed by noting that certain members of a group have a certain property. It is then concluded that any given member of the group likely will have that property.

Another type of frequently used induction is inference to the best explanation. With this type of inductive inference, the claim is that a certain conclusion is probable because it is the best explanation of a certain fact or event. For example, one might claim that it is probable that there is a green cup in front of me, because that is the best explanation of my having the belief that there is a green cup. This type of inference is sometimes called *abduction*. We will see this sort of argument in this and a later chapter.

Hume, naturally came to believe that upon hearing the chime, he would find someone at the door.

We can represent Jethro's inference in the following manner:

1. In the past, whenever I have heard the sound of the chime, I have subsequently experienced someone at the front door.
2. I am currently hearing the sound of the chime.
3. Thus, I will find someone at the front door.

(Interestingly, my dog has apparently "reasoned" to a similar conclusion. Whenever he hears a knock or the doorbell, he dashes to the front door and remains there until the front door is opened to reveal whoever is standing there.)

Undeniably, Jethro has locked on to a particular truth, and he certainly gets a lot of things right. Nevertheless, Jethro is a little worse off than we are. Jethro doesn't yet understand the connections; he doesn't understand why he is getting things right. Not only do we get a lot of things right, not only do we wind up with a lot of truths, but we think we understand why we end up believing a lot of true propositions. Again, Hume is not inclined to deny that we get a lot of things right. He is not denying that we do have true beliefs about what might occur in the future. But as we have noted, Jethro gets a lot of things right, and my dog gets a lot of things right. This, of course, is not the issue.

Hume's special interest is a certain pattern of inference, which is schematically represented in this way:

(1) All observed A's have been followed by B's.

(2) An A is currently being observed.

(3) Thus, a B will follow.

Hume's central claim is that there is no reason to believe (3) even if (1) and (2) are true. He argues for this by claiming that we are rationally entitled to accept the inference from (1) and (2) to (3) only if we can rationally accept still another principle:

> That instances, of which we have had no experience, must resemble those, of which we have had experience, and that the course of nature continues always uniformly the same.[9]

There are two parts to this principle, which, following accepted practice, we will call the Uniformity Principle (UP). The first asserts a resemblance between the unobserved and the observed, and the second asserts that nature or the world continues uniformly. The immediate problem with this principle, as many people have noticed, is that it is most likely false. Moreover, it is not easy to think of ways to modify UP in such a way as to arrive at a plausible version. But perhaps we can extract a grain of truth from UP, enough at least to let us see why Hume might think the principle to be so important.

The inference pattern just presented apparently requires us to hold that there is some sort of connection between the behavior of A's in the past and their behavior in the future—specifically, that they will bring about B's. Clearly, if we could establish this connection between past and future, we might be able to argue plausibly that the inference pattern is rational. Moreover, Hume clearly intends that in some sense, UP captures the appropriate connection. Thus, the role of UP is to license the inference from (1) and (2) to (3).

Notice that the connection captured in UP is supposed to be completely general. You press a certain sequence of keys on your computer keyboard, and the printer whirls into action; I press a button on my remote control and the television pops on. Not only are each of these and countless other similar cases repeatedly observed, but we expect these patterns to continue into the future, just insofar as these future sequences of events are like the past observed sequences. Hence, our inferences from past experience to future occurrences are based on something like UP. It now becomes clearer how we should go about establishing the epistemic legitimacy of the inference: Show that it is rational for us to accept UP.

Hume, however, has other ideas. It is precisely his argument that we have no good reason to accept UP. To show this, Hume claims that we must provide one of two types of justification for UP: (a) Show that UP is the conclusion of a deductive argument, or (b) show that UP is based on experience. Hume thinks we can do neither.

Consider first the attempt to show that UP is the conclusion of a deductive argument. By way of analogy, imagine an instance of the inference pattern you know as modus ponens, or, If P, then Q; P; therefore, Q:

(1) If it rains in April, then Sacramento will have a good almond crop.

(2) It rains in April.

(3) Therefore, Sacramento will have a good almond crop.

The validity of this argument pattern can be shown by noting that someone who accepted (1) and (2) but who also held that Sacramento would *not* have a good almond crop would be committed to a contradiction. This is a general feature of deductive arguments: The denial of the conclusion together with the acceptance of the premises is self-contradictory. Moreover, Hume thinks it is clearly not self-contradictory to deny UP. There is no contradiction involved, for example, in my believing that I press the button on my remote control but the television fails to come on. The battery in the remote may be dead; the television may not be plugged in; there may be a power failure; and so on. It is not even self-contradictory to hold that although the sun has risen every day of human history thus far, it may not do so tomorrow. Our long overdue supernova might occur just before sunrise. Nor is there any contradiction in supposing that Jethro both hears the chime and finds no one at the door. More generally, events of one kind may have always been followed by events of another kind in the past. But there seems to be no contradiction in supposing that such a connection may not hold in the future. So, the Uniformity Principle cannot be established deductively.

We might then try to justify UP by showing that it is based on what we experience, what we learn from our senses. Clearly, simple observation of *actual* cases alone will not suffice for such justification, because UP contains a reference to unobserved cases. But how, then, might a justification based on experience proceed? Perhaps something like the following will do:

(1) Reliance on UP in the past has led to true beliefs.

(2) I am relying on UP now.

(3) Hence, this use of UP will lead to a true belief.

This pattern of inference ought to seem familiar—it is merely the inference pattern we set out to establish as legitimate in the first place. We begin with a summary of our past experience, that reliance on UP has worked in the past; we further note that we are currently relying on UP. Consequently, we infer that this reliance on UP will have the desired result, acquiring a true belief. Yet it is not difficult to see that this sort of justification of UP presumes precisely what is at issue—that the future will be relevantly like the past. Hume rightly notes that we should be justly suspicious of this move. If it is our confidence in UP that is in question, we cannot use UP to justify that confidence.

We can summarize the main outline of Hume's argument. We naturally think that we can extend our knowledge through reliance on our past experiences. The typical means by which we do so is through inductive inference. Now, it is not the truth of the conclusion that Hume questions, but rather whether we have used a legitimate inference pattern to arrive at the desired conclusion. Hume thinks that inductive inferences are legitimate only if something like the Uniformity Principle licenses or permits the inference. Thus, Hume claims that our reliance on induction is legitimate only if we can justify our reliance on the Uniformity Principle. But we are seemingly unable to do so. UP is not evidently established by deductive inference. Nor is it justified by the appeal to the fact that inferences, which rely on UP, have worked in the past. This latter appeal is, for Hume, uncomfortably circular. But then we have exhausted our possible ways of justifying UP. We cannot establish it by deduction, and our attempt at justifying it based on experience has failed. We cannot claim that our inductive beliefs are based on some sort of rational deliberation. We cannot claim that we have good reasons for our inductive beliefs. According to Hume, such beliefs reflect nothing more than a habit or custom. We do it; we just do it. If you are feeling a bit more like Jethro at this point, that was Hume's intention.

Hume and Common Sense

Underlying Hume's analysis of inductive inference is a claim about the kind of reasons required for justification. This claim is worth identifying, because it is intimately connected with our commonsense view of rationality.[10] Moreover, this claim will prove important when we consider possible responses to the skeptical arguments.

As noted previously, when we say that a belief is rational, we are saying, among other things, that the person has the belief on the basis of reasons. Rational belief, however, requires a bit more than simply having reasons for the belief. For example, Sam might come to believe that he is about to win the lottery. The basis of his belief, his reason, might be another belief of his—for example, that his daily horoscope said that his financial situation is about to improve. Sam has a reason, but we might be disinclined to think that Sam has a rational belief about the lottery. Sam's

Reasons and Causes

We can take a moment to note a distinction that will be important to us in later chapters. On the one hand, when we ask why a person holds a belief, we might be referring to the person's reasons or other beliefs. More generally, we might be referring to some mental state—for example, a belief or experience or sensation—as the reason the belief is held. On the other hand, when we ask why a person holds a belief, we might be referring to the cause of the belief, or the process that produced the belief. Perception or memory typically count as such processes; it is sometimes claimed that induction is a type of cognitive process as well. Typically, the skeptical challenge is understood as asking for the agent's reasons, not the causes of the belief. Whether the source of justification is to be found in the kind of reasons or the kind of causes is heavily disputed in contemporary epistemology.

reason is not an *adequate* reason because of our view of horoscopes. The problem, then, is to specify what counts as an adequate reason.

Hume seems to think that we have good reason for the Uniformity Principle only if we have some positive reason for thinking that UP is true. Thus, Hume claims that we simply could not count (1) and (2) alone as sufficient reason for believing (3). We must first accept UP. We can, lamentably, provide no adequate reason for our reliance on UP. Of course, UP might be true. But Hume requires that we supply some reason for thinking that UP is true.

There is, however, a somewhat weaker interpretation of "adequate reason." Our ordinary, uncritical practice is to accept UP as legitimate unless we have some reason to believe it to be false. Common sense seems to accept UP for specified ranges of cases unless there is reason to think that UP is false in these sorts of case. Consider one example.

Recall that a number of years ago, several people died after taking Tylenol capsules that had been poisoned with cyanide. Consider the following inference:

(1) With respect to Tylenol, the future will resemble the past.

(2) In the past, taking Tylenol has safely relieved pain.

(3) I'm taking Tylenol now.

(4) My pain will be safely relieved.

The first claim is simply the specific form of UP applicable to this case. Notice that prior to the poisoning of the capsules being publicized, there was no reason to believe this particular application of UP to be false. After the poisoning became public, would it be rational for someone to accept this inference? Clearly not, and with this Hume agrees. Our ordinary commonsense view holds that once we know about the poisoning, we can no longer trust that the future will resemble the past. But as Hume would further claim, *prior* to the publicizing of the poisoning incidents, it still would not be *rational* to accept this inference because we have not shown any reason to believe that this specific form of UP is true.

There is a serious issue at stake here. Common sense, our ordinary practice, seems to require only that we have no special reason for believing UP (perhaps in its particularized applications) to be false. But Hume seems to be claiming that such inferences are rational only if we have some positive reason for believing the specialized forms of UP to be true. Now, we would have a response to Hume if we had some reason for preferring the commonsense account of this inference to Hume's. As yet, however, we do not have such an explanation or reason.

Regardless of how this issue turns out, an implication of Hume's arguments needs to be emphasized. These are not merely academic speculations of someone with too much time on his hands. Hume's arguments strike at the very core of our conception of what it is to be human. In particular, the arguments call into question our conception of human beings as essentially *rational* beings. Although we do not always live up to our essence, although we do not always believe or act rationally, our conception of ourselves is that *we are at the very least capable of rationality.* Indeed, we think that we have some beliefs that are rational and that we can, by means of rational methods, extend the class of such beliefs. To think, as Hume suggests we must, that ultimately we are moved by little more than a kind of *animal faith* is to invite a wholesale revision of what it is to be a human being.

SKEPTICISM AND THE DEFENSE
OF OUR COGNITIVE PRACTICES

Skepticism challenges our right to assert that we ever have knowledge or justified belief. Descartes insists that the goal of our cognitive practices is infallibility. He holds that our normal methods of acquiring beliefs—perception and some uses of reason—are inadequate with respect to this goal. According to the Dream Argument, for example, perception cannot be held to provide us with knowledge because it is always *possible* that our perceptual beliefs are mistaken. Hume, too, challenges our commonsense view of the epistemic efficacy of our normal practices. We are inclined to think that induction provides us with an effective means of extending what we have learned from perception or experience. Yet Hume questions our right to this view, claiming that we are unable to provide an adequate justification of the method of induction. The past success of induction may not be a product of our rational abilities. Rather, it may be the happy coincidence of nature's design and cooperation. Nature has so designed us to make such inferences; and at least so far, nature has been cooperative. In this, we are remarkably similar to the rest of animal creation—we've been epistemically lucky.

Must we accept the skeptic's account of our cognitive situation? Is there some way in which we can at least defuse, if not outright refute, the skeptical challenges thus far encountered? It is important to note here just how difficult the situation is for someone who wants to respond to the skeptic. One way of construing the skeptic's demand is this: Take our normal cognitive practices, our normal means of acquiring beliefs, our customary cognitive "toolbox," and set those aside. The skeptic then challenges us to provide a justification of those methods. That is, the skeptic demands that we show our methods to be up to the task without using the methods in question. The Cartesian skeptic will not permit us to use perceptual beliefs to justify the adequacy of perception. Nor will Hume permit us to use induction to justify induction. The defender of common practice consequently faces a difficult task.

Is Skepticism Inevitable?

Before beginning our analysis of responses to skepticism, it is worth noting that the skeptical conclusion can seem inevitable. An assumption of our normal view is that the world, comprising a myriad of objects and their properties, is largely independent of our beliefs about that world. Our belief that Mount Everest is the tallest mountain in the world does not make it so, any more than Newton's sincere and justified belief made it a fact that the geometry of space is Euclidean. My belief that there is a green cup on the table does not make it true that there is a green cup. To put it simply, our normal view is that our beliefs do not determine the facts. **Realism** is the view that the world is indeed mind-independent. In this sense, our commonsense view is realist.

The mind-independence of the world thus sets our cognitive task and our cognitive challenge. Our task is to acquire beliefs that accurately reflect that independent world and to avoid beliefs that do not. Our challenge is to find ways or methods that yield accurate beliefs, or *true* beliefs. However, because the world is independent of our beliefs, it seems possible that any method we employ might always fall short. Perhaps perception is simply an imperfect tool for acquiring information about the world. Perhaps induction provides us with momentary respite from our more pressing biological needs, but many evolutionary generations from now, the last human beings will realize that induction was not only risky business but a losing one at that. The more important point is that if our beliefs do not determine the facts, then our beliefs might fall short of the facts. The skeptic claims that we cannot rule out the possibility that the failure of our beliefs to reflect the facts is systematic. According to the skeptic, there is no reason to tip the scale toward trusting our beliefs as opposed to doubting our beliefs. Realism thus seems to go hand in hand with the possibility of skepticism.

Although realism implies the *possibility* of skepticism, it is an open question as to whether realism implies the *inevitability* of skepticism. Some have thought that the only way to avoid skepticism is by giving up realism, the belief in a mind-independent world. In this view, the key to knowledge and justification is to adopt idealism, the view that the world or the facts about that world are in some sense dependent on our beliefs.[11] Continuing to hold a realist view while meeting the skeptical challenge is a more difficult task, but it is the approach adopted by most epistemologists. It is the realist approach that we adopt in what follows.

Two Types of Defense

Although the skeptic's demand is an extremely stringent one, we are not entirely at a loss. In order to formulate the challenge, the skeptic had to commit, if only tacitly, to certain assumptions. We are thus at least free to ask whether there is any compelling reason to accept the skeptic's assumptions. That is, although we may not be able to show that the skeptical position is mistaken, we may nonetheless be able to show that the skeptic is not entitled to some of the claims necessary for formulating the array of skeptical arguments. The distinction between these two approaches is characterized as that between (a) refuting the skeptical position, showing that it is plainly wrong, and (b) merely rebutting the skeptic, showing that the skeptic's arguments are not compelling.

One type of refutation strategy is the attempt to show that the skeptic's position is in some way internally inconsistent. Typically, this strategy requires showing that if the skeptic accepts certain propositions, then the skeptic cannot consistently deny that we have knowledge or justified beliefs. This type of argument suggests that if one holds that we have beliefs or thoughts of a certain kind, then one is also committed to holding that we have justified beliefs or knowledge. For example, it is argued that if we mean anything by the concept "see," then we must accept that vision normally gives us true beliefs.[12] Another well-known example is the claim that if we accept that we have beliefs, which the skeptic presumably must concede, then we must also accept that most of our beliefs are true.[13] These types of arguments are sometimes called *transcendental arguments*. Such arguments attempt to show that a necessary condition of our thinking is that we do indeed have knowledge or justified belief. In the next section, we consider a particular instance of this type of argument by P. F. Strawson.

The second type of strategy attempts to rebut rather than refute the skeptic. Proponents of this strategy argue that the skeptic is committed to certain controversial claims or assumptions. Presumably, the skeptic cannot show that these claims or assumptions are compelling; the skeptic cannot provide sufficient reason for accepting these claims or assumptions. For example, the Cartesian skeptic holds that we have knowledge only if we are certain that our beliefs are infallible. As we will see in the next section, one might reasonably wonder whether knowledge requires certainty or infallibility.

This is by no means a complete survey of the variety of responses to skepticism. But this rough twofold classification is perhaps sufficient to frame the responses we consider in the next section.

RESPONDING TO THE SKEPTIC

Is Certainty Necessary for Knowledge?

The Cartesian skeptic, as we noted, holds that knowledge requires infallibility. Of course, as we also noted, skepticism is not wedded to infallibility. Neither the alternative-scenario skeptical challenge nor Hume's worry about induction is committed to the notion of infallibility. Still, we might wonder whether knowledge requires the impossibility of mistake. We are often willing to claim, for example, that Sara knows that there is a blue ball on the floor even though it is logically possible that Sara is mistaken. It will not do, however, simply to assert against the skeptic that our ordinary practice does not require the impossibility of mistake. The issue between the skeptic and the defender of our more common practice is an evaluative issue: *Should* we count the impossibility of mistake as a condition of knowledge? The question for us then is whether we are obligated to accept the standard the skeptic has identified. If we cannot find a way to reject the skeptic's standard, then our claims to knowledge or rationality will indeed seem to be mere pretensions. Our many putative claims to knowledge seem rarely to satisfy such lofty standards. We need a way for choosing between the two standards.

First, we might consider why the skeptic insists on such a lofty, stringent standard. That is, we might consider what general epistemic goal is served by the skeptic's choice of standards that is not served by our more ordinary, common one. Examine, for a moment, the requirement of certainty as a condition of knowledge. The explicit goal here apparently is the avoidance of counting something as knowledge that is in fact not knowledge at all, but rather a false belief. The skeptic thus seems to think that running the risk of mistake is detrimental to our cognitive welfare or irrational. Descartes appears to have precisely this sort of worry; he seems to think that the merely probable threatens our ability to attain knowledge. Still, we might wonder whether, in general, our weaker standard is really so detrimental.

The skeptic insists on a rather cautious epistemic policy.[14] An assumption that may underlie the skeptic's preference is that we will be epistemically confounded by our mistakes. Only by adopting the stringent skeptical standard will we be able to tell the difference between genuine items of knowledge and mere pretenders. We might interpret this as the skeptic claiming that differential epistemic assessment of our beliefs is possible only if we adopt the infallibility standard. Surely, however, we will want to know why we should accept this controversial claim. The history of our cognitive endeavors *seems* to show that we have been progressively more able to discriminate epistemically praiseworthy beliefs from those less so. We have often rooted out the mere pretenders from the genuine item. And we have been able to do this despite the fact that we have not counted the impossibility of mistake as a requirement of knowledge. Of course, this approach has sometimes required that we change our methods for making the requisite differential assessment, but this, too, we have often been able to do. Our reliance on a weaker standard still enables us to distinguish between beliefs that are mere guesses, those that are justified, and those that are instances of knowledge. What more could we want from an epistemic standard? Thus, if the skeptic is moved to adopt certainty as a condition of knowledge because of the worry that we will be unable to assess differentially the epistemic status of our beliefs, we do not yet have a compelling motivation for adopting such a standard.

The infallibility skeptic may, of course, worry that this line of response takes for granted precisely what is at issue. Our aim, however, is to show that the skeptic has not presented us with good reason to prefer the infallibility standard. The skeptic may claim that we *ought* to accept infallibility as our standard, but we may expect some reason for this "ought." We might expect, for example, that our cognitive endeavors are in some sort of disarray. But this is not *evidently* the case, as the previous paragraph attempts to illustrate.

Perhaps, however, the skeptic thinks that the requirement of infallibility is indicated by what we might take as a paradigm of knowledge.[15] The skeptic seems to hold that we know what we think. Not only do we know what we think, but apparently we are infallible with respect to what we think. We know *immediately* and *certainly* the contents of our own mind. We have a kind of direct, infallible access to what we believe. Descartes, for example, holds that he *knows* what he believes—he believes he is sitting

Descartes and the Probable

Richard H. Popkin describes a meeting in approximately 1628 at which Descartes attempted to show that if we accept the merely probable as our standard of truth, we risk accepting the false. Descartes took examples of accepted truths and, using probability as a standard, showed that these truths were false. He then took examples of falsehoods and, again using probability as the guide, constructed arguments to show that these false-hoods were indeed plausible. The audience found this shocking, and Descartes is reported to have explained to them his infallible means for at-taining truth. (See "For Further Study.")

before a fire. He is unable to tell, however, whether his belief about the fire is true. Or consider a more familiar example. Suppose you are taking a dri-ver's test to renew your license. You come to a question that asks you the speed limit when traveling through a school zone. Now, clearly, you know what you think: You think the speed limit is 25 mph. What you do not know is whether the speed limit is in fact 25 mph. Your knowledge of what you think is thus direct and infallible in the way that the actual speed limit is not. Knowledge of our own mental states, of what we think, is a clear ex-ample of a kind of infallible belief.

The skeptic might then argue along the following line: Suppose we take knowledge of our own mental states as the model of what it is to have knowledge. Because knowledge of our own mental states is always certain, then any knowledge must similarly be infallible. You might know that you *think* that there is a white cup in front of you. But, the skeptic urges, we should apply the exact same criteria to your alleged knowledge that there is in fact a white cup.

We might note two arguments against this attempt to motivate the skeptic's preferred standard for knowledge. First, it might be argued that the skeptic has assumed precisely what is at issue. Even given that we have infallible access to the contents of our own mind, it does not follow that in-fallibility is a necessary condition of knowledge. Infallibility may be simply a feature of the process of introspection. Again, imagine that you are taking a driver's test, and that you answer correctly every question. Does your per-fect score in this case imply that your *passing* any test in the future also re-quires perfection? The defender of our commonsense view might concede that infallibility is *enough* to give us knowledge. Still, the commonsense ad-vocate might argue that the skeptic has mistaken the fact that infallibility is *enough* for knowledge with the claim that knowledge is *required* for knowledge. By focusing on introspection, the skeptic has been misled into thinking that a sufficient condition is a necessary condition.

Second, it might be argued that we are no more infallible with respect to knowledge of our own mental states than we are with respect to simple perceptual beliefs under optimal conditions. We will pursue this issue in greater detail in Chapter Four. Here, it will be sufficient to note that the skeptic owes us an argument that introspection yields infallibility. That is, the skeptic cannot use introspection as a motivation for holding that knowledge requires infallibility unless the skeptic gives us some reason for thinking that we do know infallibly the contents of our own mind.

We should be careful not to lose sight of our aim here. We are looking for some reason to think that knowledge requires infallibility, as the skeptic claims. Because the skeptic claims that our commonsense view is too lax, we are looking for some reason to prefer the skeptic's view to our commonsense view. The requirement of infallibility is a substantial claim about the nature of knowledge. But we are not obligated to accept this requirement unless we can find some reason for thinking that the skeptic's view is preferable. Thus far, we have been unable to do so.

Show-and-Tell: Ruling Out That One Is Dreaming

Infallibility is not, however, a necessary feature of the skeptical challenge. The skeptic claims that if we know, we must be able to rule out alternative scenarios, such as that we might be dreaming. There must be some indication that enables us to *tell* that we are not dreaming. When pressed by the skeptic, we must be able to show that we are not dreaming by exhibiting or presenting the indications that enable us to tell we are not dreaming. The skeptic thus claims that we must be able to *show* that we can rule out competing scenarios, scenarios in which we would have the very same, yet false, belief. What is meant by "show" in this sort of case? It seems to mean that a person could provide or articulate reasons that explain why the competing scenario cannot be correct or is less preferable than our normal view.

It is important to recognize that the skeptic is making two different claims. It is certainly correct that if I know a certain proposition, P, then P is true. Thus, if I know that I am sitting at home in front of the computer, then that proposition, that I am sitting at home in front of a computer, is true. Moreover, it is plausible that I have some reasons for thinking that I am home. It is, however, not as clear how the skeptic moves from these unobjectionable claims to the more stringent claim that for any proposition incompatible with my knowledge, I have adequate reason for ruling out such incompatible propositions. More generally, we might wonder why the skeptic thinks that our reasons must be adequate to rule out *every* alternative scenario.

Consider first an ordinary case. Suppose you believe that you are having a test on a particular day; the syllabus says a test is scheduled, and the teacher reminded you of the test the previous class meeting. And you are on your way to class to take the test. Clearly, you would be justified in believing that there is a test that day. But on your way to class, a classmate stops you and tells you that there is no test today because the teacher is ill. Now, to the extent that you *cannot* rule out the claim that the teacher is ill, you would no longer be justified in believing that your hours of preparation were soon to be rewarded (or that your hours of frivolity were about to go unpunished). In fact, you might be able to do this. Perhaps your classmate is a merry prankster, or perhaps you just left the teacher's office and she looked remarkably healthy to you. Any number of reasons might permit you to rule out the competing scenario. Yet clearly, unless you could rule out the competing scenario, you would not be justified in continuing to believe that there is a test today, and *a fortiori* you would not know that there is a test today. Thus, our commonsense view of knowledge clearly requires that we be able to rule out at least *some* competing claims. It is not obvious, however, that our ordinary conception requires us to rule out *every* competing scenario, including that we are dreaming or deceived by a potent but obnoxious demon.

In ordinary cases, like the example of the test, it makes sense to suppose that a person must be able to rule out conflicting explanations. We can do this because there is something else about which you and your classmate agree. You agree about what counts as providing a justification for your belief. That is, if you were to tell your classmate that you had just come from the teacher's office, this presumably would be sufficient to establish your justification. It is not at all obvious what you might do in the case of the Demon Argument. The skeptic has precluded appeal to such commonly accepted background practices. In doing so, however, the skeptic has adopted a quite substantive claim.

The skeptic assumes that because in many instances we are able to show or provide an argument to rule out the alternative explanation, we can reasonably be expected to do so in all instances. But why should we accept this? Our ordinary intuitions are just that—intuitions confined to the sorts of case like that of knowing whether there is a test. The assumption that we would not be justified unless we could rule out conflicting accounts of the data depends on our view that some further evidence can be brought to bear. It is not at all clear that we are committed to such an assumption where *there simply is no possibility* of that assumption holding. Again, the skeptic has yet to provide us with a reason for thinking that we must always be able to engage in this bit of epistemological show-and-tell.

Let us consider one further avenue available to the skeptic. Suppose the skeptic claims that, in fact, our ordinary standards are committed to the view that we must always be able to rule out competing scenarios. Consider the following example.[16] Suppose that Sam has been trained to identify planes of various types. Sam, the plane spotter, is taught that a certain kind of plane, call it P, has identifying characteristics X and Y. Sam is not taught, however, that in his area there is a very similar but extremely rare plane, call it R, that also has identifying characteristics X and Y, as well as a further characteristic Z. Type R planes can only be distinguished from type P planes by the characteristic Z; the two types are otherwise indistinguishable. Imagine that Sam spots a plane with characteristics X and Y. Does Sam know that the plane is of type P? Because Sam cannot rule out the possibility that the plane is type R, we might very well be inclined to think that Sam does not know.

It is not clear, however, that this example helps the skeptic. Interestingly, a case very much like this occurred during the Gulf War. American pilots had to learn to discriminate friendly, French aircraft from extremely similar but hostile aircraft. That is, the pilots had to learn a feature that distinguished friendly from hostile aircraft. Suppose, however, that the French had not participated in the war and that the American pilots had not been taught to discriminate the two types of aircraft. Would we think that the American pilots did not know that a certain aircraft was hostile because of the *mere possibility* that a French plane might be in the vicinity? We might think that if there was no evidence that French planes were in the area that, in a great many cases, American pilots would indeed know. This is not to say that they could not be mistaken; a French pilot might have lost his way and wandered into the war zone. But it is at least debatable whether the mere possibility, and the Americans' inability to rule out this possibility, shows that they would not have knowledge.

These sorts of examples seem to show that which alternatives must be ruled out can vary from case to case. But it is at least questionable whether the examples illustrate the skeptic's claim that we are committed to the more stringent view of knowledge, or whether they show that our own commonsense view of knowledge requires our ability to rule out every possible competing scenario. Again, it seems less than evident that we must accept the skeptic's view of the nature of knowledge.

Skepticism and Inference to the Best Explanation

You might think that the alternative-scenario challenge should not be dismissed so quickly. On behalf of the skeptic, you might argue along the following lines: Our ordinary conception of justification requires that we have adequate reasons for our beliefs. But if we have two alternatives, and our reasons do not favor one over the other, we would not think that our reasons were adequate. Our ordinary conception specifies no limitation on the generality of the alternatives. The skeptic simply takes our notion of justification and applies it to these very general alternatives. The skeptic merely points out, for example, that everything that counts as evidence for our ordinary view of the source of our perceptual beliefs is *also* evidence for the dreaming scenario. The ordinary scenario and the dreaming scenario have the same evidence, as we noticed in the section "Cartesian Skepticism"; the weight of evidence favors neither side. So, how can we say that we are justified in favoring our normal view?

It should be noted that some have thought that this is the strongest of the skeptical challenges and that "traditional epistemology" is largely motivated by the attempt to meet this version of skepticism. Some also have argued that we do have more reason to prefer our ordinary view to the skeptical scenario simply because our ordinary view provides the *best explanation* of our experience.[17] Various strategies are used to show that our commonsense view is indeed the best explanation, but we can identify some general features of such strategies. The most important aspect of best-explanation arguments is finding some criterion for determining the best explanation. For example, simplicity might provide us with a criterion for picking out the best explanation. Or one explanation might be thought to be better than another because it is more probable. Suppose I awaken to find wet streets. One explanation of this fact is that it rained during the night; a second is that my neighbors engaged in a block party water fight (and didn't invite me). The former explanation is more probable, given what else I know. Thus, the best explanation of wet streets is that it rained last night.

One difficulty encountered with skeptical scenarios is that they claim to include all possible evidence. Consequently, our commonsense view and the skeptical scenario appear to be equally probable given the evidence— or so the skeptic claims. If we could find, however, some reason for thinking that our commonsense view is simpler or more probable than the skeptical scenario, we would have a reason for our preferred view. For example, it is argued that our commonsense view is more probable because it is simpler.[18] The Demon Hypothesis requires that we assume not only that the demon exists but also that the demon has particular states of mind associated with our consequent experiences. These assumptions are more complicated than our commonsense view, in which we need only assume the existence of the physical world. Thus, our realist view of the world is the better explanation. And because it is the better explanation, we do have reason to prefer it to the skeptical-demon scenario. One advantage of this sort of argument is that it shows that we need not automatically concede the skeptic's claim that the evidence provides no basis for deciding between our normal view and the skeptic's alternative scenario. Recall that our general strategy of rebutting the skeptic requires us only to show that the skeptic's arguments are not compelling. Best-explanation arguments suggest at least this much: The skeptic has not provided us with compelling reasons to think that skeptical alternative scenarios are as likely as our realist view of the world. Of course, we have given but a quick account of such responses to skepticism. But perhaps this is enough to provide a general sense of the approach.

Induction Again

Although there may be general support for the view that knowledge does not require certainty, there is considerably less agreement about the appropriate response to Hume's worries about induction. We confine ourselves to two strategies. The first is proposed by P. F. Strawson.

Hume worries that past experience does not provide sufficient reason or evidence for our inductive conclusions. He thinks that we are unable to show an appropriate connection between past experience and future expectations on the basis of that experience. Appeal to the Uniformity Principle is of no help, Hume claims, because we confront the same problem again. Thus, Hume claims, we are never rationally justified in accepting the conclusion of an inductive argument.

Strawson, however, argues that this is precisely what we mean by "rational." We are justified in accepting inductive conclusions only and precisely to the extent that they are supported by the evidence.

> It is an analytic proposition that it is reasonable to have a degree of belief in a statement which is proportional to the strength of the evidence in its favour; and it is an analytic proposition . . . that, other things being equal, the evidence for a generalization is strong in proportion as the number of favourable instances, and the variety of circumstances in which they have been found, is great. So to ask whether it is reasonable to place reliance on inductive procedures is like asking whether it is reasonable to proportion the degree of one's convictions to the strength of the evidence. Doing this is what "being reasonable" *means* in such a context.[19]

Strawson clearly suggests that relying on inductive inferences—*all other things being equal*—is implied by our very notion of being reasonable.

Still, we might wonder why this counts as a response to Hume. Hume claims that we are not entitled to trust our inductive inferences *unless* we can give some positive reason for thinking that such inferences generally lead to true beliefs. Strawson's apparent response is that unless there is some reason to think otherwise, induction is a model of what it is to give a positive reason for belief. Consider a simple analogy. Suppose that Sam is about to climb a ladder to do some roof repairs. Sara suggests that he is not being appropriately careful. Sam gives the ladder a shake, sees that it remains stable, begins to climb the ladder slowly, and insists that this is what it is to be careful. Something, of course, could go wrong. Sam could lose his balance; the dog might start up the ladder after him; what seemed to be solid ground might give way, causing the ladder to slide. Nonetheless, Sam could still claim he had been careful.

Strawson understands that Hume is asking why we should place our trust in the "ladder" of induction. Like Sam, Strawson understands that things could go wrong. What seemed to be a solid foundation for an inference might give way. But Strawson tells Hume that despite the risk, engaging in induction is precisely what it means to be epistemically careful. Strawson thus claims that induction is a model of human rationality, that a conceptual connection exists between rationality and reliance on induction. And, says Strawson, if Hume is asking for more, then Hume has not quite understood what is meant by justification or rationality. In a more recent work, Strawson suggests that the way to respond to the skeptic is not by means of a counterargument. Rather, we should be content to show that certain beliefs or claims are fundamental to human thought: "Our inescapable natural commitment is to a general frame of belief and to a general style (the inductive) of belief-formation."[20] Our best response, according to Strawson, is to illustrate the way in which induction plays a role in our belief system and our methods of acquiring and revising belief.

Hume might be forgiven if he finds this response somewhat frustrating. He, too, agrees that induction is part of our natural cognitive constitution (a point that Strawson recognizes). But Hume insists that we should not be taking credit for what nature has done. Nature has instilled in us and the rest of animal creation a certain style of belief formation, namely, induction. This style seems to work. But the fact that it works, Hume claims, is nature's doing, not ours. No *argument* of ours underlies the efficacy of induction. Our rational abilities do not guarantee the effectiveness of induction. At best, we can hope that nature provides the guarantee—a hope, Hume notes, we have no epistemic right to count on.

Strawson's analytic strategy attempts to assure Hume that induction is a rational strategy because we can do no better. Yet no *argument* can be given to show that induction is rational. Oddly enough, Hume and Strawson agree about precisely this latter point. Their disagreement lies in whether induction should still be called rational.

We might try to understand who is right here, Strawson or Hume, by considering a second strategy. Again, recall that Hume claims that we can trust our inferences only if we have some positive reason for thinking that past experience is a reliable indicator of what will happen in the future. Common sense, as we saw in the section "Hume, Skepticism, and Entitlement," claims that we may trust inductive inferences, as long as we have no reason for thinking that induction is inappropriate under the circumstances. The commonsense view might be strengthened if the absence of doubt could, in some way, be seen as a positive reason for trusting induction.

Hume seems to think that induction proceeds by noting that some object has a certain property, subsequently noting that still other objects of the *same* kind have the same property, and thus concluding that all objects of that kind have the property. But there is reason to doubt that this is an accurate description of our inductive practice.[21] Instead, induction always takes place against a background of other beliefs. This background licenses some inductive inferences but prohibits others. Suppose, for example, that a friend points to certain bird and says that it is an Oregon junco. On the basis of this one case, you might infer that Oregon juncos have black head feathers. Suppose also that a few moments later, the same friend points to a somewhat pudgy man walking by and says, "That's my philosophy teacher." You are unlikely to conclude on the basis of this one case that all philosophy teachers are pudgy. The difference in the two cases—that you draw the conclusion in the former case but not the latter—is due to the operation of certain background beliefs. Your background beliefs are likely to tell you that there is some lawlike connection between being an Oregon junco and having a certain coloration, but there is probably no such connection between being a philosophy teacher and being pudgy.

In this view, inductive arguments are always relative to certain contexts. If we want to understand why an inductive argument is legitimate (or illegitimate), we need to look to the context, to the relevant background beliefs. Here, the justification of a particular inductive inference is always local justification.[22] To the extent that this view is a more accurate account of our inductive practice, then Hume has *misdescribed* our actual cognitive situation. *If* Hume's skepticism depends on such misdescription, then we have some reason for thinking that Hume has not provided us with a compelling argument.

Hume is free to ask about the background beliefs that support our inductive inferences. It is important to see, however, that this changes the nature of the argument. Once we have shown that we need not accept Hume's skepticism about induction, we may use inductive methods to justify those background beliefs. There is a principled difference between asking what justifies a particular belief and asking what justifies a certain *method* of justification. If we need not accept Humean skepticism about our methods, then doubts about particular beliefs can be resolved in our normal ways. We have certain methods for determining whether all Oregon juncos have black heads, but these methods depend on the acceptability of induction. In a sense, in this view, induction always occurs against the background of a particular theory or a particular view about the way a certain part of the world works, where such theories are expressed in our general beliefs. The Humean skeptic may, of course, modify the argument to take into account the context-relative nature of induction.

Another way of putting this is to say that the skeptic assumes that we always begin with particular beliefs, beliefs about what we observe in particular cases. We then proceed to form general beliefs, beliefs arrived at by means of an inductive argument, on the basis of these particular observations. The direction of evidential support, according to the Humean, always proceeds from particular to general. But the skeptic about induction does not provide us with any compelling reason to think that this must be so. Instead, it might be suggested that we understand how particular observations support inductive conclusions *by virtue of* our having certain general beliefs about the context in which the induction occurs.[23]

Clearly, Hume will want to know what entitles us to these general beliefs that are part of the background of particular inductive inferences. We acquire such beliefs as we acquire the concepts that we use in making particular observations. The process of acquiring the concept also involves the acquisition of associated general beliefs about when certain kinds of inference are legitimate. It is then as legitimate to accept the general beliefs as it is to accept the particular observation beliefs that make use of the relevant concepts. This view of the acquisition of our concepts is, of course, an empirical claim, which the Humean skeptic may wish to reject. Nonetheless, it illustrates the sense in which the Humean view of induction depends on a certain view of how we acquire the concepts we utilize in making particular judgments about what we observe. If Hume is wrong about this, then he may well be wrong about the legitimacy of our inductively based beliefs. In any case, the Humean has yet to provide us with a compelling case for accepting the empirical claims that underlie such skepticism.

In this section, we have not tried to refute skepticism. We have merely tried to show that the skeptic's arguments are not compelling, that we have some reason for not accepting them. In particular, we have focused on why we need not accept that knowledge requires infallibility or certainty. We have also seen some reasons to reject the skeptic's claim that we must be able to rule out competing scenarios. Finally, we have suggested that we need not accept Hume's doubts about induction. If the skeptic's requirements for knowledge are indeed too stringent, we might wonder what the requirements of knowledge are. For this, we turn to the next chapter.

Key Concepts

Demon Argument	Induction
Dream Argument	Infallible beliefs
Indubitable beliefs	Realism

Review Questions

1. Why does Descartes think that the Dream Argument shows that our perceptual beliefs are intrinsically mistaken?
2. The skeptic thinks that ruling out alternative scenarios is a necessary condition of knowledge. How does the Demon Hypothesis rely on this view?
3. What is the Uniformity Principle? Why does Hume think it is important?
4. What is the difference between refuting and rebutting the skeptic?
5. Do you think knowledge requires the ability to rule out any alternative scenario? Explain.
6. Do you think Strawson's response to Hume is an effective defense of induction? Explain.
7. Do you think we are rational to rely on inductive inferences? Why or why not?

For Further Study

Descartes's *Meditations on First Philosophy* are reprinted in *The Philosophical Works of Descartes,* Vol. I, trans. Elizabeth S. Haldane and G. R. T. Ross (Cambridge: Cambridge University Press, 1968), pp. 131–199. Hume's skeptical positions are presented in L. A. Selby-Bigge, ed., *A Treatise of Human Nature,* 2nd ed. (Oxford: Clarendon Press, 1978), and *An Enquiry Concerning Human Understanding,* 3rd ed., ed. L. A. Selby-Bigge (Oxford: Clarendon Press, 1975). Barry Stroud's *Hume* (London: Routledge & Kegan Paul, 1977) and Margaret D. Wilson's *Descartes* (London: Routledge & Kegan Paul, 1978) are very accessible accounts of the main arguments of Hume and Descartes. Two further interpretative studies of Descartes are E. M. Curley, *Descartes Against the Sceptics* (Cambridge, MA: Harvard University Press, 1978), and Henry Frankfurt, *Demons, Dreamers, and Madmen* (Indianapolis, IN: Bobbs-Merrill, 1970). Two studies of Hume are Norman Kemp-Smith, *The Philosophy of David Hume* (London: Macmillan, 1941), and J. P. Wright, *The Sceptical Realism of David Hume* (Minneapolis: University of Minnesota Press, 1983).

Richard H. Popkin's *The History of Skepticism from Erasmus to Spinoza* (Berkeley and Los Angeles: University of California Press, 1979) is a classic account of the rise of modern skepticism that provides both a historical and philosophical context. Popkin's description of Descartes's critique of accepting probability as our guide to truth occurs in Chap. 9. Interesting interpretations and analyses of the major forms of skepticism can be found in Christopher Hookway, *Scepticism* (London: Routledge, 1990), and Frederick F. Schmitt, *Knowledge and Belief* (London: Routledge, 1992).

Barry Stroud's *The Philosophical Significance of Scepticism* (Oxford: Clarendon Press, 1984) is somewhat more advanced. It contains extended discussions of major attempts to respond to the skeptic's challenge. Also worth noting is Stroud's detailed consideration of the connection between skepticism and our commonsense view.

Gilbert Harman's *Thought* (Princeton, NJ: Princeton University Press, 1973) contains an accessible account of inference to the best explanation, as well as other topics in epistemology. Timothy J. McGrew provides a detailed elaboration and defense of inference to the best explanation as a response to the skeptic in *The Foundations of Knowledge* (Lanham, MD: Littlefield Adams, 1995), Chap. 7.

Notes

1. René Descartes, *Meditations on First Philosophy,* reprinted in *The Philosophical Works of Descartes,* Vol. I, trans. Elizabeth Haldane and G. R. T. Ross (Cambridge: Cambridge University Press, 1968), pp. 144–145.

2. See, for example, Keith Lehrer, *Theory of Knowledge* (Boulder, CO: Westview Press, 1990), Chap. 9, and Robert Audi, *Belief, Justification, and Knowledge* (Belmont, CA: Wadsworth, 1988), Chap. 9.

3. Margaret Wilson, *Descartes* (London: Routledge & Kegan Paul, 1978), pp. 22–23.

4. Frederick Schmitt, *Knowledge and Belief* (London: Routledge, 1992), Chap. 2, esp. pp. 37–39.

5. See, for example, Frank Jackson, "Knowledge of the External World," in G. H. R. Parkinson, ed., *The Handbook of Western Philosophy* (New York: Macmillan, 1988), pp. 140–158, esp. pp. 147–148. See also Timothy J. McGrew, *The Foundations of Knowledge* (Lanham, MD: Littlefield Adams, 1995), pp. 6–8.

6. The claim that Hume is willing to grant the truth of certain beliefs is perhaps controversial. But see, for example, David Hume, *An Enquiry Concerning Human Understanding,* 3rd ed., ed. L. A. Selby-Bigge, rev. by P. H. Nidditch (Oxford: Clarendon Press, 1975), pp. 54–55, where Hume claims that "a kind of pre-established harmony" exists between nature and our ideas. See also his *A Treatise of Human Nature,* 2nd ed., rev. by P. H. Nidditch (Oxford: Clarendon Press, 1978), pp. 173–178, where Hume lays out a set of rules "by which we may know when they [cause or effects] really are so."

    In this connection, it might be noted that Tom L. Beauchamp and Alexander Rosenberg argue that Hume was *not* a skeptic about induction. Rather, they claim, Hume argued that reason alone could not provide us with sufficient justification for inductive inferences. Hume's argument is with the rationalists, not induction. See Beauchamp and Rosenberg, *Hume and the Problem of Causation* (New York: Oxford University Press, 1981), especially Chap. 2.

7. David Hume, *An Enquiry Concerning Human Understanding* (Oxford: Clarendon Press, 1975), p. 151.

8. Barry Stroud, *Hume* (London: Routledge & Kegan Paul, 1977), p. 60. This, of course, is not the only way to interpret Hume. See "For Further Study" for additional works.

9. David Hume, *A Treatise of Human Nature* (Oxford: Clarendon Press, 1978), p. 89.

10. A more detailed discussion of the following issues can be found in Stroud, *Hume,* pp. 58ff.

11. One of the foremost advocates of this view is Hilary Putnam. See, for example, *Reason, Truth and History* (Cambridge: Cambridge University Press, 1981) and *Realism and Reason: Philosophical Papers,* Vol. 3 (Cambridge: Cambridge University Press, 1983). Although his more recent views are somewhat different, Richard Rorty has also argued against the realist view of the world; see "World Well Lost," *Consequences of Pragmatism* (Minneapolis: University of Minnesota Press, 1982), pp. 3–18.

12. Barry Stroud discusses this sort of argument in "Transcendental Arguments," reprinted in Terence Penelhum and J. J. MacIntosh, eds., *The First Critique: Reflections on Kant's Critique of Pure Reason* (Belmont, CA: Wadsworth, 1969), pp. 54–69.

13. Donald Davidson presents this view in "A Coherence Theory of Truth and Knowledge," in Ernest LePore, ed., *Truth and Interpretation* (Oxford: Basil Blackwell, 1986), pp. 307–319.

14. This type of response is along the line of argument suggested by Christopher Hookway in *Scepticism* (London: Routledge, 1990). Hookway suggests that skepticism might in part be motivated by the thought that only by adhering to a rather cautious epistemic policy will we be able to regulate our inquiries.

15. A more sophisticated version of this argument is found in Robert G. Meyers, *The Likelihood of Knowledge* (Dordrecht: Kluwer Academic Publishers, 1988), pp. 156–160.

16. This is a slight modification of an example from Thompson Clark, "The Legacy of Skepticism," *Journal of Philosophy* (1972).

17. Gilbert Harman has long advocated inference to the best explanation. See *Thought* (Princeton, NJ: Princeton University Press, 1973), Chap. 8. Harman seems to accept a type of best-explanation argument in response to the skeptic; see Chaps. 1 and 10.

18. The following is but a simplified version of the argument in McGrew, *Foundations of Knowledge,* Chap. 7. McGrew provides a detailed account and defense of the probability theory necessary for such an argument. In our Chapter Five, we will see a similar sort of argument to the best explanation.

19. P. F. Strawson, *Introduction to Logical Theory* (London: Methuen, 1952), pp. 256–257.

20. P. F. Strawson, *Skepticism and Naturalism: Some Varieties* (New York: Columbia University Press, 1983), p. 14.

21. Two examples of this sort of strategy are John H. Holland et al., *Induction* (Cambridge, MA: MIT Press, 1986), and Radu J. Bogdan, "Hume and the Problem of Local Induction," in Bogdan, ed., *Local Induction* (Dordrecht: D. Reidel, 1976), pp. 217–234. The example given is a modification of an example given by Holland.

22. See Bogdan, ed., *Local Induction.*

23. A similar line of argument appears in Nicholas Everitt and Alec Fisher, *Modern Epistemology: An Introduction* (New York: McGraw-Hill, 1995), pp. 174–178.

An Introduction to the Analysis of Knowledge

Actually, the chapter title is a bit misleading. The focus of this chapter is on the analysis of the *concept* of knowledge. As mentioned in the Introduction, concepts refer to certain properties, objects, or facts in the world. The goal in analyzing concepts is to state what must be true of some thing for it to have the property designated by the concept. So, when philosophers—epistemologists, in particular—analyze the concept of knowledge, they are attempting to state under what conditions a person knows. But we will return to this in a moment.

Most of the analyses, or theories, of knowledge considered in this chapter were developed within the past three decades. But this hardly means that prior to the latter half of the twentieth century, no philosophers other than Descartes pondered the concept of knowledge. Indeed, many contemporary epistemologists trace the general framework for thinking about the concept of knowledge back some twenty-four centuries.

Plato (c. 429–347 B.C.E.) developed an analysis of knowledge in the larger context of his metaphysical and ethical concerns. Regrettably, we must confine ourselves to a brief sketch of some of the more relevant epistemological themes. In the dialogue *Meno,* the title character, Meno, asks Socrates why knowledge should ever be preferred to true opinion or belief. Before we let Socrates answer, it is worth trying to appreciate the force of this question. Suppose you are riding with a friend and are convinced that your friend simply does not know how to get to your destination. Nonetheless, as she changes lanes and turns down streets you would rather not travel, she insists that she *knows* this is the way to go. And she smugly reminds you of this when you arrive on time. If you find her reminder a bit frustrating, perhaps it is because you are willing to concede that your friend had the right opinion or a true belief, but that she really did not *know* that this was indeed the way. Whether she had knowledge or simply true belief, this much seems apparent: You reached your destination. In this context, knowledge and true belief seem much alike in that they both get you to the same place. In other words, both knowledge and true belief get you to the right answer; they get you to the truth. It is this observation that prompts Meno's question. If both knowledge and true opinion get you to the same place, if they both get you to the right answer, why worry about having knowledge? Why not simply settle for true belief? There doesn't seem to be any difference between them.

Socrates, however, is impressed by the fact that true opinions have a disturbing tendency to "fly away." Perhaps you have also had the experience of having a true belief, but for various reasons, such as the influence of friends, you changed your mind and subsequently had a false belief, or gave the wrong answer. Now, Socrates thinks that our true beliefs are less likely to fly away if they are appropriately tied down. Our ability to tie down a true belief is merely our ability to give an *account,* or an explanation of why we think that our belief is the right or correct belief. Knowledge is distinguished from true belief by this ability to give an account or explanation. Thus, knowledge is true belief plus the account. In the vocabulary of this chapter, knowledge is *justified true belief.* It is this analysis of the concept of knowledge—the justified true belief analysis—that is called the **traditional analysis** of the concept of knowledge.[1] As we move through this chapter, we will see the first hints of a move away from an internalist conception of knowledge and toward an externalist view.

It is a bit of historical irony that prior to 1963, hardly anyone actually used the terminology of the traditional analysis—that is, who analyzed the concept of knowledge as justified true belief. After 1963, the widespread, but not unanimous, opinion has been that the traditional analysis is not quite right. Epistemologists thus have a tradition with little history and not much of a future! Nevertheless, it is plausible to think that the common core of various theories of knowledge is justified true belief. Thus, in the previous chapter, we noticed that one way of understanding the concept of knowledge is as follows:

(1) P is true.

(2) The subject or agent believes that P.

(3) P is infallible.

Notice that conditions (1) and (2) require that knowledge be at least true belief. But it is perhaps plausible to think of condition (3) as specifying the requirement for the justification of a true belief. Descartes could thus be read as claiming that for a true belief to count as knowledge, it must not be possible for the belief to be mistaken. More succinctly, infallibility is the type or kind of justification required for knowledge. So, we might view Descartes's understanding of the concept of knowledge as a variation on a theme first articulated by Plato almost 2500 years ago. Perhaps there is a bit of tradition in the traditional analysis after all.

Three matters concern us in this chapter. The first is to explain and attempt to motivate the traditional or standard analysis. Despite the fact that prior to recent decades few people actually defined knowledge as justified true belief, it is worthwhile to see why the traditional analysis provides a general framework for thinking about knowledge. The second matter relates to more recent accounts of knowledge and concerns a type of objection that led many to reject the idea that justified true belief is the appropriate way to analyze the concept of knowledge. Third, we examine three different theories of knowledge. Although our concern is the concept of knowledge, these theories focus substantially on the notion of justification and the sort of justification required for knowledge.

THE TRADITIONAL ANALYSIS

Truth Conditions

We are specifically interested in the analysis of the concept of *propositional* knowledge. Propositional knowledge differs, for example, from procedural knowledge, or *knowing how*. Knowing how seems to involve a particular skill or ability, as in knowing how to ride a bike or how to find a bit of information on the Internet. But the focus of the traditional analysis is *knowing that*. For example, Sara knows that Gödel proved the incompleteness theorems. The object of Sara's knowledge is a certain proposition or sentence. The content of her knowledge, what she knows, is given by the proposition or sentence "Gödel proved the incompleteness theorems." More generally, and somewhat schematically, the traditional or standard analysis attempts to provide the truth conditions for "S knows that P," where "S" stands for a person and "P" stands for the object or content of the person's knowledge. In attempting to provide an analysis of the concept of propositional knowledge, epistemologists aim to identify not only what is true of Sara (for example, that she knows Gödel proved the incompleteness theorems), but also what is true of Sam (for example, that he knows the ball is outside). Thus, epistemologists are attempting to give a perfectly general analysis. They want to say what is true of any person when that person has propositional knowledge. Somewhat formally, the aim of an analysis of the concept of propositional knowledge is to provide the necessary and sufficient conditions for when the following is true:

(K) S knows that P.

Less formally, the idea is to state under what conditions an agent knows something. We want to know what it is about the agent or the agent's situation that makes it the case that the agent knows and is not, say, just guessing.

Notice that when we ask this sort of question about the appropriate analysis, we are asking a different sort of question than asking when an agent is justified in *claiming* that he or she knows. For example, Newton may have been justified in thinking that space is Euclidean, but he did not actually know that. Similarly, I might be justified in claiming to know that the test will be given on Wednesday, but for various reasons I cannot foresee, the test may be postponed until Friday. Hence, although I was justified in claiming to know, it turns out that I did not in fact know. One way to express this distinction is to say that we are interested in the *truth* conditions of (K), but not necessarily the *assertibility* conditions of (K). The assertibility conditions of knowledge specify when someone is justified in *claiming* to have knowledge, regardless of whether that person actually knows. The truth conditions of (K), the necessary and sufficient conditions for knowledge, are the conditions under which someone does in fact have knowledge. Analyses of the concept of knowledge are typically concerned with the truth conditions of the concept, not the assertibility conditions. Providing the truth conditions of (K) is a way of explaining the nature of knowledge, of explaining in what knowledge consists.

Motivating the Traditional Analysis

We have already noted that it is difficult to find epistemologists who actually present the traditional or standard analysis. We might, however, consider a specific example of an analysis of the concept of propositional knowledge as a way of motivating the standard analysis. In 1956, A. J. Ayer (1910–1989) gave the following analysis:

(K_A) S knows that P if and only if:

(1) P is true.

(2) S is sure that P.

(3) S has the right to be sure that P.[2]

That condition (1) is a necessary condition for knowledge has seemed obvious to most, as it does to Ayer. This is not a recent development in the understanding of the nature of knowledge. Recall that Plato thought knowledge was at least *true* belief. But we might wonder whether we can give any explanation for thinking that knowledge entails the truth of the proposition.

One type of explanation might consist of an appeal to our normal practices, to our typical intuitions. Suppose Sam says to you, "I know that the keys are on the desk." Yet when you step over to the desk, there are no keys to be found. You might protest that Sam doesn't know, because there are simply no keys there. And you might be understandably perplexed when Sam defends himself by claiming that although he knows that the keys are on the desk, it is *false* that the keys are on the desk. Your perplexity might be traced to your presumption that knowing entails truth. In fact, you might insist that Sam *thought* he knew but in fact did not.

Perhaps one way to emphasize the oddness of this case is to think about what we expect from someone who knows. Imagine, for a moment, that your calculus teacher continually gives the wrong solutions to the assigned problems. A natural reaction might be something along the lines of "He doesn't know what he is talking about!" We expect that someone who knows can give us the right answer. That is, someone who knows has locked on to a particular truth. Refusing to acknowledge that knowledge implies truth is to collapse the distinction between knowledge and types of false belief. But we often desire to distinguish between someone who has very good reasons for what he believes but believes something false, and someone else who also has very good reasons but believes something true.

Recall that part of the aim of epistemology is to identify the standards by which we can make differential assessments of our beliefs. One natural way to do so is to distinguish between true beliefs, which pick out genuine features or characteristics of the world, and false beliefs. Moreover, to call beliefs instances of knowledge suggests that we are epistemically better off having such beliefs as opposed to false beliefs. These two thoughts together seem to motivate the idea that knowledge requires the proposition at issue to be true.

Still, we might be suspicious of this condition for at least two reasons. First, we might think that knowledge merely represents doing the best the agent can do and that in some of those cases the agent might have a false belief. Notice, however, that we can distinguish two kinds of cases: (a) one in which agents do the best they can but arrive at false beliefs, and (b) one in which agents do the best they can and arrive at true beliefs. Now, clearly, the latter case in some sense describes agents who are epistemically better off.

A second reason relates to the claim that knowledge is in some sense relative to a perspective, either an individual's or a community's. Two things can be noted in response. Even relative to a perspective, we can distinguish true from false beliefs. More generally, the truth condition does not specify what *theory* of truth is the correct theory. The condition is compatible with any number of theories of truth, including what has been called a relativist notion of truth. It is not unusual, however, to see many epistemological discussions assume an objective notion of truth, and we will do so here.

The preceding paragraphs may not provide a compelling motivation for counting truth as a necessary condition of knowledge. However, they at least make the motivation for the truth condition somewhat more apparent.

More serious questions arise with (K_A-2). Ayer suggests that the agent must be sure that P.[3] An implicit idea here is that the agent has some mental state with a particular content, which can be characterized by the proposition P. Our normal way of describing such matters is that the agent believes that P. When Sara believes that the bank closed at five, she has a

Theories of Truth

Philosophers disagree about the nature of truth. One recent classification distinguishes between nonepistemic and epistemic theories of truth. This parallels, in some respects, the distinction between realist and nonrealist views of the world. *Nonepistemic* theories of truth hold that the truth of a proposition depends on the way the world is, independently of our beliefs about the world. *Epistemic* theories hold that the truth of a proposition depends on our beliefs about the world.

A more traditional classification distinguishes between correspondence, coherence, and pragmatic views of truth. Roughly, *correspondence* theories hold that a proposition is true if and only if the proposition matches or corresponds to the way the world is (or at least the part of the world relevant to the proposition, sometimes called a "state of affairs"). *Coherence* theories hold that a proposition is true if and only if it fits or coheres with a system of propositions. *Pragmatic* theories claim that a proposition is true if "it works," that is, if acting or believing on the basis of that proposition produces the right sort of consequences.

For the purposes of this text, we assume a realist view and a correspondence theory of truth. See "For Further Study."

mental state that has a particular content. The mental state is about the bank. Being sure is a stronger requirement—for example, not only do I believe that the provost will retire, but I am sure, or perhaps convinced, that the provost will retire. But we might wonder whether being sure that P is necessary to know that P. Let's see if we can sort this out.

We might again begin by thinking of our more ordinary sense of what it means for you to know that P. Among other things, it seems fairly clear that you have acquired, in some as yet unspecified way, some bit of information P. From your perspective, this information describes some fact or feature in your environment. (We are not assuming that all information is true information; some information might be *misinformation*.) What happens when you acquire information? Well, you store it—in your memory or head or mind or brain. Note that what you have stored is the information that P, not the contradictory of P, or the contrary of P, or some other proposition, say, R. What this suggests is that you think P, and not some "competitor" of P, best describes the facts that currently interest you. This suggests that you hold P on balance to be true.

So what do we have? A mental state of yours, a representational state, purportedly of some fact, with the content P. Perhaps this is not the most elegant account, but it does bear a striking resemblance to what we think of as belief. So, at a minimum, (K_A-2) suggests that S believes that P. Do we have reason to want to state this condition more strongly?

There are two ways of understanding Ayer's "being sure" requirement. One is to interpret an agent's "sureness" in a psychological sense. The other is to construe "being sure" as indicating something about the agent's view of the epistemic status of the belief. Let us focus on the psychological construal first.

Notice that someone might "feel sure" of some belief, but for reasons that have little or nothing to do with the truth of the belief. A person who holds a belief based on mere superstition might nonetheless feel sure. Sam might feel sure that his having a flat tire is due to his having walked under a ladder. But such confidence is rarely a guide to the truth. Thus, one might object to the psychological construal on the grounds that what we are interested in is the *epistemological* issues concerning the concept of knowledge, not the psychological issues. What we need is an explanation of why a psychological state is an indication of the epistemic status of the belief: Is the belief merely a good guess? Does it qualify as knowledge? In other words, we would like to know whether a person must be sure or confident in order to know.

Suppose that Sam studied diligently for his upcoming logic test and answered all the questions correctly. But suppose also that Sam has never been terribly confident of his abilities in "abstract symbol" courses. Further suppose that were you to show Sam incorrect uses of, say, De Morgan's Rule, he would not be inclined to change the answers he gave on the test. Indeed, Sam checks his answers carefully and does not change any of them; nonetheless, Sam is reluctant to say he did well. Should we deny that Sam knows the answers? It would seem not, because there might be all sorts of irrelevant reasons for Sam's lack of confidence.[4]

This last point suggests that someone might want to understand "being sure" as indicating some epistemic concern about the belief. In particular, it might be urged that Sam's lack of confidence, in the preceding example, might indicate that he does not think he has the best of reasons for giving the answers he has. Thus, for this way of thinking about "being sure," we might argue that a person must believe that he has good reasons for holding the belief.

This line of thinking does raise important issues, some of which we will address shortly. But notice that this way of understanding "being sure" has, in effect, introduced two new considerations for knowing: (a) The person must have good reasons, and (b) the person must think that such reasons are good reasons. Both of these must be considered in their turn. Note, however, that the belief condition and considerations (a) and (b) are logically independent of one another. Because they are logically independent, it would perhaps be best to treat them separately. We will, in fact, have to look at putative conditions for knowing like (a) and (b), but for now, we rest content with the idea that (K_A-2) should be revised to read simply:

(2) S believes that P.

A few critics have objected to even this revised condition as a necessary condition of knowledge.[5] Such objections typically elicit two responses. First, there is a difference between knowing the answer and knowing the answer is correct. In our example, Sam might plausibly be said to know the answers, even if he did not know the answers were correct. Or imagine Sara as a game show contestant who gives the correct answer but is not completely confident. In this case, we might say that Sara believed that P without necessarily being confident that P is correct. This confidence may not be a necessary condition of belief.

The second point is that such cases might reasonably be considered borderline cases of knowledge. Sara, for example, may give the correct answer to a question and not be inclined to give any other answer. Yet we might not want to insist that Sara *knows*. Her lack of confidence may indicate that she does not have very good reasons for her answer or that she is simply guessing. We might want to distinguish this lack of confidence from Sam's lack of confidence about the answer on a logic test, a case in which he does have good reasons for giving the answer he does. But the important point in cases like Sara's is that in this sort of context, there is no practical difference between guessing and knowing the correct answer. Thus, we may plausibly claim that we have not yet been given a clear-cut case of knowing but not believing. Again, it is worth emphasizing that what motivates such cases is the thought that not only knowledge but also belief requires a certain sort of confidence. And we have already seen reasons to reject confidence as part of our second condition.

It is worth mentioning one further reason for thinking that knowledge does not imply belief. Suppose you ask a friend if she believes the presidential debate will be held at a local university. Her response is an emphatic "I don't just believe it; I know it!" This response is an example of a kind of "conversational rule" that agents make the strongest epistemic claim they are entitled to make. Thus, it might be claimed that if one knows that P, then one does not merely believe that P.[6] But this sort of claim does not show that knowledge does not imply belief. It merely shows that knowledge is more than simple belief.

The final condition in Ayer's analysis (K_A-3) maintains that the agent must have the right to be sure. An important feature must be noted here: "Having the right to be sure" implies that whatever grounds the agent's confidence must be an adequate ground. That is, not just anything will legitimate the agent's confidence. This suggests that there is an important normative component in knowledge, that an agent's belief must in some way satisfy a certain standard. How exactly this normative component is to be preserved or explicated remains to be seen.

We noticed in considering condition (2) that the idea of confidence or sureness raised the issue of the reasons for the agent's belief. So, one of the things that we might view $(K_A\text{-}3)$ as suggesting is that in some as yet unspecified sense, the agent must be justified in believing that P, where "justification" means "having good reasons."

A brief note on "having good reasons": There are clearly inadequate reasons for having a belief if we are interested in understanding the concept of knowledge. Suppose Sam believes, as a result of consulting a fortune-teller at a county fair, that he will someday be president. Sam does have a reason for his belief. But we might be reluctant to think that this is a good reason, that the fortune-teller's musings provide sufficient evidence for Sam's belief. More to the point, it is not a good reason if Sam is interested in believing the truth and avoiding believing things that are false. Compare this type of case with Sara's belief that there will be a test tomorrow. Imagine that she believes this because the test is scheduled on the syllabus and the teacher reminded her of the test. We would be inclined to think that Sara's belief is based on good reasons. The function of "good" is to point out that her reasons do in fact explain why she holds a true belief.

This last point brings up a further complication, one that will be significant in this and subsequent chapters. Suppose Sara has a good reason for her belief, and suppose that reason explains why she holds a true belief, in either of two senses. In one sense, the reason may be the *cause* of her belief. In this sense, the reason functions as part of a cognitive mechanism that produces Sara's belief. But there is a second sense in which the reason may explain her belief: Sara may hold her belief by virtue of the content of the reason. For example, suppose Sara notices one morning that the streets are wet. On the basis of this content, that the streets are wet, Sara infers that it rained last night. In a sense, Sara recognizes that the truth of the reason supports the truth of the belief. In the first case, the belief is an effect of the reason; in the second case, the belief is a consequence of the reason. Very informally, we might think of the difference between these two senses of "having a reason" in this way. The first sense, the causal sense, might serve to answer the question "What brought about Sara's belief?" The second sense might serve to answer Sara's question, "Why do I have this belief?" As we will see later (for example, in Chapter Six), some think that it is this latter sense that characterizes the reasons *for which* an agent holds a belief, and it is this latter sense that is necessary for justification.

At a minimum Ayer's third condition suggests that the agent must have good reasons for believing that P. That Sara studied diligently is a good reason for her to believe that a particular answer is correct (assuming the normal things we do about studying). However, condition (3) leaves open whether the agent must recognize that the reasons are good reasons or whether the agent must in fact have good reasons. Descartes offers an explicit version of the former sort of view. His "indubitability" criterion indicates not only a reason for having the belief but also the *recognition* by the agent of the indubitability as a reason for having the belief. Indeed, the classical conception of knowledge is one in which an agent not only has good reasons but recognizes that the reasons are good.

On the other hand, to some people, this latter constraint, explicitly recognizing the reasons as good reasons, might seem too strong. We cannot yet fully explain why some might want to opt for this weaker version of the condition, but we should be aware of it in our formulation of the third condition.

For the time being, we can avoid deciding between the stronger and the weaker versions of condition (3). To do so, we can maintain that an agent must minimally be justified in believing that P, without yet spelling out whether the sort of justification sufficient for knowledge is the weaker or stronger sense of this condition (or perhaps neither). As we noticed early in the chapter, Socrates distinguished mere true belief from knowledge. He did so by appealing to the notion of a person having an account or explanation for the belief. This account or explanation is what we mean by justification. The reasons for a person's belief provide the justification for the belief. The justification explains why the belief is true. Knowledge is more than a lucky guess; it is more than mere true belief. In the *Theaetetus*, Socrates argues that a jury may have a true belief without having knowledge.[7] And the notion of justification is intended to capture the difference between knowledge and mere true belief. We are thus led to the idea that a necessary condition of knowledge is that the belief is justified, that there are good reasons for the belief. We are unwilling to credit someone with knowledge unless the person has acquired the belief by "one of the accredited routes to knowledge."[8] This provides us with a schema by which to approach the analysis of the concept of knowledge:

(K) S knows that P if and only if:

  (1) P is true.

  (2) S believes that P.

  (3) S is justified in believing that P.

With the qualification that condition (3) was historically understood in the stronger sense identified in the previous paragraphs, we have arrived at the traditional or standard analysis, the *justified-true-belief* (JTB) analysis, of the concept of propositional knowledge. We will discover that criticisms of this analysis divide epistemology in ways that might never have been imagined.

GETTIER AND THE TRADITIONAL ANALYSIS

Although it is rare to find anything approaching consensus in philosophy, there was considerable agreement that something like the traditional analysis was along the right lines.[9] This complacency came to a rather abrupt halt in 1963, when Edmund Gettier published a paper entitled "Is Justified True Belief Knowledge?"[10] In this brief, three-page article, Gettier provided two examples suggesting that all was not quite right with the traditional, or JTB, analysis. His counterexamples to the JTB view suggest that the justification condition and the truth condition can be independently satisfied. That is, the circumstances that account for an agent's being justified in having a particular belief are not necessarily the circumstances that explain the truth of the belief.

Gettier-type Counterexamples

Gettier's own examples are straightforward enough, but we will consider two other examples, the first offered by Keith Lehrer.[11]

Lehrer asks us to imagine a case in which an agent, the ubiquitous S, has a coworker, Ms. Nogot. Now, S has good reason to believe that Nogot owns a Ford; imagine, for example, that S has seen Nogot driving a Ford, S has been told by persons who have in the past been reliable that Nogot owns a Ford, and so on. Hence, S has justification for her belief that Nogot owns a Ford, and from this she infers her belief that P—someone in the office owns a Ford. But Ms. Nogot does not own a Ford. Nevertheless, S's belief that someone in the office owns a Ford is true, because Ms. Havit owns a Ford.

Notice that S has a justified true belief—the belief that someone in the office owns a Ford is true. Moreover, S had good evidence for arriving at this belief; that is, S is justified in believing that P. But it is not obvious that we would want to say in this case that S has knowledge. We might think that S has been a bit lucky. It just so happened that someone did own a Ford, but not the person S thought owned the Ford. S does have reasons, but we might think that S doesn't have the right sort of reasons.

The second counterexample derives from Alvin Goldman.[12] Imagine a situation along the following lines. A man is taking his young son on a tour of the country for the first time. The man points out various things to his son and identifies them. The man points to a barn and says, "That's a barn." In fact, the man has succeeded in pointing to a barn. Unbeknownst to him, however, a film company has been in the area and has been constructing barn facsimiles. Close by the actual barn the man pointed to is just such a barn facade. Indeed, the man could not discriminate between the barn and the barn facade. Again, the agent has a justified true belief: He sees the

Bertrand Russell and Gettier-type Counterexamples

Bertrand Russell, in 1912 and 1948, provided examples that look a great deal like Gettier-type counterexamples. In *The Problems of Philosophy,* Russell suggests the following example. If a man believes that the late prime minister's last name began with "B," what he believes is true because Mr. Bannerman was the late prime minister. But he will not have knowledge because he believes that the late prime minister was Mr. Balfour. In *Human Knowledge,* Russell uses the example of someone looking at Big Ben and arriving at true belief about the time. However, the clock has in fact stopped.

Russell uses these examples to show that knowledge cannot be identified with true belief. Do you think these examples are Gettier examples? If not, can you modify them so that they would serve as Gettier examples?

barn, can recognize barns, and so on. But we might hesitate to claim that he has knowledge. After all, the man just as easily could have pointed to a barn facade and thus have had a justified, yet false belief.

Gettier-type counterexamples are abundant in the literature, but these two will serve to illustrate the points we need to make for now.[13] Two quick words of caution: First, people engaging in this debate are not skeptics. These epistemologists do think that we have knowledge; they disagree rather about the appropriate analysis of knowledge. Second, we can alter the counterexamples to make the justification as strong as we wish, so long as the evidence does not entail the truth of the belief. That is, these examples are intended to show that a true belief might be based on adequate evidence and yet fail to be a genuine instance of knowledge.

It is important to note how the two counterexamples show that the truth and justification conditions can be independently satisfied. In the Ford case, S clearly does have reasons for his belief. Yet if we were to explain why S's belief is true, we would refer not to Nogot, but rather to Havit. S's justification does not direct us to what accounts for the truth of his belief. In the barn case, the connection between the satisfaction of the two conditions is clearly more intimate. But we can still see that the justification for the father's belief does not suffice to explain why he just happened to pick out a real barn rather than one of the facades. This bit of good luck is in no way reflected in his justification. Sometimes, this feature of Gettier-type counterexamples is expressed as a belief's being accidentally true with respect to the agent's justification.

These remarks suggest a way of remedying the defect suggested by Gettier cases. The remedy is to constrain or restrict the way in which the justification condition is satisfied. One way to do this is to amend the JTB analysis so that it includes a fourth condition that specifies additional restrictions an agent's justification must meet. That is, to have knowledge, an agent must not only have a justified true belief but also be justified in a particular way. Not only must the agent have reasons for the belief, but an additional constraint is placed on how good the reasons must be. Indeed, some epistemologists hold that the attempt to deal with Gettier cases is merely an attempt to specify a fourth condition. Alternatively, we might suggest that the way to remedy the apparent defect of the JTB analysis is to change our understanding of what counts as a "justified" belief. The thought here is that the kind of justification necessary for knowledge might differ from our ordinary sense of what it means for an agent to have reasons or evidence for a belief. Of course, a response to Gettier cases might make use of both these strategies. That is, a response might not only add some further fourth condition but also amend our understanding of the justification condition. In what follows, we will talk generically of amending the JTB analysis.

Before considering how theorists have attempted to amend the JTB analysis, we need to consider a few dissenting words, for not everyone agrees that Gettier has identified a problem with the traditional analysis.

A Defense of the Traditional Analysis

The main strategy of interest here is what we might call the *entailment* strategy. Recall Descartes's insistence that the justification appropriate for knowledge requires us to show that the belief at issue is true. In particular, Descartes insists that the justificatory connections between one's evidence and the belief in question are always *deductive* connections. In this view, the justification condition and the truth condition cannot be satisfied independently.

More recently, Oliver Johnson defended the claim that properly interpreted, satisfaction of the justification condition entails that the truth condition be satisfied.[14] Johnson refers to this entailment relation as the *logical interpretation* of the justification condition. According to Johnson, if we hold the view that the justification condition does not entail the satisfaction of the truth condition, what he calls the *contingent interpretation*, then the standard analysis is rendered useless. We could not determine, for any given belief, whether the belief qualifies as knowledge. This is due to the fact that we could not tell whether the belief is in fact true; we would have no decision procedure for determining the truth of the belief. Because the truth condition is an uncontroversially necessary condition of knowledge,

Johnson thinks that our inability to demonstrate the truth of the belief renders the standard analysis useless.

On the other hand, the logical interpretation automatically guarantees the satisfaction of the truth condition. The ability to justify one's belief is merely the ability to show that the belief is true. Hence, if we accept this logical interpretation of the justification condition, Gettier-type counterexamples simply do not count against the standard analysis. After all, in the logical interpretation, the justification condition is not satisfied in Gettier cases.

The logical interpretation of the justification condition is a heroic response to Gettier. Of particular interest is that in this interpretation of the JTB view, most of the beliefs we would be inclined to count as knowledge are simply not knowledge. Consider, for example, my belief that Bob Dole lost the presidential election in 1996. I have many beliefs that support this belief. For example, I remember seeing Dole in various commercials in which he jokes about losing the election; I believe that someone else currently is president; and I hear various people remark that Dole seems much more at ease since he lost the election. In the contingent interpretation, and in our normal view, I know that Bob Dole lost the presidential election. Although I am clearly justified, none of my supporting beliefs *entail* that my belief about the outcome of the election is true. In the logical interpretation of the justification condition, I do not know that Bob Dole lost the presidential election in 1996. It is not difficult to find innumerable other beliefs, which we typically count as knowledge, that would not be knowledge if we accepted the logical interpretation. But Johnson claims that our ordinary conception of knowledge, which presumably relies on the contingent interpretation, is an incoherent conception of knowledge.

In the previous chapter, we saw some reason to reject such strong constraints on instances of knowledge. In such a view, it is difficult to see how we would ever have beliefs about the world—for example, beliefs about the kinds of objects and the properties they have—that would count as instances of knowledge. Moreover, it is not entirely clear that having knowledge requires that we be able to demonstrate the truth of the belief. We might even suggest that this is an attempt to reintroduce the infallibility requirement. Pointing out that many of our beliefs would not count as knowledge in Johnson's view does not show that he is mistaken. But it should at least make us curious as to whether there is some alternative account of Gettier problems that might not be so restrictive.[15]

Two final points can be made about Gettier cases. First, although there may be an air of unreality about some of them, cases such as Goldman's barn example surely do seem to involve genuine instances of justified belief. Second, Gettier cases can be used to draw our attention to certain aspects of knowledge. Natural Gettier cases may be rare. A recent issue of

Science News reports that researchers may have had a justified true belief that "yo-yo dieting" can cause cancer but that recent studies suggest they believed it for the wrong reasons.[16] Such a case might count as a "natural" Gettier case. However, although such cases might not be the norm, they do indicate that we are sometimes epistemically better off when our justification reflects the facts, that is, when our justification does in fact explain why the belief is true. At the very least, we might think that some Gettier cases suggest that we can have knowledge only in a generally cooperative environment. If we rely on our generally "accredited routes to knowledge," we count on the world being more or less normal. We can fail to have knowledge due to the global complications imagined by Descartes, but knowledge may also elude us when the world is less dramatically abnormal. This "failure of normality" can go undetected, and thus preclude our having knowledge, even though we have done all that we might reasonably be expected to do.

SOME STRATEGIES FOR HANDLING GETTIER PROBLEMS

After the publication of Gettier's paper, the task was to amend the JTB analysis in such a way as to preclude Gettier cases. We will be concerned with only a small and influential sample of the various specific proposals. Our aim is to get a general sense of the motivation and structure of these proposals, as well as with major difficulties each encountered. Here we will be concerned with three views: causal theories, indefeasibility theories, and the no-false-premise view. In the next chapter, we will consider in more detail a view known as reliabilism.

A General Diagnosis

It will be helpful to begin by giving at least a general account of what goes wrong in Gettier-type cases. As we already noted, Gettier cases show that as it stands, the JTB analysis permits the justification and the truth conditions to be satisfied independently of one another. That is, what accounts for the justification of the target belief (the belief that is a putative instance of knowledge) is not what accounts for the truth of the target belief. An agent's evidence or reasons for a belief may not adequately reflect the circumstances that underlie the truth of the belief. For example, S's reasons for believing that someone owns a Ford have no obvious connection to the truth of that belief. In a sense, S has evidence, but it is the wrong evidence for the belief that she has.

But you might wonder why this is a bad thing, especially given that we have apparently rejected the obvious solution: the entailment strategy. We can perhaps see what is at issue here by considering what we expect from our concept of knowledge. Rejecting the entailment strategy is in line with the previous rejection of the claim that knowledge requires infallibility. But if this particular criterion for knowledge is too stringent, what weaker demands can we make?

Gettier cases give us some hint of what we might expect from a satisfactory analysis of the concept of knowledge. The moral of Gettier cases might be this: Gettier-type cases suggest that a belief might be justified and true, but had things been just a little different, we might have had a false belief. In some sense, it was merely good fortune or a happy accident that we arrived at a true belief. Thus, in the Lehrer case, for all the evidence our omnipresent S had, it still might have been false that anyone, including Havit, owned a Ford. Or, S might simply have chosen not to make the existential generalization, in which case S would have had the false, yet justified belief that Nogot owns a Ford.[17] Similarly, in Goldman's case, it was just good fortune that the father pointed to an actual barn, rather than to a mere barn facade. Consequently, a plausible approach for dealing with the counterexamples is to find a way to amend the JTB analysis that limits the possibility of our having a false belief. To put it slightly differently, we might look for an analysis that ties our justification more closely to the truth of the belief, such that it is less of an accident that the belief turns out true, given the evidence the agent has. With this in mind, let us turn to the more specific proposals.

Causal Theories

Causal theories are a remarkably clever way of resolving the "accidentality problem." As we will see, they involve a subtly different understanding of the justification condition. Roughly, **causal theories of knowledge** hold that a belief is an instance of knowledge if the belief is true and is *caused* in the right way. Of course, we need to know something more about what it means to be caused in the right way. For the moment, we can motivate the causal theory by explaining how we can move from our more traditional understanding of the justification condition to the causal theorist's understanding of the analysis of knowledge.[18]

So far, we have been assuming that the justification condition requires that agents have evidence for their beliefs. In other words, an agent has other beliefs, which are the reasons for the target belief. As we noted previously, these are the reasons *for which* the agent holds the belief. It is not too difficult to think of this evidence as the *reason* the agent has the belief. In a legitimate sense, the evidence *causes* one to have the belief; the belief is an effect, or causal result, of the reasons. Sara has the belief that she will be flying to London tomorrow because she looks at her ticket and notices that the departure date is the following day. It is by virtue of this evidence that she comes to have the belief. Now comes the subtle shift. Instead of thinking of justification in this more traditional "evidential" sense, we can perhaps understand it in a more general "causal" sense. That is, a belief will be justified if the *reason* the belief is held—what *causes* the belief to be held—is an appropriate reason.

You might be wondering how the shift from the evidential to the causal sense of "reason" is supposed to help us with Gettier. Recall that the challenge presented by Gettier examples is to tie the justification and truth conditions more closely. We can now marry these conditions if we say that the reason the agent holds the belief is tied to the reason the belief is true. That is, some of the conditions that account for the agent having the belief must be the same conditions that account for the truth of the belief. We want at least part of what causes the agent to have the belief also to be what explains the truth of the belief. Is there a candidate for this dual role? How about the "facts"? Intuitively, the facts cause the agent to have the target belief, *and* the facts explain why the belief is true.

Consider a fairly mundane belief, that there is coffee in the cup. Why do you have this belief? You look over there, where the cup is, and see the coffee in the cup. You acquire the belief for the simple reason that that you see coffee in the cup. The fact that there is coffee in the cup causes you to believe there is coffee in the cup. If this is what we mean by being justified, then your belief clearly is justified. On the other hand, what makes your belief true? Well, how about the fact that there is coffee in the cup? Your belief is true only if there really is coffee in the cup. So, the facts explain both the justification of the belief and the truth of the belief. Moreover, this sort of analysis seems to fit with our ordinary intuitions. How do you know there is coffee in the cup? You look over there and you see it; your seeing it causes you to believe it. What more could one want from an analysis? The justification and the truth condition can no longer be satisfied independently; the two conditions are indeed intimately connected.

Your objection to the causal theory should be taking shape just about now. You are surely wondering why, in the case of the barn facades, the father's belief doesn't qualify as knowledge in this sort of causal account. Seeing the actual barn causes the father's belief, and thus he has a true belief, so why doesn't he have knowledge?

The short answer is that we are getting ahead of ourselves. Early causal accounts were designed to deal with cases like the Ford problem. The barn case will require a bit more finesse and will move us from causal accounts to reliability accounts. Alvin Goldman did offer a solution to the barn case, a kind of reliability account. But prior to giving the reliability view, Goldman offered a causal theory designed to deal with cases like the Ford problem.

Goldman's solution to this latter problem is succinctly stated in his "A Causal Theory of Knowing."[19] There, Goldman claims that

> *S* knows that *p* if and only if the fact *p* is causally connected in an "appropriate" way with *S*'s believing *p*.

Clearly, what we want to know is what the force of "appropriate" is. Goldman claims that perception and memory are appropriate knowledge-producing causal processes. But the Ford case is neither a case of mere perception nor a case of memory. Thus, Goldman adds another appropriate process. He suggests that (a) a causal chain must exist, leading from the fact to the belief, that is correctly reconstructed by inferences, each of which is warranted, and (b) the background beliefs that function in such inferences must be true.[20] (He also mentions that combinations of these three—perception, memory, and inference—count as appropriate processes.)

In the Ford case, why does S fail to have knowledge? Note that there is a causal chain leading to the fact that someone owns a Ford but that this causal chain involves Havit. S's own inferences, however, reconstruct this causal chain as involving Nogot. Thus, the inferences do not satisfactorily mirror the causal chain: S does not know.

We have already suggested that the barn case might prove problematic for this causal theory. In keeping with the spirit of Gettier, other philosophers have suggested other counterexamples. Here, it is worth noting two points. First, a somewhat technical point: Goldman's early causal analysis does not eliminate cases in which there is more than one causal chain that might account for the truth of the belief: hence, the reconstructed inferences do not mirror the actual causal chain.[21] Sherlock Holmes's faithful assistant Watson might notice a gunshot wound in the chest of a victim, take the victim's pulse, and pronounce him dead. Now, Watson surely knows the victim is dead. He knows this even though his inferences do not reconstruct the actual causal chain, say, a bite from an exotic and deadly spider released in the victim's bed. Watson is misled by the gunshot wound into thinking that this was the cause of death. Watson is right that the gunshot wound is sufficient to cause death. Poor Watson is simply unaware of how many enemies the victim had. But the gunshot is not the actual cause of the victim's demise. Thus, Watson's inference that the victim is dead, an inference based on the reasonable belief that a gunshot wound to the chest is sufficient to cause death, does not correctly mirror the actual causal chain. This reconstruction of the actual chain will be left to Holmes.

More importantly, notice the subtle shift in the notion of "reason" that is beginning here. We ordinarily think of reasons as evidence one has. That is, we often think of reasons as other beliefs the agent has, beliefs that the agent could cite as required. But there is a shift in the causal theory toward thinking of reasons as causal—that is, what caused the agent to believe that P. In a more traditional view of "reason," we might grant that an appropriate causal connection exists between a fact and a belief, but we might not be so willing to grant that an agent, say Sara, has a reason, unless she is aware of this causal connection. We can understand why she believes what she does, but we might still ask whether she is justified in believing as she does. Causal analyses of knowledge are explicit about the move from evidential to causal reasons. Marshall Swain, for example, distinguishes between "causal" and "evidential" reasons, the latter being what we would be more ordinarily inclined to think of as a reason.[22] Swain acknowledges that evidential reasons are sometimes causal reasons. However, he insists that the relevant reasons for justification are causal reasons. Consider again the belief that there is coffee in the cup. Clearly, a causal connection exists between agent and cup, namely, perception. In the causal view, the fact of this connection is enough to justify the agent's belief; there is a reason for the agent's belief. In the evidential sense of reason, however, for the agent to be justified, the existence of this causal connection is not enough. The agent must also at the very least believe that this connection exists. The causal theory counts the notion of causal reason as the primary sense of reason. We will be especially interested in this kind of move as we turn to reliability theories in the following chapter.

Indefeasibility Theories

A widely favored response to Gettier-type problems is some type of **indefeasibility theory**. The motivation for this view lies in holding that what goes wrong in Gettier cases is that the agent's justification is somehow defective. It is true that the agent's belief is justified, that the agent does have some evidence for the belief. But there is other evidence that the agent does not possess. There are other true propositions that the agent does not believe or recognize but that are nonetheless relevant to the truth of target belief. This other evidence is such that if the agent possessed it, the agent's current belief would no longer be justified; the agent's justification would be *undermined*. Thus, there is a sense in which the agent's justification is incomplete. The agent has some evidence but lacks other evidence that would render the target belief insufficiently justified to count as knowledge. This undermining evidence is called *defeating* evidence. A justification is defeasible if and only if there is defeating evidence. Hence, the sort of justification required for knowledge is not simply justified true belief but also *indefeasible justification*.

We can begin to better understand this view by noticing how an indefeasibility theorist provides plausible diagnoses of the Ford and the barn examples. In the Ford case, S believes that Nogot owns a Ford. On the basis of this justified belief, S concludes that someone in the office owns a Ford. We have not far to look to uncover a defeater: Nogot does not own a Ford. If

S believed this, then S would not be justified in believing that someone owns a Ford (recall, after all, that S had no evidence regarding Havit's owning a Ford).

In the barn case, we might identify the defeater as the proposition that there are a number of fake barns in the area that, from the highway, look exactly like real barns. Were the father to believe the proposition that there are fake barns in the area, he would no longer be justified in believing that he had succeeded in pointing to a barn.

It is worth noting what it would take for the father to have knowledge—that is, what might count as an indefeasible justification. His justification would need to be such that the information regarding the barn facades no longer threatened his justification for stating, "That's a barn." We might imagine, for example, that he pulls over and takes a closer look from different perspectives to assure himself that he is indeed seeing a real barn. Once he sees that the barn is in fact a barn, the information that there are barn facades in the area is less troubling. Indeed, even if every other barn-like object in the area is but a facade, the father seems indefeasibly justified in his belief about the real barn, for he now has reasons (specifically, his having seen the real barn from a variety of angles) that could rule out the possibility that he is looking at a fake barn. Under these sorts of conditions, we could say that the father has an indefeasible justification for his belief, and hence has knowledge.

Indefeasibility strategies thus look promising. The difficulty arises, however, in trying to formulate how the JTB analysis should be amended. As one epistemologist has pointed out, the presence of the defeating evidence is an entirely unexpected fact.[23] Indeed, the existence of defeating evidence is not something that the agent can simply introspect. As we will see, the unexpected nature of the defeating evidence makes it difficult to say what should be required for a justification to be indefeasible.

Perhaps we can approach the problem in this way: In the Ford case, S does have an *undefeated* justified true belief that someone owns a Ford. That is, S does not currently believe that Nogot does not own a Ford, so as yet her justification remains intact. S's justification is undefeated, but she does not have knowledge. Thus, we have to say that to have knowledge, S must have a justification that is indefeasible—that there are no potential defeaters lurking nearby. This means that S's actual or current justification would have to be such that it screens out or blocks all potential defeaters.

Indefeasibility theorists do not require that an agent be able to show that there are no defeaters, nor do they require that the agent believe there are no defeaters. Rather, for a justification to be indefeasible, these theorists require merely that there *in fact* be no defeaters. Whether this fact is reflected in the agent's beliefs makes no difference to the defeasibility of the agent's justification. You might notice that this is a departure from a more traditional conception of knowledge such as Descartes's. This sort of departure proves to be somewhat controversial, and we will return to it. But first, we need to consider how an indefeasibility condition might be expressed.

A seemingly natural way to state such a condition is to claim that there is no true proposition such that if it were added to S's justification, S would no longer be justified. We should note just how strong a condition this is. It claims that if there is *any* evidence that would, if believed by the agent, undermine the justification, then the agent would no longer know. Thus, according to this condition, the existence of even one defeater is sufficient to preclude knowledge. Worse, it might seem as though even *misleading* evidence could rule out knowledge.

Consider a slight modification of a case found in the literature.[24] Imagine that you attend a wedding of two close friends and that the ceremony is performed by a priest well known to you and the others at the ceremony. The wedding is conducted and concluded without a hitch. On the basis of this evidence, you come to believe that the couple is married. Clearly, your belief is justified; you have every reason to think that you know your friends are married. But let us suppose that unbeknownst to you and the others present, including the priest, the bishop has gone crazy. Among other things, the bishop falsely denounces the priest as a fraud. Now, here is a true proposition: The bishop has denounced the priest as a fraud. Were you aware of this proposition, you would not be justified in believing your friends to be married, because fraudulent priests cannot marry anyone, any more than fake barns can provide sanctuary for our barnyard friends. Despite the apparent defeater, we are still tempted to say that you know.

The crazy bishop case illustrates that a distinction must be drawn between genuine and *misleading* defeaters. Misleading defeaters are defeaters that can themselves be defeated; that is, still further evidence can be obtained that would "restore" the original justification. What further evidence defeats the defeater in the crazy bishop case? "The bishop is crazy" seems a promising candidate.

Apart from crazy bishops, misleading defeaters are illustrative of the central intuition behind indefeasibility approaches and their most difficult obstacle. According to indefeasibility theorists, defeasible justifications occur because an agent is less than ideally situated with respect to the believed proposition.[25] On the other hand, an agent's justification is indefeasible only to the extent that the agent could acquire further evidence or information without losing the original justification. An agent's knowledge ought to be extendible. According to indefeasibility theorists, an indefeasible justification cannot be undermined by the agent's acquisition of new

Strong and Weak Conditions

In the literature, a particular condition is sometimes referred to as too "strong" or too "weak." A condition is too strong if it rules out cases that we would be inclined to think of as knowledge. For example, we suggested that Johnson's logical interpretation of the justification condition is too strong because it rules out too many cases that we would be inclined to consider knowledge. A condition is too weak if it counts cases as knowledge that should not be so considered. Russell rules out identifying knowledge with true belief because those conditions are too weak; doing so would count the person who looked at the malfunctioning Big Ben as having knowledge.

evidence. There is something intuitively plausible about the extendibility of knowledge. If one knows that some object is a barn or that some couple is married, then one shouldn't lose this knowledge merely because one learns some further bit of information. The idea is that indefeasible justifications are able to withstand the acquisition of new information.

Perhaps now we can see more clearly the connection between misleading defeaters and indefeasible justifications. Misleading defeaters are true propositions. Yet when they are properly understood, they should not undermine an adequate justification. For example, the true proposition that the bishop denounced the priest as a fraud is, in a sense, not the whole story; we must also consider the bishop's insanity. So, there is some piece of information out there showing that the defeater is misleading, that it does not actually undermine the agent's knowledge. By itself, the misleading defeater *appears* to show that the agent does not have knowledge. But once the whole story is revealed, it becomes clear that the agent does know.

Yet it is not easy to see exactly how to articulate the intuition that knowledge is extendible or that we can acquire new information without losing our original justification. What is needed is a condition that will identify the defeasible justifications but will not be so strong as to rule out knowledge in those cases in which the defeaters are *misleading* defeaters. We can rule out the misleading defeaters easily enough—for example, by requiring that there be no true propositions that would undermine the agent's justification or that an agent's knowledge be extendible—but this can come at a very high price. Indeed, it has been pointed out that if we read such conditions in a very strong sense, then it would seem to result in the claim that we never have inductive or nondemonstrative knowledge.[26]

If any pocket of evidence runs counter to our legitimate inductive inferences, then on this strong reading of indefeasibility, beliefs based on such inferences could never be knowledge.

The requirement that there be no true propositions that would undermine the agent's justification should strike you as reminiscent of the skeptic's apparent requirement that to know, you must be able to rule out any alternative explanations. But there is an important difference here. Indefeasibility requires only that an agent's justification not be susceptible to *actually* true propositions that would provide counterevidence for the agent's belief. The skeptic requires that an agent be able to rule out even *possibly* true competing explanations.

This difference should not mislead us. If we still require that our current justification be such that it could survive our acquiring *any* true proposition, then there may be very few cases in which we can be said to have knowledge. And this seems to be due the fact that much of our knowledge is of the nondemonstrative or inductive sort. We come to know things inductively even though our evidence does not entail the proposition known, nor could it entail the proposition. This leaves open the possibility that certain true propositions might count against our justification.

Suppose, however, we try to find an understanding of the indefeasibility condition that does not seem to lead to this overly strong result. The idea here is that even though learning of the misleading defeater would undermine our justification, we could come to learn something else that would show us why the defeater is misleading. Although this may be a plausible idea, it is difficult to accomplish.[27]

In learning some additional information that shows the defeater to be misleading, we learn that our original justification was not defective, but merely incomplete. Our original justification is thus saved. But if we are said to have knowledge in such cases, this would seem to be due to our now being justified in believing that our original justification was nondefective. As Robert Meyers puts it, "What protects your knowledge is not the original justification but the fact that you learned the counterevidence along with the evidence that nullifies it."[28]

Let us see if we can understand what Meyers has in mind. Again, suppose that you have just witnessed the wedding of your friends. You believe that they are married, and your justification for this belief is your belief that a priest has performed the ceremony. You would thus appear to have a justified true belief. But now you learn that the bishop denounced the priest as a fraud. This new bit of information undermines the justification for your belief about the wedding. You can "regain" your knowledge by learning that the bishop is no longer trustworthy about certain matters. But now it seems as though your justification is different. Previously, your justification consisted of your belief that a priest performed the ceremony. Your "new" justification seems to consist of your belief that a priest performed the ceremony and that the bishop cannot be trusted.

Why does Meyers believe that the change in your justification matters? Perhaps for something like the following: Your original justification seemingly is *enough* or *sufficient* to give you knowledge. But attempts to rule out misleading defeaters seem to have the result that your original justification is *not* sufficient. Thus, indefeasibility analyses, which attempt to deal with the problem of misleading defeaters, fail to distinguish between justifications that are defective and justifications that are merely incomplete. In the former case, the agent is undermined by genuine defeaters; the agent does not have adequate evidence, as in the Ford case. But in the latter case, the agent's justification is adequate, but it simply does not include the misleading defeater and the relevant counterevidence. One might think that the conditions of knowledge need not require an agent's justification to include evidence sufficient to rule out any misleading defeater.

Indefeasibility theorists might respond to this as follows: A justification is adequate even if does not include evidence sufficient to rule out misleading defeaters. It is only necessary that the agent could acquire that evidence *without* changing or giving up the beliefs that comprised the original justification. For example, in learning that the bishop is crazy, you do not need to change the beliefs that comprised your original justification. Indeed, the new evidence vindicates your original justification. This strategy seems to have some promise, but we leave the matter here.

We can briefly recount the main features of indefeasibility views. We can fail to have knowledge in cases in which we have a justified true belief because our justification is not quite good enough. We might have done the best we could given the evidence we possessed. Unbeknownst to us, however, additional evidence or information is relevant to the target belief. Were we to come to know about that evidence or information, we would recognize that our original justification was inadequate; we would no longer be justified with respect to our original belief. Hence, we do not have knowledge in such cases. Although this approach may be intuitively plausible, it is difficult to find a way to amend the JTB analysis that satisfactorily distinguishes between genuine and misleading defeaters. On the one hand, the condition may be too strong and rule out legitimate cases of nondemonstrative knowledge. On the other hand, if the condition is weaker, it may fail to distinguish between defective and merely incomplete justifications. However, if there is a means of satisfactorily amending the condition, perhaps along the lines of the "vindication" approach, then the indefeasibility approach to the analysis of knowledge will have overcome one of its more significant hurdles.[29]

No-False-Premise Views

Still another way to analyze Gettier cases is to note that the agent's justification relies on a mistaken or false premise. In the Ford case, the false premise is explicit: Nogot owns a Ford. In the barn case, the false premise is more implicit but looks something like this: If it looks like a barn from the highway, then it is a barn. (Another candidate is that there is nothing unusual about the environment.) Thus, the fourth condition that might be added to the JTB analysis is that the justification does not depend on any false premises.[30]

As it stands, this proposed fourth condition is too strong. It may be that an agent believes a false premise but that this premise does not, or need not, play a central role in the agent's justification, given what else the agent believes. Consider a slight variation of the Ford case. Suppose S believes that someone in the office owns a Ford because she has seen the registration papers and seen Havit driving a Ford. Suppose, however, she falsely believes that Havit bought the car at East Ford. Finally, suppose she infers that someone in the office owns a Ford on the basis of her belief that Havit owns a Ford purchased from East Ford. We might nonetheless think that S knows that someone owns a Ford, because where the car was purchased makes no difference to Havit owning a Ford. The possibility of false, but inessential premises requires some explanation of what it means to say that a premise plays an essential role in the justification. This further explanation centers on the idea that the agent would not be justified in believing that P unless the agent also believed some further proposition Q. The proposition Q is then said to be essential to the agent's justification.

So, the fourth condition in the **no-false-premise** view is that there is no false proposition essential to the agent's justification. Or, as Robert Meyers states the condition:

> S is justified in believing *p* on the basis of *q* only if: every proposition essential to S being justified in believing *p* on the basis of *q* is true.[31]

There is a standard objection to this view. The idea behind this objection is that if an agent reasons cleverly enough, then the agent will not be committed to believing any false premises. But such objections seem to trade on the idea that if no false premise is explicitly articulated in the agent's reasoning, then the agent's justification does not depend on a false premise.

We can briefly consider an example suggested by Richard Feldman.[32] In the Ford case, Feldman argues that if S were to use existential generalization *prior* to her inferring that Nogot owned a Ford, then S's justification would not depend on the false proposition that Nogot owns a Ford. That is, if on the basis of her evidence that she had seen Nogot driving a Ford and she had been told that Nogot owned a Ford, she had immediately inferred that someone in the office owned a Ford, then S's justification would not depend on a false premise. But we might reply that whether S articulates or reasons explicitly from a false proposition, S clearly seems to believe something false. In particular, S clearly seems to believe that Nogot owns a Ford. Indeed, were it not for S having this belief, it would seem strange to us that she would infer that someone owns a Ford.

The point here is that the explicit premises in one's justification may well depend on further background beliefs. Feldman's counterexample seems to ignore these background beliefs. Doing so permits him to claim that we need only consider the explicit premises of an agent's justification. But once we recognize that some background beliefs are essential to an agent's explicit reasoning, we can see that in a legitimate sense what goes wrong in Gettier-type cases is that some false belief underlies the agent's justification.

This line of thought may be problematic. We do not want to understand this condition so strongly that every background belief held by the agent is an essential proposition for the agent's justification. But the notion of an essential proposition seems to trade on our intuition that some beliefs matter more than others for particular cases of reasoning and that some beliefs matter not at all. If this intuition proves to be well grounded, then there is much to recommend the no-false-premise view. For the moment, we will leave matters here.

THE SIGNIFICANCE OF GETTIER

The Gettier problem and subsequent work on it have not been universally prized. As counterexample spawned counterexample, as rebuttal met with rebuttal, and as yet a further subclause was added to the analysis of knowledge, some suspected that the forest had been lost, not for the trees, but for the pine needles. However, important issues have arisen as a result of this process. We will restrict our discussion to two main issues: (a) the nature of knowledge and (b) the nature of justification.

First, you may have already asked yourself what the proper response to Gettier should be. Each of the three strategies presented previously was motivated by intuitively plausible considerations, yet each faced certain difficulties. So, can we expect a return to the widespread agreement in evidence prior to Gettier?

Notice that the indefeasibility and no-false-premise views agree that justified true belief is necessary, if not sufficient, for knowledge. Depending on how we interpret causal theory, it, too, might be viewed as holding that justified true belief is necessary for knowledge. We should also notice that our justified true beliefs can be "gettierized" in many ways. These observations suggest two things. First, there may be no single account that deals with each and every counterexample. In turn, we are led to a second, perhaps more important consideration.

As characterized here, the Gettier problem results from a potential gap between the satisfaction of the justification condition and the satisfaction of the truth condition. The challenge is to find a way to close this gap. It may be, however, that this gap can arise in different ways. Indeed, we might view our three accounts as suggesting different ways in which a gap might arise between the justification and the truth conditions. Thus, different ways of closing the gap may be necessary, just as is suggested by the three views in the previous section. That is, different types of justification may be appropriate under different circumstances.

We can elaborate the idea that different responses to Gettier cases might address different ways in which the traditional analysis is inadequate. Ernest Sosa has suggested that knowledge is apt or appropriate (true) belief.[33] We can view this suggestion as a schema whereby the challenge is to identify the circumstances under which a belief is apt. We may want to distinguish, for example, between simple perceptual beliefs and beliefs arrived at as the result of a complicated chain of inductive reasoning. Thus, there may be no clear choice among the analyses presented. Still, we should keep in mind the extent to which a particular view can be extended to cover a broad range of types of counterexamples.

A second issue about knowledge arises. Do Gettier cases show, as Mark Kaplan's article title suggests, that "It's Not What You Know That Counts"?[34] Kaplan argues that finding the appropriate response to Gettier would make no difference in how we conducted our inquiries. Once an agent has made the best possible use of his or her evidence, Kaplan argues that whether the agent knows makes no difference. That further condition seemingly required by Gettier cases, which would make a justified true belief an instance of knowledge, is not something the agent can check to see if it is satisfied. What goes on in Gettier cases is that the environment has been "tricked up" in some way that normally exceeds an agent's discriminative capacities. Because such cases lie outside the agent's ability to recognize them, it is simply not clear what further requirements should be made of the agent. But then, whether the agent has knowledge seems to leave the fact that the agent has a justified true belief unaffected.

One can concede some of Kaplan's suggestion but still resist the conclusion that a solution to Gettier is unimportant.[35] In response to Kaplan's claim, it is argued that the goal of inquiry is not simply to attain a justified belief, but rather to attain knowledge. Moreover, although Gettier problems may indeed often be undetectable by the agent, in some cases further investigation may lead to genuine knowledge. Another line of response to Kaplan is the following: At the outset of this chapter, we distinguished between the assertibility and truth conditions of knowledge. Here, we might add the notion of verification conditions. Kaplan seems to be suggesting, among other things, that an analysis of knowledge is useful only if we can *verify* that we have knowledge, only if we can somehow check to see that we have knowledge. The verification conditions of knowledge are a separate issue from the truth conditions of knowledge. There clearly is an independent interest in whether an agent knows, even if the agent cannot verify that knowledge. We might want to understand the concept of knowledge despite the fact that we might not always be able to recognize every occasion that a person has knowledge. Moreover, there is reason to think that post-Gettier analyses of knowledge can make a difference to our future inquiries. Suppose, for example, that we understand the concept of knowledge along the lines of indefeasibility. Imagine that Sara knows, even though she cannot verify that her justification is indefeasible. Later, however, she may learn additional facts that explain why her justification is indefeasible, and she might be able to use these new facts to guide her future inquiries.

A distinction, which will be important to us in subsequent chapters, is that between externalist and internalist accounts of knowledge and justification. Recall from the Introduction that **externalism** is roughly the idea that an agent's justification or knowledge depends on some condition that need not be reflected in an agent's beliefs.[36] **Internalism,** on the other hand, roughly holds that a belief is justified only if the relevant justifying conditions are in some respect reflected in the agent's beliefs or cognitive perspective.

Some of the responses to Gettier may signal a move toward externalism.[37] In discussing the causal theory, we noticed the shift from evidential reasons to causal reasons. What matters is the causal mechanism that produces the agent's belief. The causal theory does not appear to insist that knowledge depends on the reasons *for which* an agent holds the belief. This has led some to think that knowledge is externalist in nature, but we still might want to hold that justification is internalist.[38] The merits of this view need not concern us here. The important point is that we notice at least the beginning of the move from internalist to externalist conceptions of knowledge and justification. In Chapter One, the traditional conception of knowledge and justification seemed largely internalist. But in the next chapter, we see a theory, which is a type of causal theory, that explicitly repudiates that traditional, internalist conception of knowledge and justification. Indeed, the contrast between internalism and externalism will concern us in several subsequent chapters.

Key Concepts

Causal theories of knowledge

Externalism

Gettier-type counterexamples

Indefeasibility theories
of knowledge

Internalism

No-false-premise theories

Traditional analysis of
knowledge

Review Questions

1. Do you think that either the Ford case or the barn case is a case of knowledge? Explain. If not, explain why each is a case of justified true belief, but not a case of knowledge. Can you construct your own Gettier case?

2. How do causal theories attempt to avoid the problem of the independent satisfaction of the justification and the truth conditions?

3. What is the difference between genuine and misleading defeaters? Do you think indefeasibility theories can resolve the problem presented by misleading defeaters? Explain.

4. Explain Feldman's objection to the no-false-premise view. Do you think this objection shows that this view is an inadequate response to Gettier? Why or why not?

For Further Study

The debate surrounding Gettier examples mainly took place in journal articles. The most comprehensive treatment of the various theories and variations on theories is Robert K. Shope, *The Analysis of Knowing* (Princeton, NJ: Princeton University Press, 1983). Early responses to Gettier, including Gettier's original paper, "Is Knowledge Justified True Belief," are reprinted in Michael D. Roth and Leon Galis, eds., *Knowing: Essays on the Analysis of Knowing* (New York: Random House, 1970). Three other worthwhile collections are George Pappas and Marshall Swain, eds., *Essays on Knowledge and Justification* (Ithaca, NY: Cornell University Press, 1978); Paul K. Moser, ed., *Empirical Knowledge,* 2nd ed. (Lanham, MD: Rowman & Littlefield); and Peter French et al., eds., *Midwest Studies in Philosophy,* Vol. V (Minneapolis: University of Minnesota Press, 1980). John Pollock also develops a version of indefeasibility theory in *Contemporary Theories of Knowledge* (Totowa, NJ: Rowman & Littlefield, 1986), pp. 180–193.

A view not discussed in the text is Robert Nozick's "tracking view." Critical appraisals of this view can be found in Steven Luper-Foy, ed., *The Possibility of Knowledge: Nozick and His Critics* (Totowa, NJ: Rowman & Littlefield, 1987).

A useful introduction to theories of truth is Paul Horwich, "Theories of Truth," in Jonathan Dancy and Ernest Sosa, eds., *A Companion to Epistemology* (London: Basil Blackwell, 1992). An accessible, yet comprensive examination is Frederick F. Schmitt, *Truth: A Primer* (Boulder, CO: Westview Press, 1995). Chapter Seven examines considers truth in connection with the analysis of knowledge and skepticism.

Notes

1. Like the *Meno,* the *Theaetetus* provides an apparent formulation of the justified true belief analysis. At 201c and following, Socrates distinguishes knowledge from true opinion, and he subsequently seems to identify knowledge with true opinion plus speech or a rationale. Both are reprinted in Edith Hamilton and Huntington Cairns, eds., *Plato: The*

Collected Dialogues (Princeton, NJ: Princeton University Press, 1961). Of course, one cannot do better than reading Plato's dialogues, but three accessible surveys and interpretations are A. E. Taylor, *Plato, the Man and His Work* (London: Methuen, 1926); Nicholas White, *Plato on Knowledge and Reality* (Indianapolis, IN: Hackett, 1976); and J. C. B. Gosling, *Plato: The Arguments of the Philosophers* (London: Routledge & Kegan Paul, 1973).

2. A. J. Ayer, *The Problem of Knowledge* (Harmondsworth, England: Penguin Books, 1956), pp. 31–35.

3. Ayer, *The Problem of Knowledge*, pp. 31–35.

4. In this connection, see D. W. Hamlyn, *The Theory of Knowledge* (London: Macmillan, 1970), Chap. 4.

5. See, for example, Colin Radford, "Knowledge—By Examples," in Michael D. Roth and Leon Galis, eds., *Knowing: Essays on the Analysis of Knowledge* (New York: Random House, 1970), pp. 171–185.

6. See Hamlyn, *The Theory of Knowledge*, Chap. 4, and Jonathan Harrison, "Does Knowing Imply Believing?" in Roth and Galis, eds., *Knowing: Essays on the Analysis of Knowledge*, pp. 155–170.

7. See fn. 1.

8. Ayer, *The Problem of Knowledge*, p. 33.

9. This is not to suggest that there was universal agreement, of course.

10. The paper was originally published in *Analysis* 23 (1963): 121–123, but it is now widely reprinted. See Roth and Galis, eds., *Knowing: Essays on the Analysis of Knowledge*, pp. 35–38.

11. See Keith Lehrer, "Knowledge, Truth, and Evidence," in Roth and Galis, eds., *Knowing: Essays on the Analysis of Knowledge*, pp. 55–66.

12. Alvin Goldman, "Discrimination and Perceptual Knowledge," in Jonathan Dancy, ed., *Perceptual Knowledge* (Oxford: Oxford University Press, 1988), pp. 41—65.

13. Robert K. Shope's *The Analysis of Knowing* (Princeton, NJ: Princeton University Press, 1983) lists some ninety-eight such counterexamples that have appeared in the literature.

14. Oliver Johnson, "The Standard Definition," in Peter French et al., eds., *Midwest Studies in Philosophy*, Vol. V (Minneapolis: University of Minnesota Press, 1980).

15. Robert Shope suggests that there are Gettier-type examples to which even Johnson's logical interpretation falls prey. Such counterexamples do not depend explicitly on the appeal to a false proposition.

16. "Does Yo-Yo Dieting Pose Cancer Threat?" *Science News* 151, p. 157.

17. *Existential generalization* is the move from a specific case (Nogot) to a more general, indefinite "some one." Some have thought that the way to preclude Gettier-type examples is to restrict such logical moves. This seems a bit arbitrary, and there are examples that do not clearly depend on such inferences.

18. It should be noted that Goldman does not consider his causal analysis to be an interpretation of the justification condition. See Alvin Goldman, "A Causal Theory of Knowing," in Roth and Galis, eds., *Knowing: Essays in the Anaylsis of Knowledge*, pp. 67–87, esp. p. 84. The aim in the following paragraphs is to motivate the causal analysis, to see how one might move from the traditional analysis to something like the causal analysis.

19. Goldman, "A Casual Theory of Knowing," pp. 67–87.

20. Goldman, "A Casual Theory of Knowing" pp. 72–75.

21. The technical name for this problem is "epistemic overdetermination."

22. Marshall Swain, *Reasons and Knowledge* (Ithaca, NY: Cornell University Press, 1981), p. 75.

23. Marshall Swain, "Epistemic Defeasibility," in George Pappas and Marshall Swain, eds., *Essays on Knowledge and Justification* (Ithaca, NY: Cornell University Press, 1978), pp. 160–183.

24. Swain, "Epistemic Defeasibility," p. 165.

25. Swain, "Epistemic Defeasibility," p. 168.

26. See Robert Meyers, *The Likelihood of Knowledge* (Dordrecht: Kluwer Academic Publishers, 1988), pp. 91ff.

27. See, for example, Shope, *The Analysis of Knowing,* Chaps. 2 and 3. Swain also addresses some of these complexities in a number of places, including "Epistemic Defeasibility" and *Reasons and Knowledge.*

28. Meyers, *The Likelihood of Knowledge,* p. 96.

29. Of course, internalists may worry about externalist features of the indefeasibility view, but we cannot pursue these matters here.

30. Robert Meyers is explicit about holding such a view, at least for cases of inferential knowledge. Others have held a similar view—see, for example, Gilbert Harman, *Thought* (Princeton, NJ: Princeton University Press, 1973)—but this seems not to be the strategy of choice.

31. Meyers, *The Likelihood of Knowledge,* p. 100.

32. Richard Feldman, "An Alleged Defect in Gettier Counterexamples," in Paul Moser, ed., *Empirical Knowledge,* 2nd ed. (Lanham, MD: Rowman & Littlefield, 1996), pp. 241–243.

33. Ernest Sosa, "Methodology and Apt Belief," in Sosa, *Knowledge in Perspective* (Cambridge: Cambridge University Press, 1991), pp. 245–246.

34. Mark Kaplan, "It's Not What You Know That Counts," *Journal of Philosophy* 82 (1985): 350–363.

35. See Earl Conee, "Why Solve the Gettier Problem?" in Moser, ed., *Empirical Knowledge,* 2nd ed., pp. 261–265.

36. This is only a rough account; the next chapter will address the needed refinements. Also, in a sense, even the traditional analysis is externalist, because whether the belief is *in fact* true is not necessarily cognitively accessible to the agent. But externalist (or internalist) views of knowledge are not intended to refer to this feature.

37. In "The Naturalists Return," *Philosophical Review* 101 (1992): pp. 53–114, Philip Kitcher suggests that one of the sources of naturalized epistemology, an externalist view, is the reaction to Gettier.

38. Representative examples of this view may be found in Robert Audi, *Belief, Justification and Knowledge* (Belmont, CA: Wadsworth, 1988), and Sosa, *Knowledge in Perspective.*

CHAPTER THREE

Reliabilism

The previous chapter considered ways of responding to Gettier's challenge to the traditional analysis of knowledge. This chapter considers a view known as **reliabilism.** Although reliabilism offers a response to Gettier examples, it is a view that is significantly influential beyond the single question of how to revise the JTB analysis. Very roughly, reliabilism holds that a belief is justified or an instance of knowledge only if there is a reliable connection between the belief and truth. Although reliabilist theories were originally proposed as accounts of knowledge, there soon appeared explicitly reliabilist theories of justification. Indeed, the principal focus of this chapter is the reliabilist view of justification.

First, we sketch two versions of reliabilist theory, each of which provides a model of perceptual knowledge. Next, we consider a reliabilist theory of justification. Finally, we present three standard criticisms of reliabilism and typical responses.

RELIABILITY AND KNOWLEDGE

Two Versions of Reliabilism

Even if causal analyses of knowledge are not quite right, they still seem to capture an intuition about the nature of knowledge—specifically, that knowledge in some sense implies that an agent's belief is an appropriate cognitive response to features of the agent's environment. The belief is appropriate only if it is causally connected to features or properties in the environment. Thus, I know that there is coffee in the cup because there is a causal connection between my belief and the coffee in the cup. Reliability theories arose as a natural extension and modification of causal theories. Today, many epistemologists subscribe to some version of a reliability theory. The virtue of reliability theories is undeniable: They make explicit the link between justification and truth. Yet we will see that some philosophers think there is a high epistemological price to pay for such a link.

Like causal theorists, reliabilists start from a very natural and plausible intuition. D. M. Armstrong asks us to consider the lowly thermometer. The thermometer registers information about the ambient environment, and it does so in a reliable way. As long as the thermometer is not defective in some way, it is a reliable indicator of the temperature in the room or the environment.[1] A still more mundane example is a simple doorbell. The ringing of a doorbell is a reliable sign that someone is at the door. Of course, the doorbell is not an *infallible* indicator; it is merely a reliable indicator. Now, perception, or the process of acquiring information via the senses, seems to be just such a reliable indicator. If circumstances are normal, then the belief that there is a cup of coffee on the table is a reliable sign that there is indeed a cup of coffee on the table. This reliable indication is due to a lawlike connection between the belief and the fact. One way to think of this is in terms of a connection between certain properties of agents and certain properties of the environment. Others have construed our beliefs to be a probabilistic indication of certain properties of the world; that is, they have posited a statistical correlation between our having certain beliefs and the existence of certain features in our environment.[2]

For the case in which there really is a cup of coffee on the table, we can see that it is no accident that someone believes that there is. Hence, it is not difficult to see why one might be tempted to think that in the **reliable indicator** view, perceptual beliefs count as instances of knowledge. But you might wonder in what sense such beliefs are justified. We will return to the reliabilist's answer shortly.

A different version of reliabilism, **reliable process theory,** views perception as a type of reliable belief-forming process. Beliefs formed as a result of the process of perception—for example, vision—tend in the main to be reliable. But what is the force of this "reliable"? The general idea is that reliable processes are those that generally produce true beliefs in actual situations and would produce true beliefs in relevantly similar situations. In "Discrimination and Perceptual Knowledge," Alvin Goldman counts perception and reasoning as two types of reliable belief-forming processes.[3] Goldman suggests that a process is reliable to the extent that it is adequately discriminative—the process will produce true beliefs under the right sorts of circumstance.

In what follows, our focus is the reliable process view. But it is worth noting that both versions, the indicator model and the process view, emphasize the connection between reliability and true beliefs. With this in mind, let us turn to Goldman's account of perceptual knowledge.

Reliabilism and Perceptual Knowledge

Recall the barn example of the previous chapter. The father's belief is the outcome of a reliable process, but we hesitate to call it knowledge because of the nature of the environment. The father's belief is the result of a reliable belief-forming process, but that process is operating in an abnormal environment. The belief might have been false. So, we need some further condition to preclude the possibility that things might go wrong.

More on Reliable Indicator Theory

D. M. Armstrong claims that there is a lawlike connection between, for example, my believing that there is a cup on the table and a cup being on the table. My having the belief, according to Armstrong, can be thought of as my having certain characteristics or properties. In this sense, my having the belief is a feature of the world, just as the cup on the table is a feature of the world. The properties that I have when I have such a belief will undoubtedly be very complicated properties, but Armstrong thinks that science can, in principle, investigate the nature of these properties. These properties are connected, in a lawlike way, to certain features of the world (in this example, the cup on the table). My having these properties—those associated with my having the belief—is a reliable indication of the cup on the table.

What is a *lawlike connection?* Laws of nature are notoriously difficult to define. The basic idea is that natural laws express or describe certain types of regularities in the world. But the problem, central to the philosophy of science, is how to distinguish accidental regularities, or events and properties that just happen to go together, from regularities that are physically necessary. Typical of this latter sort are laws that identify causal connections in the world. Although we typically think that there is a causal connection between my belief and the cup, this is not the feature that Armstrong wishes to emphasize. He seems to have in mind something like the following: Litmus paper changing color indicates the presence of an acid. The properties of litmus paper—changing color—are indicative of particular chemical properties. And this is not an accidental connection between the litmus paper and the acid; it is a lawlike connection. Like litmus paper, we reliably "change properties" in the presence of certain features of the world. Of course, we don't change color; instead, we acquire certain perceptual beliefs.

The main idea of Goldman's initial suggestion as to how to do this is that the perceptual belief arises as a result of a reliable process that is operating in an environment in which the process can't be "tricked." Think again about what is not quite right in the barn case. Suppose the father had looked just across the highway, pointed to a barn facade, and announced the false belief "That's a barn." As far as the father could tell, the two perceptual experiences—looking at an actual barn and a mere facade—would have been similar in all relevant respects. He would have had the same experience of viewing a large, red expanse with various doorlike-looking openings. Either perceptual experience would have been enough to cause the father to believe that he was indeed seeing a barn. Goldman calls such cases of perceptual experiences similar in all relevant respects "perceptual equivalents." Moreover, the barn facade was for the father a *relevant alternative*. He could just as easily have looked in a different direction; indeed, there were many places he might have looked and pointed to a facade. The notion of relevant alternatives suggests that Goldman is not simply interested in remote skeptical possibilities. If we imagine the father driving through the New Jersey countryside, the mere fact that filmmakers had constructed barn facades in North Dakota would not present a relevant alternative. Goldman claims that to have knowledge, the father would have to be able to discriminate the real from the facade in his situation, because the facades were, for him, a relevant alternative. Because he could not do this, because the real barn and the facade were for him perceptual equivalents, he did not have knowledge.

Thus, according to Goldman, to have *perceptual* knowledge, the belief must satisfy three conditions. Here, we will recount them somewhat less formally than does Goldman. First, the belief must be the result of a reliable process, which it is—vision. Second, given the agent's relevant alternatives, there must be no perceptual equivalents that could lead the agent to have a false belief. And of course, third, the actual belief must be true.

Intuitively, this account has a certain appeal. We think that perception usually yields knowledge. When I see that there is coffee in the cup, we are strongly inclined to think that I *know* there is coffee in the cup. Moreover, we think this, it might be suggested, because perceptual beliefs generally turn out to be true. Yet sometimes things can go a bit awry—Hollywood filmmakers, epistemologists, and practical jokers (imagine two identical salt shakers, one filled with sugar and the other with salt) can sometimes place "perceptual equivalents" in our way. Such abnormal environments can trick our normally reliable belief-forming mechanisms. But when our environment cooperates, when things are as they normally are, then we are inclined to think that it is the reliability of the processes involved that lead to our having beliefs that are instances of knowledge.

Reliabilism and the Traditional Analysis

One might wonder whether reliabilist accounts of perceptual knowledge hold that beliefs must be justified to be instances of knowledge. In Goldman's and Armstrong's view, there is no necessary connection between reliability and justification, at least as far as the latter notion is traditionally understood. Thus, Armstrong remarks that

> the knower himself will not have evidence for what he knows. That is the meaning of 'non-inferential'. But his own belief-state, together with the circumstances he is in, could function for somebody *else* (God perhaps) as completely

reliable evidence, in particular as a completely reliable sign, of the truth of the thing he believes. The subject's belief is not based on reasons, but it might be said to be reasonable (justifiable), because it is a sign, a completely reliable sign, that the situation believed to exist does in fact exist.[4]

The agent need have no reasons for the belief. Indeed, it is sufficient, in Armstrong's view, merely that it be true that some suitably situated observer can tell that the agent's belief is a reliable indication of the existence of some fact. In this sense of reliable indication—that the belief is an indication of some fact—an agent's belief is likely to be true. If we are thinking of justification as the likely truth of a belief, then there is a sense in which the belief is justified. But Armstrong seemingly wishes to distance himself from a more traditional internalist conception of justification and knowledge. The reasonability or the justifiability of the belief does not stem from the agent's reasons. Rather, the source of the reasonability or the justifiability of the belief is the lawlike connection between belief and environment; the belief is a reliable indicator of some feature of the world.

Goldman, too, is explicit about the sense in which his reliabilist view of perceptual knowledge departs from the more traditional understanding of knowledge:

> It [reliabilism] requires only, in effect, that beliefs in the external world be suitably caused, where 'suitably' comprehends a process or mechanism that not only produces true belief in the actual situation, but would not produce false belief in relevant counterfactual situations. If one wishes, one can so employ the term 'justification' that belief causation of *this* kind counts as justification. In this sense, of course, my theory does require justification. But this is entirely different from the sort of justification demanded by Cartesianism.[5]

However, Goldman apparently is rejecting more than just Cartesianism. Even a traditional epistemologist might agree with Goldman in rejecting the Cartesian requirement of certainty at every level of knowledge. Yet one might reject Cartesianism and still retain the view that justification requires believing on the basis of good reasons, which make the belief likely to be true. But Goldman seems to suggest that an agent's belief need only be the outcome of a reliable mechanism to be justified. Like Armstrong, Goldman seemingly claims that an agent having reasons for a belief is not necessary for knowledge. Indeed, one might wonder whether an agent having reasons is necessary for having a *justified* belief. Thus, both Goldman and Armstrong propose an externalist theory of knowledge and justification.

A brief example might serve to illustrate the issue further. Suppose Sam sees that the ball is blue and comes to believe that there is a blue ball. In one view of the internalist Cartesian model, Sam's belief is justified only if there are no grounds for doubt or it is impossible that the belief is mistaken.[6] We have seen some basis to agree with Armstrong and Goldman that this view of justification and knowledge need not be accepted. However, one might still want to hold that Sam's belief is justified only if Sam bases his belief on "good reasons." Such reasons might be, for example, Sam's other beliefs that conditions in the environment are normal, that he is not looking at the ball under special lighting, that he has a clear view of the ball, that his eyes are functioning normally, and that perception is a generally trustworthy process for acquiring beliefs. Further, one might think that Sam is or can be aware that these other beliefs are his reasons. This view places less stringent demands on justification than does the Cartesian view, but it retains the internalism of that view. But in the externalist view described by Goldman and Armstrong, reliabilism appears to hold that having reasons is not a necessary condition for justification. What matters is the connection between Sam and the world around him; what matters is how Sam is "hooked up" to his environment.

An important qualification must be noted here. Reliabilists recognize that an agent may have reasons for a belief. But they typically claim that justification depends on *how* the reasons are used. That is, reliabilists focus on the causal process by which the target belief is formed.[7] Presumably, however, the agent need not be aware of either the type of causal process or the fact that it is a reliable process.

A further, related issue can be raised here. Armstrong thinks of perceptual knowledge on the model of a thermometer. In the paragraph immediately following the preceding extract, Goldman claims that an account of knowledge should be able to explain our figurative uses of "know"—for example, an electric-eye door "knowing" that someone is coming. He remarks specifically that it would be odd to say that the door had "good reasons" or that "it has the right to be sure." Goldman concludes that his account has the advantage of being compatible with certain features of animal cognition and that our concept of knowledge is rooted in this sort of activity.

More recently, it has been suggested that we distinguish between animal knowledge and reflective knowledge.[8] *Animal knowledge* consists in our direct and relatively unreflective responses to our environment and experience; *reflective knowledge* is identified as those cases in which we understand the larger context in which belief arises. Whether one is willing to accept this contrast, it might help us to see Goldman's point a bit more clearly. It is somewhat controversial whether our "concept of knowledge" is rooted in animal cognition. Our cognitive capacities may trace back to animal cognition even if our concept of knowledge does not. But this point aside, one might still worry whether the cognitive lives of thermometers, electric-eye doors, or infrahuman species are sufficiently rich to capture at least a sense of knowledge that human beings seem sometimes to manifest. In the previous chapter, we noted that Oliver Johnson thinks our ordinary conception of knowledge is incoherent. In rejecting the Cartesianism of

Johnson, one might worry that we have set our sights a bit too low with a reliabilism that insists on thermometers or animals as the appropriate epistemic model. We return to these issues in a subsequent section.

RELIABILISM AND JUSTIFICATION

We have alluded to the fact that the reliabilist account of knowledge might be extended to provide a reliabilist account of justification. Although there are reliable indicator theories of justification, the focus here, as previously, is the reliable process theory of justification.[9]

In an extremely influential article, Goldman provides an initial version of the reliable process theory of justification:

> If S's believing p at t results from a reliable cognitive belief-forming process (or set of processes), then S's belief in p at t is justified.[10]

Again, to call a belief-forming process a *reliable* process is to suggest that the beliefs formed as a result of such processes are generally true. Plug certain information into the process (for example, the information you get about your environment via the senses, or other beliefs), and as an output of the process, you get a belief that is likely to be true. As examples of such processes, Goldman mentions standard perceptual processes, remembering, good reasoning, and introspection. Examples of unreliable processes include the usual suspects as well: wishful thinking, confused reasoning, and hasty generalization.

Goldman's characterization of this view is straightforward. The "justificational status of a belief is a function of the reliability of the process or processes that cause it, where (as a first approximation) reliability consists in the tendency of a process to produce beliefs that are true rather than false."[11] It bears emphasizing that a reliable cognitive process is merely a process generally productive of true beliefs. Recall that there is an intimate connection between justification and truth. If there is reason to think that a belief is likely to be true, then there is some reason to think that the belief is justified. A reliable process is merely a process that tends to produce true beliefs. Now, a belief that is the product of a reliable process is likely to be true. Thus, reliably formed beliefs are likely to be true, and hence, justified. Again, recall Sam's belief that the ball is blue. This belief is the product of a perceptual process. If perceptual processes tend, in general, to produce true beliefs, then such perceptual processes are reliable processes. Because Sam's belief is the product of such a process, it is likely to be true. That is, Sam's belief is a justified belief by virtue of its being produced by a reliable process.

However, we have already noticed that in the reliabilist view, instances of knowledge do not obviously require that the agent have reasons for that belief, at least not as we might normally understand "having reasons." A related issue arises here: Does the reliabilist view capture this sense of justification, that of having good reasons or adequate evidence? For the agent to have good reasons, does the agent need to believe that the processes are reliable?

Goldman's answer is instructive with respect to an underlying motivation for reliabilism. He rejects the idea that one must believe that a particular belief is reliably caused on the grounds that it would preclude children and animals from having justified beliefs.[12] We will see in a subsequent chapter that not everyone finds this type of response compelling. One might claim that children or animals have information but not justified beliefs. But the appeal to children and animals underscores a motivation for Goldman's view. Children, at least, and perhaps some animals, have true beliefs—in fact, a great many true beliefs. Small children are able to navigate the rigors of their environment, and they truly believe that the candy is in the dish or the doll is under the table. It is not mere coincidence that children have true beliefs. We are inclined to think that they are designed to acquire beliefs, which are typically true. And we think this because they are equipped with certain cognitive capacities, which enable them to acquire generally true beliefs. (Or at least, they can develop such capacities.) There is thus a connection between these cognitive capacities and the truth of the subsequently formed beliefs. Now, if one thinks that the essential aspect of justification is its connection to truth, or likely truth, then one might be disinclined to regard other features as necessary for justification. Goldman can easily suppose that children have justified beliefs because they clearly form beliefs as a result of reliable processes. But it is not quite so clear that children have views about the reliability of these processes or that they are always aware of the reasons for their beliefs. Thus, Goldman claims, it is not a necessary condition of justified belief that an agent believe that the belief is reliably produced. Similarly, one might reject the idea that the agent's awareness of the reasons for a belief is a necessary condition for justification. Thus, an agent's awareness of the reasons for belief, and the kind of reasons, does not appear constitutive of or necessary for justification, according to the reliabilist.

This suggests two ways of classifying reliabilism. Goldman describes his view as a kind of intrapersonalism.[13] A theory is *intrapersonal* if the features that determine the epistemic status of a belief are internal to the agent. Justification is a function of reliable belief-forming processes, and these processes are in at least some sense internal to the agent. When we ask about the justificatory status of a belief, we look to the cognitive process productive of that belief. Goldman clearly sees this as a desirable feature of a theory of justification.

But we might think of Goldman's theory in relation to another, more widespread type of classification, which we have already noted, that of *internalist* and *externalist* theories of justification. Recall that a theory is internalist if it requires that the features that determine the epistemic status of a belief either are or can come to be reflected in an agent's beliefs. This is sometimes characterized as the requirement that these features be cognitively accessible to the agent. Theories that reject this sort of requirement are externalist. As we have seen, Goldman rejects the accessibility constraint. The facts that determine whether a belief is justified—the source of the belief, or the reliability of the sources—need not be reflected in the agent's beliefs. Indeed, it may be that these facts cannot be found out by the agent. Thus, Goldman's view is externalist rather than internalist. The notions of internalism and externalism will figure in one of the criticisms of reliabilism encountered in the next section.

Goldman recognizes that the initial version of reliabilist justification must be modified to meet a particular kind of problem. He sees that there are occasions when it matters how an agent makes use of the available information or, more generally, the available cognitive resources. Suppose, for example, you notice a sign on your philosophy classroom door that class will meet in the media center. Later, however, you are told by a generally trustworthy friend that class will meet in the normal location. Your intuition is that your original belief would not now be justified; you should not continue believing that class will meet in the media center. The reason for this is that additional information, or additional cognitive resources, is available to you and should be used. Sometimes, such additional resources may simply be other information that is easily had; sometimes, it may be using or refraining from using certain inference methods; sometimes, it may be simply reflecting on your cognitive situation.

In a sense, we require a way of saying that agents must make the best use of their cognitive resources if beliefs are to be justified. Goldman's manner of accomplishing this is to add a clause to his initial statement of reliabilist justification. In this amended version of reliabilism, a belief is justified only if the belief is reliably formed and no other reliable process exists that the agent could or should have used that would have changed the agent's belief. Goldman specifically mentions here making use of the evidence one has.[14] We may infer that making use of the evidence one possesses is itself a reliable process, or a component of some other reliable process. But a critic of reliabilism may wonder whether "making use of one's evidence" is not a rather broad notion of a reliable cognitive process. The identification of the relevant cognitive processes is no minor worry for reliabilists, as we will see presently. Subsequently, we assume that the reliabilist account of justification refers to Goldman's amended version of a re-liabilist theory of justification.

Before we turn to the objections to reliabilism, we can briefly summa-rize the last two sections. Reliabilism is a species of causal theory. Both the reliable indicator model and the reliable process model provide accounts of knowledge. According to the first model, true beliefs, which are completely reliable indicators of certain facts, are instances of knowledge. According to the second model, a belief is knowledge if it is true and is produced by a reliable process that would have produced a true belief in relevantly similar environments. A reliable process analysis of justified belief claims that a be-lief is justified if and only if it is caused by a belief-forming process, which in general produces true beliefs, and there are no other processes that the agent could or should use. This view is internalist in the sense that the rele-vant justificatory features are internal cognitive processes of the agent. Yet it might not be counted as internalist in another sense—that the features that account for the justificatory status of the belief are or can be reflected in the agent's beliefs. Part of the motivation for these views seems to be the thought that humans are connected to their environment in such a way that, given the right circumstances, including their cognitive makeup, they are able to form true beliefs about that environment. To this extent, the epistemic status of such beliefs is compatible with a positive epistemic eval-uation of the cognitive capacities of children and certain animals.

Reliabilism, then, does seem to have its virtues—specifically, it seems to account nicely for our intuition that certain sorts of belief are normally knowledge and normally justified. The next section will focus on its per-ceived vices.

OBJECTIONS TO RELIABILISM

Although reliabilism is a popular theory, it has faced significant criticism over three issues in particular. The first has to do with the generality prob-lem; the second relates to whether a process's reliability is sufficient for knowledge or justification; and the third concerns the necessity of reliability for justification. This latter criticism has sometimes been referred to as the new evil demon problem. The generality problem is something of a techni-cal problem that has exercised both critic and reliabilist. But the latter two problems might be thought to reflect an intuition held by critics that relia-bility is not the source of epistemic justification. As one epistemologist puts it, "The beliefs are justified just because the believer is 'reasoning correctly' (in a broad sense of 'reasoning'). If one makes all the right epistemic moves, then one is justified regardless of whether his belief is false or na-ture conspires to make such reasoning unreliable."[15] Of course, intuitions notoriously differ. The objections raised by critics and the responses offered by reliabilists represent attempts to make such intuitions more precise, and to lend some independent weight to them.

The Generality Problem

How are we to identify which processes count as reliable? Obviously, the reliabilist wants us to count processes such as memory and perception as reliable. But is it clear exactly which cognitive processes are being cited? Consider, for example, some current theories about memory. Such theories identify, among other types, iconic memory, procedural memory, semantic memory, and short-term and long-term memory.[16] Do we have one cognitive process here or several? Are only some of these reliable, or are all of them? Another feature of memory sometimes noted by theorists is that we sometimes "refurbish" or "reconstruct" stored memories to aid recall. Should such reconstructive processes count as reliable? Reliabilists have tended to suggest, rightly, that which cognitive processes count as reliable is an empirical question. Presumably, this means that we will leave it to cognitive psychologists to tell us which are the reliable cognitive processes.

Yet this is not as straightforward as it seems. It is a quite substantial issue as to just how broadly or narrowly "reliable cognitive process" is to be construed. That is, depending on how we understand "reliable cognitive process," all beliefs might count as the output of a reliable cognitive process or none might. As a result, either all beliefs would count as justified or none would. Thus, we would be unable to distinguish between justified and unjustified beliefs. Richard Feldman has pursued at length this objection, which he calls the **Generality Problem.**[17]

We need a bit of terminology first. Any particular thing may be considered to be an instance, or a *token,* of any number of *types.* Consider the quarter in my pocket. What *type* of thing, or what *kind* of thing, is it? Well— it's a quarter; it's a coin; it's money; it's a round type of thing; it's the type of thing that has silver in it; and it is also the type of thing that "belongs to me." This quarter is an instance, or a token, of each of these types. So, a type may be specified by citing a characteristic or property or a group of characteristics. A token of the type will be any particular thing that has the specified characteristic.

The Generality Problem arises because any particular belief is a token of many different types of belief-forming processes. The reliabilist needs to provide us with a means for identifying a belief as a token of one type of process rather than another. It is not difficult to see why. We can determine whether a belief is justified only if we can specify the process type that produces the belief, for it is by virtue of a belief being produced by a reliable process type that the belief is justified.

A simple example will help illustrate the problem. Suppose I am walking through a supermarket parking lot, see a woman walking a dog, and come to have the belief about the breed of dog: "That's an American Eskimo." What type of process produced the belief? Was it perception? Vision? Or one of the following types: vision on a sunny afternoon; vision on a Thursday afternoon; vision across a busy parking lot in which the animal was seen for but a few seconds? We want the reliabilist to tell us at what level of specificity the process type should be described. Only once we know this can we tell whether the type is reliable, and hence whether the belief is justified.

This example also suggests constraints on the reliabilist response. On the one hand, we do not want the description of the process type to be so general that we cannot distinguish justified from unjustified beliefs. On the other hand, we do not want the type specified in such a way that it produces but a single token. This would lead to the unfortunate consequence that all true beliefs were justified and all false beliefs unjustified. This line of thought is worth exploring. As you will recall, reliabilism holds that a process that leads generally to true beliefs is reliable. So, if a process type produces only one token and that belief is true, then the type is reliable, and consequently the belief is justified. Clearly, however, the mere fact that a belief is true should not be sufficient to make it justified. Consider a simple example. Suppose I come to have the true belief that there is a glass of tea in front of me. Now, suppose we identify the type of cognitive process productive of this belief as the process of seeing a glass of tea on this particular Friday evening. This process, however, has but one token. Because that token, that belief, is true, it follows that this process type always produces true beliefs; it just so happens that it produces but one true belief. Nevertheless, every belief it produces is true. So, my belief about the glass of tea is justified.

On the other hand, we do not want to identify process types too broadly. For example, suppose we say that vision is a reliable process type. This will not quite do. Surely, some visual beliefs are justified—for example, my belief about the glass of tea—and some visual beliefs are not. Suppose I am walking on a moonless night, see a dog half a block away, and squint so that the dog is less visible than before. My belief that the dog is an Irish setter is a worthy candidate for an *unjustified* belief. Yet if all vision counts as a reliable process, then my belief about the kind of dog I am seeing counts as justified. Thus, if we identify process types too broadly, reliabilism will be unable to distinguish between justified and unjustified beliefs.

We want, then, a means of identifying process types that is neither too broad nor too narrow. Our interest here is confined to Feldman's examination of three ways by which the reliabilist might attempt to meet the Generality Problem.

We might begin our attempt to specify the reliable process types, as Goldman does, in a fairly ordinary, commonsense manner. Reliable types are those such as memory and perception, while unreliable types are those such as wishful thinking. This is initially plausible. We tend, in general, to trust memory beliefs, or beliefs formed as a result of the operations of our senses. But if the relevant type is perception or even, say, hearing, this means that all beliefs produced by this type would count as justified. However, we do not seem to count all of our perceptual beliefs as justified. If I am suffering from a bad cold and my hearing is impaired, I might very well be unjustified in believing that a friend has just said, "Is that cotton in your ear?" (when what was actually said was "It's too hot in here"). This attempt at specifying the general type, then, is much too broad and fails to distinguish justified from unjustified beliefs.

We might think that what went wrong with this first attempt is that we merely needed to be more precise about the conditions under which memory or vision or hearing are used. That is, instead of thinking of vision as the relevant type of process, we count "vision under conditions C" as the relevant type. Of course, we need to know what to substitute for the "conditions C." This leads to the second and third ways this problem might be met.

We might consider the idea that perceptual beliefs are justified only if they are produced under what we might think of as normal conditions. So, the relevant process type would be something like "vision under normal circumstances." We could then claim that my belief that there is an American Eskimo in the parking lot is justified only if I at least see it in good light, my vision is unobstructed, and my eyes are functioning normally. Yet we still have the same problem as before. Any number of visual beliefs may be produced under these normal conditions, some of them justified and some of them not. A belief that an animal is a dog and a belief that an animal is an American Eskimo may be formed under the same conditions, yet one might be justified and the other not. Intuitively, the reason for this difference seems to be that although I might be able to recognize dogs under normal circumstances, I do not possess enough information to enable me to identify the dog as a particular breed.

As you may recall, Goldman holds that a reliable process may not produce a justified belief if there is some other process the agent could and should have used instead. One type of process may override or "trump" another process. My believing that there is an American Eskimo is not justified to the extent that further thought would have led me to recognize that I am only occasionally able to tell American Eskimos from Pomeranians, or from small white dogs, for that matter.

Feldman argues that even the revised version of reliabilism faces the generality problem. It is worth taking a moment to spell this out. The problem facing the reliabilist is that a particular belief may be formed as a result of a reliable process type (even, suppose, under normal conditions), yet our intuition is that the belief is unjustified. How should the reliabilist explain this? The suggestion is that using other available cognitive processes would either prevent the belief from being produced in the first place or at least prevent the agent from continuing to have the belief.

Again, recall my belief that there is an American Eskimo, and suppose that this belief is unjustified. Moreover, suppose that were I to think about it, I would remember that I have only occasionally seen American Eskimos, I did so some time ago, and I'm not completely sure what differentiates Pomeranians from American Eskimos. So, there is another cognitive process available to me. Suppose I *do* use this process. Finally, suppose that nonetheless, I continue to believe as I originally did, confidently shouting, "Look at that American Eskimo!" I continue to hold the unjustified belief even though I make use of the other available cognitive process—the process that was to prevent me from having the belief. Thus, it is not at all clear that had I used such processes, this would have precluded me from having an unjustified belief.

Perhaps more to the point, Feldman suggests that it is not clear what this other cognitive process is. He claims that it must be a process in which I reflect on my visual belief and consider the evidence for and against the belief. But it is left unclear, Feldman claims, how we are to individuate this further reflective process.

It should be noted that this particular objection depends on a certain reading of Goldman's revised version of reliabilism. Goldman claims that a belief is justified only if there is no other process that, if used, would have resulted in the agent *not* forming the belief in question. Feldman's argument seems to be that we might use the additional process but still form the belief. Feldman thus seems to be exploiting the fact that merely using the additional process might not actually prevent me from forming the suspect belief. For the additional process to prevent me from forming the suspect belief, I must *recognize* that this additional process carries a certain "epistemic weight."

It is not immediately clear, however, that Goldman intends his revised version of reliabilism to be read in this way. Goldman may have in mind other processes that would, in fact, cause me to fail to have the belief about the type of dog before me. The sort of process that Goldman has in mind is precisely one that would preclude me from forming the belief. Because I continue to have the belief, according to Feldman's example, we have not identified the kind of process Goldman has in mind.[18] Still, we might want to know how such reflective processes are to be identified.

Is Reliability Sufficient?

It has been suggested that reliability may not be a sufficient condition for either knowledge or justification. That is, a belief might be reliable and still not count as epistemically praiseworthy; a reliably produced belief may not be justified. More informally, reliability by itself is not enough to produce justification.

Laurence BonJour was one of the first to note an implication of reliabilist analyses of knowledge.[19] Although BonJour was specifically concerned with whether reliabilism is an adequate account of knowledge, his objection, which might be termed the **clairvoyancy objection,** can easily be construed as an objection against the reliabilist view of justification as well. The basic idea is that the reliabilist view commits us to holding that there may be beliefs that the reliabilist counts as instances of knowledge but that nonetheless are *irrational beliefs.* If one also holds that justified beliefs are rational beliefs, then showing that a belief is irrational would be sufficient to show that it is unjustified. BonJour does not spell out what he means by "rational" in this context. Without distorting his argument, we may take him to mean something like the following: A belief is rational only if the agent has other beliefs that support the target belief. Further, the agent uses those supporting beliefs in a manner that the agent recognizes as legitimate—that is, the agent makes appropriate deductive or inductive inferences. This implies that the agent is aware of the reasons, the supporting beliefs, and the reasons those beliefs support the target belief. This is, of course, but one sense of "rational," but it seems to capture the idea behind BonJour's objection. Moreover, we will see that BonJour has in mind a particular kind of supporting belief.

One of BonJour's original examples is the following case:

> Norman, under certain conditions that usually obtain, is a completely reliable clairvoyant with respect to certain kinds of subject matter. He possesses no evidence or reasons of any kind for or against the general possibility of such a cognitive power, or for or against the thesis that he possesses it. One day Norman comes to believe that the President is in New York City, though he has no evidence either for or against this belief. In fact the belief is true and results from his clairvoyant power, under circumstances in which it is completely reliable.[20]

BonJour is explicit about two things. First, Norman is a completely reliable clairvoyant, although he has not the slightest inkling that he is. Now, it may seem somewhat odd to suppose that Norman is a completely reliable clairvoyant but has no knowledge of or evidence for this fact. But would he not, one might wonder, have at least some evidence for his possession of the power? Would he not have some previous experience with his clairvoyance? Perhaps not. Without speculating too much about the developmental psychology of clairvoyants, BonJour could assume that Norman's unusual powers had only recently "matured" and that this is Norman's first clairvoyant experience. Second, and more importantly, in the reliabilist view, Norman has knowledge. Moreover, it might seem that the reliabilist is committed to holding that Norman is epistemically justified in believing that the president is in New York City.

But what does *Norman* think is going on here? As BonJour notes,

> It becomes more than a little puzzling to understand what Norman thinks is going on. From his standpoint, there is apparently no way in which he *could* know the President's whereabouts. Why then does he continue to maintain the belief that the President is in New York City? Why is not the mere fact that there is no way, as far as he knows or believes, for him to have obtained this information a sufficient reason for classifying this belief as an unfounded hunch and ceasing to accept it? And if Norman does not do this, is he not thereby being epistemically irrational and irresponsible?[21]

Let us be clear what BonJour is trying to point out. One day, Norman suddenly finds himself believing that the president is in New York City. He has no evidence for this belief—he hasn't read it in the newspapers or seen it on television or been told it by a friend. This belief just suddenly pops into his head and, like a song or commercial jingle that one can't get out of one's head, stays there. But is it rational—are there adequate reasons—for Norman to believe this?

Notice that in the case of perceptual beliefs, if challenged, you could explain why you think it is rational for you to believe, say, that there is a book on the table. You would point to your belief that this particular belief is a result of the operation of your visual system, that such beliefs under normal circumstances tend to be true, that you have no reason to think that circumstances are anything other normal. But what will Norman say if asked why he believes he knows the whereabouts of the president? It will not help matters for Norman to find out that his belief is true for, from Norman's perspective, *it must surely seem accidental that he had a true belief.* The apparent accidental character of this belief is due to the fact that Norman, by hypothesis, has no reasons for this belief. Thus, clearly, BonJour assumes that justified beliefs must be rational beliefs. The justificatory status of a belief, according to BonJour, depends on the type of reasons an agent has. In the next section, we will see that reliabilists resist BonJour's claim.

Why does BonJour think that reliabilists are committed to this odd sort of consequence, that instances of knowledge might be irrational? Two points might be made. First, reliabilists reject the idea that the epistemic status of a belief depends on an agent's awareness of the source of that belief. As you will recall, reliabilists do not require that an agent *believe* that a particular belief was caused in the appropriate way. Nor does the reliability of a cognitive process depend on the beliefs of the agent. Indeed, your belief that you can ordinarily trust the operations of your visual system, in the reliabilist view, seems to have nothing to do with the epistemic status of the beliefs you have as a result of that process. Thus, the facts that explain the epistemic status of a belief need not be reflected in the agent's beliefs.

Second, part of the oddness of Norman's case undoubtedly derives from our thinking that instances of knowledge are paradigmatic of rational beliefs. Our ordinary way, and indeed the traditional epistemological way, of understanding the rationality of a belief is that the agent has good reasons for a belief and has the ability to provide those reasons under certain appropriate circumstances. We saw earlier the willingness of reliabilists to forswear traditional conceptions of knowledge and justification. Once one gives up the idea that justification requires an agent to have a particular type of reason for a belief—for example, that an agent need be aware of the reliability of a belief—cases like Norman's may appear almost inevitable. Again, we can see the sense in which reliabilist views of knowledge and justification are externalist. The features of a belief, which account for its justificatory status, need not be reflected in the agent's beliefs; those features need not be reflected in the agent's epistemic perspective.

If criticisms such as BonJour's are correct, then reliability may not be a sufficient condition of justification. It is not enough that a belief be reliably formed for it to be justified, nor will a reliably formed true belief count as knowledge. In the next section, we consider the reliabilist response to this type of example.

Evil Demons—Again

Cartesian **evil demons** can be resurrected to suggest that reliability is not necessary for justification. Again, very informally, to say that reliability is not necessary for justification is to say that a belief might be justified even though it fails to be reliably produced. This sort of objection exploits the intuition that our beliefs may be justified yet false, even on a consistent basis, so long as we have made the best use of the information available to us.[22]

Consider a world in which you have perceptual experiences just as you do in this world. As a result of these experiences, you come to have a range of perceptual beliefs, of the more or less normal sort: There is a tree; there is an Afghan hound; there is my glass of tea. The reason for holding such beliefs is that the relevant sorts of perceptual experience occur. Now, imagine that the causes of such perceptual experiences are not our familiar trees, dogs, or glasses, but rather an evil demon or collection of evil demons. In such a situation, your perceptual beliefs would clearly be *false*. There is no sense in which those beliefs would likely be true. It is, after all, a demon world. Thus, perceptual beliefs in such a case would be patently unreliable. But would such beliefs be unjustified?

The mere fact that our intuition pulls us in the direction of counting these beliefs as justified suggests a difficulty for reliabilism. Is there any accounting for such an intuition? In normal circumstances, we take our perceptual beliefs to be justified. The reason for this seems to be that we think that, given certain sorts of perceptual experience, the natural consequence is to come to have the correlative perceptual beliefs. Our perceptual beliefs are based on a certain kind of mental state, on our having the perceptual experience. Hence, we are inclined to think that our perceptual beliefs are justified. More importantly, the "source" of this justification is having the requisite perceptual experiences. Indeed, it is quite natural to think that in the normal case, we *should* have the perceptual beliefs that we do.

If this is what we should believe in the normal case, then we should also have the same beliefs in the demon world. In the demon world, we have exactly the same reasons for forming such beliefs—the same reasons, and the same justification.[23] So, if our beliefs are justified in our normal world, they are justified in the demon world.

Thus, we have a case in which an entire class of beliefs would count as justified; yet they are clearly not the result of a reliable process. This implies that reliability is not a necessary condition for justification.

RELIABILIST RESPONSES AND REVISIONS

Reliabilists take these three types of criticism seriously and have offered a variety of responses, some of which involved revisions to reliabilism. This section considers certain of these responses. We begin with the issues of the necessity and sufficiency of reliably produced beliefs for justification.

Normal Worlds and Weak Justification

Two very different responses are made to reliabilism's version of the evil demon problem. The first suggested response is that of appealing to normal worlds. According to Goldman, the reliability of a process is determined by the proportion of true beliefs it produces in normal worlds.[24] *Normal worlds* are those that are consistent with our general beliefs about our actual world. Our "general beliefs" about the actual world describe a world having certain features. Presumably, these features include the behavior of light under certain conditions and its consequent effects on our visual systems. Now, we might be mistaken about the real character of the actual world; hence, our general beliefs would be false in the actual world. Enter normal worlds. Imagine a world in which our general beliefs are true. Such a world is a normal world. Perhaps surprisingly, the actual world may not be a normal world.

In the demon case, the agent makes use of a process—perception— that would generally produce true beliefs in any world that is, in fact, the same as we believe our own world to be. Thus, despite the agent's having

Reliabilism and Skepticism

Although the demon case before us differs from the demon scenario discussed in Chapter One, we might wonder about the reliabilist's view of the skeptical challenge. Goldman, for example, suggests that one type of skepticism might be viewed as the problem of how the mind can have access to certain features of the world. Goldman suggests that causal theories attempt to explain how, in fact, we have such access. The "spirit" of causal theories is to explain how the mind receives information about the world, not whether it is possible for the mind to "make its way" to the world.

Of course, the received interpretation of the traditional view is that the skeptical problem is to explain whether and how it is possible that the mind makes its way to the world. In particular, one cannot appeal to anything other than the evidence provided by one's sensory states. One cannot begin by appealing to the reliability of the processes that produce our sensory states. This, in large part, explains the frequent charge that reliabilists in particular, and externalists in general, are simply "changing the subject."

routinely false beliefs in our demon-controlled actual world, one can say that those beliefs are nonetheless justified. The clear implication of this response is that our earlier talk of reliable cognitive processes was really elliptical. In fact, cognitive processes are reliable or unreliable *relative to normal worlds*. Goldman claims that this preserves our intuition that reliability is to be determined relative to normal situations.

Goldman himself recognizes the weaknesses of this approach. He notes that one can wonder *which* general beliefs are to determine the normal worlds and *whose* general beliefs these are, and he suggests that there can in fact be some very different normal worlds.[25] One might also wonder whether in this view, we do not actually lose part of the original motivation for reliabilist notions of justification. Part of the attraction of reliabilism is that it explains the connection between justification and truth, and the normal worlds interpretation of reliabilism diminishes this connection. This seems to be a fairly significant concession, however. We began by thinking that justified beliefs, in the reliabilist view, are those produced by reliable belief-forming processes. Our interest in such processes lay in the fact that they were *reliable;* they tended to produce true beliefs. But if our beliefs are no longer likely be true, it is indeed puzzling why the reliabilist is interested in the notion of justification. This same point is made by Richard Fumerton:

These justified beliefs will all be false [in our demon-controlled actual world] and will have been produced by processes that are terribly ineffective when it

comes to getting at the truth. Unless one has some independent reason for believing that this [our demon-controlled actual world] *is* a normal world, why
would the concept of justification even be important to a truth seeker when it is
now so obvious that having justified beliefs need not even make *probable* having true beliefs.[26]

We can put the matter somewhat simply. We think of, say, perceptual beliefs as *justified,* while we tend to think of beliefs formed as a result of
wishful thinking as unjustified. Now, a significant motivation for identifying
the former as justified and the latter as unjustified is that the former are
likely to be true. We are interested in justified beliefs precisely because of
their apparent connection to the truth. But the normal worlds interpretation
seems to sever that connection. We know that our justified beliefs are connected to truth in a *normal* world, but what reason do we have for thinking
ours is a normal world? We need some independent reason for thinking
that our actual world is a normal world. But it is not immediately obvious
that reliabilism can help us with that problem. If our interest is the truth, we
seem not to have any reason to care about justified beliefs. After all, justified beliefs have no intrinsic connection to truth in *this* world.

Goldman has more recently offered a different line of response to the
evil demon problem based on a distinction between *strong justification*
and *weak justification.*[27] A belief is *strongly justified* if and only if (a) it is
produced by a reliable process, and (b) the process is not undermined by
the agent's cognitive state. This latter condition should remind you of the
earlier account of process reliabilism, which required that there be no other
cognitive process that could or should be used.

The notion of weak justification is intended to capture the idea that
agents are blameless or not at fault for the beliefs they hold. A belief is
weakly justified if (a) the belief is produced by an unreliable process, (b)
the agent does not believe the process to be unreliable, and (c) the agent
has no evidence that the process is unreliable. (Goldman also suggests an
additional possible condition that there be no process believed by the
agent as reliable that, if used, would lead the agent to see the original
process as unreliable. Goldman, however, does not pursue this condition.)
We can note, however, the sense in which the agent is epistemically blameless. Imagine that Sara resides in a demon world and forms the perceptual
belief that a certain ball is blue. By hypothesis, she uses an unreliable
process, because in the demon world perception fails to produce generally
true beliefs. However, in a demon world, Sara seemingly has no reason to
believe that perception is unreliable. Perception seems to "work," even
though unbeknownst to Sara, it routinely produces false beliefs. Yet Sara
has done nothing epistemically wrong. All of her evidence tells her to trust
the perceptual process. Moreover, there is no apparent way for Sara to
find out otherwise. Thus, Sara does the best she can, given the cognitive

resources available to her. It is not Sara's fault that the world is so constructed that she can never find out that she routinely has false beliefs. At the very least, she deserves an "E" for effort. She is epistemically blameless.

The distinction between weak and strong justification enables Goldman to say that the demon victim has weakly justified, but not strongly justified, perceptual beliefs. Critics might be somewhat puzzled by this response. On the one hand, Goldman seems to acknowledge that there is a sense of justification that does not require reliability. On the other, he seems to disparage this sense by calling it "weak" justification. But this is precisely what is at issue: whether the sort of justification envisaged in the demon world really is "weak." Recall the quote in the beginning of the previous section, in which John Pollock claims that justification depends on whether an agent makes the right epistemic moves. The critic might then insist that weak justification is merely the fundamental sense of justification, because the agent makes the best use of his or her cognitive abilities. We seem, then, to be caught between the conflicting intuitions of reliabilist and critic.

Clairvoyancy

As you will recall, Goldman claims that for a belief to be justified, not only must it be the result of a reliable process, but there must be no other cognitive process that undermines the agent's use of the original process. This "nonundermining" clause is the focus of Goldman's response to BonJour.

Goldman, too, has trouble imagining what is going on in Norman's case. But his diagnosis is somewhat different from BonJour's:

> BonJour describes this case as one in which Norman possesses no evidence or reasons of any kind for or against the general possibility of clairvoyance, or for or against the thesis that he possesses it. But it is hard to imagine this description holding. Norman *ought* to reason along the following lines: "If I had a clairvoyant power, I would surely find some evidence for this. I would find myself believing things in otherwise explicable ways, and when these things were checked by other reliable processes, they would usually check out positively. Since I lack any such signs, I apparently do not possess reliable clairvoyant processes."[28]

There seem to be two ways in which we might understand Goldman's response.

On the one hand, Norman seemingly is to appeal to beliefs he has about the reliability of the clairvoyant process. Norman ought, according to Goldman, to reflect on his cognitive situation and form the metabelief that he has no reason to trust the process productive of his belief regarding the president's whereabouts. Thus, if Norman believes that he has no reason for thinking that he has these clairvoyant powers or that such a process is reliable, then he is not justified.[29] With this construal, Goldman seems to be admitting that beliefs about reliability are necessary for justification. Hence, mere reliability is not sufficient for justification.

Goldman may recognize this. His solution is to suggest that the proper use of evidence is a reliable process. And the proper use of evidence now seems to include an agent's beliefs about the reliability of the various processes.

On the other hand, Goldman might be arguing that Norman's justification is undermined by another available process. This additional available process is characterized by Goldman's description of how Norman should reason. Norman should reflect on his situation and realize that if clairvoyance were reliable, he would have some evidence of its reliability. Because Norman does not make use of this additional process, the justification of his belief is undermined.[30] The key idea is that this reasoning process is *available* to Norman. But the content of this reasoning process is Norman's belief about the reliability of his clairvoyant powers. Norman must have beliefs about the reliability of clairvoyance and his possession of that ability for the process to be available to him.

Recently, however, Frederick Schmitt has argued that Norman's belief is justified.[31] We might summarize Schmitt's argument as follows: We can imagine situations in which Goldman's additional cognitive process would not be available. But then, whether Norman's belief is justified depends on how we understand clairvoyance. BonJour's description of Norman as lacking any evidence regarding clairvoyance inclines us to think that it is a random, epistemically haphazard process. But if we understand clairvoyance as a cognitive process similar to perception, then we will think of Norman's belief as justified.

To illustrate this, Schmitt asks us to consider the Andromedans, who exercise reliable clairvoyant powers. Their clairvoyance plays a role similar to our perception. Abnorman, in addition to having the normal (for Andromedans) clairvoyant powers, also has reliable perceptual powers. The resulting beliefs in no way conflict with the beliefs Abnorman acquires from clairvoyance. Schmitt argues that if we count Norman's clairvoyant belief as unjustified, then we should also count Abnorman's perceptual beliefs as unjustified. But Schmitt thinks that our intuition is to count Abnorman's perceptual beliefs as justified; hence, we ought to count Norman's belief as justified.

Schmitt's view is unabashedly committed to the core reliabilist intuition. Justification depends on the reliability of the cognitive processes. This is the best one can do: Use a cognitive process that is likely to yield true beliefs. An agent's evaluation of the process is irrelevant to whether the process yields true beliefs. But this response may do little to sway the critic's contrary intuition.[32]

Perhaps we have followed this dialectic strategy long enough. What seems clear is that the reliabilist will continue to insist that what matters for justification is the reliability of the process or method. Critics no doubt think that this can obscure what genuinely accounts for the justificatory status of a belief. Using the appropriate methods can be relevant to a belief's epistemic status, but being in a position to recognize the appropriateness of the process can be an important consideration. But here, we should remind ourselves that we are confronting deeply held contrary intuitions. The reliabilist insists on our cognitive success, while the critic insists on more internalist features. However, we should not let this difference of intuition obscure the real value of the debate, for in identifying these conflicting intuitions, we have perhaps identified different core aspects of our respective concepts of justification. This is an issue we pursue further in Chapter Six.

Identifying Process Types

Can we find a principled answer for the question as to how we should identify the relevant process type? Goldman suggests one possibility.[33] We should consider the most specific description of the process that contains only causally operative properties. Goldman admits to not being completely confident of this proposal, but we can nonetheless try to see what he has in mind here.

First, consider what is meant by a property being "causally operative." Intuitively, the idea is that the property's presence (or absence) makes a difference to the outcome or end product of a causal process. For example, imagine that I am trying to light coals in a barbecue grill. That I am wearing a pumpkin-colored shirt seems to be irrelevant to my success in lighting the coals. However, that it is an extremely windy day does seem relevant: If I am unable to keep the match lighted because of the wind, I will not succeed in lighting the coals. We might then think of causally operative properties as those that are causally relevant to the belief that an agent has. More simply, causally operative properties are properties relevant to the formation of my belief. Intuitively, causally operative properties figure in determining what I believe; they figure in determining what my belief is about.

Recall the example of my looking across a supermarket parking lot at a particular dog and coming to believe, "There's an American Eskimo." The property of my seeing the dog on a Thursday afternoon does not seem causally relevant to my consequent belief. (Of course, we can imagine a much more complicated story in which it is causally relevant.) Yet the properties of my seeing the dog at a distance or from a partially obscured vantage point might very well be causally relevant. If I am seeing the dog at a distance, then I might mistake an apricot-colored dog for a white one. There is then some initial plausibility to this recommendation.

We can illustrate a potential problem for Goldman's approach by recalling the example of my wearing a pumpkin-colored shirt while trying to light coals. To know whether the color of my shirt is causally relevant, we first need to know what it is that I am doing. If I am attempting to light the coals in the grill, then we will quite naturally count the shirt color as irrelevant. But if I am trying to impress a neighbor with my stylish barbecuing attire, then my shirt color may indeed be relevant (if eventually unsuccessful). Analogously, one might suggest that I must first know the type of the belief-forming process to know what properties are causally operative. My obscured line of sight may be relevant to my *visual* belief that a certain animal is a dog. But the obscured line of sight may be irrelevant to my *auditory* belief that a certain (noisy) animal is dog. We might summarize this worry in this manner: It is by virtue of knowing the process type that we know the causally operative properties, not the other way around. Thus, Goldman's appeal to such properties is useful only if we already know the relevant type. But then, we cannot use the appeal to causally operative properties to determine the relevant process type.[34]

Reliabilism's intuition is that our epistemic successes are intimately tied to our actual cognitive successes in coping with the world around us. The controversial aspects of reliabilism stem from the manner in which reliabilism develops this original intuition, for this development occurs in a decidedly externalist manner. The demon objection and the clairvoyance objection are directed at this externalism. These objections are based on the claim that reliabilism has wrongly excluded the agent's evaluations of beliefs from the accounts of justification and knowledge. Now, in one sense, reliabilists have come closer to recognizing these features of our cognitive situation. Goldman's notion of weak justification attempts to account for the fact that agents can sometimes be blameless as they conduct their cognitive pursuits. But we can expect that the motives underlying externalism and internalism will continue to shape different accounts of knowledge and justification. As noted, we return to these issue in Chapter Six.

The generality problem presents a different sort of issue; it seems to threaten the coherency of reliabilism itself. We have seen, however, some reason to think that the problem might be manageable. Despite these challenges, reliabilism remains a widely held theory. The breadth of reliabilism's support may well be due to the fundamental nature of its underlying motivation. Doubtless, as reliabilism urges, the connection between truth and justification cannot be overlooked.

Key Concepts

Clairvoyancy objection	Reliabilism
Evil demon objection	Reliable indicator theories
Generality Problem	Reliable process theories

Review Questions

1. What is the difference between reliable indicator theories and reliable process theories?

2. What are the key features of Goldman's reliabilist account of perceptual knowledge?

3. What is Goldman's revised version of the reliabilist theory of justification? Explain why this view might be considered an externalist theory of justification.

4. Briefly explain three central objections to reliabilism. Do you think any of these objections show that reliabilism is mistaken? Why or why not?

For Further Study

Two representative reliable indicator theories are developed in D. M. Armstrong, *Belief, Truth and Knowledge* (London: Cambridge University Press, 1973), and Marshall Swain, *Reasons and Knowledge* (Ithaca, NY: Cornell University Press, 1981). Of course, Alvin Goldman's *Epistemology and Cognition* (Cambridge, MA: Harvard University Press, 1986) remains one of the central texts on reliable process views, as is his "What Is Justified Belief?" in Hilary Kornblith, ed., *Naturalizing Epistemology* (Cambridge, MA: MIT Press, 1987). Goldman's more recent views can be found in "Strong and Weak Justification," in James Tomberlin, ed., *Philosophical Perspectives, 2: Epistemology* (Atascadero, CA: Ridgeview Press, 1988), and "Epistemic Folkways and Scientific Epistemology," in Paul Moser, ed., *Empirical Knowledge*, 2nd ed. (Lanham, MD: Rowman & Littlefield, 1996). Another recent, comprehensive elaboration and defense of the reliable process view is Frederick F. Schmitt, *Knowledge and Belief* (London: Routledge, 1990).

Criticisms of reliabilism are abundant (as are the responses to the criticisms). The *Monist* 68 (1985) is devoted to both criticism and defense of reliabilism. This volume includes Richard Feldman's "Reliability and Justification," pp. 159–174. Laurence BonJour's criticisms of reliabilism are explicated in "Externalist Theories of Empirical Knowledge," in Peter French et al., eds., *Midwest Studies in Philosophy*, Vol. V (Minneapolis: University of Minnesota Press, 1980), pp. 53–73, and BonJour, *The Structure of Empirical Knowledge* (Cambridge, MA: Harvard University Press, 1985). Richard Fumerton's *Metaepistemolgy and Skepticism* (Lanham, MD: Rowman & Littlefield) is critical of the externalist aspects of reliabilism. Robert Almeder's *Blind Realism* (Lanham, MD: Rowman & Littlefield, 1992) responds to Goldman's arguments for intrapersonalism.

Notes

1. See D. M. Armstrong, *Belief, Truth and Knowledge* (London: Cambridge University Press, 1973), Chap. 12.

2. See, for example, Marshall Swain, *Reasons and Knowledge* (Ithaca, NY: Cornell University Press, 1981), esp. Chap. 4.

3. Alvin Goldman, "Discrimination and Perceptual Knowledge," in Jonathan Dancy, ed., *Perceptual Knowledge* (Oxford: Oxford University Press, 1988), pp. 41–65.

4. Armstrong, *Belief, Truth and Knowledge,* p. 183.

5. Goldman, "Discrimination and Perceptual Knowledge, pp. 63–64.

6. As we will see in Chapter Four, there is a "neoclassical" version of internalism that does not require the impossibility of mistake as a condition of justification for every belief.

7. See, for example, Frederick F. Schmitt, "Justification as Reliable Indication or Reliable Process?" *Philosophical Studies* 40 (1981): 409–417, esp. 413–414.

8. Ernest Sosa, *Knowledge in Perspective* (Cambridge: Cambridge University Press, 1991), Chap. 13.

9. Again, see Swain, *Reasons and Knowledge*, Chap. 4.

10. Alvin Goldman, "What Is Justified Belief?" in Hilary Kornblith, ed., *Naturalizing Epistemology* (Cambridge, MA: MIT Press, 1985), pp. 91–113.

11. Goldman, "What Is Justified Belief?" p. 100.

12. Goldman, "What Is Justified Belief?" p. 109. This line of thinking is not atypical. We will see in a subsequent chapter that William Alston makes use of this line of argument. See also Frederick F. Schmitt, *Knowledge and Belief* (London: Routledge, 1992), p. 168.

13. Alvin Goldman, *Epistemology and Cognition* (Cambridge, MA: Harvard University Press, 1986), pp. 75ff.

14. Goldman, "What Is Justified Belief?" p. 109.

15. John Pollock, *Contemporary Theories of Knowledge* (Totowa, NJ: Rowman & Littlefield, 1986), p. 116.

16. For an introduction to these issues, see Roberta Klatzky, *Human Memory: Structures and Processes*, 2nd ed. (New York: Freeman, 1980).

17. Richard Feldman, "Reliability and Justification," *Monist* 68 (1985): 159–174.

18. This line of response was suggested by an anonymous reader.

19. Laurence BonJour, "Externalist Theories of Empirical Knowledge," in Peter French, et al., eds., *Midwest Studies in Philosophy*, Vol. V (Minneapolis: University of Minnesota Press, 1980), pp. 53–73. Others have raised this issue as well. See, for example, Richard Foley, "What's Wrong with Reliabilism?" and Steven Luper-Foy, "The Reliabilist Theory of Rational Belief," both in *Monist* 68 (1985). Also see Pollock, *Contemporary Theories of Knowledge*.

20. BonJour, "Externalist Theories," p. 62.

21. BonJour, "Externalist Theories," pp. 62–63.

22. The evil demon objection to reliabilism is raised in Stewart Cohen, "Justification and Truth," *Philosophical Studies* 46 (1984): 279–295.

23. Interestingly, the general principle that if two agents have the same reason, then their beliefs have the same justificational status is challenged in Schmitt, "Justification as Reliable Indication or Reliable Process?" p. 413. Schmitt's rationale for this is that it matters not only what reasons an agent has but how those reasons are used. Clearly, in the demon world under consideration, the reasons are used in exactly the same way as they are in the normal world we take ourselves to be in.

24. Goldman, *Epistemology and Cognition*, p. 113.

25. Alvin Goldman, "Strong and Weak Justification," in James Tomberlin, ed., *Philosophical Perspectives, 2: Epistemology* (Atascadero, CA: Ridgeview Press, 1988), p. 62.

26. Richard Fumerton, *Metaepistemology and Skepticism* (Lanham, MD: Rowman & Littlefield, 1995), pp. 114–115.

27. Goldman, "Strong and Weak Justification," pp. 51–69.

28. Goldman, *Epistemology and Cognition*, p. 112.

29. Goldman presents a somewhat different analysis in Alvin Goldman, "Epistemic Folkways and Scientific Epistemology," in Paul Moser, ed., *Empirical Knowledge* (Lanham, MD: Rowman & Littlefield, 1996), pp. 423–446. There, he suggests that Norman's belief might be considered "nonjustified."

30. This interpretation was suggested by an anonymous reader.

31. Schmitt, *Knowledge and Belief*, pp. 179–180.

32. See, for example, Fumerton, *Metaepistemology and Skepticism*, p. 116.

33. Alvin Goldman, "Reliabilism," in Jonathan Dancy, ed., *Companion to Epistemology* (Oxford: Basil Blackwell, 1992), and Goldman, *Epistemology and Cognition*, pp. 50–51.

34. Goldman's more recent work may contain a suggestion as to how he thinks this problem will eventually be managed. Cognitive science may be able to identify the kinds and the number of elements necessary for an agent to form a belief of a certain type. For example, to see that something is an animal, it may be that only, say, two of six factors must be present. To identify the animal as a dog and then as a French poodle, increasingly more factors will be required. These factors are called "parameters." It may be, then, that a sufficiently scientific epistemology could identify the *type* of process with the number and kinds of parameters required for successful identification. See Goldman, "Epistemic Folkways and Scientific Epistemology," pp. 423–446.

    Because such research is still in the early stages, we cannot fully assess it here. Suffice it to say that there is still likely to be an indefinitely large number of types of belief-forming processes, and there may be no clear boundary between some of the types. To the extent that this would generate single token types or would fail to distinguish adequately reliable from unreliable types, reliabilism would still face the generality problem.

    One other sustained attempt to deal with the generality problem should be mentioned. Frederick Schmitt devotes the majority of a chapter of his *Knowledge and Belief* to the problem (see Chap. 6). This text cannot do justice to the detailed considerations Schmitt offers, but a couple of points can be briefly mentioned. Schmitt identifies (and argues for) five different constraints that individuation of process types should satisfy. The *folk process constraint* claims that the relevant process types are folk processes. That is, the way in which ordinary agents typically think of and describe belief-forming processes constrains the way in which the reliabilist ought to identify the relevant types. Consequently, Schmitt argues against Goldman's scientific epistemology approach. The reader is urged to consult Schmitt's work on this topic.

Structure and Sources of Justification: Foundationalism

At least sometimes, we support a claim that a particular belief is justified by citing other beliefs. For example, I think my belief that the gardener will not come today is justified because I believe that it rained last night and that he does not like to mow when the grass is wet. My belief about the gardener derives its justification from my other beliefs. I explain why I think the belief is justified by indicating a certain connection among my beliefs. More specifically, I cite these other beliefs as the basis or support for my belief. In doing so, I explain that one belief depends or rests on other beliefs. I describe a certain *structure* by virtue of which my belief is justified. In describing this structure, I am claiming that some others of my beliefs provide the justificatory support for my belief about the gardener.

Suppose, however, that I am interested not only in beliefs about gardeners but in the nature of justification more generally. One feature that I would then be interested in is the *structure of justification.* That is, I would be interested in the kind of justificatory connections among my beliefs. In this and the following chapter, we will be looking at this notion of the structure of justification.

The concern with the structure of justification signals a perhaps deeper issue, one that has already been in the background of some of our discussions. The notion of structure signals a concern about the *source* of justification or knowledge. How is it that our beliefs obtain their initial epistemic credibility? How is it that our beliefs initially come to be justified? One answer to this question is **foundationalism,** which is the view that at least some of our beliefs are justified, but do not depend on other beliefs for their justification. Such beliefs are epistemically independent of and the foundation of our other beliefs. Foundationalist theories are the focus of this chapter. Foundationalism is a theory about the structure of justification, but it is also a theory about the *initial source* of justification. Because the Regress Argument is thought to indicate where we might look for this initial source of justification, we begin the chapter with an informal account of the Regress Argument. We then consider why foundationalists think that the Regress Argument provides a motive for foundationalism. Then, in the bulk of the chapter, we outline in more detail the nature of foundationalism and principal criticisms of the theory.

THE REGRESS ARGUMENT

The **Regress Argument** begins with the quite natural supposition that a belief is justified only if there is some evidence for it. Typically, we think of this evidence as other beliefs we have. Think again of my belief that the gardener will not come today. My evidence for that belief is my other beliefs that it rained last night and that he does not like to mow when the grass is wet. Still, I might think that my belief about the gardener is only as good—only as justified—as my evidence. That is, my beliefs regarding rain and the gardener's desire to avoid wet grass must also be justified. Intuitively, we can begin to see the start of a regress. If I now offer other beliefs in support of these justifying beliefs, we can again ask what justifies these supporting beliefs. This may strike you as a bit reminiscent of Hume. The core of Hume's objection is not only that we have a justifying argument, that other beliefs justify a particular belief, but that the justifying beliefs are themselves justified. Indeed, it is precisely this dialectical move that is constitutive of the Regress Argument—a belief can be justified by other beliefs only if they are justified.

But here the troublesome feature of the Regress Argument appears. Our everyday beliefs—the ones about books, cups, and trees—are justified only if they are supported by other beliefs. Obviously, the dialectical regress requires that the supporting beliefs be justified. More importantly, there seems no obvious end to this dialectical regress. Yet the argument implies that our beliefs are genuinely justified only if we can end the regress. We might summarize the argument in this way: Beliefs are justified only if they are supported by other evidence. Supporting beliefs can justify only if they are themselves justified. Thus, for any belief we cite as evidence or support, we seemingly must always ask why that belief is justified. In turn, apparently, we would have to cite still further beliefs as evidence. Thus, no belief can be justified unless there is some principled way to end the regress.[1]

We can look a bit more closely at this argument, beginning with a commonsense observation. Many of our beliefs are indeed inferential—that is, are based on other beliefs. My belief that it rained last night is based on my beliefs that I heard rain outside my window last night and that the deck was wet early this morning.

The Regress Argument adds two important points to this commonsense observation. First, the argument holds that any belief that can serve as evidence or justify some other belief must itself be justified. This alone can be a prescription for a very long regress. Second, however, the argument holds that none of our beliefs legitimately count as justified unless we can end the regress. Notice that this leads to a construal of the Regress Argument as re-quiring that there be an *initial source* of the justification of our beliefs if we want to think that any of our beliefs are justified. That is, the argument claims that our beliefs are not justified unless there is such an initial source. We can see from this why questions about structure are also questions about the initial source of justification (or knowledge). We are able to provide a principled answer to the regress only if we can explain how there might be justified beliefs about which the regress question cannot be asked.[2]

MOTIVES FOR FOUNDATIONALISM

In this section, we discuss why the Regress Argument is thought to motivate foundationalism. Standard approaches to the Regress Argument hold that there are four possible responses. In rejecting three of these as unsatisfactory, foundationalists seek to provide a motive for their preferred view. The first two possible responses are held to be unsatisfactory, as is, ultimately, a third, more substantive response. Rejection of this third approach, however, leaves but one response to the Regress Argument—foundationalism.

Options for the Regress Argument

As noted, four possible responses to the Regress Argument seem to be available:

1. The regress might terminate in beliefs that are not justified.
2. No end is ever reached in the process of justification.
3. Justification forms a kind of network, or beliefs seem to be mutually supporting.
4. The regress terminates in beliefs that do not depend on other beliefs for their justification.

Option 1 is unsatisfactory because it implies that ultimately all of our pretensions to justification, and hence to knowledge, rest on beliefs that appear arbitrary from an epistemic standpoint. If we allow our justifying beliefs to be unjustified, then any belief could come to count as justified. Indeed, to accept option 1 seems to require abandoning a central feature of justification exploited by the Regress Argument: that we have not just reasons, but good reasons for our beliefs. At a minimum, this seems to require that our justifying beliefs are the sorts of belief for which there is some evidence. That is, these beliefs are themselves justified.

Option 2 seems not much better. For one thing, justifications that never come to an end are not the sort of justifications we typically prize from the standpoint of learning more about our world. For another, option 2 seemingly would commit us to the idea that humans have an infinite chain of beliefs. For each belief that we cite, there is yet another justifying belief to be cited, ad infinitum. Although the normal person undoubtedly has an indefinitely large number of beliefs, that person is unlikely to have a limitless supply of beliefs. Notice that rejecting option 2 seems to suggest that there must be a point at which the justificatory chain of beliefs can be traced no further.

A Motive for Foundationalism

Option 3 is taken to be descriptive of a family of views known as coherence theories. As the principal alternative to foundationalism, *coherentism* roughly holds that justification derives from the system of our beliefs. Such views are thought by some to be suspect for specific reasons that we will consider in detail in the next chapter. But we need to sketch briefly why some hold that coherentism is suspect, and hence, why foundationalism is considered the best response to the Regress Argument.

The principal objection goes under different names and variations. Typically, it is referred to as the *isolation objection;* sometimes, it is known as the *independent warrant objection.* A brief summary of the objection follows (we will consider this objection in more detail in Chapter Five). Proponents of coherence views claim that justification derives from the system of beliefs held by an agent. Suppose, however, that what we mean by the notion of a justified belief is that the belief is likely to be true, that there is some reason to think that the belief "matches up" with the world. Now, with the isolation objection, the question becomes, How is it that this likelihood of matching up is to derive from the agent's other beliefs? We must appeal to something outside the agent's beliefs to explain how any particular belief is justified. But this is precisely what coherentism prevents us from doing. As we will see in the next chapter, one way of characterizing this line of thought is that coherence alone is never a source of justification.

Consider now where this leaves us. We reject the first two responses to the Regress Argument because they require us to give up essential features of the notion of justification. Coherentism is held to be unacceptable. But if we still think that we have justified beliefs, we have remaining only option 4. According to this view, at least some beliefs are justified but do not depend on other beliefs for their justification. Such beliefs are *foundational.* Indeed, they are the source of justification for all our other beliefs. Now, foundationalists do not claim that the Regress Argument categorically shows that foundationalism is the correct approach to justification and knowledge. Rather, their claim is hypothetical. If there are any justified beliefs, then there must be some foundational beliefs, beliefs that are justified but that do not depend on other beliefs for their justification. Foundational beliefs are **basic beliefs,** beliefs that do not depend on other beliefs for their justification.

Of course, how exactly there can be such foundational beliefs is a fundamental issue. What sorts of beliefs are foundational? Why should we view them as justified, and what is their justificatory connection to other nonfoundational beliefs? These questions and the foundationalist responses will occupy us the rest of this chapter.

TWO TYPES OF FOUNDATIONALISM

The Basic Structure

The structure of justification as pictured by foundationalism is that there are two classes of belief. As noted previously, basic beliefs are beliefs that are justified, but not by virtue of their connections to other beliefs. Thus, basic beliefs are held to be self-justified or directly justified in that they are *epistemically independent* of other beliefs.[3] According to foundationalists, basic beliefs are justified by virtue of some feature of the beliefs themselves.

The notion of epistemic independence is crucial for foundationalists, and it must be distinguished from other types of dependence. Foundationalists do not object to the idea that basic beliefs may be *causally* dependent on other beliefs. Recall my belief that the gardener will not come today. Suppose, only for illustration, that my believing that the grass is wet counts as a basic belief. (Not all foundationalists will agree that it should count as a basic belief.) Clearly, my having this belief depends on my having many other beliefs, including beliefs about grass, about water, and about the property of wetness. I would not have this particular belief *unless* I possessed these concepts and associated beliefs. Foundationalists can agree that having any particular belief requires having a range of concepts and the ability to apply those concepts appropriately. This is sometimes referred to as a coherence theory of concepts, which must be distinguished from a coherence theory of justification or knowledge.[4] But according to foundationalists, these other beliefs are not what justify my belief. In this sense, my belief is *psychologically dependent* without being *epistemically dependent;* that is, these other beliefs do not explain why my belief about the wetness of the grass is likely to be true.[5] This might suggest that epistemically basic beliefs are in some sense psychologically nonbasic.

This is a rather cursory account of this distinction. But the key point, which will be significant for the next section, is that foundationalists acknowledge that *having* or *forming* a belief may depend on having other beliefs. Foundationalists also claim, however, that this is not relevant to the epistemic dependence or independence of the belief.

Basic beliefs, then, are the ultimate source of justification for all other beliefs. Beliefs that ultimately depend on basic beliefs for their justification

Foundationalism as a Theory of Knowledge

Although our concern in this chapter is with foundationalism as a theory of justification, foundationalism can also be a theory of the structure of knowledge. In such a view, there are foundational items of knowledge. These foundational beliefs are similarly epistemically independent of other beliefs. Not only are they justified, they also satisfy whatever other conditions are necessary for a belief to be knowledge.

are called *nonbasic beliefs*. The connections between basic and nonbasic beliefs are inferential, but the nature of these inferential connections varies with the type of foundationalism espoused. Again, recall my belief that the gardener will not come today. Initially, I might appeal to other nonbasic beliefs as my justification, and in fact, I might appeal to a good many of them. However, when asked what justifies these justifying beliefs, eventually I will, in the foundationalist view, appeal to basic beliefs. Thus, the structure of justification, according to foundationalists, is that of an inverted tree or pyramid. In principle, claim foundationalists, we can trace the justificatory support for any nonbasic belief back to one or more basic beliefs.

In this view, all justification terminates in basic beliefs, and a nonbasic belief qualifies as knowledge only if its justification is eventually traceable to some basic beliefs. Descartes's view is, of course, a familiar and paradigmatic example of foundationalism, as is Hume's, at least in some construals. Hume claims that all justification must terminate in either beliefs about the present contents of our mind (sense impressions), beliefs recalled from memory, or relations of ideas. In some sense, Hume rejects the appeal to the Uniformity Principle because such a foundational justification cannot be given.

Two questions arise at this point. First, what types or classes of belief are these basic beliefs? Second, what is the character of the relations between basic beliefs and nonbasic beliefs? The answers to these two questions give rise to the two forms of foundationalism we will be considering.

Strong Foundationalism

The classic Cartesian type of foundationalism holds that basic beliefs are infallibly justified, that they cannot be false. Simply having the belief is enough to guarantee that the belief is true. Moreover, foundationalism of this type requires that nonbasic beliefs be infallibly justified as well. Of course, the only way to ensure this infallibility of the nonbasic beliefs is to require that the inferential connections between basic and nonbasic beliefs be deductive. Any justified nonbasic belief is ultimately a deductive consequence of the set of basic beliefs. We will call this view **strong foundationalism,** although it is also known as *infallible foundationalism* or *Cartesian foundationalism.*

What types of belief might count as infallibly justified? Requiring that the belief cannot be mistaken clearly restricts the range of candidates. It is sometimes held that beliefs about simple logical or arithmetical truths cannot possibly be mistaken, and hence are infallibly justified. More important for our purposes is the claim that beliefs about the contents of our own minds are infallible. Accordingly, beliefs that arise as a result of introspection count as basic. The content of these beliefs may vary; they may be about certain sensations that one is having, certain feelings that one has, or simple beliefs about what one is thinking. Comparing "introspective beliefs" with perceptual beliefs might provide an initial sense of why the former are thought to be infallible.

Obviously, perceptual beliefs are liable to error, even very simple beliefs such as "That's a red thing." The lighting, for example, might not be normal, and I might mistake a piece of white paper for a red piece. This possibility of error is endemic to the class of perceptual beliefs. But why are introspective beliefs seemingly not liable to this possibility of error? Perhaps introspective beliefs are direct in a way that perceptual beliefs are not. There seems to be no intervening "gap" between the belief and that which it is about, as there appears to be with perceptual beliefs. It is this directness of introspective beliefs that is thought to account for their infallibility. After all, how could I possibly be mistaken about what I am thinking? I'm merely reading my own mind. Moreover, with perceptual beliefs, in a certain sense, it is not up to me as to whether an object is red or fuzzy, or even whether there is an object in front of me. But introspective beliefs seem different. Who else but me would be in a position to say what the contents of my own mind are? Again, apparently, the immediacy of introspective beliefs account for their infallible character. Whether this intuitive approach to the infallibility of introspective beliefs can be cast in a more rigorous manner that will withstand criticism is addressed in the following section.

For the sake of argument, assume that certain classes of belief, like introspective beliefs, are infallibly justified. The infallible foundationalist's task would only be half complete. We will still want to know how the infallible foundationalist plans to move from beliefs such as "I am having the sense impression of a red thing" to the infallibly justified belief "There is a red thing before me." Descartes famously—or, some might say, "infamously"— invoked divine benevolence to vouchsafe such connections. Hume, on the other hand, was less sure of such supernatural benevolence and seemed willing to put his faith in nature's more parsimonious benevolence. But this, of course, was no epistemic guarantee of the infallibility of the belief. The challenge for the infallible foundationalist should be obvious by now: What sort of deductive connection is there between introspective beliefs and beliefs about external objects and their properties? Descartes thought that at least some truths about the external world could be known by deductive argument—again, depending on divine benevolence. This suggests that one option for the infallible foundationalist is to hold that a sufficient number of inference principles might be underwritten by reason alone. Such principles would then provide the deductive arguments needed to carry us from our beliefs, from what's inside our minds, out into the natural world. Few in the history of philosophy have seriously attempted this project. Nor will we pursue further the issue of deducing truths about the world from basic infallible beliefs. When we move to consideration of objections to foundationalism in the next section, the focus for strong foundationalism will be whether basic beliefs are infallibly justified. Yet we should not forget that half the task of the strong foundationalist is to show us how we might move from basic beliefs to infallibly justified beliefs about the world around us.

Neoclassical foundationalism

Elements of a variant of strong foundationalism are discernible in the work of a number of twentieth century epistemologists. We might call this view **neoclassical foundationalism.**[6] Neoclassical foundationalism holds that certain basic beliefs are incorrigibly justified. A typical kind of basic belief is belief about the contents of our sense experiences. Other types of belief also might count as basic. Bertrand Russell, for example, holds that we are directly acquainted not only with the content of our sense experiences but also with our own thoughts and feelings and the deliverances of memory. The important feature of this acquaintance is that it is direct; consequently, in Russell's view, such beliefs cannot be mistaken.[7] In general, the neoclassical view holds that basic beliefs are certain in the following sense: If one believes that P, then P. Again, the essential idea is that there is no gap between the belief itself and the object of the belief.

The essential difference between the neoclassical and the Cartesian versions of strong foundationalism is the justificatory link between basic and nonbasic beliefs. Whereas the Cartesian version requires a deductive link between basic and nonbasic beliefs, the neoclassical view does not. Inductive or probabilistic connections, inferences to the best explanation, and Russell's "psychological inferences" are examples of the type of link permitted by various neoclassical positions. This change from the Cartesian version allows that nonbasic beliefs may be justified, although they are not certain. An advantage of the neoclassical view, according to proponents, is that it provides an explanation of our knowledge of the world while buttressing that knowledge against the claims of the skeptic.[8]

Modest Foundationalism

Modest foundationalism, sometimes known as *minimal foundationalism,* derives its name from the fact that proponents require only that basic and nonbasic beliefs be *fallibly* justified. Fallibly justified beliefs are likely, but not guaranteed, to be true. The justification of such beliefs can be overridden or defeated; we might later come to see that some belief we previously counted as basic must be revised or rejected in light of new evidence. For example, suppose Sam has the basic belief that the ball is blue. The modest foundationalist claims that Sam might acquire further evidence that undermines the justification of the basic belief—for example, move to a different part of the room, see the ball from a different angle, and decide that it is green. Or consider a type of belief that modest foundationalists typically count as basic: memory beliefs. Sam might believe, on the basis of a "memory experience," that his appointment with Sara is tomorrow evening. After checking his calendar, however, he notices that he has written in the appointment for this evening, which means he must reassess his basic belief. In general, the type of evidence that undermines the justification of a basic belief may come in the form of another basic belief or as a result of nonbasic beliefs.

The second important feature of modest foundationalism is that the inferential connections between basic and nonbasic beliefs may be inductive. Notice again that this sort of inferential connection is fallibilist. Though we might have very good inductive evidence for a belief, we ultimately might have to reject it because of new evidence. Induction, recall, is risky business.

Two different thoughts might motivate one to be a modest rather than a strong foundationalist. First, some hold that there are basic beliefs, but not any infallibly justified beliefs. Another sort of motivation for modest foundationalism stems from the recognition of Descartes's difficulty, moving from infallible basic beliefs to beliefs about the world. As suggested previously, it is hard to see how we could ever come to have much in the way of empirical knowledge. According to modest foundationalists (and others), it is difficult to see how we can extend our basic knowledge to account for what we normally think of as our knowledge of the world if we are required do so only by infallible means. Modest foundationalists seek to redress these difficulties by (a) holding that justification is fallible, and thus counting different types of belief as basic, and (b) allowing inferential connections between basic and nonbasic beliefs to be inductive.[9]

Different types of modest foundationalism countenance different types of belief as basic. We will not explore most of them in detail, but it will be

Can Reliabilists Be Foundationalists?

Clearly, reliabilists cannot be strong foundationalists, because they do not claim that beliefs, which are the result of reliable belief-forming processes, are guaranteed to be true; they are, at best, very likely to be true.

That reliabilism might embrace modest foundationalism is another matter. Certain types of belief—for example, perceptual and memory—seem to be justified independently of our other beliefs, according to the reliabilist. Recall that what accounts for the justification of my belief that there is a cup in front of me is simply that such beliefs are likely to be true in the relevant situations. This seems to make such beliefs epistemically independent in the requisite sense. Reliabilism and foundationalism might also be thought incompatible because reliabilism is an externalist theory whereas foundationalism historically has been internalist. Note, however, that the Regress Argument does not rely on internalism, any more than it relies on infallibilism. Thus, reliabilism can satisfy the essential condition of foundationalism—there are beliefs that do not depend on other beliefs for their justification.

useful to describe two of the more prevalent types. The first type we might call **doxastic foundationalism.**[10] Doxastic foundationalists count beliefs about one's perceptual experiences or sensations, or simply appearance beliefs, as basic. Doxastic foundationalists claim that our appearance beliefs *inductively support* our consequent perceptual beliefs. Appearance beliefs provide a fallible justification for our beliefs about objects and their properties.

The second type of modest foundationalism, which will receive more of our attention, might be called **nondoxastic foundationalism.** In this view, memory beliefs and perceptual beliefs, for example, count as basic beliefs. Sam's perceptual belief that there is a glass in front of him is a basic belief according to the nondoxastic foundationalist. Basic beliefs are epistemically dependent on the contents of the perceptual experiences or sensations, but these contents are not themselves beliefs. For example, if Sara sees a purple book, then she has a certain visual experience or sensation. The visual experience is Sara's experience or awareness of the visual properties—for example, the shape, color, and size—of the book. Now, this experience or sensation is not itself a belief; it is a nondoxastic mental state. Visual experiences are, of course, not unique to Sara. As you look up from what you are reading and glance about your environment, you are having certain visual experiences related to the colors, sizes, shapes, and distances of the objects around you. As you run your hand over the surface of the chair or the grass on which you are reclining, noting the texture and feel of these surfaces, you are having tactile experiences. Such perceptual experiences are especially important for foundationalists. It is by virtue of her visual experience that Sara comes to have the perceptual belief "There is a purple book." Accordingly, nondoxastic foundationalists would claim that her belief, "There is a purple book," is justified independently of other beliefs. Sara's belief is likely to be true because she has the appropriate visual experience; hence, her belief is justified. Because the visual experience itself is not a belief, Sara's belief doesn't depend on any other belief for its justification, and so her belief satisfies the conditions for a basic belief.

This example highlights the principle difference between doxastic and nondoxastic foundationalism. Doxastic foundationalists claim that Sara has a belief about her visual experience. It is this belief about her experience that is basic. Her perceptual belief that there is a purple book, then, is a nonbasic belief. As noted previously, however, nondoxastic foundationalists hold that our normal perceptual beliefs are based on the nondoxastic contents of our experiences. Thus, normal perceptual beliefs count as basic beliefs. Doxastic foundationalists count beliefs about the properties of our mental states, appearance beliefs, as basic; nondoxastic foundationalists count perceptual beliefs, or beliefs about our environment, as basic.

One might wonder how significant this difference is. Why prefer one version to the other? In attempting to answer this question, we touch on issues more complex than we can fully consider here. Indeed, some of these issues overlap the philosophy of the mind.

One thought that might motivate the adoption of nondoxastic foundationalism is the view that we do not usually have beliefs about our visual experiences.[11] If so, that would mean that the justification of our ordinary perceptual beliefs would be more cumbersome. If we only occasionally have beliefs about appearances, then it will be more difficult to supply the inductive links to the vast range of our perceptual beliefs. This is not to imply that doxastic foundationalism is wrong, but rather to point out that some have thought that perceptual beliefs are our primary doxastic contact with the world.

Now, doxastic foundationalists do have a line of response to this sort of view. First, they hold that there is perception without belief; that is, agents can make perceptual discriminations without having beliefs. The ability to make perceptual discriminations without having beliefs shows, in the doxastic foundationlists' view, that appearances are psychologically prior to perceptual beliefs. The psychological process of perception begins with appearances and then proceeds to beliefs. Second, they claim that we often cite how things appear to us to justify our perceptual beliefs.[12] Sara's belief that there is a purple book might be defended by citing how it appeared to her—for example, "It looks purple." That we can appeal to how we are appeared to (recall that this is only a way of talking about our visual experience or sensation) purportedly shows that we do have beliefs about the contents of the appearance and that our perceptual beliefs are epistemically dependent on our appearance beliefs. Perhaps more importantly, argues Alan Goldman, a doxastic foundationalist, perceptual beliefs cannot be justified on the basis of perceptual experiences. In Goldman's view, appearances do not involve concepts; they are unconceptualized. The perceptual experience is, in a sense, too "nondoxastic." There is, of course, a content to our experience, but it is the wrong sort of content to be of use in the justification of belief.[13] We will see later that critics of foundationalism exploit just this sort of claim.

Note that the nondoxastic foundationalist will want to be careful about challenging the first claim. The nondoxastic foundationalist agrees that perceptual experiences are essential to the justification of perceptual beliefs. But the nondoxastic foundationalist will no doubt object to the claim that appearance beliefs must inevitably be cited in the justification of perceptual beliefs. One way to begin the objection is to recall the earlier distinction between causal and epistemic dependence. If I believe I see a green glass in front of me, I might cite not only my belief that it seems to me to be green but also my beliefs that I know what glasses are and that my eyes are in good working order. But the fact that these beliefs are psychologically relevant does not entail my belief being epistemically dependent on them. The nondoxastic foundationalist may press further by claiming that many of our perceptual beliefs are simply not accompanied by (much less preceded by) appearance beliefs. Having a perceptual belief does not necessarily entail having correlative appearance beliefs. If this were so, then many of our perceptual beliefs seemingly would be unjustified, which runs counter to a very strong intuition. A similar line of argument might run as follows: The nondoxastic foundationalist might grant that we appeal to appearance beliefs as a means of *showing* that we are justified, but appearance beliefs are not necessary for *being* justified. This distinction between showing that a belief is justified and a belief in fact being justified proves central in arguments considered later. We might illustrate the distinction by a simple example. Suppose you go to a bookstore and notice a sign indicating that students receive a 5 percent discount. You open your billfold to retrieve your student ID only to find that you have removed it. Now, you are in fact a student. Your inability to *show* that you are a student does not make you any less a student; it only makes you a poorer student. You have the property of being a student no matter where your ID might be. Similarly, a belief might have the property of justification despite one's inability to show that the belief is justified.[14]

Finally, the nondoxastic foundationalist may view appearance beliefs as unnecessary. If appearance beliefs are justified by appeal to the content of the experience or appearance, then why could it not be the case that the experience or appearance also was the basis of the justification for the perceptual belief? As long as this connection holds, appearance beliefs might seem to be unnecessary. Nondoxastic foundationalists can then claim to have the best of both views without the more controversial element of doxastic foundationalism. How we are appeared to plays a significant epistemic role in nondoxastic foundationalism, but the further controversial claim that these appearances are the contents of beliefs is avoided.

Clearly, this issue is too complicated to pursue further now. However, other questions have been raised about foundationalism in general and about modest and strong foundationalism in particular. In the next section, we canvas the principal criticisms of foundationalism and some of the ways in which foundationalists have responded.

Features of Modest Foundationalism

Before turning to criticisms of foundationalism, it might be useful to summarize the essential features of modest (nondoxastic) foundationalism. The two primary features are, of course, fallibilism and inductive connections between basic and nonbasic beliefs. Modest foundationalists are committed only to fallibly justified basic beliefs. They hold that the source of justification for basic beliefs is independent of other beliefs. Such justification can, however, be overridden. Indeed, some foundationalists allow that the lack of coherence among beliefs may be sufficient to override the justification of a basic belief.[15]

The conditions for the justification of a basic belief are typically expressed by certain epistemic principles. Robert Audi presents four principles of direct justification, principles that explain the source of justification for types of basic belief. We might briefly consider his perceptual principle as an example:

> If S has a spontaneous perceptual experience in which S has the impression that x is F, and on this basis attentively believes that x is F, then this belief is prima facie justified.[16]

Suppose, then, that Sara has the belief that the book is purple. Also, suppose that Sara has this belief as a result of her having a particular perceptual or visual experience, the experience of a purple book. Thus, the *source* of the justification for her belief is the perceptual experience. But the experience is not itself a belief. So, the justification of her belief about the book does not depend on other beliefs. Sara's belief that the book is purple thus satisfies the conditions for a basic belief. Of course, this justification can be overriden, and that is the point of calling the belief *prima facie* justified.

You might wonder why Audi's view—and views like it—is not a version of reliabilism. Clearly, Audi counts perceptual beliefs as likely to be true. But Audi thinks that the epistemic basis of a perceptual belief is in principle accessible to the agent. Note that in the preceding principle, the agent must *attentively* believe *on the basis of* a perceptual experience. Audi thus holds that the accessibility of one's reasons is a necessary condition for the justification of belief. This is sufficient to distinguish Audi's view from reliabilism, although Audi is clearly committed to the reliability or likely truth of perceptual beliefs.

Audi is typical of modest foundationalists in that he holds that perceptual beliefs, memory beliefs, introspective beliefs, and a priori beliefs all are types of basic belief. Although we have presented only the principle of direct justification for perceptual beliefs, Audi also presents similar principles for memory, introspective, and a priori beliefs.[17]

OBJECTIONS TO FOUNDATIONALISM

Most theorists are willing to concede that beliefs either deductively or inductively derived from justified beliefs are themselves justified.[18] Predictably, then, challenges to foundationalist projects occur with respect to the notion of basic beliefs. Critics of foundationalism want to know why there should be thought to be self-justified beliefs. Put simply, are there basic beliefs? This question can arise in two different ways. First, with respect to the notion of infallibility, are there *infallibly* justified beliefs? Second, and more generally, are there indeed beliefs that are justified, whether fallibly or infallibly, but that nonetheless are *epistemically independent* of other beliefs? We begin this section by looking at the notion of infallible justification. We then consider why the notion of epistemic independence has seemed troubling and how the foundationalists have responded.

Strong Foundationalism and Basic Beliefs

A standard claim of the strong foundationalist is that we have infallible access to the contents of our own mind. This means that one cannot be mistaken about what one is thinking about, sensing, desiring, wishing, and so on. If you ask me, for example, what I am thinking about, and I tell you I am thinking I need more coffee, we typically accept—assuming I am not lying or impaired—that, of course, that is what I am thinking about. Indeed, what better evidence could there be than the typical deliverances of introspection?

How could I possibly be wrong? And if I could not possibly be wrong, then this is precisely what we mean by an infallibly justified belief. Thus, beliefs about the contents of my own mind are infallibly justified. The feature that accounts for the infallibility of these beliefs is simply that they are the result of introspection. But do we have reason to hold that beliefs arrived at via introspection are likely to be not just true, but infallibly true? Two different kinds of reason for thinking that this is not so have been suggested.

First, for any belief we might have as a result of introspection, we might also have arrived at the belief by means of an inference. Now, if such beliefs are arrived at via inference, then the inference may be based on mistaken or false premises or, indeed, be merely a faulty inference. This type of objection is illustrated by the following example from Keith Lehrer.[19]

Suppose I am thinking that Francis Bacon is the author of *Hamlet*. Further, suppose I falsely think that, if most scholars are to be believed, Bacon is Shakespeare. This false belief that Bacon is Shakespeare is not occurrent; I am not thinking of it at the moment. But when you ask me what I am thinking, I reply that I am thinking that Shakespeare is the author of *Hamlet*. Now, am I correct in believing that this is what I think? Lehrer argues that I would not be correct. Notice that there are a number of things that are true of the former content that are not true of the latter, even if we allow that I do have the mistaken belief about the identity of Shakespeare.

This is undoubtedly a controversial example. First, note why Lehrer thinks I would have *misidentified* the content of my belief. That Shakespeare is the author of *Hamlet* is true. However, if I had told you that I was thinking that Bacon was the author of *Hamlet*, you would have worried that the old guy (me) was not just old but a bit senile as well. A second point is more important for our purposes. Lehrer might be understood as pointing out that we can be mistaken about whether introspection is a *direct* process. Introspection may, on the surface, seem to us to be direct: that is, there are no intervening inferences—we simply "look inside" and "see" what we are thinking. But suppose introspection is not like this. Suppose that on at least some occasions, what goes on is something like an inference, an inference that is hidden from us. Such unconscious inferences do occur. The troublesome point for the infallibilist is that it seems possible for these two cases to go undistinguished. That is, it is possible that we may not be able to tell when introspection is direct or when it is the result of inference. This possibility, in turn, opens up the possibility that introspection may *not* be an infallible process.

Although Lehrer's case may seem a bit odd, it is worth bearing in mind that the reliability of introspection, much less its infallibility, is a subject of much empirical investigation. Even some of the introspectionist psychologists of the early twentieth century held that not just anyone is a "reliable introspecter." Rather, the ability to introspect required some practice and learning. More recently, studies indicate that only under certain conditions can the deliverances of introspection be held to be reliable or, even more problematic, infallible.[20] This should not be surprising. We know, for example, that the mechanisms that underlie our visual capabilities occasionally break down. This is part of the source of the fallibility of perception. But if we analogously think of introspection as a mechanism, then we might also think that it, too, could break down. But imperfect mechanisms are unlikely to underwrite infallibility.

However compelling these objections to the infallibility of introspection may be, there is still the strong temptation to think that I simply cannot be mistaken about what I am thinking. If I am thinking about a red balloon, then that's all there is to it—I'm thinking about a red balloon. It is worth looking at this idea in a bit more detail. Suppose I have the introspective belief that I am having the sensation of purple. Now, it seems possible to have a sensation and yet to have the wrong belief about the current sense impression. Suppose, for example, that I mistakenly believe that indigo is a type of purple, and I come to have the belief that I am having the sensation of indigo. But I am not; I am having the sensation of purple.

A standard response to this objection is to claim that I am not mistaken about the nature of my sensation; I have only misdescribed it. The assumption that underlies this response is that there is a difference between *recognizing* that I have a certain sensation and *describing* it, or characterizing it as being of a certain type. The recognition is held to be infallible; my description has simply been in error. My mistake has occurred in applying the wrong concept. In this way, at least, introspection is still infallible.

One might object on the ground that no clear-cut line separates recognition from description. Even with very low-grade forms of recognition—for example, recognizing something as familiar as purple—one might object that I must have some beliefs about the nature of the sensation. I must be able to characterize or describe the sensation in at least some ways, and here the possibility of error arises.[21] For me to characterize the sensation as being of a certain type requires that I have discriminating beliefs about what qualifies as an instance of being of a certain type. The greater this descriptive component in recognition, the greater is the chance of error.

There is a related reason for thinking that the line between recognition and description may not be as clear-cut as the strong foundationalist requires. Introspection is putatively a source of beliefs. More specifically, it is a source of beliefs about the contents of our own minds. This, after all, is part of the aim of strong foundationalism—to identify *beliefs* that are infallibly justified. Now, whatever else beliefs may be or involve, having a belief about something seems to require not only having concepts but also applying those concepts. Suppose we think of applying concepts to sensations as a type of description. If we adopt this line, then having a belief involves a descriptive component, because having beliefs involves applying concepts. But this line of thought tends to blur the distinction between recognizing and describing sensations. If recognizing a sensation is a belief, then recognizing involves describing or applying concepts. In this view, having a belief ineluctably involves this descriptive or identifying component. If introspection is a source of belief, and if having a belief requires the use of concepts, and if using concepts involves a risk of misusing or misapplying concepts, then introspection is not an infallible source of belief about the contents of our own minds.

A last defense of infallibility is to claim something like the following: I cannot be mistaken about the fact that I am thinking *this,* where we are to understand the force of the "this" as a kind of mental pointing. Critics counter that this line of thought sacrifices much of the content of these basic beliefs. With this sort of specification of the content of an introspective belief, the belief might be thought to contain very little content; the belief doesn't say very much. One might then be somewhat dubious that the strong foundationalist can hope to use these sorts of belief as the *foundation* for our more customary beliefs about glasses, red balloons, and all the familiar objects of our world.[22]

Although the preceding seems to cast some doubt on the possibility of infallible beliefs, there remain defenders of infallible belief. Evan Fales, for example, argues in support of infallible beliefs, and in particular, introspective beliefs.[23] Fales contends that it is a mistake to understand infallibility as the *logical* impossibility of mistake. Rather, he construes infallibility as a kind of self-evidence. We have access to the contents of certain mental states, access that guarantees we cannot be mistaken about those contents. Fales designates this sort of access as *cognitive transparency.* Unfortunately, the richness of Fales's argument precludes a detailed consideration of his perception. But we might make a suggestion about the future direction of this argument.

Evidently, much of the argument between advocates and critics of infallibility turns on the nature of introspection itself. Advocates, such as Fales, argue that introspection is the sort of process or mechanism that guarantees the requisite type of access for infallibility. This is, it should be noted, an empirical claim. It is not self-contradictory to assert that the deliverances of introspection might sometimes be mistaken. Consequently, we might profitably turn to cognitive psychology for data that might suggest whether introspection does provide the requisite sort of access. Indeed, William Lyons attempts to construct a model of introspection that takes account of research in cognitive psychology. Now, this is not to claim that Lyons's model of introspection is preferable to Fales's. Lyons is aware that the research is not conclusive. Rather, the suggestion here is that certain empirical results ought to be integrated into any adequate model of introspection. For example, empirical studies regarding the nature of attention and perception and the interaction between the two might lead us to doubt that we have a direct or guaranteed access to the contents of our perceptual experiences.[24] If this modest suggestion is right, then the issue between infallibilists and their critics may turn on our understanding of the results of the work of cognitive psychologists.

Levels of Justification

Fundamental to any foundationalist view is the claim that there are basic beliefs that are justified but that are epistemically independent of other beliefs. Understandably, the central criticism of the foundationalist perspective focuses on just this aspect of foundationalism. Critics of foundationalism have argued that the notion of a justified but epistemically independent belief cannot be sustained. Simply, there are no basic beliefs. The first argument to be considered is sometimes called the *levels ascent argument.*[25]

If basic beliefs are justified, there is some feature of those beliefs by virtue of which they are justified. Once we have identified this feature, we can ask why it is a justifying feature—that is, how it makes the truth of the basic belief more likely. (In the case of strong foundationalism, we would ask why the feature guarantees the truth of the basic belief. For simplicity, we focus on fallible foundationalism.) Thus, we have two "premises" supporting the claim that any putative basic belief is justified: (a) The belief possesses some feature, F, and (b) beliefs possessing F are likely to be true. The conclusion of this argument is that some particular belief is likely to be true, and hence justified. A bit more formally, the argument can be put thus:

(1) Basic belief B has the feature F.

(2) Beliefs having F are likely to be true.

(3) Thus, belief B is likely to be true, hence, justified.

Premise (1) states that basic beliefs will have some property F by virtue of which they are justified. It is a matter of some dispute, even among foundationalists, whether the agent must be able to recognize that the belief has the property, but at the very least, the belief must have the property. Premise (2) makes an explicit claim about the connection between the property F and the likelihood of truth. Now, on the face of it, this seems to be an empirical claim. To talk of the likelihood of truth is to talk about the way the world actually is, or at least probably is. But now we can highlight the problem that concerns critics.

If something like this argument is required for the justification of any basic belief, then the basic belief seemingly depends on at least one other empirical belief, the belief described in premise (2). But this would mean that the basic belief is not epistemically independent of other beliefs. Thus, it fails to satisfy the key condition for being basic. Further, if the agent does not accept this argument, then there seems to be *no reason* for thinking the basic belief is true. Hence, the basic belief would not be justified.

Foundationalists respond to the levels ascent argument by distinguishing between *showing that a belief is justified* and *being justified in believing*. Foundationalists agree that if in order for a belief to be justified one must show that it is justified, then something like the previous argument is needed. But foundationalists claim that showing that a belief is justified is not a necessary condition of its being justified. Recall the example of being a student and showing that one is a student. There are conditions by virtue of which Sara is a student: The appropriate documents (and money) have been presented to the appropriate people at a university in the lower reaches of California. Still, Sara might not be able to show that she is a student; she might not have access to the appropriate papers, or she may have misplaced her ID. The *fact* that she is a student is independent of her ability, or lack thereof, to *show* that she is a student. Similarly, foundationalists claim that whether a belief is justified is independent of whether one can show that it is justified. (Beliefs that are justified are sometimes said to be first-order justified; showing that the belief is justified is a type of second-order justification.) Foundationalists further claim that beliefs are justified by virtue of their satisfying certain conditions. Recall, for example, Audi's principles of direct justification. Sam's memory belief that the ball was left outside is justified by virtue of Sam's forming the belief as a result of his having a "memory experience." It is by virtue of these conditions obtaining—his forming the belief on the basis of his memory experience—that Sam's belief is justified. According to foundationalists, it is quite another matter as to whether Sam could actually show that his belief is justified, as to whether he could actually produce some sort of argument that highlights the connection between memory beliefs, memory experiences, and the likelihood of truth.

These considerations enable us to pinpoint one source of the disagreement between foundationalists and their critics. Critics claim that a necessary condition of an agent being justified in believing is that, in principle, the agent have available a kind of argument *showing* that the belief is justified. Many foundationalists counter that all that is necessary for a belief to be justified is that the belief actually satisfies the conditions required by the relevant epistemic principles—for example, Audi's principles of direct justification. If it is an epistemic principle that appropriately formed memory beliefs are justified, then if Sam has a genuine memory belief that Sara will be late, his belief is justified. It does not matter, claim foundationalists, that Sam is unable to give the following argument:

(1) My belief about Sara is a memory belief.

(2) Memory beliefs are likely to be true.

(3) Hence, my belief is likely to be true, and thus justified.

Why do foundationalists reject the requirement that an agent must have a justifying argument, or be able to show that a belief is justified? One reason typically given is that many people—for example, children—are unable to give such justifying arguments. Yet we are inclined to think that even children have justified beliefs. If we are right about this, then *showing* that a belief is justified apparently is not a necessary condition of a belief being justified.[26]

The levels ascent argument clearly highlights one difference between advocates and critics of foundationalism. A virtue of the argument is that it relies on our intuition that an agent must have reasons for a belief if that belief is to be justified. Yet, if accepted, the argument clearly does impose a serious restriction on when a person has justified beliefs. There may be reason to think that the argument is too strong as it stands. It is one thing to hold that an agent must have reasons for believing what he does if his beliefs are to be justified. But the levels ascent argument seems to require more than this. It requires that the agent be able to recognize the "metareason" that these reasons for which he believes have the appropriate connection to truth. It requires that the agent be able to recognize *why* these reasons are *justifying* reasons. A bit more technically, it requires that the agent have beliefs about the *epistemic status* of justifying beliefs. This can be illustrated by recalling the general schema of the levels ascent argument. Premise (2) requires that the agent recognize that beliefs having the property F are likely to be true. This is a belief about the epistemic status of another belief.

We can highlight, then, three distinct requirements that one might impose on justified beliefs. It is one thing to require an agent to have reasons for believing. It is another to insist that the agent believe on the basis of these reasons and, in some sense, have access to these reasons. Many foundationalists accept these two requirements in one form or another.[27] It is, however, a much stronger requirement to say that the agent must recognize or even believe that the reasons are justifying reasons. That is, the agent must have beliefs about the epistemic status of the justifying reasons. The more explicit this recognition is required to be, the fewer justified beliefs people will have (and the fewer people will have justified beliefs). This third requirement imposed by the levels ascent argument thus seems to be too strong.

There is, however, another kind of argument that exploits the same intuition underlying the levels ascent argument but without imposing such constraints. This argument is the focus of the next section.

Independent Information and Modest Foundationalism

An intuition motivating the levels ascent argument is that whatever accounts for the justification of a belief must be the right sort of thing to provide justification. For example, nondoxastic foundationalists explain the direct justification of perceptual beliefs by citing the experience that grounds the perceptual belief. Thus, one can ask just why it is that the experience is sufficient for the justification of the correlative perceptual belief. There are two ways this issue can be pursued. The first concerns the notion of independent information. The second is somewhat more complicated and concerns the nature of the experience itself—that is, whether experiences are the right sort of thing to ground the justification of beliefs. Nondoxastic foundationalism provides a representative framework for us to pursue these questions.

By now, we understand how the nondoxastic foundationalist explains the direct justification of a perceptual belief. Suppose I see a computer screen in front of me. Let us further suppose that as a result of seeing the screen, I come to have the basic belief that there is a computer screen in front of me. My seeing the screen causes a visual experience. The visual experience, in turn, leads to my having the belief about the computer screen. The normal, typical cause of such experiences is simply that there is a computer screen in front of me. It is by virtue of my having the experience that my belief is likely to be true. Thus, my belief is justified. However, because the visual experience of the computer screen is not itself a belief, the belief is justified independently of other beliefs. Hence, it is directly justified.

Keith Lehrer questions whether this sort of explanation really does show that basic beliefs are independent of other beliefs.[28] He claims that having a basic belief requires that an agent possess *independent information*—specifically, beliefs about the character and nature of the content of the basic belief. For example, if I have the perceptual belief that there is a computer screen in front of me, Lehrer claims that I must be able to recognize or discriminate this type of object from other types of object. I must have available to me the identifying features of computer screens, and I must draw specifically on this information in coming to have the belief that there is a computer screen in front of me. Or, as Lehrer puts it, I must have information about how computer screens look, and that information must be sufficient to enable me to discriminate such screens from keyboards. If I did not know that computer screens looked this way and not some other, how could I be justified in believing there was a computer screen in front of me? This would seem to require that I draw on other beliefs, specifically empirical beliefs, in the explanation of the justification of this basic belief. Thus, according to Lehrer, we have not yet identified a basic belief.

Here, we can see the importance of the distinction between causal dependence and epistemic independence. Foundationalists concede that there

are other beliefs I must have if I am to have the belief that there is a computer screen in front of me. My belief is causally dependent on these other
beliefs. Yet this, foundationalists claim, does nothing to show that the basic
belief is epistemically dependent on the beliefs that provide the necessary
independent information. According to foundationalists, the explanation of
why my belief is likely to be true is the fact that I have that belief as a result
of a visual experience of a certain sort. On the other hand, my believing that
computer screens have colorful displays whereas computer keyboards do
not does nothing to show that my belief that there is a screen in front of me
is likely to be true. The visual experience, not the independent information
beliefs, explains why the belief is likely to be true, and hence justified.

How should we go about determining whether basic beliefs are genuinely epistemically independent? As a first step, we need to recognize that
a basic belief is justified if there is some reason to think that it is more likely
to be true. Now, the independent information beliefs do provide some reason for thinking that the basic belief is likely to be true. If I believe that
monitors look like *this,* and my visual experience is of *this* sort, then my belief about the way computer screens look clearly makes my belief more
likely to be true. But foundationalists are willing to accept two ideas. As we
saw in the previous section, they are willing to accept the claim that having
any belief requires having other beliefs. Second, and more importantly,
they are willing to accept that the independent information beliefs can and
do help to justify the basic belief. Coherence with other beliefs can increase
the justification of a basic belief. However, foundationalists claim that this is
a case of epistemic overdetermination. It is still the case that certain kinds
of experience, such as visual experiences, are *sufficient* to justify the basic
belief. The justificatory contribution of the independent information beliefs
is a bit of *lagniappe,* a little extra epistemic support. The basic belief would
still be justified, even without the justificatory support of the independent
information beliefs.

Before we proceed, it would be worthwhile to recount briefly the foundationalists' claim. They do not deny that independent information is necessary to form the basic belief in the first place. They grant the causal,
psychological dependence of the basic belief on the independent information beliefs.[29] Nor do foundationalists deny that the independent information beliefs contribute some justificatory support to the basic belief.
What they deny is that this justificatory support is *necessary* for the justification of the basic belief. Now, it becomes clearer what critics of foundationalism must maintain. What needs to be shown is that the experience, which
is the alleged ground of the justification of the basic belief, is not epistemically *sufficient* to justify the basic belief. The critics must argue that the experience *by itself* cannot account for the justification of the basic belief. It is
to this critical issue that we now turn.

The Cognitive Status of Experience

Recall that what drives the Regress Argument is the idea that one belief can justify another belief only if it (the justifying belief) is itself justified. Foundationalists accept this idea. Indeed, it is precisely this idea that leads them to countenance the notion of basic beliefs. To maintain that basic beliefs are epistemically independent but justified, foundationalists appeal to the thought that an experience of a relevant sort is the source of the justification of the basic belief. At this point, critics have a question: If this experience—whatever it is—can serve to justify the basic belief, then why doesn't it need to be justified? Isn't this just what the Regress Argument is about? Don't foundationalists accept this feature of the Regress Argument, that to be a "justifier" requires being justified? So, why doesn't the experience need to be justified? If the answer is that it doesn't need to be justified, then how can it be the sort of thing that justifies beliefs of any sort?

The dilemma that faces foundationalists can be put in the following form, what we might call the cognitive status argument:[30]

(1) If experiences are capable of providing justification for basic beliefs, then they need to be justified.

(2) So, either experiences themselves need to be justified, in which case the regress has yet to be terminated, or experiences are not the source of the justification of basic beliefs.

Clearly, foundationalists want to claim that experiences provide the necessary justification for basic beliefs but are themselves in no need of justification. That is, foundationalists claim, and critics question, whether there can be nonbelieflike or nondoxastic sources of justification. (Laurence BonJour refers to such mental states as noncognitive.) Obviously, this is a significant issue for both foundationalists and nonfoundationalists, as well as a rather complicated one.

Let us start with a simple example. I look out the window, and I come to have the belief that a bird (which is no longer in view) has just left the bird feeder. I believe this because I see that the bird feeder, which is suspended by a chain, is swaying, and I can see from the stillness of the leaves on the trees that there is no wind blowing. Obviously, there are a lot of other potentially relevant beliefs (for example, that the swaying was not caused by a neighborhood cat playing on the deck), but for simplicity, let us focus on the two beliefs I have mentioned. Now, as we have had occasion to note, these two beliefs justify my belief about a bird visiting only to the extent that they make the latter belief more likely to be true. But how do they do this? The thought seems to be that given the *content* of those two beliefs, along with the necessary inferential relation, the content of my belief about the visiting bird is more likely to be true. That is, it is by virtue of the *contents* of my justifying beliefs that the contents of my belief is likely to be true. The key notion here is that beliefs are contentful mental states.

Let us restate two key points from our previous discussion of strong foundationalism. Beliefs have the contents they do by virtue of the concepts that are constitutive of them, and concepts are the sort of things that can be misapplied or used incorrectly. Applying concepts is part of our general cognitive ability, and states that involve concepts are cognitive states. It follows that mental states that have content are cognitive states. My belief about the visiting bird is a cognitive state, as are my beliefs that the bird feeder is swaying and there is no wind blowing.

We can now see how these issues bear on the notion of justification. To say that my belief about the bird is likely to be true—justified—is to say that I likely have the right mental state content, and the reason for thinking that I do is by virtue of the contents of my other two beliefs. Two principal claims can now be made explicit. First, it is because beliefs are contentful, that is, cognitive, that we want to know whether they are justified. We want to know whether our beliefs are the *right* contents. Second, it looks as if the only potential justifiers are other contentful states, other cognitive states. These two claims allow us to recast the antifoundationalist's worry.

Suppose experiences are contentful mental states. Then we will want to know whether these experiences have the *right* contents, that is, whether they are justified. Why aren't they just like any other belief that requires justification? Hence, the regress will not have ended. On the other hand, suppose the experiences are not contentful mental states. Then we will want to know how it is that they can support the justificatory status of basic beliefs. How can they serve as the justificatory source for basic beliefs?

Foundationalists like to respond in something like the following way.[31] If we have any hope of our beliefs turning out to be true, and not sheer fiction, then at some point there must be a contact, an interface, between our cognitive states and the world. Somehow, what's going on out there in the world has to get in here, in our heads, in the form of contentful mental states. We need a way of translating physical, natural information into mental information. The means by which this happens is experience—that is, our first-level interaction with the world. Granted, experiences are contentful, but the way to explain why those experiences probably have the right contents is not by continuing the epistemological story, but rather by telling a physical or causal story. At some point, the physical-causal story becomes an epistemological story. That's where experiences come in. For example, when someone has the perceptual belief that the bird feeder is swaying, that belief is likely to be true if it is caused by a visual experience of the appropriate sort. In turn, the visual experience is likely to be of the appropriate sort if it is caused by the appropriate physical events: a bird departing the feeder, which causes it to sway; light reflecting from the swaying feeder and striking the retinas, which sets in motion a complex neurological process, which culminates in an experience of a certain type. Experience thus plays the crucial transitional role, and when a person does have an experience of the appropriate sort, that experience explains why the belief is likely to be true. Only if there is something like experience can we hope that our belief contents are the right contents to have.

The original objection and the foundationalist's response are both powerful; each points to fundamental epistemological questions. We can raise three matters that both foundationalist and critic need to address. First, if we are to accept the foundationalist response, we clearly will want to know more about the nature of the experiences. Are the appearances or experiences that are to support the basic beliefs cognitive? If they are, is the content of the experience of the same type as the content of the basic belief it is to support? Second, we will want to know whether foundationalists have the empirical story right. Is their account of the genesis of experience, especially those states we have characterized as appearances, correct? Finally, even if they are right about the nature of experience and the correlative empirical story, are they right about the epistemological role experience plays? Is it really by virtue of the experiences themselves that basic beliefs are justified, or is it by virtue of our beliefs about the connection between experience and the world?

Common to all types of foundationalism is the idea that certain beliefs are epistemically prior to other beliefs. These basic beliefs do not depend on other beliefs for their justification. As we can see now, basic beliefs are the ultimate *doxastic* source of the justification of other beliefs. Doubts about infallibility may lead to doubts about strong foundationalism. Neoclassical foundationalists, however, have mounted a vigorous defense of the idea that certain basic beliefs are immune to error. With modest foundationalism, the problem of infallibility disappears. The more pressing issue for the modest foundationalist is the sense in which basic beliefs do not depend on other beliefs for their justification. Although basic beliefs are doxastically basic, there is indeed an ultimate *nondoxastic* source of the justification of basic beliefs, and indirectly of all beliefs. In response to the cognitive status argument, we saw that modest foundationalists invoke experiences as the ground of the justified status of basic beliefs. Without this ground, foundationalists claim that we will be unable to explain how our beliefs ever receive their initial epistemic credibility.

Key Concepts

Basic beliefs	Neoclassical foundationalism
Doxastic foundationalism	Nondoxastic foundationalism
Foundationalism	Regress Argument
Modest foundationalism	Strong foundationalism

Review Questions

1. Why do foundationalists think that the Regress Argument provides a motivation for foundationalism?

2. What is the difference between modest and strong foundationalism? Do you think there are infallible beliefs? Why or why not?

3. What reasons might be given for preferring nondoxastic to doxastic foundationalism? Do you think these reasons are compelling? Explain.

4. Discuss the central features of the levels ascent argument. Do you think foundationalists have an adequate response to this criticism? Why or why not?

5. Why does Lehrer think that the notion of independent information undermines the notion of basic beliefs? Do you agree with Lehrer?

6. The cognitive status argument presents a dilemma to foundationalists. What is this dilemma? Why is it important to know the "cognitive status" of experiences? Evaluate the foundationalist response to this argument.

For Further Study

There has been a resurgence of interest in foundationalism in recent years, and there are a number of variations on the theme. Of course, the classic strong foundationalism is Descartes's *Meditations,* which is variously reprinted. Evan Fales's *A Defense of the Given* (Lanham, MD: Rowman & Littlefield, 1996) defends the infallibility of beliefs about our perceptual experience. Roderick Chisholm defends the idea that we have beliefs about our experiences and that these are self-presenting, which he classifies as indubitable. See his *Theory of Knowledge,* 2nd ed. (Englewood Cliffs, NJ: Prentice-Hall, 1977) and *The Foundations of Knowing* (Minneapolis: University of Minnesota Press, 1982), esp. Chap. 1. An articulate and sustained defense of neoclassical foundationalism is Timothy J. McGrew, *The Foundations of Knowledge* (Lanham, MD: Littlefield Adams, 1995), in which he considers in detail many of the challenges to foundationalism. Richard Fumerton also defends foundationalism in *Metaepistemology and Skepticism* (Lanham, MD: Rowman & Littlefield, 1995). Fumerton's view might be described as neoclassical; he adapts the notion of acquaintance in his defense of basic beliefs.

Robert Audi has for some time defended and elaborated modest nondoxastic foundationalism. His *Belief, Justification, and Knowledge* (Belmont, CA: Wadsworth, 1988) provides an accessible introduction to his view, and his *The Structure of Justification* (Cambridge: Cambridge University Press, 1993) presents a sustained and elaborate account of his view. William Alston also defends modest foundationalism, although his more recent view leans more toward externalism, but see *Epistemic Justification* (Ithaca, NY: Cornell University Press, 1989), esp. Chaps. 1–3. Alan Goldman argues at length for modest doxastic foundationalism in *Empirical Knowledge* (Berkeley: University of California Press, 1988). Susan Haack attempts to move beyond foundationalism and coherentism in *Evidence and Inquiry: Towards Reconstruction in Epistemology* (Oxford: Basil Blackwell, 1993).

A survey and critical analysis of types of foundationalism can be found in John Pollock, *Contemporary Theories of Knowledge* (Totowa, NJ: Rowman & Littlefield, 1986).

Both Keith Lehrer and Laurence BonJour critique foundationalism. Lehrer's critique can be found in *Theory of Knowledge* (Boulder, CO: Westview Press, 1990), and BonJour's in *The Structure of Empirical Knowledge* (Cambridge, MA: Harvard University Press, 1985).

Notes

1. It should be noted that the Regress Argument receives different formulations. What we are calling the Regress Argument is sometimes called the Regress Problem, and the op-

tions presented in the next section are identified as the Regress Argument. Robert Audi, in *Belief, Justification, and Knowledge* (Belmont, CA: Wadsworth, 1988), p. 86, seems to take this line. Richard Fumerton identifies both an epistemic and conceptual regress argument in *Metaepistemology and Skepticism* (Lanham, MD: Rowman & Littlefield, 1995), Chap. 3.

2. In this section, I have relied on both the dialectical and the structural form of the Regress Argument. The former characterizes the argument as an agent attempting to show or exhibit the grounds for a belief, as she might do in answer to the question "Why do you believe that?" The structural form instead focuses on the identification of the basis or grounds for justification. See Robert Audi, *The Structure of Justification* (Cambridge: Cambridge University Press, 1993), Chap. 4. In the rest of the chapter, the primary concern will be the structural form.

3. As it is used here, the term *self-justified* means only that the belief does not depend on other beliefs for its justification. Some have taken the term to mean that the belief itself is the source of the justification—for example, that the belief is self-evident.

4. See, for example, William Alston's *Epistemic Justification* (Ithaca, NY: Cornell University Press, 1989), Chap. 3.

5. Robert Audi takes up these matters in more detail in *The Structure of Justification*, Chap. 3.

6. The term *neoclassical foundationalism* is from Timothy J. McGrew, *The Foundations of Knowledge* (Lanham, MD: Littlefield Adams, 1995), p. 57. McGrew presents a detailed articulation and defense of neoclassical foundationalism.

7. See Bertrand Russell, *The Problems of Philosophy* (London: Oxford University Press, 1959), Chap. 5.

8. See McGrew, *The Foundations of Knowledge*, p. 59.

9. Paul Moser canvases these issues in Moser, ed., *Empirical Knowledge*, 2nd ed. (Lanham, MD: Rowman & Littlefield, 1996), pp. 1–34, esp. pp. 1–11.

10. The terms *doxastic* and *nondoxastic foundationalism* are perhaps not the best for distinguishing these two types of modest foundationalism. But there seems to be no consistent terminology. The term *appearance foundationalist* seems to describe someone like Alan Goldman (see fn. 11), but there is unfortunately no obvious corresponding term for foundationalists like Audi. The terms are intended to capture but one contrast—that between foundationalists who think appearance beliefs are necessary to explain the source of justification and those who do not. (Understood in this way, reliabilist foundationalists would count as a type of nondoxastic foundationalist.)

11. Discussions of this issue can be found in John Pollock, *Contemporary Theories of Knowledge* (Totowa, NJ: Rowman & Littlefield, 1986), Chap. 2, and Alan Goldman, *Empirical Knowledge* (Berkeley: University of California Press, 1988), Chap. 5. Pollock dissents from the view that we typically have beliefs about appearances, while Goldman defends a form of doxastic foundationalism. Roderick Chisholm also seems to be a doxastic foundationalist, although he construes appearance beliefs adverbially. See, for example, his *The Foundations of Knowing* (Minneapolis: University of Minnesota Press, 1982), Chap. 1. Robert Audi is a fairly clear case of what I am calling an nondoxastic foundationalist.

12. See Goldman, *Empirical Knowledge*, p. 149.

13. Goldman, *Empirical Knowledge*, p. 148.

14. Audi makes this point in *Belief, Justification, and Knowledge*, p. 95. We will see that this position is not unique to Audi; yet the position is not uncontroversial.

15. For example, Robert Audi makes this sort of claim. See his *The Structure of Justification*, p. 9, and *Belief, Justification, and Knowledge*, Chap. 6.

16. See Audi, *The Structure of Justification*, Chap. 10.

17. See Audi, *The Structure of Justification*, Chap. 10.

18. Hume, of course, had reservations about induction. There are two further complications that we will not be considering here. First, some have challenged whether deduction preserves justification. For discussions of this issue, see Audi, *Belief, Justification, and Knowledge*, and Stephen Luper-Foy, ed., *The Possibility of Knowledge: Nozick and His Critics* (Totowa, NJ: Rowman & Littlefield, 1987). Second, some might wonder whether inductive inferences from basic beliefs, which are typically about particular objects or properties, can yield justified general beliefs.

19. Keith Lehrer, *Theory of Knowledge* (Boulder, CO: Westview Press, 1990), pp. 49–50.

20. See, for example, William Lyons, *The Disappearance of Introspection* (Cambridge, MA: MIT Press, 1986), Chap. 1. Note that Lyons does not accept the traditional account of introspection as a mechanism for "viewing" the contents of one's mind. Rather, he thinks that introspection is the "employment of perceptual memory and imagination to find out about our motives, thoughts, hopes, desires, and the like" (p. 114). In short, introspection is the (creative) replay of perception.

21. A. J. Ayer, for example, argues that there is always the logical possibility of error, because I might be uncertain about the nature of the experience or because further evidence, in principle, could arise that would cast doubt on my belief about the experience. Ayer does not deny that one's experience is the best grounds possible for the consequent belief, and in this sense such beliefs are incorrigible. See his *The Problem of Knowledge* (Harmondsworth, England: Penguin Books, 1956), pp. 52–68.

22. Ayer suggests this objection in *The Problem of Knowledge*, pp. 66–67. For a response to this "not-much-content" objection, see McGrew, *The Foundations of Knowledge*, Chap. 7.

23. Evan Fales, *A Defense of the Given* (Lanham, MD: Rowman & Littlefield, 1996), esp. Chap. 6.

24. Lyons makes this point in *The Disappearance of Introspection*, Chap. 6. In Chap. 5, he also notes that there is a growing body of evidence that might be discomfiting to those who hold that introspection "is some kind of direct private access to occurrent mental or brain states or event, which in turn bestows special status, if not unique reliability, on introspective evidence" (p. 100).

25. The version of the argument given here can be found in Laurence BonJour, *The Structure of Empirical Knowledge* (Cambridge, MA: Harvard University Press, 1985), Chap. 2.

26. William Alston explores these issues at length in the first three essays of his *Epistemic Justification*. Audi also is explicit about the distinction; see, for example, *Belief, Justification, and Knowledge*, p. 95. We will see in the next chapter that coherentists like Lehrer do not find adverting to children compelling.

27. That Audi holds this position was pointed out in the previous section. William Alston's acceptance of these two requirements can be found in his *Epistemic Justification*, Chap. 9. Roderick Chisholm also seems to accept both these conditions. See, for example, his *The Foundations of Knowing*, Chap. 1.

28. Lehrer, *Theory of Knowledge*, Chap. 4.

29. Some foundationalists do deny this—for example, Timothy J. McGrew.

30. Laurence BonJour gives this sort of argument in his *The Structure of Empirical Knowledge*, pp. 69ff.

31. I think this line of argument can be found in both Audi, *The Structure of Justification*, Chap. 10, and James van Cleve, "Epistemic Supervenience and the Circle of Belief," *Monist* 68 (1985): 90–104.

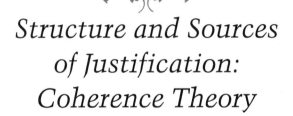

CHAPTER FIVE

Structure and Sources
of Justification:
Coherence Theory

There is no exit from the circle of one's beliefs.
KEITH LEHRER, *KNOWLEDGE*

The principal alternative to foundationalism is a family of views known as coherence theories. A **coherence theory** holds that the justification of a belief derives from the coherence of an agent's beliefs. This general understanding of coherence theory incorporates both a positive and a negative claim. Coherence theorists deny that any beliefs are epistemically independent of other beliefs, and hence deny that there are epistemically basic beliefs. The positive thesis of coherence theory is that justification derives from the mutual support among an agent's beliefs. The views of two prominent coherentists, Laurence BonJour and Keith Lehrer, have attracted substantial attention of late. Although BonJour and Lehrer agree on general features of the coherentist theory of justification, there are important differences between them, just as there are important differences among foundationalists. In this chapter, it will prove convenient to highlight these differences by detailing BonJour's and Lehrer's particular views. But first, we present an intuitive motivation for coherence theory. We also discuss standard criticisms of coherentism and typical coherentists' responses, as well as the more substantial criticism of coherentism.

THE INTUITIVE IDEA

Mutual Support and Responsibility

Two interrelated thoughts seem to motivate coherence theory: epistemic responsibility and the idea of mutual support among beliefs. We can begin with the idea of mutual support.

The intuitive idea of mutual support is that our beliefs *fit* or *hang together*. We are inclined to give greater epistemic weight or credibility to beliefs that fit together better. It is not difficult to see why this is so. Any particular belief gives us a picture or a representation of the world; it gives us a bit of information. We might have doubts about whether to trust any particular bit of information. But as we find that the particular information *fits* with other pieces of information in our possession, our trust in that belief increases. A single belief is a bit like a piece of jigsaw puzzle. By itself, it does not make a lot of sense. Yet once we see how the piece fits together with other pieces, once we see the way it interlocks with other pieces, we understand where the piece fits in and why we need it. That is, once we see how various beliefs fit together, once the overall picture begins to take shape, we understand better the role and importance of the individual beliefs.

Some beliefs might seem to make sense all by themselves, to not require other beliefs for support or epistemic credibility. Take, for example, seeing and consequently believing that there is a purple book on the table. Surely, you might protest, other beliefs aren't needed to support this belief. But the coherentist asks you to look a bit closer. You remember your brother mentioning that the color of the book cover matches his shirt; you remember seeing him leave the book there; you believe that there is nothing unusual about the situation. Indeed, you probably would not be so confident of this particular belief *unless* you also believed that your vision was quite normal and that you could certainly perform the routine perceptual task of identifying the type of object and its color. You know a book when you see one! As you begin to see that the belief about the color of the book fits with so many of your other beliefs, you also begin to see the source of your "epistemic confidence." Your recognition of the way in which this belief is tied to other beliefs enhances the belief's epistemic credibility.

But notice that this support is, in a sense, a two-way street. Your belief that you know a book when you see one is supported by all the particular occasions on which you have seen books—whether purple books, blue books, or an intriguing little black book. Your belief that you have normal vision is supported by all the individual occasions on which you have managed to navigate your way through a room or reached for an object you thought you saw and, indeed, found an object there to be grasped.

The metaphor of the "web of belief" has become commonplace in recent decades. This idea includes the thought that beliefs are mutually supportive and that they hang or fit together. Notice that a web has no real starting point; no one place in the web is more basic than any other. This is precisely what the coherentist has in mind: No one belief, no one type of belief, is epistemically basic. Rather, each belief has a role to play, but that particular role makes sense only in the context of the whole set of beliefs. The web of belief hangs or falls together. It is this intuitive idea of beliefs hanging together that the coherentist is attempting to make more precise in the claim that justification derives from the relations of mutual support among beliefs.

The idea of mutual support contains an implicit prescription. As epistemic agents, we should count a belief as epistemically legitimate only if we have some reason for it, only if we have other beliefs that support the particular belief. We should count a belief as epistemically legitimate only if we have some reason for thinking that the belief is true or is likely to be true. We would be epistemically irresponsible were we to do otherwise. (Imagine an extreme case of believing that you will win the lottery because you believe it will make your life simpler, and then shopping accordingly. Surely, the belief is irresponsible.) The notion of epistemic responsibility motivates BonJour's commitment to coherence theory. BonJour holds that the constitutive aim of epistemic justification is that of truth. Thus, a belief is justified only if there is some reason for its truth. More precisely, BonJour holds that an agent is justified in accepting particular beliefs only if the agent is in cognitive possession of a reason for thinking the belief is likely to be true. "To accept a belief in the absence of such a reason," BonJour claims,

> is to neglect the pursuit of truth; such acceptance is, one might say, *epistemically irresponsible*. My contention here is that the idea of avoiding such irresponsibility, of being epistemically responsible in one's believings, is the core of the notion of epistemic justification.[1]

According to BonJour, beliefs derive their epistemic support from an agent's other beliefs. More to the point, an epistemically responsible agent accepts beliefs only if those beliefs are supported by the agent's other beliefs. An agent pursues the truth most responsibly when the agent recognizes that the epistemic credibility of a belief derives from its interlocking connections with other beliefs.

Two Views of Coherence

The intuitive characterization of coherence as beliefs hanging together can be understood in different ways, but two are important for us. We might say that our beliefs "hang together" because any particular belief somehow fits with or is related to at least some of our other beliefs. But we might understand "hanging together" a bit more globally or holistically, in terms of all of our beliefs hanging together in some way. The former views coherence as a relational property, while the latter construes coherence as a global or holistic property.[2] BonJour takes coherence to be fundamentally a global or holistic property, while Lehrer understands coherence as a particular type of relation. These two construals of coherence significantly affect the understanding of justification. According to the globalist, a belief is justified if it is a member of a coherent system of beliefs. According to the relationalist, a belief is justified *only* if it coheres or fits with *at least some of* an agent's other beliefs. We begin with the idea of global or holistic coherence.

Global or holistic coherentism is the idea that within an agent's total set of beliefs, the individual beliefs are interrelated in various ways. Any particular belief is connected in some way to other beliefs, and these in turn are severally connected to still other beliefs. Thus, individual beliefs or subsets of beliefs in a coherent system hang together, by virtue of the various types of relation, "so as to produce an organized, tightly structured system of beliefs, rather than either a helter-skelter collection or a set of conflicting subsystems."[3] As a simple analogy, think of a quilt comprised of various types and pieces of fabric. We can, of course, talk about the particular relations between the various pieces. We can describe the different kinds of fabric or the different kinds of stitches that hold the pieces together. But the whole quilt provides the warmth. A particular sequence of stitches would be the wrong place to look for the warmth the quilt brings. Indeed, if certain parts of the quilt were tightly stitched but there were holes in between, the quilt would not provide much warmth. Holistic coherence is a little like the warmth of the quilt. Relations among particular beliefs are important. Subgroups of beliefs may be tightly connected, but if these subgroups are not connected to one another, the system as a whole is not tightly connected. It is only with the entire system that coherence appears. Just as warmth comes from a well-made quilt, analogously, coherence comes from a well-made system of beliefs, a system in which the parts are stitched together tightly. In the next section, we discuss BonJour's view of the types of relations that increase the coherence of a system of beliefs. The point here is that holistic coherentism is the idea that coherence is a property of an entire system of beliefs. Justification arises as a consequence of the coherence of a system of beliefs. More technically, the coherence of a set of beliefs is the property that generates the epistemic property of justification.[4]

Coherence can also be understood as a relational property. The **relational view of coherence** is sometimes intuitively expressed as the idea that a belief is justified if it coheres with an agent's other beliefs. My belief that there is a glass of tea on the table coheres with my other beliefs—for example, that I see the glass and that I remember drinking from it a moment ago. My belief that there is a glass of tea on the table is justified by virtue of its cohering with my other beliefs. The task, of course, of a relational theory is to articulate the nature of this coherence relationship. Lehrer's theory, discussed later in the chapter, holds this relation to be one of comparative reasonability.

Although Lehrer and BonJour differ about coherence as a relational or holistic property, they agree about the two fundamental aspects of coherence theory. First, they both reject the foundationalist assertion that some beliefs are epistemically prior to other beliefs. Second, and related, they agree that any belief depends on other beliefs for its justification. Thus,

Linear Coherence

The coherentist response to the Regress Argument is sometimes described as the idea that justification proceeds in a circle. A natural way of explaining this "circular" idea of coherentism is that we trace the justification of a belief from one justifying belief to another. That is, we proceed in a *linear* fashion from belief to belief. Because this linear regress cannot go on forever, we eventually must return to the original belief. So, a belief justifies itself. This notion of *linear coherence* is not widely accepted and will not figure in either BonJour's or Lehrer's views.

both Lehrer and BonJour adopt a version of coherentism that is sometimes called positive coherentism as opposed to negative coherentism. **Negative coherentism** is generally understood as the claim that one belief coheres with an agent's other beliefs if the agent's other beliefs provide no reason to question the truth of the candidate belief. One might think that negative coherentism provides a plausible model of the justification of perceptual beliefs. Unless there is reason to the contrary, our normal perceptual beliefs are justified. **Positive coherentism,** however, requires an agent to have reasons for the belief. Indeed, both Lehrer and BonJour think that the justification of any belief, including perceptual beliefs, requires the agent to have some positive reason for the belief.

As we turn to the details of the two theorists, it will be useful to keep in mind two overarching issues. The first concerns the nature of coherence: What does it mean to say that a set of beliefs is coherent or that one belief coheres with other beliefs? The second concerns the connection between justification and coherence: How does the theorist view coherence as generating justification? Why does the coherence of our beliefs make them likely to be true?

EPISTEMIC RESPONSIBILITY AND COHERENCE: BONJOUR'S THEORY

The commitment to epistemic responsibility as the core aspect of justification evidences BonJour's commitment both to internalism and coherentism. According to BonJour, epistemic responsibility requires that an agent believe on the basis of reasons. But the reasons are not the *agent's* reasons unless the agent is aware of those reasons. Thus, BonJour claims that, in principle, the reasons for which an agent accepts a belief must be cognitively accessible. A reason is cognitively accessible if the agent can, on reflection, become aware of the reason. For example, when I casually look over and see that I left my glass by the chair, I might not be aware that I believe my vision is normal and is operating under normal conditions. But on sufficient reflection, I can become aware that this is my reason for believing that the glass is by the chair.[5] The cognitive accessibility of one's reasons defines internalism, according to BonJour. This notion of epistemic responsibility also motivates BonJour's commitment to coherentism, and it is not difficult to see why. In his view of epistemic responsibility, a belief is justified only if an agent has reasons for the belief. But these reasons are simply an agent's other beliefs. Thus, the justification of a particular belief depends on other beliefs. As we proceed with an outline of BonJour's theory, bear in mind how his commitment to epistemic responsibility influences his particular view of coherentism.

An Outline of BonJour's Theory

BonJour's theory is somewhat complicated in that it involves both relational and holistic or global elements.[6] Thus, we take a broad overview of his account of justification before focusing on the particular elements in more detail. The full justification of a particular belief involves four stages or arguments, according to BonJour:

1. Show that a candidate belief is appropriately connected to other beliefs in the agent's system of beliefs.
2. Show that the system of beliefs is coherent.
3. Show that the system of beliefs is likely to be true.
4. Show that the candidate belief is justified by virtue of its membership in a coherent, and hence justified, system of beliefs.

Stage 1, the *justifying argument,* expresses the relationship between a candidate belief and other beliefs in the agent's system. It is this stage that we ordinarily think of when we think of the justification of beliefs. But BonJour evidently considers this but the first step. Stage 2 reflects his understanding of coherence as a global property. It is the system of beliefs that is coherent, not particular subgroups of the system. A belief can be justified only if it is appropriately connected to a coherent belief system. The subsequent exposition of BonJour's theory begins with these first two stages.

Arguably the most problematic, and the most crucial, stage is that articulated in stage 3. This stage requires showing that a coherent system of beliefs is likely to be true; hence, stage 3 links coherence to justification. Failure to show that coherence yields justification would bankrupt BonJour's theory. Satisfying stage 3 requires an explanation of why a coherent system of beliefs yields a system that has beliefs *that are likely to be true*. Justification thus is ultimately a global or holistic property. Although stage 3 is critical for BonJour's enterprise, we will postpone consideration of it until the rest of the theory is elaborated.

It is relatively easy to see that stage 4 follows from stages 1–3. Stage 1 establishes that the candidate belief has the right membership credentials and thus is a member of the agent's belief system. Stages 2 and 3 show that the belief is a member of a coherent, justified system of beliefs. Hence, the candidate belief is justified by virtue of its membership in this coherent, justified system of beliefs. Stages 1–4 are encapsulated in the succinct claim that *a particular belief is justified by virtue of its membership in a coherent system of beliefs*.

The Holistic Character of Coherence and Justification

BonJour accepts the intuitive characterization of a coherent belief system as a system of beliefs that "hang together" or "fit together." But he also recognizes that difficulty rests in stating more precisely what it means for beliefs to hang together. As a first approximation, an agent's system of beliefs is coherent if a sufficient number of connections exist among the particular beliefs. BonJour provides a rough gloss of these connections.[7]

In general, beliefs are connected if there is some type of relation between them. You, for example, are connected to various people by virtue of certain relationships that hold between you and these other individuals. They may be biological relationships, such as sister or parent. Or they may be institutional relationships, such as "being a student at" or "being the roommate of." Beliefs, too, have certain relations to other beliefs. We might start with those relationships that are broadly logical in nature. A system of beliefs is consistent if they can all be true at the same time. As the number of inconsistent beliefs decreases and as the system approaches logical consistency, the system's coherence increases.[8] Mere logical consistency, however, is but one constraint on the agent's belief system.

BonJour also accords greater coherence to a system in which the beliefs are probabilistically consistent. Here is a very simple example of beliefs that are probabilistically inconsistent. Suppose Sam believes it is more probable that he will have chicken for dinner than that he will have fish. He also believes it is more probable that he will have fish for dinner than that he will have pork. Given this, we would normally expect Sam to believe that it is more probable that he will have chicken than pork. This is a kind of transitivity relation: If A is more probable than B and B is more probable than C, then A is more probable than C. But suppose Sam's beliefs do not exhibit this transitivity; that is, suppose he believes it is more probable that he will have pork than chicken. Sam's beliefs would then be probabilistically inconsistent. We commonly associate this type of inconsistency with a person holding irrational beliefs. Belief systems that avoid such inconsistencies possess a greater degree of coherence.

Of more interest for BonJour are the types of *inferential* relationships that hold among beliefs. If Sara believes that Socrates is mortal because she believes that Socrates was Greek and all Greeks are mortal, there is a deductive connection between these beliefs. On the other hand, if Sara believes that Socrates is mortal because her philosophy teacher told her so and because she believes that her philosophy teacher usually tells her the truth, then there is an inductive connection among these beliefs. Inductive connections can be construed broadly to include one belief making another belief more probable, or more likely to be true. Sara's belief, for example, that her philosophy professor owns a Mercedes makes more probable her belief that the professor is well paid for her efforts. A belief system acquires a greater degree of coherence as the number of inductive and deductive inferential connections increases.

We might wonder why one should epistemically value having these kinds of connections among beliefs. BonJour's internalism provides one evident reason. If one or several of Sara's beliefs are disconnected from her other beliefs, then Sara clearly will not have reasons for those beliefs. In one sense, inductive and deductive connections are the *model* of what it is to have reasons. Sara has the best sort of reasons for her belief that Socrates is mortal. But the real epistemic payoff lies in the thought that if someone has a coherent belief system, then that individual is more likely to have true beliefs. The first step to obtaining truth is by having beliefs that are linked together. A coherent belief system has an instrumental value, according to BonJour: It helps to put us in a position to attain our real goal, which is believing what is true. Of course, we want to see just how BonJour connects coherence to truth, a matter to be taken up shortly.

So far, we have been discussing what makes an agent's beliefs coherent. The answer, says BonJour, is that the beliefs are connected to one another in the right way; the beliefs are logically and probabilistically consistent and inferentially related. We now need an explanation of the relation between the coherence of a system and the justification of a particular belief. BonJour views the connection between coherence and justification as operating at two different levels. The fundamental level is that of global justification, or the justification of a system of beliefs.[9] Thus, justification is also a holistic property of a belief system. Illustrating the connection between a coherent belief system and justification requires showing that a coherent system contains beliefs that are likely to be true. Again, we will take this issue up shortly. Our present concern is the justification of a particular belief or, as BonJour calls it, local justification.

Suppose a person has a coherent belief system, and assume for the moment that such a system is globally justified, that it contains beliefs that are

Global and Local Justification

A coherent system is globally justified if the beliefs in that system are likely to be true. According to BonJour, we show that our beliefs are likely to be true in relation to the system as a whole. Thus, when BonJour talks of "local justification," he does not mean showing that a particular belief is likely to be true. On the contrary, particular beliefs are likely to be true if and only if they are members of a coherent system. "Local justification" refers to the connection or relation between a particular belief and other beliefs in the system. In this sense, local justification is the starting point for coherence, or for a system of beliefs that hang together.

likely to be true. A particular belief is justified by virtue of its membership in the belief system. The internalist character of BonJour's theory requires that an agent have a reason for thinking that a particular belief is likely to be true. Moreover, BonJour thinks that such reasons are premises for the particular belief. Thus, a particular belief is a member of the belief system if the agent has a *justifying argument* for that belief. A justifying argument provides reasons for thinking a belief is likely to be true, given what else the agent believes. Imagine that Sara has a coherent belief system and that she is considering whether to accept the belief that a certain rock is from the Painted Desert. Suppose she already believes that her father said the rock was purchased at the Painted Desert's gift shop, where rocks from that desert are sold. Notice that this belief about her father's remark does not yet give her reason to think that the candidate belief is likely to be true. Sara may not believe that father knows best, but she must at least believe that her father's testimony about such matters is credible. It is only something like this latter belief that gives her some reason to think the target belief is likely to be true. Laid out explicitly, Sara's justifying argument is this:

(1) My belief about the origin of this rock is based on my father's testimony.

(2) Beliefs based on my father's testimony are likely to be true.

(3) So, my belief about the origin of this rock is likely to be true.

It is by virtue of this sort of justifying argument that Sara's belief is a member of her system of beliefs. A belief is worthy of membership in a system only if it is connected in the right way, only if the agent has a justifying argument. So, Sara's belief is a member of a coherent system. But BonJour claims that a coherent system is also a justified system of beliefs. So, the particular belief is justified by virtue of its membership in such a system.

Particular beliefs acquire their justified status because they belong to a system that is coherent and, consequently, justified.

Sara's justifying argument reflects certain general features that any justifying argument must have. Notice that the first premise specifies a certain type of belief—in this case, beliefs based on her father's testimony. More generally, one premise of the argument specifies a feature of the candidate belief. That feature may be that the belief is based on testimony, or that it is a memory belief, or that it is supported by an inductive argument. The more important premise is the second, which expresses the agent's recognition of the connection between beliefs having such a feature and the likely truth of that type of belief. The justifying argument thus has the general form:

(1) This belief has the feature F.

(2) Beliefs having the feature F are likely to be true.

(3) Thus, this belief is likely to be true.

Membership requires an argument. But does membership require that the agent actually give the argument? Must Sara actually think to herself that her belief about the rock's origin is based on her father's testimony and that he is credible about such matters? Although BonJour does not require that an agent actually give or be aware of the justifying argument, he does hold that such an argument be within the agent's cognitive grasp. Were Sara, for example, to reflect on the matter, she could come to see that she at least has a tacit reliance on such beliefs.[10]

The Doxastic Presumption

BonJour claims that the core notion of justification is epistemic responsibility: A person's belief is justified only if the person has a reason for that belief. Now, imagine that Sara, acting as a conscientious and well-versed epistemic agent, reflects on her belief that the rock before her comes from the Painted Desert. Sara approvingly notices her justifying argument. So far, so good. But the justification of her belief depends on the coherence of her belief system. Now, for Sara to believe that her belief system is coherent, *she must first know what she believes.* If Sara has no way of telling what she believes, she obviously cannot judge that those beliefs form a coherent system. Enter the *Doxastic Presumption.* BonJour claims that Sara has an approximate grasp of her overall belief system, that she knows approximately what she believes. According to BonJour, we must *presume* that agents have a general understanding of what they believe.

It is worth emphasizing the general feature of BonJour's theory that makes the Doxastic Presumption necessary. Of course, coherence is a necessary condition of justification. But BonJour recognizes that his fundamental commitment to epistemic internalism requires not only that a belief system be coherent but also that such coherence be accessible to the agent. This further requires that agents know what they believe. The Doxastic Presumption is thus necessary if an agent is to have some reason for thinking that his belief system is coherent. We can draw this point out further.

BonJour suggests that the Doxastic Presumption is the necessary backdrop against which epistemic reflection takes place.[11] When Sara considers whether to accept a belief that a rock is from the Painted Desert, we must *take for granted* that she has an understanding of what she believes. She could not seriously entertain the question of whether to accept the belief unless she had some sense of what she believed. BonJour claims that having a grasp of what she believes is a necessary condition—not a premise—for reflecting on or thinking about what she believes. The Doxastic Presumption is not itself a premise in an argument or a metabelief, a belief about other beliefs an agent has. Instead, BonJour suggests, it is a description of a kind of relation between persons and their overall belief systems. Agents' cognitive endeavors—the questions they set themselves, the beliefs they considers worthy of acceptance, the inquiries they undertake—presume or presuppose that agents have an approximate understanding or representation of what they believe. The Doxastic Presumption, BonJour claims, is an unavoidable aspect of our cognitive practice.

BonJour may be right that the Doxastic Presumption is a feature of our cognitive practice. Yet some have objected that access to the coherence of one's beliefs is not the simple matter BonJour's account of the Presumption seems to make it.[12] More precisely, some object that often we do not have access to the *actual* coherence of our beliefs. This objection is worth considering in more detail.

First, recall BonJour's claim that a belief is justified only if it is a member of a coherent belief system. Notice what BonJour does not say: He does not say that a belief is justified if it is a member of a system that the agent *believes to be coherent*. The belief, according to BonJour, must be a member of an *actually* coherent system. (As an analogy, consider the difference between your *thinking* you have done a trigonometry problem correctly and the *actual* correctness of your solution.) Second, some urge that it is a quite daunting task for ordinary agents like Sam and Sara to determine correctly whether their beliefs are, for example, consistent. The actual logical and inferential relations among beliefs may be quite obscure and, for all practical purposes, impossible for a normal agent to determine. We can now understand the objection to claim the following: An agent's beliefs about the coherence of a system are an unreliable guide to its *actual* coherence. It is the latter, the actual coherence, that is required for justification. An agent may, for example, think that a certain belief is deductively connected to other

Is the Doxastic Presumption True?

Independent of BonJour's claim that the Doxastic Presumption is a pre-supposition of our cognitive practice, we might wonder whether there is reason to think that the Presumption is true. Intuitively, we do seem to have at least a sense of some of the things we believe. For example, if you are asked why the Allies won World War II, it may take you but a few moments to determine whether anything you believe bears on this question. It is clearly a more difficult matter to determine whether, in general, people have a reasonably accurate grasp of their overall belief systems. Some recent studies on memory suggest that people are reasonably accurate predictors of whether they have certain beliefs. For example, if asked whether one knows Thomas Jefferson's home state, a person will generally be able to answer this question correctly. It has also been claimed that certain belief contents generally are readily accessible. These contents are "state-of-the-world" memories such as who and where we are, what we are doing, and what our current effective goals and plans are. Evidence such as this may suggest some initial plausibility to the Doxastic Presumption. (See "For Further Study.")

beliefs but be mistaken about what constitutes a deductive connection. The Doxastic Presumption seemingly only guarantees an agent's cognitive access to the agent's *beliefs about* the coherence of the belief system.

BonJour agrees that more attention needs to be given these issues.[13] In response, he offers two remarks. First, he suggests that the coherence of one's belief is accessible, *at least to a degree.* It is not as though the actual coherence is completely inaccessible to an agent. Thus, an agent has an *approximate* sense of the actual coherence of the belief system. Second, he allows that the actual coherence of an agent's belief system may differ from the agent's sense of the coherence of the system. This is, however, unobjectionable because there are degrees of justification. Thus, a person will be more fully justified only to the extent that the person's sense of the coherence of the belief system matches its actual coherence.

The Doxastic Presumption is evidently central to BonJour's coherentist theory of justification, especially insofar as that theory is internalist. To preserve the internalist character of his theory, BonJour insists that an agent does have sufficient cognitive access to the contents of his or her belief system and to the actual coherence of those contents. This, as just noted, is a controversial claim. Waiving this problem, we have this much of BonJour's view before us: A particular belief derives its justification from its membership in a coherent system. That belief's membership credentials are established by a justifying argument. But a crucial piece of the puzzle is missing. BonJour claims that coherent systems of belief are *justified* systems of belief. Thus, we still need to see why BonJour thinks coherence generates justification. More specifically, we need to see why coherent systems of belief contain beliefs that are likely to be true.

Observation and Global Justification

Perhaps the ultimate test for coherence theories is the justification of perceptual beliefs. BonJour recognizes that if we have justified beliefs about the world, then there must be some way for information about the world to enter agents' belief systems. The challenge for BonJour can be brought out in the following way. The first step in the justification of any belief is that it can be inferred from other beliefs the agent holds. This requires, as we have seen, that the agent have a grasp of a justifying argument, which derives from the agent's belief system. But consider Sam's perceptual belief that he sees a purple book. It is not immediately obvious what other beliefs Sam has that would make it more probable that he sees a *purple* book rather than, say, a chartreuse book. But if Sam's belief system does not contain these supporting beliefs, then the belief about the purple book does not possess the requisite credentials for membership in the system. Hence, the belief fails, according to BonJour's theory, to be justified.

To resolve this difficulty, BonJour exploits the notion of *cognitively spontaneous beliefs*. The mark of cognitively spontaneous beliefs is that the agent does not infer them, nor do they seem to be the result of any explicit or implicit deliberative process. Such beliefs are in a sense involuntary. When Sam turns his head, he simply comes to have the belief, regardless of his current thought processes, "There's a purple book." Of course, simply having the belief is insufficient for the coherentist to count the belief as justified. Sam must have some reason to accept the belief.

BonJour suggests that Sam indeed has a justifying argument. Like the rest of us, when Sam has perceptual beliefs, they have a definite content. The book is at a certain distance and angle and has a particular shape and color. Moreover, Sam forms this belief under particular conditions of normal lighting, normal angles of vision, and the normal functioning of his visual system. This suggests the following schema for a justifying argument:

(1) I have a cognitively spontaneous belief that P which is of kind K.

(2) Conditions C obtain. [That is, the lighting is normal and so on.]

(3) Cognitively spontaneous beliefs of kind K in conditions C are very likely to be true.

(4)   Thus, my belief that P is very likely to be true.

(5)   Thus, (probably) P.[14]

BonJour argues that a person does have reasons to accept each of these premises. Here, however, we will limit our concern to the reasons he offers for premise (3), because that is our special concern.[15] Indeed, the likely truth of premise (3) can seem rather puzzling when a coherentist offers it. Why should we think, solely on the basis of what else we believe, that our perceptual beliefs are likely to be true? Are not foundationalists right in claiming that the justification of perceptual beliefs must, at some point, appeal to the facts? BonJour, however, is rather sanguine about this matter. He claims that the justification of (3) consists in the agent believing that when premises (1) and (2) hold, (3) is a likely result. More precisely, BonJour holds that the agent must consider premise (3) to be a kind of empirical law that is justified by other beliefs the agent has. Thus, when Sam spies the purple book lurking on the corner of the desk, he must take it that there is more than an accidental connection between his having the belief that he does under current conditions and his belief being true. Sam must believe that while matters may sometimes go awry, *his having the belief is a reliable indication of the truth of the belief.* BonJour characterizes this requirement as the *Observation Requirement.* An agent must attribute reliability to at least some types of cognitive spontaneously beliefs.[16]

We are now at the crux of the issue. The Observation Requirement demands only believed reliability. But why think that a coherent system of beliefs, even one that satisfies the Observation Requirement, is likely to be true? Again, recall the trigonometry example: Your *actual* reliability in solving trigonometry problems is judged not from your perspective, but from an independent perspective, say, a teacher's perspective. Perhaps annoyingly, actual reliability is not determined by what you believe. More precisely, for BonJour, the question becomes, Do agents have reason to believe that the coherence of beliefs is in any way connected to the likely truth of those beliefs?

BonJour's answer is detailed and complex, but its essential outlines are fairly clear. Assume you have a system of beliefs that has remained coherent over a period of time and that satisfies the Observation Requirement. The point of this last clause is that the belief system is sensitive to the evidence presented by the senses, and because such beliefs are accorded a special status (believed to be reliable), other beliefs are modified accordingly. At least some beliefs—for example, perceptual beliefs—are recognized by the agent as reliable. BonJour claims that the long-run stability of such a system is best explained by the probable truth of the beliefs that make up the system.

Suppose that my belief system is coherent and has remained so over time. Suppose also that my belief system satisfies the Observation Requirement.

This latter point requires that I count certain beliefs as reliable—for example, perceptual beliefs. When I see a purple book or I notice that my Arizona rock is somewhat reddish in color, these beliefs are accorded a type of special status. These perceptual beliefs do not have this status wholly independently of my other beliefs; nonetheless, they have a kind of *prima facie* reliability. Now, what would explain my having these beliefs? What would explain my having the belief that there is a purple book or that somewhere in eastern Arizona is a vast expanse of land that has a reddish hue? One explanation, the best explanation according to BonJour, is that *there really is* a purple book and parts of the Arizona desert plateau *really are* reddish in color. The best explanation of a stable, coherent, observationally sensitive belief system is that the world *really is* the way the belief system represents it to be! But if that is the way the world really is, then my beliefs are likely to be true. I thus have a reason for thinking that my beliefs are likely to be true—that is the best explanation of my having this coherent, observationally sensitive system. So, my overall system of beliefs is justified. Coherence, together with the Observation Requirement, generates justification.

The two preceding paragraphs may seem just a bit hasty. What reason do I have for thinking that I have hit on the *best* explanation? Indeed, the complexities of BonJour's argument arise when he turns to justifying the claim that this (the world is the way I believe it to be) is the best explanation. As indicated, we can only sketch the outline of these arguments.

BonJour attempts to show that the correspondence of an agent's beliefs to the world is a better explanation than any other for the coherence and stability of the agent's belief system. Let us call this preferred explanation the *correspondence explanation.* BonJour identifies two competing explanations, the *chance explanation* and the *demon explanation.* According to the chance explanation, the coherence and stability of a belief system is mere chance; it turns out that an agent simply has come to have beliefs that cohere, even though they do not represent the way things actually are. The stability of the agent's cognitive system is but a cosmic coincidence. The demon explanation suggests that the coherence of a belief system is due to a demon that causes an agent to have certain beliefs rather than others. BonJour argues that the correspondence explanation is the best of these three because we have more reason to believe it rather than the chance or demon explanations.

The key to BonJour's argument is the fact that an agent continues to accept cognitively spontaneous beliefs while the overall belief system remains coherent. Or as BonJour puts it, cognitively spontaneous beliefs continue to be coherence-conducive.[17] BonJour's argument against a sophisticated version of the demon explanation indicates his line of reasoning. Imagine a demon that has both the power and the desire to cause an agent to have cognitively spontaneous beliefs, beliefs that contribute to the coherence of the agent's belief system. BonJour claims that initially this explanation is very unlikely. Unfortunately, it is no more unlikely than the correspondence explanation. There doesn't seem to be any reason to prefer the correspondence explanation to the demon explanation. However, BonJour asks us to consider the following: The demon doesn't really care what beliefs a person has. The demon's only concern is that apparent perceptual beliefs are coherence-conducive in producing the illusion of a physical world. For example, the demon is unconcerned with whether perceptual beliefs are about unicorns or antelope. The demon's sole desire is that whatever the content of the apparent perceptual beliefs, the cognitive system continues to be coherent. Somewhat loosely, then, it is "doubly unlikely" that (a) there would be a demon causing us to have coherence-conducive beliefs *and* (b) we would be having cognitively spontaneous beliefs about antelopes rather than unicorns. On the other hand, the correspondence explanation presents us with a world in which we would *expect* to have beliefs about antelopes rather than unicorns. If the world were like the world pictured in the correspondence explanation, there would be a sort of predictability to the content of the beliefs we would have in such a world. We would expect a certain orderliness to our beliefs. Thus, the correspondence explanation is initially no more likely than the demon explanation. Yet when we look to what types of beliefs we would expect to have based on the two explanations, the correspondence explanation seems to give a better account of the beliefs we actually do have. Thus, there is more reason to believe the correspondence explanation than the demon explanation.

The line of argument has brought us to this point. We began by asking how coherence could yield justification. If a coherent system yields beliefs, which are likely to be true, then the system is justified. BonJour then argues that the best explanation of a coherent, observationally sensitive system is that the system represents the world more or less accurately. That is, the best explanation of the coherence of a system, which also satisfies the Observation Requirement, is the likely truth of the system's beliefs. The final piece in the puzzle is to argue that the correspondence explanation is indeed the best explanation; it is better than either the chance or demon explanations. If this argument is successful, we have reason to believe our beliefs are likely to be true, that is, justified. We might note here that while BonJour utilizes inference to the best explanation, Keith Lehrer's version of coherence theory, which is considered in the next section, does not do so.

The stages of the justification of a particular belief are thus complete. An agent has cognitive access to a justifying argument, which links that belief to the agent's belief system. The Doxastic Presumption is invoked to explain the agent's cognitive access to the coherence of the system. But it is not just coherence that generates justification. The justification of the system requires not only a coherent system but also a system that accords reliability to certain types of cognitively spontaneous beliefs. BonJour argues for the justification of a stable, coherent, *observationally sensitive* system. Particular beliefs then are justified by virtue of their membership in such a system. In BonJour's view, the ultimate source of justification is a system that is coherent and that accords reliability to some types of cognitively spontaneous beliefs, a coherent system that satisfies the Observation Requirement.

CYCLES AND LOOPS: LEHRER'S VIEW OF COHERENCE

For some time, Keith Lehrer has been articulating, defending, and revising a coherence theory of knowledge and justification. This section focuses on his more recent account of justification.[18] Lehrer formulates his coherentist view with three core concepts: acceptance, an acceptance system, and comparative reasonability. **Comparative reasonability** is the relation that is, in Lehrer's account, constitutive of coherence. Lehrer's theory thus views coherence as a relational property and is succinctly summarized in the following:

> (L) A person is personally justified in accepting P if and only if P coheres with that person's acceptance system at that time.

We first explain the related notions of acceptance and acceptance system, and then turn to comparative reasonability. Although this will provide us with an outline of Lehrer's coherence theory, there will still be one further matter to address. Lehrer attaches considerable importance to the idea that to act as epistemic agents, we must accept ourselves as trustworthy evaluators. The notion of trustworthy evaluators is central not only to Lehrer's defense of coherence theory against standard objections but also to explanations of the mutual support among the various items a person accepts. Ultimately, this mutual support becomes the central feature of coherence theory.

The Elements of Lehrer's Coherence Theory

A distinctive feature of Lehrer's view is the pivotal notion of acceptance rather than that of belief. Lehrer describes **acceptance** as a functional notion. In particular, a person accepts a proposition if "he is in a certain kind of functional state which typically arises when a person reflectively judges that p with the objective of judging that p if and only if p."[19] There is an explicit appeal here to the idea of an agent's cognitive goal or aim. For Lehrer, this cognitive goal is that of obtaining truth and avoiding error. Acceptance is thus an explicitly epistemological notion, and in this sense, it is to be distinguished from that of belief. Belief states are in the first instance psychological states. The content of a belief state may indeed be what a person accepts. But by using the term "acceptance," Lehrer intends to restrict his attention to the cognitive practices of persons when they are acting as epistemic agents, that is, when they are pursuing the cognitive goal of truth. A person thus accepts a proposition when the person is attempting to decide what propositions, or beliefs for that matter, will best serve the cognitive goal of gaining truth and avoiding falsehood. It is relative to this cognitive goal that the *functional state* of acceptance arises. The function of accepting is the evaluation of the contents of our beliefs.

We can further illustrate Lehrer's point. I look across the table, see a candle, and consequently come to have the belief, "There's a candle." Many beliefs are formed in similar automatic fashion. Sometimes perceptual beliefs are formed attentively; sometimes they are formed as a result of but a casual glance. In general, beliefs may be formed without care or attention, but they may also be formed as a result of conscious deliberation. These beliefs may or may not contribute to the cognitive goal of obtaining truth and avoiding error. Now, I may or may not be able to control whether I come to have certain beliefs. I can't control my believing that there is a candle. Put a candle three feet in front of me in good light, and I will have the belief that there's a candle. But I can control my *evaluation* of this belief. I can judge that this belief of mine is a step toward truth and away from error. My accepting that there is a candle is my judging or evaluating that this content satisfies the cognitive goal of obtaining truth. For Lehrer, acceptance is the positive evaluation of beliefs.[20] In this sense, acceptance is a *second-order* mental state; it is the evaluation of other mental states.

It might appear that acceptance is always explicit, that acceptance arises only as the result of conscious reflection. Lehrer denies this.[21] It does seem to be true, however, that what a person accepts is in principle cognitively accessible. I can in principle come to know what I accept. Perhaps one further advantage of understanding acceptance in this way is that it permits Lehrer to avoid commitment to the sometimes unwieldy notion of tacit belief. Tacit beliefs are beliefs that a person has but has never thought about. An example of a tacit belief is that 2047 is greater than 5. Now, I have never thought of this particular content before. Only now did I haphazardly type out the sequence 2047. Yet I would, without even minimal reflection, be inclined to think that 2047 is greater than 5. But it quickly becomes evident that if this type of content is a tacit belief, then I have a great many others—for example, that 2048 is greater than 5, that 2049 is greater than 5, and so on. With but a little effort, I can generate potential tacit beliefs about all kinds of subject matter. This seems to involve my having an indefinitely large number of tacit beliefs, and to some philosophers, this has seemed problematic. Yet in any given cognitive situation, there seem to be any number of contents to which I am functionally committed.

There is an important consequence of this view of acceptance. Although an agent may never have explicitly considered a proposition, that proposition may nonetheless play a role in the agent's cognitive endeavors. Just as I might set out on Interstate 5 to drive from Southern to Northern California without explicitly considering that the highway is passable, so I might engage in particular cognitive endeavors without explicitly representing various propositions. Nor need it be the case that these propositions are implied by anything else I believe. Yet the propositions play a role in my current project. As we will see, Lehrer is interested in a general sort of functional commitment, that of an agent's trustworthiness with respect to evaluating certain kinds of belief. A person may accept evaluative principles, principles that indicate the kinds of proposition a person should accept. An ordinary person might be functionally committed to such evaluative principles even though the person might not ever explicitly represent or recognize these principles or have actually formulated an argument for such principles. Lehrer's notion of acceptance thus permits him to articulate a genuinely coherentist and internalist theory of justification that reflects an agent's actual cognitive abilities and practices.

Closely related to the concept of acceptance is the idea that personal justification is relative to a person's *acceptance system.*[22] This acceptance system is the set of statements describing what the person accepts at a particular time. It is worth noting that Lehrer does not describe this as what a person thinks or believes one accepts. This is in part due to Lehrer's view that what some agent accepts is not always explicitly thought of by the agent. Nonetheless, the agent is functionally committed to these propositions in the course of various cognitive endeavors, and it is relative to the set of these functional commitments, some explicit and some not, that coherence is to be judged. A person's acceptance system is the background against which particular acceptances are determined.

A simple example will illustrate the two additional concepts required to explain adequately Lehrer's view of coherentist justification: (a) the notion of *epistemic competitors* and (b) the pivotal notion of *comparative reasonableness.* Imagine that Sam is trying to decide whether to accept that he can purchase a computer more cheaply later in the summer. Other propositions are epistemic competitors of this proposition; that is, certain propositions either deny or cast doubt on the proposition in question. "Computers will be more expensive later in the summer" is a proposition that denies the proposition Sam is considering, whereas "The availability of microprocessors will diminish during the summer" is a proposition that casts doubt on that proposition. Suppose that these are the only epistemic competitors. Intuitively, we might expect that Sam would be justified in believing that computers will be cheaper later in the summer only if it would be epistemically better for him to believe this than either of the competitors. In Lehrer's view, this intuitive idea becomes the notion that the proposition must be comparatively more reasonable for Sam to accept than either of the competitors. More precisely, Sam is justified in accepting the proposition if and only if it is comparatively more reasonable than any epistemic competitor, given what else Sam accepts. If other propositions accepted by Sam provide sufficient evidence to rule out the competitors, then the proposition that computers will be cheaper later in the summer is comparatively more reasonable. Lehrer's technical term for the balance of evidence favoring a proposition is that the competitors are *beaten* or *neutralized*. Thus, if relative to Sam's acceptance system the competitors are beaten or neutralized, the proposition is comparatively more reasonable.

We are now in a position to specify Lehrer's view of coherence. Suppose an agent's acceptance system is adequate to rule out the competitors of a given proposition. Now, if a proposition is comparatively more reasonable, given a person's acceptance system, then that proposition *coheres* with the acceptance system. Coherence is thus defined in terms of the relation of comparative reasonability, given what else an agent accepts. The positive element of coherence is just this defensibility of the claim against epistemic competitors.[23] A person is *justified* in accepting a proposition only if that proposition coheres with the person's acceptance system, that is, if the proposition is comparatively more reasonable. Propositions are justified for an agent because they "fit better" with what else an agent accepts, which is to say that they are comparatively more reasonable.

The intuitive appeal of Lehrer's theory might be brought out in the following: Suppose I am vacationing in the mountains with my family. Walking along the banks of a lake, my sister points to a particular indentation along the shore and asks what kind of animal made that track. Imagine that on looking at the impression, I instantly form the belief that it is the paw print of a mountain lion. Consider how we might ordinarily determine whether I am justified in accepting that a mountain lion made the track. If my sister is sufficiently skeptical of my claim, she might ask whether I can distinguish mountain lion tracks from the tracks of large dogs, deer, raccoons, or even small bears. These options are merely the epistemic competitors of my belief that a mountain lion has recently walked where we are now enjoying mountain vistas. Unless I have sufficient reason to rule out these other options, my sister might reasonably conclude that this was but another instance of my pretending to know when I did not. But what will provide me with sufficient reason to rule out these sibling-inspired options? It would seem that what else I accept would provide the reason, including my confidence in my ability to identify such tracks, or my recent conversation with one of the locals that mountain lions were coming increasingly closer to town in search of food, in particular the deer that inhabited the meadow along the lake. Moreover, we might intuitively think I was justified only to the extent that these other bits of information were sufficient to defend my claim against its competitors. My view about the source of the track is justified if it fits with what other evidence I have available to me at the time. Apart from some terminological differences, this intuitive explanation of my justification seems to capture the essence of Lehrer's theory. It is also worth noting that we frequently make judgments of comparative reasonability. When I get in my car and notice the gas gauge, I judge that on balance it is more reasonable to believe that the gas gauge is functioning properly and I have sufficient gas to reach my destination. We routinely make these sorts of comparative judgments on the basis of what else we believe or accept.

We now see two points: (a) why Lehrer views coherence as a relational property, and (b) why his view is nonetheless a *coherence* theory. First, comparative reasonability requires only that the candidate proposition be more reasonable relative to *some* other things I accept. Comparative reasonability does not depend on everything I accept. Indeed, Lehrer explicity denies that coherence is a global feature or property of the system.[24] Second, and perhaps more important for our purposes, Lehrer's view is coherentist. The salient feature of coherence views is the claim that any belief depends on other beliefs for its justification. Apart from the terminological distinction between belief and acceptance, Lehrer's view has this feature: Comparative reasonableness always depends on *what else a person accepts*. It is this latter feature that accounts for the coherentist character of Lehrer's view. Justification always depends on other propositions a person accepts. There are no independently acceptable propositions. This is just what we would expect of a coherentist theory of justification—that justification depends on other beliefs, or in this case, other accepted propositions.

We now have the principal elements of Lehrer's theory of justification. Justified acceptance arises when, relative to what else a person accepts, a proposition is comparatively more reasonable than any of its epistemic competitors. But this still leaves a further question unanswered. Recall that an assumption of the Regress Argument is that only *justified* beliefs can serve to justify other beliefs. We might then ask, given Lehrer's view, in what sense the elements of an agent's acceptance system are justified. How is it that an agent's background evidence, the acceptance system, is justified? Answering these questions requires our canvasing Lehrer's view of agents as trustworthy evaluators.

Justifying Trustworthiness

It seems credible to suppose that some kinds of propositions are comparatively more reasonable relative to other things we already accept. For example, Sam accepts certain propositions regarding the marketing practices of computer manufacturers, and these propositions bear on whether he is justified in accepting that computers will be cheaper later in the summer. But there seem to be certain classes of proposition for which this is not obviously the case. In fact, these kinds of proposition seem quite independent of what else we accept. We are, of course, referring to types of proposition or belief that the foundationalist refers to as basic. Indeed, it is not immediately clear how, for example, simple observational contents are more reasonable given what else we accept.

Imagine that Sara sees a blue bird. Is she justified in accepting that there is a blue bird? According to Lehrer, Sara is justified if, relative to what else she accepts, this content is more reasonable than any of its competitors. Consider but two possible competitors: that she sees a red bird and that she sees a squirrel. Now, exactly what else does Sara accept that will either beat or neutralize these competitors? Surely, what else Sara accepts, prior to her actually seeing the bird, is neutral between it being a *red* or *blue* bird. How could anything she already accepts tell her what color she is about to see? Similarly, how could anything Sara already accepts tell her whether she is about to see a squirrel or a bird? Sara's acceptance system would not seem to provide the requisite sort of evidence to determine what is comparatively more reasonable for her to accept.

The problem illustrated by this example is that on many occasions, the specific contents of our observations seem logically and often probabilistically independent of what else we accept. These types of content apparently do not accord well with the coherentist view set out by Lehrer. There simply do not appear to be any already accepted propositions that could serve to tell us whether the content of our perceptual beliefs is more reasonable to accept. Now, the foundationalist will, of course, be happy to resolve this difficulty. Simply concede that there are basic beliefs, the foundationalist advises. But how can a coherentist like Lehrer resolve the problem? It is precisely here that the importance of our accepting ourselves as trustworthy evaluators appears. To see how, recall Sara and her seeing a blue bird.

Sara sees a blue bird. Her aim is to obtain truth and avoid error. Does she have some reason for thinking that her accepting that there is a blue bird will lead to truth? According to Lehrer, Sara does as long as she also accepts that she is a *trustworthy evaluator* of these types of matters. Sara must accept that she is a trustworthy evaluator—that she tends to get it right—of these types or kinds of propositions. If Sara accepts that more often than not, under these kinds of circumstances, she is capable of telling blue from red, or birds from squirrels, then there is "something else" she accepts that is relevant. This "something else" is her acceptance that she is a trustworthy evaluator. Indeed, this "something else" makes it comparatively more reasonable for her to accept that she sees a blue bird rather than the epistemic competitors. Lehrer himself considers brown birds and headaches:

> Consider . . . for example, my seeing a brown bird. Does my being justified in accepting this depend on anything else I accept? Yes it does. It depends on my accepting that I can tell a brown bird when I see one in the present circumstances. Consider my having a headache. Does my being justified in accepting

this depend on anything else I accept? It depends on my accepting that I can tell a headache when I have one. . . . What makes foundationalism plausible is that we accept that we can tell whether or not certain things are true, without reasoning, and so we can. But if we did not accept that we could, if we had no idea whether we were trustworthy in such matters, our beliefs about them would not seem basic.[25]

Lehrer points out that he does not claim that it is his acceptance of his trustworthiness with respect to observation beliefs *in general* that justifies his acceptance of seeing a brown bird. Rather, Lehrer's justification for accepting that there is a brown bird depends on his accepting that he is trustworthy with respect to *seeing brown birds in these sorts of circumstances*. Similarly, Sara's justification for accepting that she sees a blue bird depends on her accepting that she is trustworthy with respect to seeing that there are blue birds.

Lehrer's remarks in this passage about foundationalism are also instructive. Lehrer does not hold that our justification depends on us having, either explicitly or implicitly, an argument. We accept such things "without reasoning." Sara's acceptance that she is trustworthy with respect to telling that something is a blue bird is epistemically relevant to her justification, but this "background acceptance" is not a premise in an argument for her belief that she sees a bird of a certain feather. Thus, although Lehrer and BonJour agree that the justification of the agent's perceptual belief depends on other members of the agent's acceptance or belief system, they differ about the ways in which these members are related to the perceptual belief.

Lehrer also claims that accepting oneself as a trustworthy evaluator explains the plausibility of the foundationalist's appeal to basic beliefs. It is not that Sara or Lehrer are justified by virtue of their having some visual sensation or other experiential state. Rather, it is that each of them counts him- or herself trustworthy in such matters. Accepting that one is a trustworthy evaluator of the relevant subject matter explains why it is more reasonable to accept a belief or proposition than any of its competitors. An agent is justified in accepting the candidate proposition by virtue of the agent's acceptance of his or her trustworthiness. Notice that because the justification depends on something else one accepts, the main feature of a coherentist account of justification is present. Justification ultimately depends on what else one accepts.

The preceding, however, may seem more than a little reminiscent of reliabilism. To accept that one is a trustworthy evaluator of the color of birds or the kind of bee buzzing about is but another way of saying that one accepts that he is *reliable* under those circumstances. Lehrer does acknowledge his commitment to a kind of reliabilism. He holds that we are naturally constituted to accept that we are trustworthy with respect to the deliverances of the senses and memory. But the crucial difference between

Lehrer's view and the reliabilist's lies in Lehrer's claim that justification requires an agent's *acceptance* of his reliability. The reliabilist, recall, merely requires that one in fact be reliable and have no reason for thinking this reliability is undermined.

At this point, you might be recalling the Regress Argument. With that in mind, you might be tempted to say something like the following to Lehrer:

> The Regress Argument showed us that a belief could be justified only by other *justified* beliefs. Now, you claim that a person is justified in accepting some particular perceptual belief if that person accepts that she is trustworthy in those circumstances. But what justifies *that*? What *justifies* a person's accepting that she is a trustworthy evaluator under those kinds of conditions? After all, if she is not justified in accepting her trustworthiness as an evaluator, then her simply accepting that she is trustworthy won't justify her accepting that she sees a red bird, blue bird, or anything.

Lehrer anticipates this type of response. His answer involves the notion of mutual support, but he designates this mutual support as "cycles of coherence" and what he now refers to as a "keystone loop":

> Just as my justification for accepting particular claims may depend on the inclusion of some general principle of my trustworthiness, so my justification for accepting the general claim may depend on the inclusion of specific claims of obtaining truth and avoiding error in my acceptance system. . . . No justified statement is an island. Coherence cycles.[26]

Lehrer seems to be suggesting that there is an interplay between more general claims of trustworthiness and more specific claims of trustworthiness. We will take matters a bit slowly here in order to see what he might have in mind. Consider my accepting the following:

(C) I am a trustworthy evaluator of whether a coffee cup is blue.

Why is my acceptance of (C) justified? According to Lehrer, it is justified, in part, because I accept this:

(G) I am in general a trustworthy evaluator of what I accept.

Of course, what we now want to know is why my acceptance of (G) is justified. Lehrer's answer has two aspects. First, accepting (G) is in part justified by my acceptance of (C). It may be, as John Bender suggests, that I have come to accept (C) by virtue of my past success in identifying the color of coffee cups.[27] Thus, my acceptance of (G) supports my acceptance of (C) and my acceptance of (C) supports my acceptance of (G). But Lehrer seems also to suggest a somewhat deeper reason. To the question "Why should I consider myself worthy of trust?" he responds, "I accept that I am worthy of my trust because of my best efforts to be so."[28] Recall that when we accept a proposition, we do so with the aim of obtaining truth and avoiding error. If I am committed to this cognitive goal, then I will try to avoid error and accept only propositions that have a reasonable chance of truth.

A brief analogy might help. Suppose you have been baking something in a very hot oven. As you start to remove the pan, your mother reminds you to be careful. Your response is that, of course, you will be careful. But why should your mother, or you, for that matter, count you as trustworthy with respect to your being careful? Is not the answer to that question simply that you *want to be careful*? That you are simply *trying to be careful*? Of course you will be careful; you don't want to get burned! It is precisely your wanting to be careful that vouchsafes your being careful.

Similarly, your wanting to obtain truth and avoid error vouchsafes that you should accept your trustworthiness in these matters—after all, you don't want to be burned by the false! Two points bear notice. First, just as your trying to be careful doesn't guarantee that you will avoid getting burned, so your trying to obtain the truth does not guarantee that you will avoid the false. Even the most trustworthy people sometimes disappoint. Pursuing the analogy but one step further can bring out the deeper point. Your success in your efforts to be careful requires that you are *able* to be careful, that you can put your hands where you want and avoid putting them in more dangerous places. Similarly, it might be thought that my trustworthiness as an evaluator of cups and coffee, or of birds and bees, requires that I am able, for the most part, to succeed in my evaluations of the truth. This point may lie behind Lehrer's claim that we naturally trust the deliverances of our senses.

This last point suggests a crucial distinction. There is a difference between accepting that one is trustworthy and one's actually being trustworthy. The former implies only that one should accept that one is doing the best one can do, from the epistemic point of view. But this in no way implies that one succeeds in obtaining truth and avoiding falsehood. Thus, doing one's epistemic best does not imply that one is actually trustworthy.

We are now in a better position to see how "coherence cycles." Specific principles of trustworthiness, like (C), depend for their justified acceptance on more general principles, such as (G). But Lehrer claims it is reasonable to accept principles such as (G), because my interest in obtaining truth and avoiding error is evidenced by what I do when it comes to matters such as detecting the color of cups or birds.[29] The general and specific principles are mutually supporting. It is this mutual support, which Lehrer calls the "keystone loop," that underlies our justified acceptance of (G) and specific principles like (C).[30] But this is what we would expect of a genuinely coherentist theory. No propositions are justified independently of what else a person accepts.

Lehrer claims that acceptance of a proposition is justified if that proposition coheres with an agent's acceptance system, and a proposition coheres if and only if it is more reasonable than any of its competitors. The immediate source of justification of a proposition is this relationship of comparative reasonability. But we have just seen that the acceptance system can provide this "support" for a proposition only if the system contains the keystone loop. That loop is the recognition by an agent that acceptance of his or her general trustworthiness is mutually supported by acceptance of his or her trustworthiness about particular propositions. Thus, the *ultimate* source of coherentist justification, in Lehrer's view, is the keystone loop.

OBJECTIONS TO COHERENCE THEORY: LIBERAL OR CONSERVATIVE?

To put it mildly, coherence theory is not without its critics. In this and the following section, our attention turns to some of the more natural and more substantive criticisms of the coherentist theory of justification. We then examine the resources for answering these questions that can be found in BonJour's or Lehrer's theories. In this section, we consider criticisms that coherentism is either too liberal or too conservative. We will see, however, that even these more natural objections turn on what is undoubtedly the most substantive charge against coherence theory, which is examined in the next section.

The coherentist view that relations among beliefs are the principal source of justification prompts two natural questions. Roughly, the theory holds that if an agent's beliefs are related in the right way, then the beliefs are justified. This would seem to mean that any belief might count as justified so long as it is related in a certain way to the agent's other beliefs. Could not any belief turn out to be justified? This question suggests that coherence theory is too tolerant or too liberal. But we might also wonder whether coherence theory could ever countenance an agent revising or changing beliefs. How could an agent ever come to accept evidence or beliefs that conflicted with already held beliefs? This question suggests that coherence theory is too conservative. It is the twin charge of liberality and illiberality that is our focus here.

Liberality

Both Lehrer and BonJour view the justification of a belief as dependent on the other beliefs held by the agent. These background beliefs, in effect, determine the types of beliefs that might come to be justified, given those background beliefs. In principle, seemingly, someone having the right background beliefs might come to believe that the moon is made of Styrofoam, and this belief could count as justified. Another person having a different set of background beliefs might come to believe that the moon is made of green cheese, and this belief, too, could count as justified. A more realistic example comes from the history of science. It was once thought that a substance called phlogiston was responsible for the process we now call oxidation. Specifically, it was believed that phlogiston was given off during the oxidation of a substance. However, observation showed that some substances actually weighed more after oxidation. But rather than counting this as a defect of phlogiston theory, it was instead held that phlogiston had negative weight.

More recent examples might be found among conspiracy theorists—for example, those who believe that the earth is flat and that there is an international conspiracy to make us believe otherwise. Some may be inclined to dismiss such people as irrational. But it is not obvious that phlogiston theorists were irrational.

The point of the liberality objection instead seems to be that coherence theory places no *external* constraints on the contents of justified beliefs. The justification of belief is too serious a matter to be left solely to the guidance of an agent's own belief system.

The following point can be made on the coherentist's behalf. First, the coherentist might ask whether dubious beliefs really are members of a coherent system. Suppose someone did have beliefs about the shape of the earth, namely, that it is quite flat. Notice all of the things that this person would also have to believe for this flat-earth belief to count as justified. Newspapers, television, radio, commentators, reporters, casual bystanders, witnesses—all would have to be engaged in selective misrepresentation. Thus, for instance, newspapers would report the truth except for matters pertaining to space. Moreover, notice that this same person—if only moderately well informed—would have to believe that governments can't even keep secrets about what they say in confidential meetings. Yet thousands, and even hundreds of thousands, of people have cleverly managed to keep this truth from the benighted among us. On the face of it, these beliefs seem to count against the flat-earth belief as cohering and thus justified.

Suppose, however, the incoherence of the controversial belief(s) is only apparent. One of two reactions seems appropriate. The first is to claim that there is nothing wrong with the existence of incompatible, coherent systems. It is plausible to hold that in 1543 Copernican and Ptolemaic theories were equally coherent and mutually incompatible. It should not be the point of epistemological theory to legislate a priori which systems of empirical belief are acceptable and which are not.

The coherentist's second reaction should be to challenge the critic's lurking suspicion that coherence theory makes it difficult, if not impossible, for an agent ever to accept competing evidence.

Conservatism

The critic of coherence theory will no doubt concede that in the middle of the sixteenth century evidence existed for the incompatible but coherent geocentric and heliocentric models of our solar system. Both systems of belief were justified. But, the critic contends, coherence theory seems unable to explain how someone could change or revise beliefs. Astronomers changed—justifiably—their beliefs; the beliefs did not simply die off. The conservatism objection holds that coherence theory is unable to explain justified revisions of our beliefs. A new belief counts as justified only if it fits with the already accepted and justified beliefs of an agent. For Lehrer, this requires that the new belief be comparatively more reasonable, *given what else the agent already accepts*. For BonJour, this requires that the new belief be inferable *from the agent's other beliefs*. Suppose, however, the agent comes across a bit of information that conflicts with already held beliefs. Imagine, for example, that everything I believe justifies the belief that my keys are on the desk. Suppose, however, that I now walk to the desk and look very carefully at the broad, brown, *empty* expanse. My other, already held beliefs seem to overrule this single proposition that my keys are *not* on the desk. If coherence theory is unable to explain why I should change this mundane belief, can the theory ever hope to account for beliefs about the structure of the solar system?

The first thing to notice is that revision of our belief system is, in the usual case, conservative. Moreover, there is some reason to think that belief revision ought to be conservative. At any given time, a person has a large number of beliefs. Now, what should his attitude toward what he believes be? It seems almost obvious that the person would not have the beliefs in the first place unless he thought of those beliefs as likely to be true. It does not follow from this that he thinks that all of his beliefs are true, only that the vast majority of them are. Both BonJour's and Lehrer's theories provide a rationale for an agent having this positive evaluation of already held beliefs.

This might motivate the conservative nature of belief revisions, but it still leaves open the question of how actual revisions of currently cohering beliefs occur. The important point about such revisions is that conflicting beliefs are in fact often supported by other beliefs the agent has. For example, consider my belief that I see the empty surface of the desk. Recall that in Lehrer's view justified acceptance of such beliefs requires that, among other things, I accept that I can tell whether the desk surface is empty. If I accept my reliability under such circumstances, then there is some reason to accept the new belief. Similarly, BonJour's view allows for the attribution of reliability to cognitively spontaneous beliefs, such as perceptual beliefs. It may well be the case that accepting a conflicting belief occasions the revision of still other beliefs. But such revision is at least plausible in the coherentist view.

A critic of coherentism could offer this complaint: This sort of response to the conservatism charge tacitly concedes what is most troubling about coherence theory. If the coherentist view can allow for some input from the world, some connection between our beliefs and the world, then the charges of liberality and conservatism no doubt can be met. But this is just what is most troubling about coherence theory—it seems not to allow for a connection between beliefs and the world. The coherentist must recognize some nondoxastic connection between belief systems and the agent's environs.

THE ISOLATION OBJECTION

If there is no exit from the circle of belief, then there is no entrance into it, either. This is the crux of the family of objections discussed in this section. Although they differ in formulation or perhaps in emphasis, the objections clearly have but one aim: to show that the intimate connection between truth and justification is severed by coherence theories. C. I. Lewis expressed the concern somewhat metaphorically, claiming that coherence theory gave us no more assurance of the likely truth of beliefs than "a well-written novel." More recently, the same sort of worry is expressed in the claim that coherence is never the source of justification. This fundamental concern is sometimes referred to as the absence of independent warrant for our beliefs. The essence of the **isolation objection** is expressed in the claim that coherence theory cuts justification off from the world. This metaphor, while forceful, requires some clarification.

That coherence theory seems to be at odds with the essence of justification is illustrated by the following:

(1) Justification of beliefs implies the likelihood of truth of those beliefs.

(2) Truth is not merely a function of internal relations between beliefs.

(3) Coherentist justification is merely a function of internal relations among beliefs.

(4) Thus, coherentist justification does not imply the likelihood of truth.

(5) Thus, coherentism cuts justification off from the world.

The first two statements make a claim about the nature of truth and its connection to justification. Statement (1) articulates a feature of our intuitive understanding of justification. Statement (2) makes explicit the idea that whether our beliefs are true depends on the way the world is. The truth (or falsity) of my belief that my keys are on the desk depends on something about the world, whether *in fact* the keys are on the desk. As we have seen, however, coherence is fundamentally either a relation between beliefs (Lehrer) or a global property of relations between beliefs (BonJour). This feature of coherence is expressed by (3). The intermediate conclusion in (4) claims that there is no way to get from coherence, or relations among beliefs, to likely truth, which involves relations between beliefs and the world. In this sense, coherentism cuts justification off from the world.

The isolation objection presupposes that justification begins only if there is some belief-independent connection between our beliefs and the world. We must acknowledge that at least some of our belief contents are legitimated not by other beliefs, but by the fact that there is a connection between our cognitive capacities and the world around us. It is the existence of this connection, the very fact that the connection exists, that explains the likelihood that our beliefs are true. However, coherence theory seems to allow only connections between beliefs to play a role in justification. There seems to be no place for the connection between our belief-forming capacities and the world. Hence, there seems to be no way for coherence theory to explain the likelihood of the truth of our beliefs. There seems to be no way to explain the initial epistemic credibility of some of our beliefs, given only their relation to other beliefs. The essence of the isolation objection is that the world can't have any impact on the epistemic status of our beliefs.

We touched on this issue in the previous chapter, but a simple example will serve to illustrate the matter further. Consider my perceptual belief that there is a glass of tea on the table. Simplifying matters, my belief is the result of the causal interaction between the glass and the tea, an interaction that includes my having a certain visual experience. Why is my belief likely to be true? According to the critic of coherence theory, the belief is likely to be true because, in the normal course of things, my having the experience is a pretty darned good indication that there really is a glass of tea on the table. Moreover, the critic claims, the fact of this experience and its connection to the actual glass of tea seems to have little to do with my other beliefs. Indeed, if I were to draw only on my other beliefs, I would never have any reason to think that there was a glass of tea before me and that my thirst would soon be quenched. My senses, not my other beliefs, are my window to the world.

Put very crudely, the critic of coherentism—the foundationalist—says that sooner or later, the justificatory chain gets started by the world influencing, impacting, causing us to have some belief content, say, a glass of tea, rather than some other content. By definition, this influencing, impacting, causing is *outside* the content of our other beliefs. The influencing is evidenced by the existence of nonbelief mental states—for example, visual experiences. Yet mere relations among our other beliefs can never supply the content supplied by the influencing or impacting. My other beliefs

The Isolation Objection and Its Cousins

With this exposition of the isolation objection, we can illustrate the claim that this objection is closely connected to other objections mentioned at the outset of this section. For example, Robert Audi has claimed that coherence is never a source of justification; coherence is not what brings about justification. It is a straightforward matter to construe Audi's objection as the claim that coherence cannot be the source of the likely truth of our beliefs. This is at least the spirit of the isolation objection. A second example comes from Robert Meyers, who has argued that coherence theory cannot explain the initial, independent epistemic credibility of our beliefs. To say that our beliefs are epistemically credible is to say that at least some of the beliefs have independent credibility; our beliefs must allow for some epistemic input. It would not be too far amiss to suggest that this epistemic input is input from the world to our belief system, whether this input comes from perceptual experiences or "basic beliefs" of some sort. Thus, to say that our beliefs are epistemically credible is to say that we have reason to think they are true. A very hasty gloss of Meyers's view is that coherence theory at most allows that we have reason to think our beliefs are epistemically credible or likely to be true *if* we have reason to think some of our beliefs are initially credible or likely to be true. Unhappily, coherentism cannot explain where we get that *initial* reason to think our beliefs are true. Again, evidently, the core problem for coherence theory is explaining the connection between coherence and truth. These examples are not intended to show that all substantive objections to coherentism are but variants of the isolation objection. Rather, the point is that the isolation objection focuses attention on a deep concern for any coherentist.

cannot tell me that there is a *glass of tea on the table*. Hence, coherence theory isolates our beliefs from the world.

At this point, a coherentist like BonJour is likely to protest. Recall BonJour's argument for the connection between coherence and justification. A key component of that argument was that a cognitive system must be coherent and *the system must satisfy the Observation Requirement*. That is, a cognitive system contains beliefs likely to be true only if it is observationally sensitive. More formally, the agent must attribute a special reliability to that class of beliefs we call perceptual beliefs. Observational sensitivity is the link between our beliefs and the world. Lehrer, too, acknowledges that his theory incorporates a type of metareliabilism. We accept that we are trustworthy with respect to the deliverances of our senses. Thus, the coherence theories of both BonJour and Lehrer acknowledge that there is something special about our perceptual beliefs; there is a kind of reliability that attaches to such beliefs. If we make just one more move in this dialectic, we will be able to see the core disagreement between the critic and the coherentist.

The foundationalist's frustration is likely to be patent at this point. Instead of calling them "cognitively spontaneous beliefs of kind K," why not just call them "basic" and be done with it? Attributing reliability and special status to such beliefs, argues the foundationalist, is merely one way of saying they are not justified solely by virtue of their connections to other beliefs. The justification of such beliefs is a function of the connection between our beliefs and the world. The price of such a belief–world connection, claims the foundationalist, is recognizing the existence of basic beliefs.

A quick inventory is in order. The isolation objection asks the coherentist to explain the nature of belief–world connection, which assures that the belief systems are something more than well-written novels and that the world has some influence on our beliefs. Genuine justification arises only if there is such a connection, the critic claims. The coherentist responds by noting that our belief system does acknowledge a special status for perceptual beliefs. BonJour does so by invoking the Observation Requirement, while Lehrer appeals to a type of metareliabilism. The critic retorts that this is but a back door to basic beliefs.

Very simply, the coherentist's response is that it is our *assessment,* our *evaluation* of the belief–world connection that is pivotal for justification, not the mere existence of the connection. Underlying the justification of our beliefs is our recognition of the fact that we are the kind of beings that are impacted by the world. When Lehrer claims that "what is special about human mentality is our capacity for metamental ascent," he is claiming, among other things, that the distinctive feature of human beings is their ability to evaluate information they receive.[31] Neither the mere existence of a certain visual experience nor the causal connection between the world and that experience justifies my acceptance that there is a glass of tea on the table. My justified acceptance that there is a glass of tea requires my acceptance that I am trustworthy when it comes to discerning glasses of tea. Similarly, BonJour requires that I have a justifying argument that my belief about the tea is of a certain kind and that my having such beliefs is generally a good indication that there are glasses of tea in the vicinity. In general, how does any belief gain its initial epistemic credibility? It does so through one's assessment or evaluation that one has obtained the belief by a legitimate method, whether by inference or by more spontaneous, automatic processes.

It is this issue that fundamentally divides foundationalist from coherentist. Foundationalists zealously insist that we cannot always appeal only to other beliefs to establish the epistemic credibility of our beliefs. At some point, we must appeal to some sort of "truth connection," a belief–world connection that explains why our beliefs are likely to be true. Coherentists, equally fervently, maintain that the relevance of the belief–world connection is to be found in an agent's evaluation of the epistemic worth of the information obtained from such a connection. And this epistemic worth is to be sought in what else an agent believes or accepts.

The argument can, of course, be pursued down still further avenues. We will have occasion to revisit some of them. But for the moment, we leave matters here. The coherentist response to the isolation objection begins with the acknowledgment that some classes of belief are deserving of special recognition. These classes are indicative of a connection between world and mind. Second, and most importantly, the epistemic value of this connection is to be sought in what else an agent believes or accepts, in particular, the agent's evaluation of the belief–world connection. The ultimate source of epistemic justification is our reflective and evaluative capacities, which are manifested in the circle of belief.

Key Concepts

Acceptance	Isolation objection
Coherence theory of justification	Positive and negative coherentism
Comparative reasonability	
Global or holistic coherentism	Relational view of coherence

Review Questions

1. How do coherentist theories differ from foundationalist theories?
2. What are the stages or elements of the justification of a belief, according to BonJour?
3. What is the Doxastic Presumption, and what role does it play, according to BonJour? Do you think that BonJour is right to accept the Doxastic Presumption?
4. According to Lehrer, when is a person justified in accepting a proposition? What does it mean for one proposition to cohere with others, according to Lehrer?
5. Both Lehrer and BonJour provide an account of the justification of perceptual beliefs. Can you explain these accounts? Which do you think is better? Why?
6. What is the isolation objection? How does the coherentist respond to it? With whom to do you agree, the critic or the coherentist? Why?

For Further Study

Laurence BonJour and Keith Lehrer are two of the important contemporary coherentists. BonJour's *The Structure of Empirical Knowledge* (Cambridge, MA: Harvard University Press,

1985) contains not only an elaboration and defense of his view but also an extended critical discussion of foundationalism and externalism. Lehrer's *Knowledge* (Oxford: Oxford University Press, 1974) contains his earlier view, but the broad outlines of the earlier view are similar to his current view. This work contains a useful discussion of explanatory coherentism. The most recent statement of his view is contained in *Self-Trust: A Study of Reason, Knowledge, and Autonomy* (Oxford: Oxford University Press, 1997).

John Bender, ed., *The Current State of Coherence Theory* (Dordrecht: Kluwer Academic Publishers, 1989), is an excellent collection of essays on both BonJour's and Lehrer's views. Bender's introduction, "Coherence, Justification, and Knowledge: The Current Debate," is extremely useful, as are the replies by BonJour and Lehrer.

Robert Audi's discussion of coherentism in *Belief, Truth and Knowledge* (Belmont, CA: Wadsworth, 1988), Chap. 6, is sympathetic, if critical. Although Audi maintains that coherence, by itself, is never a source of justification, he holds that coherence can increase the epistemic credibility of a belief. Two other critiques of coherentism can be found in Robert Meyers, *The Likelihood of Knowledge* (Dordrecht: Kluwer Academic Publishers, 1988), Chap. 7, and Richard Fumerton, *Metaepistemology and Skepticism* (Landham, MD: Rowman & Littlefield, 1995), Chap. 5. John Pollock's *Contemporary Theories of Knowledge* (Totowa, NJ: Rowman & Littlefield, 1986), Chap. 3, contains a useful classification of various types of coherence.

An important coherence theorist whom we have not discussed in the text is Donald Davidson. The two essays, "A Coherence Theory of Truth and Knowledge" and "Empirical Content," provide an introduction to Davidson's view. Both essays are in Ernest LePore, ed., *Truth and Interpretation: Perspectives on the Philosophy of Donald Davidson* (Oxford: Basil Blackwell, 1985), pp. 307–332. Part V of LePore's volume also contains responses to Davidson's view. W. V. Quine's view is also sometimes characterized as coherentist, although the more frequent characterization is holistic. Quine's holism is most succinctly presented in "Two Dogmas of Empiricism," reprinted in *From a Logical Point of View,* 2nd ed. (New York: Harper, 1961), pp. 20–46. For a recent defense of coherentism based on connectionism, a theoretical view of the structure of the mind, see Paul Thagard, *Conceptual Revolutions* (Princeton, NJ: Princeton University Press, 1992).

For a discussion of whether we know what we believe, see Asher Koriat, "How Do We Know That We Know? The Accessibility Model of the Feeling of Knowing," *Psychological Review* 100 (1993): 609–639, and George Mandler, "Memory: Conscious and Unconscious," in P. R. Soloman et al., eds., *Memory: Interdisciplinary Approaches,* (New York: Springer-Verlag, 1989), pp. 84–106.

Notes

1. Laurence BonJour, *The Structure of Empirical Knowledge* (Cambridge, MA: Harvard University Press, 1985), p. 8. The phrase "accept a belief" is frequent in BonJour's work. Although BonJour does not elaborate on what he means by this phrase, he apparently has in mind something like an agent's willingness to use a belief in his cognitive endeavors. BonJour is not disputing that we involuntarily come to have a great many beliefs. His concern is rather with a person's "decision" to utilize the belief in his inquiries and whether the agent does so because he has some reason to think the belief is likely to be true. These reasons are, of course, other beliefs of an agent. Thus, an epistemically responsible agent accepts a belief only if he has other beliefs, which support the likely truth of the accepted belief. For doubts about the connection between internalism and epistemic responsibility, see Frederick F. Schmitt *Knowledge and Belief* (London: Routledge, 1992), Chap. 5. See also Hilary Kornblith, "Justified Belief and Epistemically Responsible Action," *Philosophical Review* 92 (1983): 33–48.

2. The distinction between global and relational understandings of coherence is drawn by both Michael Williams, *Unnatural Doubts* (Oxford: Blackwell, 1991), pp. 276ff., and John Bender, "Coherence, Justification, and Knowledge: The Current Debate," in John Bender, ed., *The Current State of Coherence Theory* (Dordrecht: Kluwer Academic Publishers, 1989), pp. 2–3. John Pollock utilizes the contrast between linear and holistic conceptions

of coherence in his *Contemporary Theories of Knowledge* (Totowa, NJ: Rowman & Littlefield, 1986), Chap. 3.

3. BonJour, *The Structure of Empirical Knowledge,* p. 93.
4. BonJour's view of these issues is succinctly recounted in Timothy Joseph Day, "Circularity, Non-linear Justification, and Holistic Coherentism," in Bender, *The Current State,* pp. 134–141.
5. In Chapter Six, "Externalism and Internalism," we consider the notion of cognitive accessibility in more detail.
6. BonJour describes the relational element as linear. His point is that any belief must be related to some of the agent's other beliefs by a "justifying argument." But BonJour insists that coherence is not to be identified with this relation.
7. BonJour, *The Structure of Empirical Knowledge,* pp. 93–101.
8. BonJour does acknowledge that, in certain cases, accepting beliefs that are inconsistent can be cognitively fruitful. He also acknowledges that he is unable to identify the nature of such inconsistencies.
9. BonJour, *The Structure of Empirical Knowledge,* p. 91.
10. BonJour, *The Structure of Empirical Knowledge,* p. 151. However, in the same section, BonJour goes on to say that "the account of justification offered here represents at best an idealization which is only loosely approximated by ordinary cognition."
11. BonJour, *The Structure of Empirical Knowledge,* pp. 101–102 especially.
12. Hilary Kornblith has addressed this issue in two articles, "How Internal Can You Get?" *Synthese* 73 (1988): 27–41, and "The Unattainability of Coherence," in Bender, *The Current State,* pp. 207–214.
13. Laurence BonJour, "Replies and Clarifications," in Bender, *The Current State,* p. 285.
14. BonJour, *The Structure of Empirical Knowledge,* p. 123.
15. See BonJour, *The Structure of Empirical Knowledge,* pp. 124–132, for a discussion of these premises.
16. BonJour, *The Structure of Empirical Knowledge,* p. 142.
17. BonJour, *The Structure of Empirical Knowledge,* p. 183.
18. An earlier, exhaustive presentation is in Keith Lehrer, *Knowledge* (Oxford: Oxford University Press, 1974). More recent statements of Lehrer's view can be found in "Reply to My Critics," in Bender, *The Current State,* and *Self-Trust: A Study of Reason, Knowledge, and Autonomy* (Oxford: Oxford University Press, 1996), esp. Chaps. 1–3. As indicated in the text, the exposition here will rely on these more recent formulations.
19. Lehrer, "Reply to My Critics," p. 253. See also Lehrer, *Self-Trust,* p. 90.
20. Lehrer, *Self-Trust,* pp. 1–4.
21. Lehrer, *Self-Trust,* p. 4. It still might be true that most acceptance arises as a result of conscious reflection, even if such reflection is not necessary for acceptance.
22. In *Self-Trust,* Lehrer uses the broader notion of an agent's *evaluation system,* which includes not only what a person accepts but also what a person prefers. Preference is the positive evaluation of what an agent desires. For our purposes, we can ignore this difference.
23. Lehrer, *Self-Trust,* p. 29.
24. Lehrer, *Self-Trust,* p. 32. Bender, in "Coherence, Justification and Knowledge," p. 3, suggests a sense in which coherence is a global property in Lehrer's view.
25. Lehrer, "Reply to My Critics," pp. 270–271.
26. Lehrer, "Reply to My Critics," pp. 274–275. In Bender, *The Current State,* pp. 8–9, Bender describes this as a kind of "bootstrapping process."
27. See fn. 13.
28. Lehrer, *Self-Trust,* p. 14.
29. From this, we can see why one might be tempted by Bender's "bootstrap" interpretation that our initial acceptance of, for example, perceptual beliefs would not be justified (see fn. 13). There might be reason to think that Lehrer would not find this interpretation too uncomfortable. Elsewhere, he suggests that children and animals do not have knowledge; what they have is information. Knowledge, and presumably justification, that is

"characteristically human" depends on an appreciation of the distinction between truth and error. See, for example, Bender, *The Current State*, p. 271. In *Self-Trust*, p. 9, Lehrer claims that it is reasonable for me to accept the principle I have called (G) by virtue of other things I accept, "remembering that what I accept constitutes my best effort to accept what is worth accepting as true and avoid accepting what is not." This sort of remark seems to indicate that Lehrer thinks of the relationship between principles (C) and (G) as mutually supportive, or what he calls the "keystone loop."

30. Lehrer, *Self-Trust*, pp. 9–10, 33–34. The relation between reasonable acceptance and justified acceptance is more complex. Lehrer counts the former as necessary but not sufficient for the latter (p. 29). I take it that the epistemological move from reasonable acceptance to justified acceptance of (G) is described on pp. 33–34. In sum, I take the argument to be that I am justified in accepting (G) rather than its competitor (G*: I am not a trustworthy evaluator of what I accept) because (G) is more reasonable in light of what else I (reasonably) accept. Again, Bender's "bootstrap" metaphor might be helpful here. It should be noted that some will worry that this move is circular.

31. Lehrer, *Self-Trust*, p. 78. Similarly, see Lehrer, "Reply to My Critics," p. 271.

CHAPTER SIX

Externalism and Internalism

In previous chapters, we occasionally characterized a certain theory as internalist or externalist. We described reliabilism, for example, as an externalist theory of knowledge and justification. In this respect, reliabilism seemed to depart from the internalist character that historically typified epistemological theories. On the other hand, the coherentism of BonJour and Lehrer was identified as internalist. It is now somewhat commonplace to classify a theory of justification or knowledge as externalist or internalist. Indeed, the received view is that, as with foundationalism and coherentism, the contrast between externalism and internalism is a fundamental dividing line in epistemological theory. Epistemologists disagree about whether and to what extent an adequate theory should be externalist or internalist. There is, however, no single view of how best to draw the contrast.

Debate typically centers on two notions: cognitive accessibility and epistemic responsibility. Internalism holds that either cognitive accessibility or epistemic responsibility, or both, are necessary for justification. Externalists tend to deny that either is necessary for justification. The focus of this chapter is the debate over cognitive accessibility and epistemic responsibility. We begin by considering features of the concept of justification and the reasons these features might be thought to motivate either externalism or internalism. We then present some of the standard arguments concerning epistemic responsibility and cognitive accessibility and outline two theories that attempt to combine features of both externalism and internalism. Finally, we consider both an optimistic and a pessimistic outlook for resolution of the debate.

The internalism/externalism debate is a metatheoretical or metaepistemological debate. Epistemological theories explain or analyze certain target concepts, such as knowledge or justification. For example, reliabilist theories explain the concept of justification in terms of reliability of one type or another. A Cartesian theory of knowledge explains the concept of knowledge as infallibly true belief. A *metatheory*—a theory about theories—tells us what are the admissible or appropriate ways of analyzing or explicating the target concepts. Internalism, for example, holds that an appropriate analysis of justification must include some essential reference to the agent's perspective. Internalism is thus a metatheory about theories of justification. In this sense, the internalism/externalism debate is a metatheoretical debate; it is a **metaepistemological** debate about the nature of epistemological theories.

EXTERNALIST AND INTERNALIST FEATURES OF JUSTIFICATION

Although the contrast between externalism and internalism is a relatively late arrival on the epistemological landscape, the concept of justification can be seen to motivate each side of the distinction. To say that a belief is justified is to say that, among other things, the belief is likely to be true. This aspect of justification derives from the recognition that the goal or aim of justification is truth. One approach, then, to a theory of justification is to emphasize those features or conditions that make it likely that a belief is true. Now, whether an agent's belief is true, or is likely to be true, seems to be largely independent of one's cognitive perspective, which is the thoughts, ideas, and beliefs that make up one's outlook on the world and guide one's cognitive activities. The truth of Sara's belief that there is a glass of tea on the table does not depend on what Sara thinks, believes, or wishes. Her belief is true if and only if there is a glass of tea on the table. Similarly, the likely truth of Sara's belief depends on conditions or features that are *external* to her cognitive perspective. The likelihood that a toss of a pair of dice will produce a seven is independent of a person's beliefs or fervent wishes. That likelihood depends on the environment and the nature of the tumbling dice. Analogously, the likely truth of Sara's belief depends on her nature and her relation to her environment—for example, the quality of her eyesight, her ability to distinguish tea from coke, and the conditions under which she sees the glass. Again, the significant aspect of these conditions or qualities is that they are *external* to Sara's cognitive perspective. Emphasizing that a theory of justification must explain the likely truth of our beliefs thus leads naturally to emphasizing the external aspects of justification. The importance attached to explaining the likely truth of justified beliefs is perhaps the defining characteristic of externalist theories.

There is, of course, another intuition about the nature of justified belief, which is clearly in evidence in the theories of Descartes and Hume. This intuition is familiar even in our ordinary discourse and disputation. One person claims that the crime rate has gone down in, say, New York, and another claims that there is insufficient *evidence* for that claim, that there is no *good reason* for believing that the crime rate has decreased. Entrenched in the epistemological tradition is the similar thought that a belief is justified only if the agent has good reasons for having the belief. It is also sometimes held that justification is a matter not simply of whether a belief is likely to be true, but of whether an agent has good reason for thinking that the belief is true. For Hume, recall, the likely truth of our beliefs about the world is inadequate to justify these beliefs. Hume requires that we have good reason for our beliefs about the nature of the external world.

A view that insists that a belief is justified only if the agent has good reasons is internalist in a dual sense. First, it is quite natural to think that the reasons for a belief are part of the agent's cognitive perspective. The justification of Sam's belief that the speed of light is 300,000 km/sec depends on Sam having other reasons for this belief—for example, remembering a comment by a trusted physics professor. Sam's memories are a part of *his* cognitive outlook; his reason is internal to his perspective.

Second, the thought that an agent must have *good* reasons for the belief introduces the notion of an agent's reasons satisfying a standard. Again, it is natural to think that such standards are, or can be, internal to the agent's cognitive outlook. Hume, for example, frequently admonishes us that we have good reasons for a belief only if we can show that the belief derives from some experience or results from a deductive argument. Epistemic agents are thus epistemically responsible for assuring that their reasons for a belief are appropriate with respect to a given standard. Whether a person's beliefs are epistemically responsible is evidently an internalist matter. Of course, it is no small task for an internalist theory of justification to identify the appropriate standards.

Internalism, it might be suggested, thus holds justified belief to be a kind of reasonable belief. More importantly, the reasonability of a belief is judged relative to the agent's cognitive perspective. In this sense, justification depends, at least in part, on what is happening *inside*. A theory is internalist if it holds that justification depends on features internal to the agent's cognitive perspective.

An obvious thought at this point is to suggest that a theory of justification include both external and internal features. Indeed, as we will see in a later section, such combinations are proposed. But the internalist and externalist aspects clearly can pull in different directions. You are no doubt familiar with persons who believe that they will do well in performing some task, such as playing in a sports event or taking a test, because they have prepared appropriately. We might grant that they have a good reason for their optimism. But it is not difficult to imagine that their reason is not a very good indicator of their success. We might doubt that there is a "truth connection" between their reason and their actual performance. In such a case, would you count their belief as justified? As noted, many theories do attempt to include both internalist and externalist aspects. When push comes to shove, however, a theory might be identified as externalist or internalist to the extent that it emphasizes the likelihood of truth of an agent's beliefs or the reasonability of a belief.

EPISTEMIC RESPONSIBILITY

The notion of epistemic responsibility is sometimes thought to characterize internalist theories of justification. The claim that an adequate theory of justification requires an appeal to the notion of epistemic responsibility is often challenged, however. Such challenges typically appeal to whether beliefs are voluntary, whether we can decide what to believe. As we will see, the involuntary character of belief is thought to count against requiring epistemic responsibility as a condition of justification.

Responsibility: Goals and Means

We might begin with a brief recounting of what it means in general for a person to be responsible. One sense of this term is that people have obligations or duties that they are required to fulfill. If Sam is responsible for cleaning the kitchen, then he has a duty or obligation to clean the kitchen, and his mother may reasonably expect him to do so. We might think of this as a kind of familial or practical responsibility. There are also legal and moral responsibilities. If Sara is a public defender, then she has both a moral and a legal obligation to provide her clients with the best possible defense. Other people, including her clients, may reasonably expect that she satisfy her obligations. Notice that these responsibilities include a goal—a clean kitchen or an able defense—and an appropriate means for satisfying the goal. Running the garden hose through the kitchen window and giving the place a good dousing is not an appropriate means to attain the goal of a clean kitchen.

Epistemic responsibility differs in an important respect from these more general familial, legal, and moral responsibilities. Epistemic responsibility concerns beliefs, not individual actions. Nonetheless, the notions of a goal and an appropriate means to that goal suggest how we might understand the idea that a person might be epistemically responsible with respect to beliefs. We have seen before the idea that our *epistemic goal* is to have true beliefs and avoid false beliefs. Epistemic responsibility, then, is assessed in part by the extent to which an agent aims at having true beliefs and avoiding false beliefs. But just as it matters *how* Sam reaches the goal of having a clean kitchen, so it matters how a person comes to satisfy the relevant epistemic goal. Sam might bribe a sibling to clean the kitchen for him. We would not think him *responsible,* despite his having achieved the goal. Similarly, Sam might be epistemically lucky. He might, through good fortune, avoid false beliefs and acquire true beliefs. He acquires true beliefs from reading *Newsweek,* but just as he is turning to this week's tabloid and the inevitable acquisition of false beliefs, he is reminded of his familial obligation in the kitchen. An epistemically responsible agent employs the appropriate means to achieving an epistemic goal. Specifically, an epistemically responsible agent has good reasons for his beliefs. Those reasons are good reasons if they indicate the likely truth of or are evidence for the beliefs. Perhaps now we can pull things together. An epistemically responsible agent has the epistemic goal of having true beliefs and avoiding false beliefs, and because of this goal, the agent holds beliefs on the basis of good reasons, which indicate the likely truth of those beliefs. More succinctly, an epistemically responsible agent does the best he can to achieve epistemic goals.

It may now be more apparent why the notion of epistemic responsibility is thought to be essential for an understanding of the notion of justification. Considered as a kind of reasonable belief, justified beliefs are beliefs held on the basis of good reasons. Now, the claim of the responsibility theorist is that reasons are *good* reasons only if the agent, in some sense, recognizes that they are good reasons. The agent must recognize that given such reasons, the beliefs are likely to be true. Consequently, an agent has justified beliefs only if the agent aims at the appropriate epistemic goal and comes to have beliefs as a result of trying to satisfy that goal. There are questions that can be raised about this argument, which we will return to shortly. For the moment, this line of argument is reminiscent of Bon-Jour's constraints on an adequate theory of justification. BonJour, however, is not the only advocate of epistemic responsibility. Roderick Chisholm defends a slightly different version in which we are subject to the intellectual requirement of trying our best to accept a proposition if and only if that proposition is true.[1] Later, we will also consider a notion of epistemic responsibility suggested by Richard Feldman.

It is also not difficult to see the connection between internalism and epistemic responsibility.[2] Internalism holds that the justification of a belief must depend on some aspect of the agent's perspective. Now, beliefs are epistemically responsible beliefs if an agent holds those beliefs on the basis of good reasons, with the aim of attaining her epistemic goal. Both the reasons and the goal are evidently part of the agent's cognitive perspective. Sara's goal, for example, of having true beliefs and avoiding false beliefs leads her to accept what she reads in *Newsweek* and ignore the nearby tabloid. The epistemic goal is part of her cognitive perspective. Not every internalist theory, however, is committed to the notion of epistemic responsibility. A theory might be internalist for other reasons, such as a commitment to the notion of accessibility, but not be committed to the notion of epistemic responsibility as a condition of justification.[3] That is, a theory might not insist that Sara view herself as having epistemic goals and forming beliefs on that basis. We can summarize this by noting that a sufficient condition for a theory to be internalist is that it requires justified beliefs to be epistemically responsible. It does not seem, however, that epistemic responsibility is a necessary condition for a theory to be internalist.[4] A theory that requires epistemic responsibility as a condition of justification is sometimes thought of as a type of **deontological theory of justification,** because epistemic responsibility theories view agents as having epistemic obligations.

Are Beliefs Voluntary?

There is a central objection to holding that justified beliefs must be epistemically responsible. Theories of epistemic responsibility seem to presuppose that our beliefs are voluntary. We can *decide* what to believe and what not to believe. One can argue, however, that our beliefs are not like that; we do not typically decide what to believe. Indeed, it is claimed, many of our beliefs are clearly involuntary. We must then either give up the notion of epistemic responsibility or the thought that we have many justified beliefs. Critics urge abstinence from the former.

It is natural to suppose that a person is responsible for some act or behavior only if that person has some control over the act or behavior. Recall that Sam has an obligation to clean the kitchen. That he is responsible suggests that he is *able* to clean the kitchen, that he has it in his power to do so. Sam's failure to clean the kitchen will be viewed as an irresponsible act, in part, because it was in his power to clean it. More generally, we assign responsibility to a person only if the person is capable of meeting that responsibility.

If we try to extend the notion of responsibility from actions to beliefs, we seem to face a difficulty. Too many of our beliefs seem to be *out of our control.* Compare Sam's decision to browse the World Wide Web instead of cleaning the kitchen with his belief that he now hears a friendly parental reminder that the kitchen is *his* responsibility. Sam can choose whether to browse or clean; but can he similarly choose to believe that he hears his father? Perceptual beliefs are a kind of belief that is evidently out of our control. I do not choose to believe that I hear the bird chirping. The bird chirps; I hear it chirp, and automatically, involuntarily, I believe that the bird is chirping. William Alston offers the more dramatic example of seeming to see a truck coming down a street. I do not, he claims, "have the capacity to believe or refrain from believing at will."[5] Nor need the involuntary character of belief be restricted only to perceptual beliefs. Beliefs based, for example, on simple deductive arguments may be similarly involuntary.

The idea that many of our beliefs are involuntary runs counter to the idea that we first consider the reasons we have for a *prospective* belief, decide that those reasons are good, and finally form or come to have the belief. Very often, beliefs simply happen to us; they are not obviously the products of deliberation or reflection. Now, if beliefs are often out of our control, in what sense can we be held responsible for them? Consider

Doxastic Voluntarism

Doxa is a Greek word meaning "opinion" or "belief." Doxastic states are beliefs. *Doxastic voluntarism* is the view that our beliefs are voluntary or that we are capable of controlling what we believe. Doxastic voluntarism probably should be distinguished from a view that might be called *epistemic voluntarism*. Descartes, for example, recognized that certain beliefs, such as that a square is four-sided, are psychologically irresistible, but he thought we could refrain from giving them our "epistemic approval."

Sam once more. Imagine that he has nearly finished cleaning the kitchen. More dramatically, imagine that just as he is wiping down the last counter, he glances through a window barely in time to see a truck hurtling down the road, out of control, and crash into the kitchen wall (you can imagine the results). Could Sam be held responsible for the mess? The more natural intuition is that he could not, that there would be something unreasonable about assigning responsibility to him. Analogously, we would be disinclined to hold Sam responsible, for example, for his perceptual belief that he sees a plate on the counter.

The critic of deontological theories of justification claims that the involuntary character of many beliefs leads to a formidable objection. Deontological theories are at odds with the facts about actual belief acquisition. If many or most of our beliefs are out of our control, then those beliefs are not epistemically responsible beliefs. They are not formed as a result of some deliberative process. If these involuntary beliefs are not epistemically responsible, then they are not justified. The dilemma facing the responsibility theorist is now evident. Either many of our beliefs are not justified or epistemic responsibility is *not* a constraint on a theory of justification. The crucial claim in this line of reasoning is that epistemic responsibility is a viable notion only if our beliefs are voluntary.

One possible response is to distinguish between belief and acceptance, as Lehrer does. Voluntarism might fail at the doxastic level, at the level of beliefs, but might hold at the epistemic level of acceptance. We can assess whether our beliefs, however they are formed, are the sort of opinions we would hold on appropriate reflection. Beliefs, which meet the test of appropriate reflection, may then play a part in our future cognitive inquiries. Recall that Lehrer thinks of acceptance as what typically results from reflection, when our epistemic goal is to accept what is true and avoid what is false. We might come to have, for whatever reason, beliefs that we would not judge on reflection to be true. I might have acquired the belief that the stock market will continue to rise indefinitely. Yet I might refrain from accepting the proposition because, after due reflection, I come to recognize that the proposition has unbeaten competitors. Further, I undertake this reflection with the goal of believing the truth.

Interestingly, Descartes can, at times, be interpreted as making this sort of suggestion. In Meditation I, for example, he claims that he ought to refrain from "giving credence to these opinions," the opinions arrived at by means of the senses. He does not suggest that he ought to refrain from having the beliefs (opinions); he suggests that he merely ought to refrain from giving them credence, from recognizing such opinions as epistemically valuable.

Yet a different line of response suggests that we are capable of controlling our beliefs. Although our beliefs may not be under our direct control, we can indirectly control them by altering our policies or habits of belief formation. A person might study logic or statistics, which might help to preclude forming certain kinds of beliefs. A person might take other precautions as well. For example, if I am aware that I tend to accept uncritically the views of unreliable but enthusiastic orators, I might make it a point to become aware of opposing views. In this view, our epistemic responsibility is to engage in a bit of epistemic training. There are, of course, difficulties in spelling out how *much* epistemic training we are obligated to undertake.

The critic of epistemic responsibility might suggest that this line of response fails to take account of the *unavoidability* of believing. Short of a very unattractive alternative, we are "hostage to our senses."[6] While we may try to make the best use of our sensory abilities, we cannot avoid, at some point, acquiring perceptual beliefs. If, however, perceptual beliefs are unavoidable, it might be argued that they are not in our control. It is up to nature, not us, as to which perceptual beliefs we acquire. Thus, some—probably most, the critic urges—of our perceptual beliefs are of this involuntary sort. But if these perceptual beliefs are justified, then epistemic responsibility is not a necessary condition of justified beliefs. Now, the responsibility theorist may fall back on the first kind of response, arguing that we are responsible for our epistemic evaluations of or our acceptance of those beliefs. Or the responsibility theorist may pursue a third line of thought.

The third response that we consider to the voluntarism objection is to deny that we are epistemically responsible for our beliefs only if our beliefs are under our control.[7] Richard Feldman suggests that we may have obligations to perform certain acts even though we are unable to do so. If Sam takes out a mortgage on his house and later becomes *unable* to make payments, he still has the *obligation* to pay. If Sara's printer breaks down hours before a project is due and she *cannot* complete the project, her obligation does not disappear. Of course, critics of epistemic responsibility might argue that our beliefs are not like mortgages or projects. Beliefs are not like mortgages in that we decide to undertake the latter; we cannot decide to avoid having beliefs. The similarity between beliefs and mortgages is that we can take appropriate precautions in undertaking mortgages—for example, mortgage insurance—and we can take precautions with respect to our belief-forming habits. These examples suggest that beliefs are under our indirect control in the same way that our ability to make mortgage payments is under our indirect control.

The responses we have been considering suggest that epistemic responsibility is a viable constraint on theories of justification even if our beliefs are not formed voluntarily. However, William Alston, a principal critic of the notion of epistemic responsibility, argues that there is still a fundamental defect in attempts to meet the voluntarism objection. He claims that deontological theories of justification, theories that appeal to the notion of epistemic responsibility, do not "hook up in the right way with an adequate truth-conducive ground."[8] Alston claims that a person may have satisfied all his epistemic responsibilities, yet there is no reason to think that his beliefs are likely to be true. Hoping to improve his habits of perceptual belief formation, Sam may, for example, conscientiously study logic and probability texts and learn as much as he can about the operations of his visual system. He may indeed do more than can reasonably be expected of someone. Yet, Alston urges, none of this suggests that his beliefs are likely to be true. Ultimately, the task of a theory of justification is to elaborate the connection between justified beliefs and the likely truth of those beliefs.

We might elaborate this a bit further by means of Lehrer's notion of acceptance. The critic of epistemic responsibility might grant that someone like Lehrer could meet the voluntarism charge. Still, the critic might urge that a view such as Lehrer's does not adequately connect acceptance to likely truth. An agent's conscientious attempt to obtain the truth does nothing to assure that reasons or grounds for accepting a proposition make that proposition likely to be true. A student's conscientious efforts to give the right answers are, on occasion, insufficient to make it likely that the answers are indeed right. An epistemic agent may be similarly well intentioned. But simply doing the best one can, given one's own perspective, is inadequate. Satisfying one's epistemic obligations doesn't seem connected, in any obvious way, to the truth. Epistemic obligations apply only to one's perspective, to what one can do. But the likelihood of truth is independent of the agent's perspective. Thus, the critic claims that there is no way to get from epistemic responsibility to the likelihood of truth.

Defenders of the notion of epistemic responsibility may be unmoved by this argument. First, they may argue that the critic has at most shown that satisfying one's epistemic responsibilities is not sufficient for justification.

But the critic has not shown that satisfaction of one's epistemic obligation is not necessary for justification. Indeed, arguably, coherentists like Lehrer and BonJour make the "truth connection" on other grounds.

There are, however, some who argue that the notion of epistemic responsibility *does* connect appropriately with the notion of truth. Feldman, for example, argues that our epistemic obligation is to believe that which is supported by the evidence.[9] If we understand by "evidence" that which makes a belief likely to be true, then there is a connection between our epistemic obligation and the likely truth of our beliefs. Of course, this does not tell us what sorts of things—for example, other beliefs or visual experiences—count as evidence. That is the project of theories of justification. Our aim here, however, is to scout certain metaepistemological issues.

Let us grant for the moment that something like Feldman's suggestion can meet the "truth connection" worry raised by Alston. Determined internalists might be concerned that this concedes too much. Suppose an internalist argued in the following way:

> Internalism claims that justification depends on features internal to the agent's perspective. But in relying on the notion of evidence, "that which makes a belief likely to be true," we really are not very internalist any longer. "That which makes a belief likely to be true" is, in a real sense, external to the agent's perspective. It is a question of *fact* whether other beliefs or visual experiences or causal relations, or anything else for that matter, makes our beliefs likely to be true. It doesn't depend on *my* perspective whether my having certain visual experiences makes my belief that there is a glass of tea on the table likely to be true. Indeed, a reliabilist like Goldman could be very happy with this "internalist" notion of epistemic responsibility. How can this be a genuine internalism when I do not seem to have any connection to this evidence? There has to be more to internalism than simply whether I succeed in believing on the basis of evidence. We don't have a genuine internalism unless this evidence is *my* evidence, unless there is some sense in which I see it as my evidence.

This argument ought to sound reminiscent of both BonJour and Lehrer. But many noncoherentist internalists would be moved by just such an argument. The fundamental claim here is that it is not enough that beliefs are based on factors that make it likely that those beliefs are true. Internalists are not satisfied with the idea that a belief is justified merely on the basis of causal connections that make the belief likely to be true. Rather, the internalist requires that the agent have evidence or reasons for which the belief is held. What is needed, according to internalism, is that this evidence is something that is the agent's or is in the agent's perspective— that the agent, in some sense, has *access* to the evidence.

COGNITIVE ACCESS

The immediately preceding discussion leads us to a second approach to contrasting internalism and externalism. Internalism, as characterized by the notion of epistemic responsibility, could meet worries about the involuntary character of belief. In order to meet worries about the "truth connection," we seem to be led to a notion of evidence that is not obviously internalist. Internalist scruples, however, might be satisfied if the evidence is part of the agent's perspective, if the evidence is accessible to the agent.

The second approach, then, understands internalism in terms of the notion of the **cognitive accessibility of reasons.** Very simply, the idea is that justification depends on the agent's actual or possible awareness of why a belief is held. The intuition behind this approach has two aspects. First, a belief is justified only if it is based on the agent's reasons for thinking the belief is true. This is, by now, a quite familiar requirement. Sara has a justified belief that the president will visit San Diego only if she holds the belief on the basis of some reason, such as having read it in the *San Diego Union,* that supports the likely truth of the belief. So, a justified belief must be held for reasons, which support the likely truth of the belief. We might call such reasons *supporting reasons.* Supporting reasons are both the basis of the agent's belief and the reasons the belief is likely to be true. Now, the second aspect is that the supporting reasons must be *cognitively accessible.* That is, the agent can become aware that these are the reasons that support the belief. We then have the following characterization of internalist theories of justification: Internalist theories hold that a belief is justified only if the agent can become aware of the supporting reasons for the belief.

Strong and Weak Accessibility

It is possible to identify both stronger and weaker versions of the accessibility requirement. Recall Sara's belief about the president coming to San Diego. The stronger version insists that Sara must actually be aware of the supporting reasons as leading to her belief. On this strong sense of cognitive accessibility, Sara comes to have her belief about the president because she recognizes that she has supporting reasons. For example, she might come to have this belief about the president because she recognizes that she has a supporting reason, namely, her having read of his planned arrival in the paper. At times, BonJour seems to prefer this stronger notion of accessibility.

Many internalists subscribe to a weaker notion of accessibility. A weaker version of cognitive accessibility merely requires that the agent *could* become aware of the supporting reasons. I might believe that there is a glass of tea on the table. In the normal case, I have this sort of belief because I see the glass. The supporting reason is my seeing the glass. But I do not always reflect on my seeing the glass as my reason for having the belief. I simply form the belief. I could, however, become aware that seeing the glass is the supporting reason for my belief. Chisholm, for example, seems to support this weaker notion when he claims that a subject *can* know on any given occasion what are the grounds or reasons for a belief.[10]

The weaker notion of accessibility might be preferred on two counts. First, the strong version might be criticized as psychologically unrealistic. It is unrealistic because many of our beliefs are justified, but we do not normally explicitly consider the supporting reasons for the belief. Some beliefs, of course, are the result of conscious deliberation. We are often aware of the reasons for those beliefs arrived at as a result of computation or inference. However, we simply form or acquire many beliefs without actually rehearsing the reasons we have for thinking that the belief is likely to be true. The second reason for preferring the weaker version is that it is more widely applicable. Various forms of foundationalism clearly seem to be internalist in nature yet do not require strong accessibility.[11] The weak version thus more naturally captures a broader notion of internalism. Although these two points do not show the strong version of accessibility to be fundamentally mistaken, we will assume the weaker version in what follows. The weaker version simply requires that were agents to reflect on the matter, they could become aware of the supporting reasons for their beliefs. Similarly, Earl Conee and Richard Feldman claim that a belief is justified "only where the person has cognitive access to evidence that supports the truth of the belief. Justifying evidence must be internally available."[12] Notice that they require only that the justifying evidence, our supporting reasons, be internally *available*. The evidence, or the supporting reasons, is part of the agent's perspective, in the sense that the agent could become aware of them after sufficient reflection.

Objections and Responses

We can anticipate two likely objections. First, it might be claimed that although small children have justified beliefs, they do not have access to the supporting reasons.[13] In response to such objections, Lehrer, for example, has urged that children and even certain kinds of animals undoubtedly possess information, or the ability to discriminate certain features of the world, but we should resist identifying the mere possession of information with knowledge or justification. Children and lower animals thus provide at best inconclusive evidence for whether an adequate theory of justification is internalist or whether access to reasons is a necessary condition for justified belief. Indeed, one's view of this matter likely is determined by one's prior stand on whether justification is internalist or externalist.

A more threatening objection is the claim that *competent agents* either do not keep track of their reasons for their beliefs or are sometimes mistaken about the actual causes of their beliefs. There are some complicated issues here. We need to distinguish between the reason for which an agent believes and the causes of an agent's beliefs. The agent may not recognize the causes of belief as the reasons he believes what he does. So, we will take matters somewhat slowly.

Consider first the claim that we sometimes mistake the actual causes of our beliefs. An agent may count one set of reasons as the cause of a belief when in fact an entirely different set of reasons is the basis of the belief. In ordinary situations, we sometimes refer to this kind of case as rationalization. Imagine that Sam insists that his belief that affirmative action is unfair is based on his belief that the principle of equality is the fundamental principle of justice. Suppose, however, that Sam's belief is actually based on his belief that he was not accepted to law school due to affirmative action. This kind of case, in which an agent misidentifies the actual reasons for his belief, is thought to undermine the claim that justification requires cognitive accessibility.

Internalists can make two responses. First, it might be thought that internalists need not require *infallible access* to the reasons for the belief. Thus, the kinds of cases would be more troubling if they could be shown to be the norm or typical. Apparently, one does have access to the supporting reasons for many beliefs. Perceptual beliefs and beliefs based on simple inferences, for example, might be thought to be of this variety. But internalists cannot rest easy with this response. Accessibility internalists claim that the accessibility of one's reasons is a *necessary* condition of justified belief; a belief is not justified unless the agent has access to the supporting reasons. Consequently, the internalist cannot suggest that there are cases in which a person has a justified belief but the reasons are not accessible.

The accessibility internalist might then try a second defense. The advocate of accessibility can insist that what matters is whether the actual reasons are *in principle* accessible to the agent. The actual reasons may not be immediately accessible; they may not be "luminous," that is, accessible after a cursory introspective glance. The accessibility theorist might hold that the reasons need only be *dispositionally accessible.*[14] Somewhat crudely, dispositional accessibility says that seek—long enough—and ye shall find. In this view, the accessibility of one's reasons is not guaranteed to be a quick and easy matter. It may take someone like Sam a long time to realize that his real opposition to affirmative action is based not on beliefs about equality, but on his belief about why he was rejected from law school. But if you think that people can eventually come to know what their reasons are for their beliefs, then you lean more to the *eventual* accessibility of one's reasons. This may be enough, however, because the eventual accessibility of one's reasons is compatible with the weak version of accessibility.

This leaves open cases in which agents lose track of their reasons. Suppose Sara believes that a certain formula is a theorem in modal logic because she remembers having once worked out the proof, but she no longer remembers the particular steps of the proof. It is plausible that Sara has a justified belief, but how might the accessibility theorist explain this, given that Sara has forgotten her reasons? It could be argued that there are *two* sources or bases of Sara's belief. One obvious source is her actually having done the proof. But Sara has another source or basis for her belief, namely, her belief that this completed computation is a proof. Now, Sara remembers this "second-order" belief that she has a proof, and this second-order belief is the *accessible* reason for her belief that the formula is a theorem in modal logic.[15] More generally, an agent might have more than one appropriate source for the justification of belief. But accessibility need not require that she have access to the original reasons for her belief.[16]

If these considerations are along the right lines, then a weak version of accessibility appears defensible. Advocates of accessibility may well have plausible responses to worries that agents are either misled about the nature of their reasons or that these reasons might be inaccessible.

There is still one further and significant issue to be addressed. Suppose Sam believes that there is a glass of tea in front of him. Suppose, were he to be asked why he believes that, Sam responded that his visual experience is that of seeing a glass of tea. Thus, Sam has access to the reason his belief is likely to be true. But does Sam also need access to the fact that, normally, he has such a visual experience because of a causal connection between the experience and the glass of tea? More generally, does the agent need to be aware of *why* his reason is an adequate reason?

The issue here might be illustrated by a rather simple analogy. Suppose I have learned, through a series of distinct but equally annoying experiences, the sound the starter makes when my car battery is, if not dead, very close to death's door. Suppose I do not understand very much about cars, including why batteries go dead or why exactly they are so important. Now, imagine that I attempt to start my car one morning and hear this familiar, distressing sound of a battery about to give up the ghost. Am I justified in believing that my car will not start because the battery is dead? Analogously, does Sam need to know or be aware of the causal connections that underlie his seeing the glass of tea and his consequent belief that there is a glass of tea? Does he need to be aware of the physical mechanisms that explain the likely truth of his belief that there is a glass of tea?

It is important to understand why this concern is significant. We have seen that if internalism is to be plausible, it must in some way account for the likely truth of our beliefs. Often, the likely truth of our beliefs is explained by appealing to various causal connections. We are undoubtedly familiar with one way to tell this story. The glass of tea deflects light to

Sam's eyes, causing a visual experience. This visual experience in turn causes Sam's belief. Thus, we are able to explain the likely truth of Sam's belief. Yet these causal relations are not evidently part of Sam's internal perspective. These are merely facts about certain physical, physiological, and mental processes. At least on the surface, the causal explanation of the truth of Sam's belief appears incompatible with internalism. What we have seen so far is that accessibility requires that Sam have access to the reasons for his belief. The issue now raised is whether, in general, agents must also have access to *how* these reasons explain the likely truth of their beliefs.

Internalists seem generally inclined to doubt that such a requirement is necessary. Earl Conee claims that an agent needs to have justifying evidence, but the agent need not know why it is justifying evidence.[17] Robert Audi, too, seems to resist such a requirement.[18] Recall also that Lehrer holds that we must believe that we are reliable with respect to perceptual beliefs, but he does not also require that we be aware of how it is that we are reliable.

Again, a simple example might help to illustrate why the internalist might not accept this further requirement. Suppose Sam tells Sara that he believes that Sacramento will have a good almond crop this year, because if it rains in April, then Sacramento has a good almond crop, and it rained in April this year. Suppose, on a bit of prodding from Sara, Sam claims that he is justified in believing the conclusion of this argument because it is reached by an application of modus ponens. Sam, however, is unable to explain why modus ponens is a valid argument form. Thus, Sam has access to the reason for his belief without also having access to how this reason supports his belief. But Sam's inability to demonstrate the validity of the argument does not undermine the fact that he does indeed have a justifying reason and that he does have access to that reason. To require more than access to the justifying reason seems to imply that justification requires showing that one is justified.[19] Certainly, externalists are not in the position of insisting that an agent must have access to the finer causal details that underlie belief. Moreover, the accessibility theorist might argue that to insist on access to the details of the causal facts is to become enmeshed in a kind of level confusion. It is to fail to distinguish between being justified and proving that one is justified.

We might characterize the situation like this: Likelihood of truth is a necessary condition of justification. The explanation of the likely truth of a belief is typically a causal story, hardly an encouraging thought for internalists. But the internalist suggests the following: When we spell out the sequence of causal relations, we encounter an agent's reasons as one of the causal links, as one feature that sustains belief. Now, it is enough that the agent have access to this particular causal link—the supporting reasons—without also having access to the whole causal story. The whole truth may be understood only in cases in which the whole story is understood. Justification, however, only requires that the agent have access to that part of the story that supports a target belief. The internalist claims that as long as the agent is able to hook into, or access, the causal story in the right place, then the agent has a justified belief. An agent's reasons are the link to the likely truth of a belief, whether the agent understands the whole story of why these reasons are the link to the likelihood of truth.

Earlier in the chapter, we considered the notion of epistemic responsibility. This led to the thought that an agent's belief is justified only if it is based on evidence, which makes the belief likely to be true. To preserve the internalist character of such a view, we were led to the notion of accessibility. In principle, the agent must be able to become aware of the supporting reasons for her belief. But a difficulty arises here. The supporting reasons explain the likely truth of the agent's belief. Just how these reasons link belief to likely truth is often external to the agent's perspective. Yet the fact that there is such a link seems necessary for justification. The internalist can accept this, however. The internalist claims that the agent need not have access to the causal facts, only access to reasons that indeed are part of the causal story. As long as these reasons are the reasons for which the agent has the belief, then the belief is justified, according to the access internalist.

ATTEMPTED RECONCILIATION

Critics of internalism still argue that epistemic responsibility and cognitive accessibility are inadequate to justify belief. The properties by virtue of which a belief is justified must be truth-conducive, and there is nothing in the two notions of epistemic responsibility and cognitive accessibility that is appropriately truth-conducive. The explanation of justified belief given by the access internalist, for example, does not explain why the beliefs are likely to be true. The likely truth of a belief depends on the way in which the belief is acquired or the means by which it is formed. Beliefs are likely to be true because they are formed in the right kind of environment under the right kind of conditions. The environment and conditions under which a belief is formed or acquired are *externalist* features. The agent's perspective need not reflect these externalist features. Consequently, a theory of justified belief must account for these externalist features. In Chapter Three, we considered the predominant form of externalism, reliabilism. Here, we will consider two views that attempt to combine externalist and internalist features: Alston's internalist externalism and Ernest Sosa's virtue perspectivism. But we will also see that both views have a marked affinity with reliabilism.

Alston's Internalist Externalism

Alston claims that a belief is justified if and only if the belief is based on an adequate ground.[20] Although he characterizes the view as having an internalist aspect, it is primarily an externalist view. He holds that the view resembles reliable indicator theories. Further, Alston rejects the idea that there is any suitable internalist interpretation of adequacy. And it is the notion of adequacy that forms the cornerstone of his theory.

Alston wants to combine the plausible features of internalism and externalism. Thus far, we have noted that externalist theories are marked by an emphasis on truth-conduciveness. We must be able to identify, according to externalism, properties or characteristics of a justified belief that account for the likely truth of the belief. Our considerations in the previous two sections lead to the idea that accessibility is a central, defining feature of internalism. In what follows, our interest is chiefly the manner in which Alston accommodates these features of internalism and externalism. We need to begin with the concept of a ground.

Justified beliefs are based on grounds, according to Alston. Although the notion of basing is a difficult one, Alston suggests two features. First, a belief is based on a ground if it is causally dependent on the ground. Second, the belief is based on a ground if it is in some sense guided by that ground.[21] An example may help to illuminate this notion of being based on a ground.

Suppose that as a result of looking at the table, Sam believes that there are apples in the bowl. The ground of Sam's belief is his perceptual experience. In this case, the ground is an experience; in other cases, the ground might be other beliefs. Very generally, we might think of grounds as the evidence an agent has for the belief, but we must be careful not to think that evidence is restricted to propositions or other beliefs. In this example, Sam's evidence, his ground, is simply the perceptual experience. His consequent belief is *caused by* the experience. Sam would not have had the belief unless he had the perceptual experience of seeing apples in the bowl. The ground of a belief is the causal basis of the belief.

But there is more to the notion of being based on a ground than simple causal dependency. Thus, Alston claims that a belief is based on a ground only if it is formed *in light of* or *guided by* the ground. Alston seems to have in mind the idea that certain features of the ground are particularly relevant to the subsequently formed belief. Our belief-forming mechanisms are sensitive to and take account of these features. Now, which features these are will vary from case to case. The redness and the roundness of the apples will be such guiding features, but the proximity of the apples to the flower vase will not. When the ground is an experience of some sort, the relevant guiding features are some aspect of the experience. When the ground is other beliefs, the relevant guiding features are undoubtedly the content of those beliefs. Although Alston does not put the matter this way, we might suggest that the guiding features of the ground must be features that are relevant to the truth of the belief. There is some reason to interpret Alston in this way, especially in light of his accessibility requirement. With this in mind, we can understand Alston's notion of a belief being based on a ground in the following way: A belief is based on a ground if it is at least partially caused by features of the ground, features that are relevant to the truth of a belief.

In a very weak sense, this notion of being based on a ground is internalist. The ground of a belief is something internal to the agent; it is some state or belief of the agent. Yet Alston has in mind a stronger internalist condition. Specifically, he thinks a belief is justified only if the ground of the belief is accessible to the agent.

Earlier, we noted that Alston defends foundationalism in part by distinguishing between a belief being justified and the activity of justifying a belief or showing that the belief is justified. Alston sees an interesting and intimate connection between these two. Exploiting this connection enables him to explain why a satisfactory theory of justification must have a kind of accessibility requirement. Alston does not attempt to prove that accessibility is necessary for justification. Rather, he contents himself with explaining why an accessibility condition should be present.

Consider that humans clearly have been and are engaged in the activity of critically reflecting on their beliefs. Had we never heard of epistemology, we would still critique our beliefs. As a matter of fact, we look at the beliefs that "work" and those that do not. Our critique of these beliefs is geared toward identifying features of them that explain their differential success. It is in our interest, if only for purely practical reasons, to identify the features that make beliefs work and the features that prevent them from doing so. Imagine seeking out a tutor for your calculus class. Initially, you would no doubt trust the tutor. You would have some confidence in your solutions to various problems because they were based on the advice and counsel of the tutor. If a classmate were to ask you why you had this confidence, you likely would cite the tutor's explanations as your reason. Now, were you to discover that your tutor-inspired answers were consistently at odds with the instructor's solutions, you might begin to rethink your reliance on the tutor. This practice of reason giving and subsequent critiquing is clearly not confined to calculus homework. We routinely engage in this practice—that is, we routinely cite our *grounds* or our *reasons* for our beliefs.

Alston suggests that we would not be interested in whether our beliefs are justified unless we had such a practice of evaluating our reasons. If our beliefs were never challenged, either by the recalcitrant features of the world or by other humans, we would not care whether our beliefs were justified. We would not be interested in the grounds or reasons for which we believe.

Alston claims that we are thus led to an understanding of what it is for a belief to be justified. What justifies a belief is what we need to cite to defend successfully our beliefs. Imagine, for example, that Sara asks Sam why he believes that there are apples in the bowl. What will it take for Sam to justify successfully his belief? It would be a simple matter of Sam's citing the fact that he *saw* the apples. Or suppose that you have a quiz scheduled in your logic class. You believe that your logic instructor misses class only under the most extreme circumstances; indeed, you strongly suspect that your teacher actually enjoys logic and would not miss class even if he were ill. But a classmate tells you that class is canceled. When you ask how she knows, she cites her *seeing* signs on the classroom door and on his office door. Generally, the citation of a perceptual experience is enough to defend successfully a belief. Put somewhat differently, perceptual experience is a legitimate ground because it is what we would cite in explaining why our belief is justified. Of course, this connection between being justified and the activity of justifying, of defending our beliefs, is not confined to perceptual experience. Explaining that a belief is based on expert testimony or is the conclusion of a sound argument is generally sufficient to defend a belief. Thus, expert testimony and deductive arguments are legitimate bases for our beliefs.

Alston takes this to explain the need for an accessibility requirement for a theory of justified belief. If our grounds are what we would cite in the course of justifying our beliefs, then, in some sense, we must be able to come to know what such grounds are. The ground must be cognitively accessible to the agent if it is to figure in the agent justifying the belief. Alston does not think that the ground must be immediately accessible, but he does think that after sufficient reflection on the situation, an agent must be able to identify the grounds on which the belief is based. The internalist aspect of Alston's theory is manifested in this accessibility requirement.

Given Alston's view of the relation between the activity of justifying a belief, or giving the reasons for a belief, and a belief being justified, one might wonder why Alston views his theory as an internalist externalism instead of an externalist internalism. After all, it appears as though the activity of justifying is the fundamental feature, because it is what seems to lead us to the more externalist notion of what, in fact, makes a belief justified. Indeed, others have suggested that this activity of justifying, of giving reasons, is the central feature of justification. This view is explicit in coherentists like Lehrer and BonJour, but it can also be found in non-coherentist views.[22]

It would seem that the answer to the question of why Alston's view is ultimately externalist lies in his notion of adequacy. A ground is an *adequate* ground only if it makes the belief likely to be true. An agent may be able to give reasons for a belief, but the belief counts as justified only if the reasons or grounds cited by the agent make it likely that the belief is true. We can perhaps see here why Alston is attracted to a version of reliabilism. The grounds of a belief are adequate if and only if they indicate that the belief is likely to be true. However, Alston does not believe that this likelihood of truth is something that can be subjected to an accessibility condition. That is, Alston does not think an agent will always have access to the fact that the grounds of a belief are indeed adequate. We cannot get into the details of Alston's argument, but we can briefly sketch some of the reasons he thinks that accessibility to the adequacy of a ground is not necessary to have a justified belief.

To see precisely what is at issue, recall Sam's belief that there are apples in the bowl. The ground of Sam's belief is his perceptual experience, which has a certain character including redness and roundness. As we have seen, Alston holds that Sam must be able to offer his seeing the apples as his ground for his belief. Sara's challenge leads Sam to a moment's reflection, which leads to his identifying the ground of his belief. This much Alston accepts as a necessary condition. He rejects, however, a further condition, which we might put as follows: Sam has a justified belief only if he is able *to show* that because his belief is based on perceptual experience, the belief is likely to be true. Thus, Alston rejects the idea that an agent must be able to show that beliefs based on certain types of ground are likely to be true. Alston provides two kinds of reason for his rejection.

Again, recall Sam's belief that there are apples in the bowl. Suppose Sam is but a few years old. Alston argues that Sam may have the perceptual experience of the apples and thus have an adequate ground. But Sam may lack the conceptual sophistication to explain that because his belief is based on his seeing the apples and because beliefs based on perception are likely to be true, then his ground is indeed an adequate ground. We have seen this type of argument before. Externalists frequently argue that children have justified beliefs, but children often do not satisfy internalist constraints. Thus, the internalist constraints are not necessary. We have also seen, however, that internalists are unmoved by this sort of argument. Alston, however, provides a second reason that does not rely on the cognitive abilities of children.

By way of introducing this second reason, consider the following *internalist* argument: Again, consider Sam's belief that there are apples in the bowl. Suppose that Sam lacks the conceptual sophistication to argue that his grounds are adequate. Although Sam doesn't have the sophistication to produce the needed argument, he does have all the evidence he needs. During the course of his short life, he has had innumerable perceptual experiences that led to true beliefs. Indeed, if little Sam is anything like the rest of us, then he has the evidence for a pretty good inductive argument that his grounds are indeed adequate, that given his perceptual experience of the apples, his belief is likely to be true. What Sam lacks, continues the internalist, is the ability to put his evidence in the form of an inductive argument. But he has the evidence, and a bit of Socratic inquiry would indeed show that his evidence is accessible to Sam.

Alston's response to this argument is that he doubts that "we store enough observational evidence to constitute adequate evidence for the thesis that normal sensory experience is an adequate ground for our beliefs about the physical environment."[23] This remark might seem a bit puzzling. Clearly, Alston does not object to the thesis itself—that normal sensory experience is an adequate ground. Reliabilists typically cite perceptual beliefs as a paradigm case of justified beliefs. Rather, his objection is that the *quantity* of evidence possessed by the typical agent is insufficient to justify the claim that perceptual experience constitutes an adequate ground. Unfortunately, Alston does not explain why he thinks the typical agent fails in this regard. In one construal, agents have an immense quantity of evidence at their disposal. Imagine that you and a friend are appropriately bored one evening. You decide to recount what you saw, whether mundane or magical, during the course of the day. Although you might not be able to recall all that you saw, you would certainly be able to cite *a lot of things*. During your protracted boredom, it is not improbable to suppose that you would be able to cite numerous cases of your perceptual experience resulting in true beliefs. (It is worth noting that Alston does not rely on circularity to reject the accessibility requirement.) The point here is not whether this is "enough observational evidence." Rather, the point is that Alston has provided us with no indication of how we might determine what counts as enough evidence. Failing such an indication, it is at least controversial whether Alston has shown that the adequacy of our grounds is largely inaccessible.

It might be possible, however, to interpret Alston as making the following sort of claim: The typical agent does not store enough observational evidence to believe justifiably that the perceptual experience is the result of the normal causal relations, which underlie perception. This seems at least consistent with Alston's general view. He argues, recall, that the *adequacy* or the truth-conduciveness of our grounds is not generally accessible. For example, Sam's belief that there are apples in the bowl is the result of a perceptual experience. But Sam may not have sufficient evidence that the perceptual experience is the result of the normal causal relations that are constitutive of perception. If Sam does not have access to this fact, then Sam does not have access to the likely truth of his belief.

An advantage of interpreting Alston in this way is that it explains his view that there is an inescapable externalist component in an acceptable account of justification. Moreover, we might make one further note on Alston's behalf. Some internalists think it is quite difficult to show that an agent's grounds are indeed adequate. That is, it is difficult for an agent to have access to the fact that the supporting reasons do indeed support the likely truth of the agent's beliefs.[24] Now, this is not a minor concession on the part of internalists. Suppose for a moment that an acceptable theory of justification must account for the "truth connection." That is, suppose that a necessary condition of justified belief is that the belief is likely to be true. In Alston's terminology, this is the requirement that a belief have adequate grounds. Now, if having adequate grounds is a condition of justified belief, and if the adequacy of one's grounds are not cognitively accessible, then there is a significant feature of justification that is not purely internalist.[25]

Alston recognizes that there are two, sometimes contrary features of a theory of justified belief. He attempts to accommodate both the thought that agents themselves have access to the reasons for their beliefs and the thought that justification has an intimate connection to truth or likely truth. Alston denies that a theory of justification can be completely internalist, because he claims that we do not generally have access to the adequacy of the grounds of our beliefs. That is, because likely truth is a condition of justification, and because likely truth is in some sense independent of the agent's beliefs, it is hard to see how the *actual* likely truth of a belief is something accessible to the agent. The likely truth of a belief seems to depend on facts that simply may not be in the agent's possession or accessible to the agent.

Sosa's Virtue Perspectivism[26]

Ernest Sosa recognizes the tension that exists in a theory of justification. He is aware of our natural tendency to hold that justification consists in an agent doing his or her cognitive best, relying on the available reasons. There is a seemingly unavoidable internalist dimension to justification. But Sosa also recognizes that there is an externalist dimension, a dimension he thinks is manifested in our conception of knowledge as justified true belief. This externalist dimension is, of course, the by-now familiar thought that justification must be connected to truth. Sosa attempts to resolve the tension by distinguishing between the justification of a belief and its *aptness* and by distinguishing between animal knowledge and reflective knowledge.

Sosa's theory is a particular version of **virtue epistemology.** Virtue epistemology holds that our beliefs are justified, or instances of knowledge, if they exhibit or manifest certain intellectual virtues. More generally, justification or knowledge arises as the result of certain character traits, what we might call, in this case, intellectual traits. Virtue epistemologists tend to think of justified beliefs as depending on intellectual virtues or traits, rather than depending on whether the belief satisfies a certain principle or rule.

We might try to motivate Sosa's view in this way: Humans have certain cognitive capacities or faculties, some of which enable us to cope with our environment. Perception is such a capacity, as are memory and deductive reasoning. But we might also think of wishful thinking or daydreaming as capacities that humans have. In one sense, even these latter capacities help us cope with our environment. They may make, for example, the routine seem less dreary. Sosa has in mind, however, capacities that enable us to cope effectively with the world around us—specifically, capacities that enable us to form a greater preponderance of true rather than false beliefs. Thus, Sosa is interested in those faculties or abilities that are appropriately related to truth. A capacity is intellectually virtuous if and only if it enables us to acquire more true than false beliefs. Perception is intellectually virtuous because, as a result of its exercise, we form more true beliefs than false beliefs about the visual, auditory, gustatory, olfactory, and tactile properties of our world.

Compare such abilities, for a moment, with the skills and abilities of a talented athlete. A baseball player, using the appropriate technique, is able to bunt the ball so that a runner is advanced. We call it a "good bunt." A diver performs a certain dive, exhibiting an appropriate form or technique, resulting in what we again call a "good dive." We *praise* the proper use of skill and ability. Similarly, we might be inclined to praise the proper use of intellectual skill or abilities. As a result of an agent's proper use of a capacity or ability, we might want to say that the agent has a "good belief." It is a good belief by virtue of its arising from the proper use of a capacity. Of course, the term we have been using for such beliefs is "justified." There is a sense, then, in which justified beliefs arise as a result of the proper use of those cognitive capacities that are attuned to the truth. Moreover, when these cognitive faculties function properly, they can yield beliefs that are instances of knowledge.

As we have noted, internalists might balk at calling beliefs "justified" simply because they are the product of certain faculties. Sosa recognizes this. Still, he insists that there is something epistemically praiseworthy about such beliefs. And there is something right about this. Sara has the visual experience of a sugar bowl in front of her, acquires the belief "There is the sugar," and reaches for the spoon. Now, this is just what we want vision to do for us; there is something right about Sara's belief. Or as Sosa remarks, Sara's perceptual belief is *appropriate* or *apt*. Given the environment, given the particular faculty, vision, that Sara used, she acquired an entirely appropriate belief. *Apt beliefs* are beliefs that result from a particular truth-producing faculty. Sosa's definition is actually a bit more complicated than this. He holds that the truth-producing character of a faculty is relative to a

Do Externalists Change the Subject?

One objection sometimes raised against externalism is that it changes the subject and nature of the traditional epistemological enterprise. As we saw in the Introduction, one view of the traditional epistemological project is to decide whether we ever have good reason to think our empirical beliefs are true and to explain why the reasons are good reasons. Now, this view is conceived as fundamentally internalist. Moreover, in this traditional picture, we cannot appeal to the success or proper functioning of our belief-forming mechanisms until we have given some reason for thinking that those mechanisms are reliable. After all, in the traditional picture, the challenge of the skeptic precludes such an appeal. As we have seen in previous chapters, it is not unusual for externalists to admit that they are adopting a different notion of justification and knowledge. Recently, however, it has been argued that a different reading of the tradition is possible—for example, that there are externalist strains in Hume. Indeed, it is not unusual in philosophy for advocates of a revisionary view to return to historical sources to find foreshadowings of their view. (See "For Further Study.")

certain environment, in particular, the normal environment for the faculty.[27] In this sense, aptness depends on the context or the environment. Some faculties are suited to some environments while others are not. There is a perspectival character to aptness; hence, we see why Sosa thinks of his view as virtue perspectivism. To put this in terms we have seen before, Sosa thinks of apt beliefs as those arising from reliable cognitive processes, which are operating in their normal environment. Aptness is an external feature of beliefs, a feature that arises as a result of connections between beliefs.

Those favorably disposed to internalism might wish to voice the following complaint: We were hoping for a theory of epistemic justification, but we have instead a theory of *aptness*. Recall that internalism is partly motivated by the idea that one must have reasons for believing. Beliefs derive their justification from their connections to other beliefs, or at least to other cognitively accessible states of the agent. Internalists frequently worry that reliabilism holds that beliefs are justified, despite the agent's lack of beliefs about the reliability of the process. As we have seen, Sosa is inclined to agree with reliabilism that there is something *epistemically appropriate* about beliefs formed by the right faculties or abilities. Sosa's response to pure internalism is that there are various ways for a belief to be apt, and one way is being justified. Justification is thus a species of aptness.

Sosa concedes that justification is an internalist notion, but it is nonetheless connected to intellectual virtue and depends on such virtue. Thus, the basic notion, for Sosa, is aptness. Aptness is what a belief must have for the belief to qualify as knowledge (in addition to being true and un-Gettierized, of course). In holding that aptness is the basic notion, Sosa thus suggests that justification may not be the fundamental epistemological notion that we have always thought.[28]

Justification, according to Sosa, depends on an agent's awareness of or beliefs about the source of a particular belief. Recall Sara's apt belief about the sugar bowl. The aptness of the belief is independent of Sara's other beliefs. But she might also become aware that this belief is the result of a capacity of hers that is particularly trustworthy. Now, if Sara believes that her visual capacity is trustworthy and that it is operating in a normal environment, then these other beliefs support her belief about the sugar bowl. Beliefs supported by other beliefs are justified beliefs. Sosa suggests that we come to recognize a capacity as trustworthy by a kind of induction. We are aware that over a period of time, a certain faculty or ability, when used in a certain environment, produces more true than false beliefs. In this regard, Sosa seems to disagree with Alston. According to Sosa, we have the ability to become aware of the source of our beliefs. He refers to this as our *perspective* on the source of our beliefs.

Sosa thus clearly holds that justification is internalist. Not only does it require a connection to other beliefs that one has, but it also requires that the agent be aware of this connection. In this sense, Sosa's perspectivism is committed to a type of accessibility requirement for justification. But it should also be clear that Sosa thinks that it is the aptness of our beliefs that lies at the bottom of justification. Justification comes about only because we recognize that our beliefs come from the *right kind of source.* Having the right source constitutes the aptness of a belief.

The distinction between aptness and justification gives rise to a further distinction between **animal knowledge** and **reflective knowledge.** Animal knowledge is our immediate, unreflective, and direct response to our environment.[29] Sara sees the sugar bowl; without thinking, she immediately forms the belief that there is the sugar. The very name suggests that it requires no thought. It is merely the automatic, discriminative response of a capacity to certain features of the environment. (To count as knowledge, these beliefs must, of course, satisfy the other necessary conditions of knowledge.) Reflective knowledge, however, requires an understanding of the place of the belief. Understanding the place of the belief means understanding both the source of the belief and its connection to our other beliefs. Sosa also characterizes reflective knowledge as believing out of virtue and being aware that one is doing so.[30] Both animal and reflective knowledge have their source in the proper exercise of generally truth-producing faculties. As with the notion of justification, reflective knowledge requires something more on the part of the agent. The agent must recognize that the belief arises from a source, operating in its proper environment, and that the source is indeed a virtuous source. With reflective knowledge, belief is not only apt but also justified. For example, suppose that Sam and his young son, Junior, both see an apple on the table. Now, Junior has animal knowledge that there is an apple, but he is too young to appreciate the source of his belief. He simply sees apples, grabs them, and eats them. Still, his belief is apt; it is the appropriate belief for him to have, given his environment. Sam, on the other hand, is aware of why he believes that there is an apple. In response to Sara's question about whether Sam is sure that there is an apple left for Junior's lunch, Sam confidently replies that he is indeed *looking* at the apple this very moment. Sam possesses an understanding of the location of his belief in his overall cognitive perspective. Thus, Sam's belief is not only apt but also justified. Moreover, Sam *reflectively* knows that there is an apple on the table by virtue of the fact that his belief is justified. Reflective knowledge thus evidently has an internalist component, which derives from the fact that justification is an internalist notion, in Sosa's view. Still, we must not overlook the fact that the fundamental notion for Sosa is that of apt belief. The possibility of reflective knowledge and justification depends on the fact that we have abilities or faculties that are especially suited to producing true beliefs.

At this point, we might consider why Sosa adopts the language of virtue, rather than resting content with notion of reliable mechanisms operating under normal conditions. The Greek word for "virtue" suggests the idea of excellence in performing a function. Character traits, which we might be inclined to think of as virtues, enable humans to perform their function *as humans* well. Generosity, honesty, and courage are character traits that enable humans to be *good* humans. People who possess these virtues not only do what humans are supposed to do but in some sense do it well. Of course, this presupposes that we have some idea of what the goal or the aim of human nature is. Because we think we have some idea of what it is to be a good human, certain character traits are then picked out as contributing to a person's ability to attain the goal or the aim. Virtue makes it possible for a human to *do the right thing*.

Sosa is particularly interested in *intellectual virtues,* or those traits or abilities that enable humans to perform well their intellectual functions. Again, to identify these traits, we must have some idea of the goal of our intellectual abilities or capacities. Sosa shares the widely held view that the goal of our intellectual capacities is obtaining true beliefs. The *virtuous* capacities, then, are those that enable humans to perform well their intellectual function. Capacities or abilities that routinely produce true beliefs contribute to humans attaining their intellectual goal. The intellectual virtues don't so much let humans do the right thing as *believe the right thing*.

Somewhat speculatively, we might suggest that talk of intellectual virtue has this advantage over talk of reliable mechanisms. Although Sosa does characterize certain beliefs as apt, as mere animal responses to our environment, there is nonetheless the suggestion that our unreflective responses are what we are *supposed* to believe. Given that we have these kinds of capacities and abilities—perception, memory, reasoning, and so on—there are certain kinds of belief that we *ought* to have in certain situations. This is the best we can cognitively do under the circumstances. More importantly, this provides the basis for a natural extension to cases of justified belief or reflective knowledge. Sosa suggests at one point that reflective justification is our best intellectual procedure.[31] Humans have an ability to reflect on the source of their beliefs and on the trustworthiness of that source, and to revise or accept beliefs accordingly. Humans have the ability to assess whether their beliefs make sense in light of their other beliefs. Sosa wagers that this reflective ability, like our more animal, unreflective abilities, helps us to make the best use of our cognitive faculties, helps us to believe the right thing. And the right thing, of course, is that which is likely to be true.

PROSPECTS FOR RECONCILIATION

The hope, evidenced in a view like Sosa's, is that internalism and externalism might be united in a single theory. And there may be reason for optimism here. The source of this optimism can be traced to the notion of cognitive accessibility. Not only internalists but also some theorists drawn to externalism allow a role to cognitive accessibility. Thus, we saw that Alston and Sosa think that the accessibility of an agent's reasons is a plausible constraint on a theory of justification. The cognitive accessibility of an agent's reasons might then be common ground between externalism and internalism.

Yet any theory that attempts to unite two often contrary themes must inevitably count one as more basic than another. BonJour and Lehrer, recall, acknowledge a kind of reliability at work in our cognitive endeavors. But for them, reliability plays an epistemic role only because we have reason for believing that certain belief types are generally reliable. Internalist notions count as basic for them. Someone like Sosa, however, holds the externalist notion of aptness to be the primary notion. Although reflective justification is our best intellectual procedure, it nonetheless depends on the initial aptness of at least some of our beliefs. We can easily imagine BonJour and Lehrer objecting that any belief has positive epistemic status only if it is appropriately related to our other beliefs. The dispute, then, seems to be over which aspect of justification is basic, the internalist or the externalist.

The source of the dispute is hinted at in Lehrer and is somewhat more explicit in Sosa. Richard Foley is quite explicit about the source of the dispute; moreover, he is somewhat pessimistic about our chances of resolving it. Foley suggests that we might view epistemology as either of two projects. We might view it as the epistemology of knowledge. If we pursue this approach, we will tend to emphasize such things as reliability or proper cognitive functioning.[32] We will tend to emphasize aspects of cognitive endeavors that seem to provide some assurance of the truth or likely truth of our beliefs. Interest in an epistemology of knowledge will then naturally draw us toward externalism. We may, however, pursue a different project, one that Foley calls "egocentric epistemology." The focus of egocentric epistemology is the rationality of belief. More importantly, the goal of rational belief is not truth, but that beliefs make sense from an agent's point of view. Egocentric epistemology is motivated by the thought that our beliefs must be reasonable, given our other beliefs. In this sense, egocentric epistemology is a type of internalism.

Foley's pessimism about reconciling these two projects is evident in his claim that no single notion of rational or justified belief can unite these two projects. This, Foley claims, is the lesson of Descartes and epistemology's subsequent skirmishes with skepticism.[33] We are forced to conclude that the internal rationality or justification of our beliefs will not vouchsafe the truth of our beliefs. We might interpret this in the following way: On the one hand, we can begin with the idea that we are already connected to the world, that we are out there in the world, and that our natural cognitive response is the acquisition of true beliefs. The epistemologist's task is specifying the appropriate conditions that enhance our acquisition of true beliefs. The epistemologist attempts to specify the *external* conditions that must be satisfied by any epistemically praiseworthy belief. On the other hand, we might begin with the idea that we start in here, with our beliefs, and ask to what extent these beliefs, as a system, make sense. Now, what we simply *cannot* do, according to Foley, is start *in here* and arrive *out there*. There is no process that will simultaneously show us that our beliefs make sense, that they fit together, and that they are very likely to be true. We are thus faced with an epistemological choice. To put it bluntly, in Foley's view, we might focus on justification or we might focus on knowledge. The former will lead to more internalist theories; the way of the latter is the way of externalism. Of course, the internalist (and the traditionalist) will want to claim that it is not so easy to divide up the epistemological landscape. They will claim that externalists are rejecting the justification condition of knowledge, at least as that condition is traditionally conceived.

Externalists, however, are undeterred. They think that there is indeed something significant to the epistemological project, even if that project abandons some of its more traditional roots. Indeed, externalists are inclined to think that there is philosophical value in pursuing a scientific study of the mind.[34] Externalism thus leads to the temptation to see what becomes of epistemology in a more naturalistic setting. The attempt not only to externalize epistemology but also to *naturalize* epistemology is the concern of the next chapter.

Key Concepts

Animal versus reflective knowledge

Cognitive accessibility of reasons

Deontological theories of justification

Metaepistemology

Virtue epistemology

Review Questions

1. Can you explain how the concept of justification motivates both externalist and internalist theories of justification?

2. What are the principal criticisms of internalist theories that hold that epistemic responsibility is a condition of justified belief?

3. What is the difference between weak and strong cognitive accessibility?

4. Must internalists accept the idea that agents must have access to the causal relations that underlie a belief? Explain.

5. Why does Alston think that a theory of justification should have an internalist feature? Why does he think that a theory of justification must have an externalist feature?

6. What is the difference between apt and justified belief, according to Sosa? What is your assessment of Sosa's attempt to reconcile internalist and externalist features?

For Further Study

William Alston devotes considerable attention to the issue of externalism in *Epistemic Justification* (Ithaca, NY: Cornell University Press, 1989), Part III. Robert Audi also treats the issue extensively in various essays in *The Structure of Justification* (New York: Cambridge University Press, 1993). In *Blind Realism* (Lanham, MD: Rowman & Littlefield, 1992), Chap. 2, Robert Almeder presents a sustained defense of internalism, considering in detail arguments by Alvin Goldman and William Alston. Frederick F. Schmitt's *Knowledge and Belief* (London: Routledge, 1992) is a book-length treatment of the internalism/externalism controversy. Schmitt defends an externalist view; in Chaps. 4 and 5, he argues against internalism. Interestingly, Schmitt also argues that externalism is not simply a contemporary development, but that externalist concerns are evidenced in the views of Descartes and Hume. In "The Internalism/Externalism Controversy," in James Tomberlin, ed., *Philosophical Perspectives 2,*

Epistemology (Atascadero, CA: Ridgeview Press, 1988), pp. 443–459, Richard Fumerton argues that the key issue between internalists and externalists is whether epistemic terms are reducible to purely causal notions. Fumerton elaborates on these and other issues in *Metaepistemology and Skepticism* (Lanham, MD: Rowman & Littlefield, 1995). Ernest Sosa's *Knowledge in Perspective: Selected Essays in Epistemology* (New York: Cambridge University Press, 1991) contains the essays referred to in this chapter, as well as a number of other essays on epistemology. See also Linda Zagzebski, *Virtues of the Mind: An Inquiry into the Nature of Virtue and the Ethical Foundations of Knowledge* (New York: Cambridge University Press, 1996).

Of course, one of the classical elaborations and defenses of externalism is Alvin Goldman, *Epistemology and Cognition* (Cambridge, MA: Harvard University Press, 1986), esp. Chaps. 3–5. Laurence BonJour's *The Structure of Empirical Knowledge* (Cambridge, MA: Harvard University Press, 1985) is a sustained defense of coherentist internalism; Chap. 4 provides detailed consideration of arguments for and against externalism. Keith Lehrer also has long defended the virtues of coherentist internalism. See his recent *Self-Trust: A Study of Reason, Knowledge and Autonomy* (New York: Oxford University Press, 1997), esp. Chaps. 1–3, and "Coherence and the Truth Connection: A Reply to My Critics," in John Bender, ed., *The Current State of the Coherence Theory* (Dordrecht: Kluwer Academic Publishers, 1989), pp. 253–275.

Notes

1. Roderick Chisholm, *Theory of Knowledge,* 2nd ed. (Englewood Cliffs, NJ: Prentice-Hall, 1977), p. 14.
2. Frederick Schmitt argues against such a connection. At least he doubts that epistemic responsibility can be used to motivate *perspectival internalism,* the view that a belief is justified if and only if it is sanctioned by the agent's cognitive perspective, including the agent's views about what counts as a justified belief. See his *Knowledge and Belief* (London: Routledge, 1992), Chap. 5. See also Hilary Kornblith, "Justified Belief and Epistemically Responsible Action," *Philosophical Review* 92 (1983): pp. 33–48.
3. Robert Audi's theory of justification seems to eschew a commitment to epistemic responsibility, although it is clearly internalist on other grounds. See, for example, "Justification, Truth, and Reliability," in Audi, *The Structure of Justification* (New York: Cambridge University Press, 1993), pp. 299–321.
4. See fn. 2.
5. William Alston, "What's Wrong with Immediate Knowledge?" in Alston, *Epistemic Justification* (Ithaca, NY: Cornell University Press, 1989), p. 77.
6. The phrase is due to Frederick Schmitt.
7. Richard Feldman suggests this line in "Epistemic Obligation," in James Tomberlin, ed., *Philosophical Perspectives 2, Epistemology* (Atascadero, CA: Ridgeview Press, 1988), pp. 240ff. The mortgage example in the text is Feldman's.
8. William Alston, "Concepts of Epistemic Justification," in Alston, *Epistemic Justification,* p. 95. See also p. 201.
9. Feldman, "Epistemic Obligation," p. 254.
10. Chisholm, *Theory of Knowledge,* p. 17.
11. Audi's foundationalism seems to fall into this category. Also see Timothy J. McGrew, *The Foundations of Knowledge* (Lanham, MD: Littlefield Adams, 1995); still another example seems to be the view advocated by Richard Fumerton in *Metaepistemology and Skepticism* (Lanham, MD: Rowman & Littlefield, 1995).
12. Earl Conee and Richard Feldman, "Evidentialism," *Philosophical Studies* 17 (1985): 15.
13. Recall that in Chapter Three, we saw Armstrong make a similar claim.
14. The notion of "dispositional accessibility" is from Robert Audi, "Causalist Internalism," in Audi, *The Structure of Justification,* p. 343. Audi counts cases in which the reasons are luminous as *occurrently accessible.*
15. Audi suggests this line in "Causalist Internalism," p. 345.

16. There is, of course, a limit to what internalists should allow as counting as an alternative reason. If Sara simply says that she believes the theorem but cannot recall any reason why, accessibility internalists may want to resist the claim that Sara is justified. Externalists would count such a case as a case of justified belief.

17. Earl Conee, "The Basic Nature of Epistemic Justification," *Monist* 71 (1988): 389–404. See esp. p. 401.

18. Audi, "Causalist Internalism," pp. 336–349.

19. Audi, "Causalist Internalism." See esp. pp. 336–340.

20. See William Alston, "An Internalist Externalism," in Alston, *Epistemic Justification,* pp. 227–245.

21. Alston, "An Internalist Externalism," pp. 228–229.

22. See Robert Almeder, *Blind Realism* (Lanham, MD: Rowman & Littlefield, 1992), Chap. 2. On pp. 83ff, Almeder argues specifically against Alston's claim that showing one is justified is not necessary for being justified.

23. Alston, "An Internalist Externalism," p. 241.

24. For example, see Fumerton, *Metaepistemology and Skepticism,* Chap. 7.

25. Of course, an internalist like BonJour does think we can provide something of an argument that the grounds of belief are indeed adequate.

26. Ernest Sosa's virtue theory is elaborated in a number of essays contained in *Knowledge in Perspective* (New York: Cambridge University Press, 1991). See esp. Part IV.

27. Sosa, *Knowledge in Perspective,* p. 289.

28. Sosa, *Knowledge in Perspective,* p. 255.

29. Sosa, *Knowledge in Perspective,* p. 240.

30. Sosa, *Knowledge in Perspective,* p. 278.

31. Sosa, *Knowledge in Perspective,* p. 291.

32. Richard Foley, *Working Without a Net* (Oxford: Oxford University Press, 1993), p. 87.

33. Foley, *Working Without a Net,* p. 85.

34. See, for example, Hilary Kornblith, "Naturalism: Both Metaphysical and Epistemological," in Peter A. French et al., eds., *Midwest Studies in Philosophy, Vol. XIX* (Notre Dame, IN: University of Notre Dame Press, 1994), pp. 39–52.

Naturalized Epistemology

Presumably, the natural sciences are a rich source of justified beliefs, and if we are duly circumspect, of knowledge as well. We know, for example, that earthquakes are the result of the activity of various geologic plates at neutral plate boundaries and that "genes are coded sequences of smaller molecules arrayed along a segment of a much larger molecule called DNA."[1] For many of us, science not only provides the model for the acquisition and extension of our knowledge but also tells us what types of things exist. Genes and molecules are real; phlogiston and caloric are not. We are confident that science vouchsafes even more mundane examples of knowledge—for example, that the traffic light is red. As scientific novices, we might not have the scientific explanation, but someone, somewhere could explain how it is that we come by the knowledge, for example, that the light is red. Even the television sports commentator John Madden is confident that there is a scientific explanation as to why the bigger football player exerts a greater force than the smaller player does. The thought that all of our knowledge and justified beliefs are ultimately linked to science is pervasive, even if controversial. In such a view, all knowledge is natural knowledge. Any legitimate theory that claims to identify some property, some object, or some state of affairs must explain how that property, object, or state of affairs is linked to nature. *Genuine* properties or states of affairs ultimately are *natural* states of affairs or properties.

Given that we often assume this naturalistic background, we might wonder about the status of epistemology. Epistemological theories aim in part to identify the nature of certain properties or certain states of affairs. Those theories specify the conditions under which beliefs have the property of being justified or the conditions under which an agent knows a particular proposition. In the naturalistic view, the epistemic property of being justified is a genuine property only if we can show that it has a natural source, that justification is rooted in natural properties. Thus, if we want an adequate epistemology, we had better keep an eye on how epistemic properties will eventually connect with natural properties. We had better keep an eye on one or more of the sciences so that we can see the most "natural" place to locate the connection between the epistemic and the natural. If epistemology is a legitimate enterprise, then it had best display its naturalistic credentials.

But there is a long tradition that sees epistemology as *independent* of the natural sciences, precisely because epistemology supplies the foundation or the grounding for our natural knowledge. Descartes, you may recall, sought to find a firm and lasting foundation for the sciences. He thought that we must first identify the epistemological principles that underlie and secure our cognitive endeavors. Until our epistemology is in place, looking to the sciences is a fool's errand. We must rely on our epistemology to show us which of the sciences provide us with knowledge and justified belief, and hence, which properties are the genuine natural properties.

It is a metaepistemological issue whether epistemology is best viewed as *naturalized* or in its more traditional guise. In any case, this chapter focuses on **naturalized epistemology.** Perhaps unfortunately, naturalized epistemology is like its more traditional cousin in that it has a number of variations, but our interest is confined to certain major themes. In particular, we identify three distinctive aspects or features of traditional epistemology: (a) the autonomy of epistemology, (b) the normative character of epistemology, and (c) the a priori character of epistemological claims. Naturalized epistemology might be characterized by its typical rejection of one or more of these features, and so we sketch the relevant features of naturalism, which motivate the rejection of traditional epistemology. We begin with the view of W. V. O. Quine, perhaps the most influential spokesman for naturalized epistemology. Then we consider different ways in which one might naturalize epistemology, as well as the likely responses of the more traditional epistemologist.

TRADITION AND NATURALISM

A Traditional Picture

The contours of traditional epistemology no doubt may be found in the writings of Plato, Aristotle, Descartes, Locke, Hume, Kant, and others. According to one epistemological tradition, reason enables us to identify or apprehend the content of our cognitive or epistemic goal. In some interpretations, for example, Plato holds that the *ideal* epistemic goal is apprehension of the interconnected system of truths about reality. A more modest epistemic goal might be seen in the *Phaedo,* that of attaining the most consistent and defensible set of beliefs. In previous chapters, we characterized the epistemic goal as obtaining truth and avoiding error. Whatever the goal, it is reason that enables us to identify it. But merely having a goal, without a way to get there, is not much good. The traditional conception of the epistemological enterprise holds that reason enables us to articulate a set of principles—a methodology—that serves a dual role. The methodology first provides a standard for the evaluation of our beliefs. We can evaluate our beliefs as reasonable and justified, as instances of knowledge, or, if they do not measure up, as irrational or unjustified. The methodology or set of principles is simply the content of epistemological theories encountered in previous chapters. Again, it is of limited use to know that our beliefs do not measure up if we have no way of fixing or revising them. Thus, the methodology further articulates how we might revise our beliefs so as to align them with our epistemic goal. One example of this is Descartes's method of doubt, which not only sets a goal but provides a procedure for achieving that goal. Hume's more dramatic exhortation to commit to the flames any belief that is not traceable to an original impression or a description of the relation between ideas is another example. Interestingly, traditional epistemology also holds that we have the resources to justify the methodology. Skirmishes with the skeptic are just such attempts to legitimate, to defend the preferred methodology.

Three features of this traditional picture are of interest in this chapter. First, knowledge of the principles that guide belief evaluation and revision is a priori knowledge. We do not arrive at these principles by means of empirical investigation (although we may arrive at it by reflection on particular instances of knowledge or justification, as Chisholm suggests[2]).

Second, traditional epistemology is essentially normative. The identification of goals and methods, which counsel us as to how we might attain the goal, provides a standard or norm by which we evaluate our beliefs and belief-forming strategies. Epistemology is thus thought to differ from empirical studies, whose aim is primarily *descriptive*. Empirical studies aim to identify the facts or the way things are and to provide us with theories that explain the connections between facts. Cognitive psychology, for example, may tell us *how* we come to have certain beliefs. Traditional epistemology's normative character is less concerned with the how and more concerned with what we *ought* to believe.

Third, traditional epistemology is **autonomous;** it is an independent discipline. Both the subject matter and the methodology of epistemology are independent of progress in the empirical sciences. Although he knew much of the science of his day, Descartes conducted his meditations independent of that science. If epistemology is independent of the sciences, then his injunction to accept as instances of knowledge only indubitable beliefs is not imperiled by the development of quantum theory or progress in the sociology of knowledge.

The picture of traditional epistemology may not fit any one philosopher exactly. But naturalized epistemology arose as a reaction to something very much like this picture. In particular, naturalized epistemology rejects the claim that epistemology is independent, in subject matter and method, of the empirical sciences. Closely allied with the rejection of the independence of epistemology, many proponents of naturalized epistemology also doubt the extent to which our knowledge of epistemological principles is a priori. Most, however, accept that epistemology is normative in character. One of the issues at the center of debate about naturalized epistemology is the reconciliation of the naturalistic character of epistemology with its normative character. Before looking more closely at particular naturalized epistemologies, we need to outline some of the main features of naturalism.

Naturalism and Epistemology

Naturalism holds two central doctrines, one ontological and one epistemological.[3] The ontological doctrine, a doctrine about what exists, holds that everything that exists is natural. Objects and their properties are real precisely to the extent that they are natural objects or properties. But this does not yet tell us which objects and properties are the natural ones. Thus, the epistemological doctrine claims that the natural is whatever figures in the explanations and theories offered by the natural sciences. Quine, for example, claims that naturalism is "the recognition that it is within science itself, and not in some prior philosophy, that reality is to be identified and described."[4] We recognize, discover, or identify what is natural by means of the methods of the natural sciences, which include observation, hypothesis and prediction, and experimentation. What is distinctive about these methods is that they are empirical, or dependent on our experience. Notice that this view of the acceptable methods of inquiry might seem to rule out the sort of inquiry undertaken by Descartes in the *Meditations*, because this type of inquiry seems prior to or independent of experience. In this sense, naturalized epistemology is incompatible with the idea that epistemological principles can be arrived at by means of a priori reasoning. Of more importance for us at the moment, natural science is characterized by its method. Natural objects and properties are thus those susceptible of study or investigation by the scientific method.

There are two ways in which an object or property might be susceptible to scientific methods, and hence count as a natural object or property. An object or property might be *reducible* to clearly natural objects or properties, or the object or property might *supervene* on clearly natural objects or properties. Let us suppose for a moment that clearly natural objects or properties are those countenanced by physics, chemistry, biology, and other natural sciences, such as geology or astronomy. Quarks and their flavors are natural, as are the earth's crust and supernovas.

Reducibility and supervenience are two different relationships between groups of objects and properties. **Reduction** is a very strong relationship,

Facts and Values

Philosophers have sometimes distinguished between facts and values, suggesting that the former, but not the latter, are the province of the sciences. Judgments about facts are thought to describe the way things are. But evaluative judgments, or judgments about the value of something, express the way things ought to be or that a certain thing satisfies some standard of what ought to be. For example, calling a sculpture a work of art is thought, at least by some, to be an evaluative judgment. The significant feature of the distinction is that there are no factual judgments that "add up to" the judgment that the sculpture is a work of art. Factual and evaluative judgments are different in kind, according to this view.

Analogously, it might be thought that epistemology aims to explain the conditions for evaluative judgments, or judgments about certain epistemic properties, such as being justified in believing. In one sense, the topic of this chapter is whether the evaluative judgments of the epistemologist can be explained in terms of some set of factual judgments.

in that it identifies a property or object with other, underlying natural properties or objects. A property or object is reducible if it can be *identified* with certain other properties or objects. Water, for example, is simply H_2O. Because hydrogen and oxygen are paradigmatically natural objects, so, too, is water, in that it is reducible to those natural objects. As another example, consider rainbows. Rainbows are natural objects because they can be identified with certain properties of light, specifically light's refractory properties. The significance of this for naturalized epistemology is that one way to show that epistemic properties are natural properties is to show how they are reducible to, say, biological properties. Very loosely, reducibility requires that there is an exact correspondence between one group of objects or properties and another. (This correspondence is expressed in what are called "bridge laws," laws that describe the connection between different domains or groups.)

It is not always a simple matter to find criteria that would enable us to reduce one domain to another. Indeed, it can be a quite complicated, if not intractable, process. Thus, some naturalized epistemologists think that epistemic properties are natural not because they are reducible to other natural properties, but because epistemic properties supervene on natural properties. This **supervenience** relation is a weaker relation than that of reduction; supervenience does not require laws connecting one domain to another. We can work with an informal characterization of supervenience. Suppose epistemic justification is a supervenient property. There are then certain other underlying properties, called base properties, associated with justification. The relevant base property might be something like being a reliable indicator, being some feature of the environment, or being the product of a certain type of cognitive process. Now, anything that has the identified base properties also has the property of justification. Moreover, if the property of justification is lost or changes, it is because of some change in the base properties. Very informally, then, epistemic properties are intimately tied to certain natural properties, but they are not identified with those properties.

Ernest Sosa provides a somewhat more formal definition of the supervenience of normative properties. Suppose that some A has a normative property P. There is then some non-normative or nonevaluative base property Q such that (a) A has Q, and (b) necessarily, whatever has Q has P.[5] A belief, then, has the property of justification by virtue of the belief having other non-normative or nonevaluative base properties. Anything that has the relevant base properties will also have the property of justification. Thus, one view of the task of the naturalized epistemologist is to identify the natural properties on which epistemic properties supervene.

We can now understand naturalized epistemologists' reaction to the three features characteristic of traditional epistemology noted previously. Clearly, naturalized epistemology rejects the ontological independence of epistemology. There are no epistemic properties that are neither reducible to nor supervenient on natural properties. About the methodological independence of epistemology, as we will see, there is somewhat more controversy. Some consider the a priori methods of traditional epistemology to be objectionable, because such methods appear at odds with the empirical character of the scientific method. There is, however, wide agreement that any naturalization of epistemology must retain the normative character of epistemology. How to retain the normative character is still more controversial, as we will see with Quine's proposed naturalization of epistemology.

QUINE'S VIEW OF NATURALIZED EPISTEMOLOGY

Although there are other historical and conceptual sources, Quine's view of naturalized epistemology represents the seminal framework for naturalized epistemology.[6] Quine accepts something very much like the picture of traditional epistemology just sketched. In a sense, Quine is motivated by the same questions that have historically motivated traditional epistemological theories. He sees that we have a very sophisticated and complicated understanding of the world around us, an understanding that nonetheless grew from quite ordinary and commonsense beginnings. Quine, too, wants to understand the sense in which our beliefs about the world are justified, although some of his critics do not think that he is interested in this issue.

Quine, however, regards *the way in which* traditional epistemology attempts to justify our beliefs about the world as either a failed or a moribund project. It is in part because of the *failure* of traditional epistemology that Quine thinks we ought to turn to a naturalized epistemology. Within a naturalized epistemology, we can see the sense in which our beliefs about the world are justified. It is best to begin with a brief sketch of Quine's view of the failure of traditional epistemology.

First Philosophy

As Quine understands traditional epistemology, it is engaged in what he calls *first philosophy*. Independently of the knowledge afforded us by the sciences, the traditional epistemologist attempts to identify and defend the principles by which we might justify our beliefs about the world. The traditional epistemologist first attempts to identify those norms or principles that enable us to sort our beliefs about the world into those that are genuine instances of knowledge and those that are not. The traditional epistemologist then attempts to defend these principles as the *legitimate* principles of knowledge and justification. That is, the traditional epistemologist must answer any skeptical doubts. Why does Quine consider these two interrelated tasks to be *first* philosophy? In carrying out these tasks, the traditional epistemologist cannot rely on other beliefs about the world precisely because we do not know yet which empirical beliefs are trustworthy. Traditional epistemology is first philosophy because it is conceptually prior to the knowledge afforded us by our routine and scientific inquiries. We must first be in possession of the principles or methods that tell us which of our empirical beliefs we can trust. Remember, for example, that Descartes embarks on his epistemological meditations *in order to* put science on a firm and lasting foundation. Epistemology provides the principles that tell us which beliefs are genuinely scientific and which are mere pretenders. But the task is not complete until the principles themselves are legitimated or defended. This defense must also be completed independently of our beliefs about the world and without reliance on any of the empirical methods of science. The methods of the traditional epistemologist are, in this sense, a priori. Both tasks of traditional epistemology must be completed before we can turn our attention to the natural world. Epistemology must precede science; epistemology must come first.

But Quine rejects the notion of first philosophy, of an epistemology that precedes science. He rejects the idea that epistemology is logically or conceptually prior to science. In doing so, however, he does not reject the idea that we can identify and defend principles of justification and knowledge. Rather, he rejects the traditional epistemologist's view that these principles are *outside of and prior to science*. But let us begin with Quine's

Quine and the Rejection of the A Priori

In the next chapter, we will examine another of Quine's claims, which also figures as a motivating factor in his move toward naturalized epistemology. Quine argues that we cannot clearly separate the human contribution to our knowledge from the world's contribution. Very loosely, we cannot separate the information the world gives us from our way of thinking about or characterizing that information. For Quine, this has the consequence that our cognitive endeavors cannot begin a priori; we cannot begin with a first philosophy that is wholly independent of the world. The view that naturalized epistemology can easily do away with a commitment to the a priori is disputed, however. It is argued that if we do not have at least some a priori justification, then we can never have good reason to believe anything beyond what we can observe. (See "For Further Study.")

rejection of traditional epistemology's attempt to justify our beliefs about the world.

Traditional epistemology, according to Quine, unfortunately carries an insurmountable burden. In his view, traditional epistemology attempts to accomplish its aim within the framework of a strong form of foundationalism.[7] Thus, as Quine interprets it, traditional epistemology attempts first to identify infallible basic beliefs and then to show how we might infallibly derive our more complicated beliefs about the world from these basic beliefs. The typical starting point, the set of basic beliefs, is simply our infallible awareness of our own sensory impressions. From this awareness of sensory impressions, we are to deduce our more interesting beliefs about the world. That is, from "I have an impression of a reddish, roundish patch," we are to deduce "There is an apple in front of me." Now, even if we accomplish this epistemological feat, it is still a long way to "Hydrogen has one electron." Yet traditional epistemology can succeed only if we can deduce our more complicated beliefs about the world from our basic beliefs, beliefs about the contents of our minds. Like others, Quine thinks that neither rationalist nor empiricist can accomplish this. Epistemologists, of whatever persuasion, are unable to show that our beliefs about the world are derivable from our awareness of our sensory impressions. Traditional epistemology thus fails to show us the way from *in here,* in our minds, to *out there,* the natural world. Quine refers to the process of justifying our beliefs about the world on the basis of the contents of our mental states as *rational reconstruction.* Because the process of rational reconstruction shows no evident signs of life, Quine claims we are better off settling for replacing traditional epistemology with psychology. If we cannot identify and legitimate the principles that tell us what we *ought* to believe, then we should be content with knowing *how* we came to believe what we do in fact believe. "Better," Quine says, "to discover how science is in fact developed and learned than to fabricate a fictitious structure to a similar effect."[8] Despite this replacement, Quine claims, perhaps surprisingly, that epistemology, "or something like it," still continues. It is the sense of this "something like it" that is of interest.

The Normative Character of Naturalized Epistemology

There are three issues we might consider in order to understand whether we should follow Quine's injunction to adopt a new epistemology. First, as just noted, Quine identifies traditional epistemology with a strong form of foundationalism. It is the failure of foundationalism, classically conceived, that leads Quine to his preferred alternative, psychology. There are, however, several claims that might be distinguished here. Epistemology indeed aims at the identification and defense of principles of justification. A broad task of epistemology is to provide a principled means for discriminating justified from unjustified beliefs. But it is a quite different matter to insist that the only means of accomplishing this task is to adopt a strong or infallible foundationalism. We have seen throughout that not only are there less stringent forms of foundationalism, including neoclassical and modest versions, but there are also coherentist theories, which articulate and defend principles of justified belief. One could concede that the hope of the strong foundationalist is inevitably frustrated without also conceding that the hope of traditional epistemology in general is inevitably frustrated. To share with Descartes or Hume the hope of justifying our beliefs about the natural world is not simultaneously to share their view of *how* to justify our beliefs.

The second issue comes closer to what most worries Quine's critics. In an often cited passage, Quine summarizes his view of the connection between traditional and the new psychologized "epistemology":

> But I think at this point it may be more useful to say rather that epistemology still goes on, though in a new setting and a clarified status. Epistemology, or something like it, simply falls into place as a chapter of psychology and hence of natural science. It studies a natural phenomenon, viz., a physical human subject. This human subject is accorded a certain experimentally controlled input—certain patterns of irradiation in assorted frequencies for instance—and in the fullness of time the subject delivers as output a description of the three-dimensional external world and its history. The relation between the meager input and the torrential output is a relation that we are prompted to study for somewhat the same reasons that always prompted epistemology, namely, in order to see how evidence relates to theory, and in what ways one's theory of

nature transcends any available evidence. . . . But a conspicuous difference be-tween old epistemology and the epistemological enterprise in this new psycho-logical setting is that we can now make free use of empirical psychology.[9]

Because epistemic subjects are a natural phenomenon, just like any other animate creatures, we can study them just as we would the rest of the animal kingdom. The discipline that studies our representations, or our picture, of the world, rather than our biological or physical properties, is psychology. Quine further suggests the old and the new epistemology are prompted by much the same reasons—to see how theory relates to evi-dence. That is, both traditional and naturalized epistemology are motivated by the desire to understand the basis for our beliefs about the world.

Quine's rather sanguine identification of the motivation of the two proj-ects has met with less than universal approval. At the core of the dispute is Quine's apparent failure to recognize that epistemology is a fundamentally normative discipline while psychology is a descriptive enterprise. The claim is that "how theory relates to evidence" is understood in different ways by the two disciplines. Jaegwon Kim's reaction is typical. Kim insists that psy-chology studies the *causal* relation between the information provided by our senses and our consequent beliefs. Psychology describes the processes that lead from our initial sensory excitations to our beliefs. The causal story, which interests the naturalized epistemologist, is not the story of justified or reasonable belief. But the justificatory story is the interest of the traditional epistemologist.[10] Hume, for example, has an interesting theory about the *causes* of our beliefs about the natural world: Nature has deemed the ex-planation of our beliefs about the world too important an affair to leave to our meager abilities, so imagination fills in the cognitive gaps. But Hume insists that causal relations are not justificatory relations. *Knowing how* we come to believe what we do does not yet tell us that we *ought to believe* the way we do. In thus emphasizing the descriptive task of identifying the causal relations that underlie our beliefs, naturalized epistemology forsakes its normative ancestry. An epistemology, however, that is not essentially normative has no right to the name; naturalized epistemology fails to be epistemology because it fails to retain the normative dimension.

In Quine's defense, we might note that it is not quite true that science is a purely descriptive enterprise. Science, too, has its principles for distin-guishing legitimate from illegitimate claims. Indeed, science typically is identified with its *method,* its procedure for identifying acceptable hy-potheses. In Quine's view, naturalized epistemology retains its normative character insofar as, like any other branch of science, it is aimed at truth and understanding. The normative, in Quine's terms, is the "technology of truth-seeking." Quine might then be construed as claiming that the norms of naturalized epistemology have evolved in the same way as the norms of

Science Studies Science: The Strong Programme

Instead of thinking of the acquisition of knowledge and justified belief as a purely individual enterprise, some have turned to studying the dynamic interaction between members of a community that plays a causal role in the acquisition of knowledge. One such view in the sociology of knowledge is known as the Strong Programme. The aim of the Programme is to identify what scientific beliefs are held by a community, why such beliefs are held, and how those beliefs are defended and disseminated. Advocates of the Programme, who typically consider themselves naturalists, attempt to understand the actual social mechanisms and factors by which beliefs, both rational and irrational, are generated and sustained. Some critics maintain that the Programme is committed to the view that scientific knowledge is socially constructed rather than discovered. (See "For Further Study.")

other sciences, in response to the pressures of discovering the truth and increasing our predictive powers.

We can elaborate on this a bit more. Quine holds that psychology will identify the causal mechanisms that produce our beliefs about the natural world. While this appears to be a purely descriptive enterprise, Quine nonetheless has an interest in how we might evaluate our beliefs. More precisely, his interest lies in those beliefs that get us closer to the truth, and the evidence for greater proximity to the truth is enhanced predictability. Thus, a more appropriate characterization of naturalized epistemology is that it aims to identify the causal mechanisms that produce true beliefs, or beliefs that enhance our understanding of the natural world. Beliefs caused by our perceptual processes are to be preferred to beliefs caused by wishful thinking or astrology precisely to the extent that they contribute to our overall *scientific* picture of the world. We *ought* to accept beliefs formed as a result of perception because science shows us that perceptual beliefs are part of the natural order. Consequently, the normative character of naturalized epistemology derives from the normative character of science itself. If the objection to Quine's naturalized epistemology is that it is insufficiently normative, Quine seems to have a line of reply. The norms or principles for belief evaluation are simply the norms and principles accepted by science. Quine looks to science for the norms and principles of belief evaluation; he rejects traditional epistemology's view that the relevant norms and principles are independent of science. Identifying the standards for belief evaluation is, in Quine's view, part of the scientific process.

One might still object that Quine has resolved but half of the issue that confronts him. Traditional epistemology seeks not only to identify the norms or principles of justification but also to legitimize those very norms or principles. A significant part of the traditional epistemologist's task is to *defend* the principles of belief evaluation. In particular, the traditional epistemologist must answer various skeptical doubts. Now, the skeptic is not asking which belief-forming practices are reliable. The skeptic is not even asking for a scientific explanation of how we came by our belief-forming practices. Rather, the skeptic asks why we should believe that those practices are reliable or legitimate *in the first place*. Recall that Hume questions whether we can provide adequate justification for our inductive practices. Quine's turn to science for the norms that identify the appropriate belief-forming practices still leaves us to wonder what justification can be given for accepting those norms. For example, we now have a fairly detailed *causal* story of the formation of our perceptual beliefs. Together, various sciences provide us with a causal explanation of our perceptual beliefs. *Given or assuming that scientific background,* science even tells us that we should trust our perceptual beliefs. Quine is perhaps able to explain why naturalized epistemology is normative, but he has not explained why these norms, inherited from science generally, are themselves justified or acceptable. He has not explained why we should trust their scientific ancestry.

A fundamental difference between naturalized and traditional epistemology, as Quine conceives them, is revealed in his response to this matter. According to Quine, once we realize that the strong foundationalist projects an unreachable aim, "once we have stopped dreaming of deducing science from observations," we can apply science in responding to skeptical questions.[11] Elsewhere, Quine remarks that he is free to use inductive generalizations to justify induction because he rejects the notion that philosophy can provide us with the a priori justification of science. There is no first philosophy; there is only the philosophy that is continuous with science.[12] Rejecting the foundationalist's project thus leaves us with a *different* justificatory task. Responding to the skeptic is, in principle, no different from responding to a rival scientific theory. We may freely use all the empirical information and theory at our disposal. Significantly, Quine holds that "the skeptical challenge springs from science itself, and that in coping with it we are free to use scientific knowledge. The old epistemologist failed to recognize the strength of his position."[13]

There are two important aspects to this claim. First, all skeptical doubts are essentially scientific doubts. The skeptic, according to Quine, presupposes our generally scientific framework. The skeptic can offer a challenge only if he or she has already accepted our commonsense world of objects:

> Scepticism is an offshoot of science. The basis for scepticism is the awareness of illusion, the discovery that we must not always believe our eyes. Scepticism battens on mirages, on seemingly bent sticks in water, on rainbows, after-images, double images, dreams. But in what sense are these illusions? In the sense that they seem to be material objects which they in fact are not. Illusions are illusions only relative to a prior acceptance of genuine bodies with which to contrast them. . . . Rudimentary physical science, that is, common sense about bodies, is thus needed as a springboard for scepticism.[14]

Quine believes that scientific inquiry begins with our rudimentary commonsense inquiries—for example, "Can I cross this stream by walking across this fallen tree?" or "If I build my house here, can I reasonably expect that it will be safe from flooding?" In Quine's view, our most sophisticated cognitive claims—including scientific claims—begin with such ordinary commonsense inquiries. These commonsense inquiries take objects for granted. Now, we might later come to revise our beliefs about these physical objects, but this is precisely the fallibilistic attitude that we must adopt, says Quine. Still, the important point is that our knowledge begins with our assumption of the existence of physical objects. According to Quine, the skeptical challenge arises against the background of this assumption. Skeptical doubts about whether perception is a reliable source of knowledge presumes that we are sensing beings in the midst of a natural world not of our own making. The realization that skeptical doubts are scientific doubts thus allows the naturalized epistemologist to make free use of science, both in its commonsense and more theoretical guises, in responding to the skeptic.

For Quine, there is an important consequence of this line of thought: All justification is *scientific justification.* The rejection of traditional epistemology is the rejection of an unobtainable first philosophy. But when we reject first philosophy, we reject the idea that we can appeal to norms that are external to our natural cognitive inquiries. Our initial, mundane and commonsense inquiries are the source of our principles of belief evaluation. We can revise these principles, just as we revise our beliefs about the world. But what we cannot do is start from scratch. We cannot put aside all of our beliefs about the world or the principles of evaluation implicit in those beliefs. But this means, for Quine, that skeptic, scientist, and ordinary person alike must appeal only to scientific norms. There are no extra-scientific norms or principles to which we may appeal. Beliefs, hypotheses, theories, even methods and cognitive goals—all are justified by the extent to which they contribute to our understanding of the world.

We are now in a position to highlight the essential features of Quine's naturalized epistemology. Quine thinks that the task of deducing our beliefs about the world from basic beliefs has no hope of succeeding. In this sense, traditional epistemology must be abandoned, but we can still learn lessons from this failure. The beginnings of our empirical knowledge lie in our ordinary interaction with familiar objects and in our inquiries regarding those objects. These humble beginnings provide us not only with our initial beliefs about the natural world but also with the initial norms or principles for evaluating our beliefs. It is the extension and revision of these initial beliefs and norms that lead to the endeavor that we more commonly recognize as science. The crucial point for Quine is the recognition that while we may revise particular beliefs or particular norms, we cannot put in abeyance *all* of our beliefs and *all* of our principles of evaluation. Skeptical doubts may arise, but they arise *within* the general context of our inquiries. Indeed, skeptical doubts make sense only within the context of inquiry. We are thus free to respond to skeptical doubts with whatever information is at our disposal.

The Goal of Inquiry

Implicit in Quine's rejection of first philosophy and his consequent acceptance of naturalized epistemology is his conception of the goal of inquiry. In a brief passage, Quine suggests that normative epistemology is a technology, the "technology of truth-seeking, or in a more cautiously epistemological term, prediction."[15] Elsewhere, Quine suggests that the overarching goals of science are technology and understanding.[16] This yields a rather broad notion of the goal of inquiry. On the one hand, we are sometimes moved to inquire into the world around us simply for the sake of understanding. We want to know how and why the world works the way it does and how we can function in and represent that world. In more recognizably scientific contexts, the general goal of understanding may be refined to the goal of truth seeking. Our understanding is enhanced to the extent that we have true beliefs about the way the world works. Now, the clue that we have attained true beliefs is our enhanced ability to predict the kinds of experience we are likely to encounter. Rival beliefs are tested by the extent to which they allow us to anticipate that we will have certain experiences under certain conditions. This is no less true for policies of belief evaluation. Rival belief-forming policies are tested by the extent to which they legitimate classes of belief, which allow us to navigate the world in which we find ourselves. The task of the epistemologist—to identify and defend principles of belief evaluation—thus falls into place as part of science. But unlike Descartes, who desires to find the principles on which to *found* science, the Quinean naturalized epistemologist identifies the principles that arise from within our various cognitive and scientific endeavors. Quine thus claims that all our knowledge is natural knowledge, or more specifically, scientific knowledge, and naturalized epistemology is concerned with but a special branch of this knowledge.

The Goal of Inquiry: Normative and Natural

If Quine is right, then both the descriptive and the normative character of naturalized epistemology flow from science. This would seem to imply that the way in which we acquire our beliefs is the way in which we ought to acquire our beliefs. But we can spell out a bit more how this situation arises. Naturalized epistemology seeks to describe the processes by which we actually acquire our beliefs, or by which the "meager input" becomes the "torrential output." Not only our ordinary commonsense beliefs but our scientific beliefs as well are the products of these processes. One task of the naturalized epistemologist is then a clearly descriptive task. But according to Quine, naturalized epistemology also retains something of the normative character of the more traditional enterprise precisely to the extent that the methods governing science are the methods by which we acquire our beliefs. The methods of science, of course, are aimed at the acquisition of true beliefs, because this is the goal of inquiry.

Quine thus seems to be suggesting that how we actually acquire our beliefs is also the way we ought to acquire our beliefs. Consider, for example, induction. Many of our beliefs are, of course, the result of inductive inference. Quine thinks that our use of induction is "efficacious."[17] Induction gets us to where we want to be—acquiring true beliefs. Not only do we actually use induction, but we *ought* to use induction. But how should we explain this happy coincidence? Recall that Hume, too, thinks that we use induction, but he is unable to suggest any reason for thinking we *ought* to rely on inductive methods. So, what exactly is it that Quine sees that Hume does not? The Quinean answer is, Darwin. If natural selection is true, then this helps to explain why induction is efficacious.[18]

Quine does not spell out this argument, but it is detailed by Hilary Kornblith.[19] According to Kornblith, nature has endowed us with certain cognitive capacities that are biased toward truth. Through natural selection, we retain belief-forming processes that generally lead to true beliefs. But if we are naturally predisposed to the acquisition of true beliefs, then the way we *in fact* acquire our beliefs is the way we *ought* to acquire our beliefs. For example, we acquire many beliefs as a result of vision. Now, the Darwinian naturalized epistemologist tells us that were such beliefs generally false, they would not have much survival value. Cognitive psychology tells us that the periphery of the retina primarily detects motion; it is not very good at detecting color. And this seems to have some survival value. For example, if I am about to step off the curb into the street, I need to be able to detect the *moving* truck, not the color of the truck. If a certain color of berry is poisonous, I need a reliable way of detecting that color. Were my visual beliefs generally false—that is, were I unable to detect motion or color—I would be a less likely candidate for survival. Thus, vision actually produces true beliefs, the beliefs I ought to have. In describing how we acquire our beliefs, the naturalized epistemologist is also telling us the ways in which we ought to acquire our beliefs. The normative character of belief acquisition is thus reduced to the evolutionary explanation of how we come to acquire our beliefs.

The success of this argument clearly depends on the claim that natural selection operates so as to select generally truth-conducive cognitive processes. There is some doubt, however, about the truth of this claim. Stephen Stich, for example, argues that false beliefs may often have survival value.[20] If false beliefs lead us to avoid situations that are life threatening or simply injurious to our well-being, then natural selection may indeed favor belief-forming mechanisms that produce a good many false beliefs. *Erring* on the side of caution is arguably of greater survival utility. As Stich remarks elsewhere, natural selection does not care about truth but about reproductive success.[21] The animal that refrains from fleeing in order to find out whether it has a true belief that a predator is nearby may unfortunately have a "pathetic but praiseworthy tendency to die out before reproducing [its] kind."[22] Moreover, it is problematic whether many of our scientific beliefs, even if true, contribute to our survival. Nature seems, at best, indifferent to whether we truly believe that quarks have flavors. Consequently, there is some reason to reject the argument from natural selection.

Where does the rejection of the argument from natural selection leave Quinean naturalized epistemology? Quine promises that abandonment of the traditional epistemological enterprise still leaves us with a discipline that is sufficiently normative. Moreover, Quine promises that we can explain the normative character of naturalized epistemology by appealing to the very science of which naturalized epistemology is a part. Quine's apparent suggestion, elaborated by Kornblith, is that we appeal to natural selection. Natural selection explains why we have the goal of acquiring true beliefs and why our methods are generally adapted to this goal—namely, their survival value. But the failure of the argument from natural selection would seem to leave the naturalized epistemologist with an *unnaturalized* normative property. Consequently, we seem to be faced with two options. We might give up the idea that naturalized epistemology is a normative discipline. In this case, Quine's critics would be right; naturalized epistemology bears little or no resemblance to epistemology traditionally conceived. Quine might be right to reject strong foundationalism, but he has failed to show us that traditional epistemology cannot be rehabilitated and that our sole option is naturalized epistemology. A second option is to hold that epistemic properties supervene on natural properties.

Evolutionary Epistemology

Evolutionary epistemology holds that we can understand the growth of knowledge and our acquisition of justified or rational beliefs based on the model of evolution—specifically, natural selection. One type of evolutionary epistemology holds that certain types of belief-producing mechanisms are selected, in much the same way that other biological traits are selected. In this view, the selection and transmission of various scientific claims can be explained by the fact that humans have particular capacities that have evolved in response to certain environmental needs. This view is sometimes criticized on the grounds that natural selection is blind, but the growth of knowledge is not "blind" in this way. Another type of evolutionary epistemology seeks to avoid this problem by suggesting that the growth and revision of the methods and strategies by which we acquire our beliefs can be understood as paralleling the structure of evolution; it takes evolution as a metaphor. The argument in the text is relevant to the first type of evolutionary epistemology. (See "For Further Study.")

NATURALIZED EPISTEMOLOGY AND SUPERVENIENCE

Recently, some have argued that we should view naturalized epistemology in the following way. We can, through the analysis of certain concepts, identify certain features that any adequate epistemology must have. These features may include the nature of our epistemic goals or assumptions necessary for epistemology. It is worth noting that this analysis of concepts might plausibly be considered to be a kind of a priori reasoning. The methods of traditional epistemology are not wholly abandoned, as Quine suggests. Still, there is a further test of the adequacy of epistemological theory. Epistemic concepts, such as justification, are to be explained by citing naturalistic criteria or conditions. We can look briefly at two proponents of this view, Jaegwon Kim and Alvin Goldman.

There are two issues of interest with Kim's view: (a) the source of the normative character of epistemology, and (b) the reason we might nonetheless seek a naturalistic epistemology, albeit one quite different from that espoused by Quine. Kim argues that the normative character of epistemology derives from the concept of belief, which is itself intrinsically normative. According to Kim, our attributing certain beliefs to a person requires that we assume that the person meets certain minimal standards of rationality. Indeed, it would make no sense to suggest that a person had beliefs at all unless some minimal rationality were present.[23] Thus, the concept of belief necessarily involves the notion of evaluation. A mental state cannot be a belief unless it belongs to system that can be evaluated as minimally rational. This does not imply that we never have irrational beliefs. Rather, Kim suggests that we must presume at least some discernible evidential relationship among a person's beliefs.

This is but a brief gloss of Kim's argument, but two facets deserve attention. First, Kim seems to deploy a kind of a priori argument. He argues that a precondition of our intelligible use of the concept of belief is our seeing this as a normative notion. But this evidently a priori argument does not stop here. Implicit in Kim's argument is the claim that a genuine epistemology must make use of the concept of belief. Because the concept of belief is a fundamentally evaluative or normative concept, then epistemology is itself a normative discipline. Commitment to the notion of belief entails that one "cannot dispense with normative concepts or disengage himself from valuational activities."[24] We are thus led to the second facet, the source of the normative character of epistemology. Epistemology is a normative discipline because it traffics in beliefs. Kim thus presents an a priori argument for the normative character of epistemology.

While Kim thinks that epistemology is inherently normative, he also holds that the possibility of normative epistemology depends on our ability to give naturalistic criteria for normative, epistemic terms. That is, normative epistemology is a feasible area of study only if the specifically epistemic terms, such as justified belief, can be given a naturalistic explanation. It is here that the concept of supervenience appears.

According to Kim, epistemic properties supervene on naturalistic facts. Consider, for example, justified belief. If we think that Sara has a justified belief that it is raining outside, there must be some reason that the belief is justified—the reason must be "grounded in the factual descriptive properties of that belief."[25] These factual descriptive properties are criteria or conditions that specify when a belief is justified.

For example, Kim suggests that the factual property of being caused by a certain perceptual experience might serve as the requisite *naturalistic* condition or criterion for the justification of perceptual beliefs. The normative property of justification is thus based on a particular causal, psychological property, which is a factual property. Kim also suggests that recognizing logical relations might serve as a naturalistic criterion for justification, since "recognizing" is a psychological process. Notice the pattern implicit in Kim's examples. Beliefs that have the normative property of justification will also have certain other naturalistic or factual properties, which are then identified as the criteria of justification. It is worth pausing to see why this sort of view is thought to offer some comfort to the naturalistically inclined epistemologist.

The normative character of epistemology presents a daunting obstacle to the naturalization of epistemology. On the one hand, epistemology suggests that we may value our beliefs differently; we assign a positive value to justified beliefs and a negative value to unjustified beliefs. The business of epistemology is the identification of *normative* or *evaluative* properties that account for or explain these different evaluations. There is seemingly no doubt that as humans, we engage in the activity of evaluating, either positively or negatively, our many beliefs. More importantly, we are strongly inclined to think that there is some point to this evaluative activity. That is, when we describe as justified Sara's belief that it is raining but describe as unjustified Sam's belief that it is snowing, we think that we have described some *genuine* difference between the two beliefs. The view that epistemology is a legitimate and worthwhile activity is intimately connected with the view that normative epistemic differences are real or genuine differences. Rather colloquially, there *really is* a difference between Sam's and Sara's beliefs. Epistemology aims to identify this real difference.

But now consider the point of view of the naturalist. The naturalist looks to science to identify the real objects and properties. It is the scientist's method that reveals the structure of the world around us. In doing so, science reveals to us *facts:* Hydrogen has but a single atom; life on earth began some 4 billion years ago; the shifting of geologic plates causes earthquakes. Science does not reveal to us values or evaluative properties. Science describes and explains. In doing so, it presents us with only "factual descriptive properties." When the meteorologist predicts that the hurricane will turn north and miss the coast, she is not evaluating the behavior of the hurricane. Nor, in distinguishing between tropical storms and hurricanes, is she evaluating features or properties of the hurricane.

The naturalist then has a choice: Either reject normative or evaluative properties or explain them by appeal to natural facts or properties, or to non-normative facts or properties. If the naturalist thinks that a certain kind of normative property is a genuine property, then it must be connected to, or as Kim suggests, grounded in, natural descriptive facts or properties. Thus, the normative character of epistemic properties must be explained by showing how they are connected to properties that are "scientifically or naturalistically respectable." We might suggest that a property is naturalistically respectable if we can reasonably expect that science is able to explain to us the nature and origin of these respectable properties. Of course, this may be a rather complicated story, as in the case of perceptual experience. The naturalist has two ways of grounding normative properties, reduction or supervenience. Previously, we discussed one reason for thinking that normative epistemic properties are not reducible to evolutionary facts. Nonetheless, naturalists, such as Kim, think that epistemic properties are *real* properties. Consequently, they rely on the notion of supervenience to explain how evaluative properties like justification arise. Whenever we find a type of naturalistic property or a collection of naturalistic properties, we have some naturalistically acceptable reason for attributing the relevant normative epistemic property. Supervenience thus permits naturalized epistemology to retain the commitment to naturalism while allowing that there are genuinely normative epistemic properties. The task of the naturalized epistemologist is to identify the naturalistic properties on which the epistemic properties supervene.

If the task of the naturalized epistemologist is to identify the naturalistic properties on which epistemic properties supervene, then he must know where in the world to look for the relevant natural properties. There are infinitely many natural properties possessed by agents as they acquire various beliefs. Sara and Sam are both living, breathing, conscious beings, but only Sara's belief that it is raining outside is justified. Thus, there must be some principled way of sorting through all the different natural properties and selecting those that are the criteria or conditions for having a justified belief. It is here that the idea of the goal of inquiry or the aim of justification becomes important. Happily, Alvin Goldman is quite explicit about the methodology of the naturalized epistemologist, and it is to his view that we turn.

We are attempting to understand how the naturalistic epistemologist might reasonably decide which natural properties constitute the supervenience base, or the ground of evaluative epistemic properties. One way to approach the matter is to consider that we evaluate objects or properties relative to some goal or end. We praise, for example, Sara's volunteering to work with disadvantaged children because it furthers a certain end, perhaps the betterment of society. Similarly, we might think that the notion of justification is relative to some goal. Indeed, we have seen throughout the text the widespread presumption that justification is aimed at truth. We prize justified beliefs because they are more likely to be true. Now, if our goal is to have beliefs that are more likely to be true, this could provide the needed clue for identifying the relevant descriptive or natural properties. We look for the naturalistically respectable properties that contribute to the formation or acquisition of true beliefs. Consequently, we have some means of identifying the relevant natural properties *if* we have some explanation of why we choose the particular goal that we do. Quine, for example, thought the goal of having true beliefs might be explained by their survival value, but we saw reason to reject this notion.

Goldman, as we know from Chapter Three, also holds that the goal of justification is to have beliefs that are likely to be true. However, Goldman defends likely truth as the goal, not on the basis of some empirical investigation, but on the basis of a conceptual analysis, or what might be described as a kind of a priori investigation. Goldman thinks that the process of identifying the nature of justified belief and of knowledge begins with a kind of conceptual or semantic investigation. Thus, he claims that his preferred initial principle expresses "a semantic truth about the language of justified belief" and that it is a necessary condition of justified belief.[26] The significant point, for our purposes, is Goldman's contention that our search for an acceptable principle of justified belief begins with conceptual investigation or analysis. Indeed, although Goldman clearly holds that psychology is relevant to epistemology, this relevance is rationalized or explained by specific conceptual analyses of key epistemic terms. It is by virtue of a certain conceptual investigation that the epistemologist is enjoined to look to empirical disciplines such as psychology.[27]

Once we have undertaken the initial conceptual analysis, once we have identified our basic "starting principle," as it were, there may still be rival accounts of justified belief that satisfy that initial or starting principle. Different theories may look, for example, to the notion of coherence or indubitability. We thus require some means for selecting from among rival theories. Why should we prefer reliability theories to, say, coherence theories? Goldman's preferred method for choosing between these rival accounts is "considered judgments in reflective equilibrium."[28] Once we have identified the initial principle, which specifies a necessary condition for any adequate theory of justification, we test rival theories against our intuitions, our commonsense notion of which beliefs are justified. Our intuition, for example, is that most of our perceptual beliefs, formed under normal conditions, are justified. If a theory has the implication that perceptual beliefs formed under normal conditions are generally *unjustified,* then this would count against the theory. Notice, for example, the extent to which we have relied on something like this method. Our consideration of reliabilism involved testing the theory against our intuitions concerning Norman, the clairvoyant. Similarly, we noticed that critics of coherentism suspect that perceptual beliefs are unjustified according to coherentist process. Goldman is urging that this is the general means by which we choose among competing theories. Of course, during this process, we may come to revise our original intuitions. But we continue to balance theory against intuition until we arrive at an acceptable theory. Interestingly, Goldman explicitly rejects the idea that we appeal to empirical psychology or social science at this stage of epistemological theorizing. In fact, he rejects various approaches to a theory of justified belief largely on conceptual grounds. His rejection, for example, of what we might call social theories of justification turns largely on the claim that what a community thinks counts as a justified belief may not in fact be a justified belief. The community might have misidentified the base properties on which justification supervenes.

Our interest here is not with the particular theory Goldman supports; we know from Chapter Three that he is committed to a process reliabilism. Our interest is rather Goldman's methodology for epistemological theorizing. What we are seeing is that Goldman holds that epistemological theory begins not with the empirical, but with the conceptual. We begin with "semantic truths" about the language of justified belief. We begin by attempting to understand the concept of justification. Now, we might appeal to some of our commonsense judgments about clear cases of justified beliefs. But we have not, as Quine would have us do, admitted that our epistemological theorizing starts within science and that we look to science alone for our evaluative principles.

Although the beginning of epistemological theory lies in a conceptual investigation, it certainly cannot end there, in Goldman's view. Thus, he claims that "a central problem for epistemology, equally, is the factual basis on which epistemic evaluations are made."[29] Goldman, like Kim, holds that epistemic evaluations supervene on purely factual states of affairs. The task, then, for the epistemologist is to identify the factual, substantive conditions on which epistemic properties supervene. The epistemologist must identify the *naturalistic* criteria that are necessary and sufficient for epistemic evaluations. If you will recall, Goldman holds that epistemic properties supervene on the functioning of reliable cognitive processes. It is here, in the last stage of epistemological theory, that empirical psychology and other disciplines become relevant, because it is an empirical matter which of our cognitive processes are sufficiently reliable. More importantly, notice that, like Kim, Goldman holds that our epistemic evaluations are not autonomous, that is, are not independent of the natural order.

With this account, albeit brief, of the nature of epistemological theory, we see both the sense in which Goldman is committed to a naturalistic epistemology and the sense in which Goldman's view is continuous with traditional epistemology. Unlike Quine, Goldman seems less suspicious of a priori theorizing.[30] At the very least, Goldman thinks that epistemological *method* begins with conceptual analysis. We might even suggest that Goldman's use of the method of reflective equilibrium is at the very least consistent with traditional epistemology's method. These features of Goldman's method may distance him from someone like Quine and place him in closer proximity to the traditional enterprise. Descartes, for example, began with certain conceptual claims—among them, that knowledge implies infallibility. Goldman does, however, think that the natural sciences have a role in epistemology. But this role clearly occurs at a late stage of the epistemological process, after much of the theoretical heavy lifting has been done.

Perhaps the most significant similarity between Goldman-style epistemology and traditional epistemology is the commitment to the essentially normative character of the discipline. An epistemology that is not normative in character, as Kim emphasized, is simply not deserving of the title. Of the three features of traditional epistemology noted in the first section of this chapter, Goldman clearly endorses one of them, the normative aspect, and does not entirely oppose another, the role of conceptual analysis or a priori theorizing in epistemology. We need to look elsewhere if we are to see why Goldman's epistemology is a naturalistic epistemology.

Common to Quine, Kim, and Goldman is the claim that epistemic properties are not some special sort of property, independent of the natural order. Justification enters the world by way of natural properties, whether these are causal relations, types of cognitive process, or some other natural, factual property. Thus, it might be suggested that the naturalistic character of Goldman's epistemology lies in the rejection of the claim that epistemology is autonomous. But this view might apply to naturalized epistemology more generally. Apparently, what characterizes the naturalistic approach to epistemology is the rejection of the autonomy or independence of epistemology. From the naturalist's perspective, the legitimacy of epistemology rests on its ability to show the connection between natural properties and epistemic properties. The key to the naturalist's endeavor is rejecting the autonomy of epistemology while continuing to hold that there are nonetheless genuinely normative, epistemic properties. Naturalistically inclined epistemologists, like Kim and Goldman, thus are moved to a quite special notion. Supervenience enables the naturalist to shun autonomy while embracing normativity. A recognizable epistemology thus finds its place in the natural order.

TRADITION, REDUCTION, AND SUPERVENIENCE

Quinean and Modest Naturalized Epistemology

To what extent is naturalized epistemology compatible with the more traditional enterprise? For convenience, we can distinguish between a Quinean version of naturalized epistemology and a more modest version. **Quinean naturalized epistemology** is principally characterized by two claims. First, it espouses a methodological claim that epistemological theorizing begins within scientific theorizing. The conceptual tools and the methods available to the epistemologist are the identical tools and methods utilized by the empirical scientist. Second, the Quinean version has a greater affinity for reduction. Epistemic properties are more acceptable precisely to the extent that they can be identified with properties described by the empirical sciences. **Modest naturalized epistemology** relies not on reduction, but on supervenience. The modest version also has a different view of the methodology of naturalized epistemology. It recognizes an appropriate role for conceptual analysis at the beginning of epistemological theory. With these cursory distinctions in mind, let us consider the relative compatibility of these two versions of naturalized epistemology with the more traditional version.

Clearly, the Quinean version is less hospitable to traditional epistemology. Even if we waive worries about whether the Quinean version is sufficiently normative, there is still an obvious disparity between it and traditional epistemology. Perhaps this is most evident in the Quinean version's rejection of the traditional approach. Again, setting aside worries about whether the traditional view is committed to strong foundationalism, Quinean naturalized epistemology insists that the epistemological theory is rooted in science. The Quinean version rejects the idea that epistemology first marks the places where we might find knowledge or justification and that science follows, harvesting what fruit it can. Instead, the Quinean version holds that science first leads us to knowledge, and epistemology is but science become self-conscious. Epistemology, in the Quinean view, follows after science, attempting to explain why it is so successful. If the traditional view holds that epistemology can begin outside science, if it holds that epistemology can begin independently of science by asking general questions about the nature of knowledge and justification, then the traditional view and the Quinean version are clearly at odds. The Quinean version's injunction to "Let psychology do it" is not quite what the traditional epistemologist had in mind.

Quinean naturalized epistemology's affinity for reduction of epistemic properties is also inhospitable to the traditional view of such properties. Epistemic properties are normative properties, and the traditional view would regard with suspicion the attempt to identify them with purely descriptive properties. Indeed, as we saw earlier in the chapter, the attempted identification of the normative aspects of belief acquisition with certain aspects of natural selection is not entirely compelling.

Modest versions of naturalized epistemology may be more compatible with traditional epistemology. If not common ground, then at least neutral ground with room to maneuver might be found in their conceptions of the method of epistemology. By allowing an initial role to conceptual analysis, the modest version may be more in line with the traditional view. Significantly, the modest version recognizes that epistemology is an inherently normative discipline. It does not *identify* normative properties with factual or descriptive properties, but it does hold that certain factual properties are the basis for the normative properties. Thus, an advocate of the modest version could hold that among the various types of *natural* property in the world—for example, physical, chemical, biological, or psychological—there are also epistemic properties. Epistemic properties are natural by virtue of their connection to other natural properties; hence, a complete catalogue of the features of the world will include epistemic properties.

We might put these considerations very informally. Traditional epistemology begins by saying "Here's where we want to go" (this is the epistemic goal, the aim of our cognitive endeavors) and proceeds with "It's possible to get there" (the response to the skeptic) and "Now, here's the best way to get there" (the principles of belief evaluation). Quinean naturalized epistemology begins instead with a rather triumphant "Look where we are!" (we already know things; we already are engaged in scientific activity) and then offers to interested parties "And here's how we got here" (naturalized epistemology). Now, the traditionalist is none too sure that the Quinean is actually where he thinks he is. And, not surprisingly, the Quinean is none too sure that the traditionalist will ever *start* on the journey, much less actually get there. If scientists were still waiting on the traditionalist, we might still be nervously sailing wooden ships across inhospitable seas, still thinking that flight was for the birds, and still hoping someone would tell Benjamin Franklin to go fly a kite.

On the one hand, the Quinean seems to have a point. If you want to show that something is possible, show that it is actual. If you want to show that knowledge is possible, take a look at science. On the other hand, the traditionalist seems to be correct in maintaining that the Quinean is far too hasty in the treatment of evaluative matters. Other than the claim that science is indeed successful and that the foundationalism of Descartes is a failure, the Quinean has given no reason for thinking that principles of belief evaluation come *only* from science.

The modest naturalized epistemologist's recognition that epistemology begins in conceptual analysis lends additional support to the traditional enterprise. Questions regarding the goal of our inquiries and the best way to attain to that goal can be intelligibly posed independently of science. But the modest naturalist's reliance on the notion of supervenience appears to depart from the traditional enterprise.

The traditionalist claims that the evaluative aspects of epistemic properties are not *fully* explained by appeal to natural properties. Identifying the natural properties that are the criteria for epistemic properties might explain our cognitive success. But the traditionalist might object that the fact of our success does not yet explain why we should believe that we are successful. In one sense, this is the heart of the traditionalist enterprise. Hume does not doubt that we are cognitively successful, even in matters of induction. Rather, he despairs of our ever having sufficient reason for believing that we are successful. To use Lehrer's terminology, Hume despairs of having adequate reason for thinking we are trustworthy in inductive matters. Quine counsels that the Humean predicament is the human predicament and suggests that we find comfort in forsaking Hume's task for science's— the technology of truth seeking. Now, the traditionalist claims that the Humean predicament is not only the *human* predicament but also the *epistemologist's* predicament. No epistemology that forsakes the evaluative process is a genuine epistemology. And supervenience offers cold comfort to the traditionalist. The traditionalist appears to reject even a modest naturalized epistemology, due to the traditionalist's insistence that the notion of supervenience will not adequately explain the evaluative character of epistemology.

Three Options

We can conclude this chapter by informally considering the general position you would be committing yourself to if you took one of the three options we have discussed. We cannot consider all the consequences of these positions, but we can clarify the broad outlines of the general positions. So, let us consider our three options.

The Quinean naturalized epistemologist is committed to the idea that epistemic notions or properties are *reducible* to nonepistemic, or purely factual, properties. Were you to choose this option, here is part of what you would be saying. In principle, some law, some scientific law, states that the property of being justified, for example, is some set of factual or descriptive properties. Such factual properties might be having some sort of biological structure or perhaps some complex of psychological properties. Regardless of what these properties are, the Quinean naturalized epistemologist says that we could talk *only* about these factual properties and not miss anything in our explanation of the epistemic endeavors of humans. As we noted, reducibility is a very strong notion. The Quinean naturalized epistemologist holds that epistemic properties are *identical* to certain descriptive properties. We can continue to talk in our commonsense way about a person being rational or justified, about a person knowing, but this is merely a shorthand way of talking about more complicated scientific phenomena. For example, the property of being a good person is an evaluative property, as is being justified in believing. Now, we should be careful about pressing the analogy too far, but the analogous Quinean position suggests that being a good person is merely a shorthand way of talking about certain other kinds of facts or descriptive properties, perhaps biological, psychological, or sociological. Given a sufficiently developed science, the Quinean suggests, we could eventually discover the scientific laws that are true of all good people. Once we discovered these laws, we would no longer need to talk about being good. We could, instead, simply talk about the (obviously very complicated) factual properties identified by the law. Nor, the Quinean suggests, would we lose anything in our understanding of "being a good person." As a matter of fact, the Quinean urges, we might actually learn a little bit more about what it is to be a good person! Similarly, the Quinean naturalized epistemologist suggests that we might actually understand better our epistemic judgments and activities if we were to discover the relevant laws. In any case, we should dispense with traditional epistemology and turn to the relevant sciences for these laws. Again, we should not press the analogy too closely; but if you think that it is plausible that there are laws, whether biological, psychological or sociological, explaining what it is to be a good person, then perhaps you share some sympathies with the Quinean naturalized epistemologist.

The second option belongs to the modest naturalized epistemologist. The modest naturalist, recall, rejects reducibility but is committed to the idea that epistemic properties supervene on natural properties. Terminology can become complicated here very quickly. For example, as we discussed, Goldman commits himself only to the supervenience of epistemic properties on factual properties. Yet Goldman is sometimes identified as being committed to the reducibility of epistemic concepts.[31] We can contrast the modest with the Quinean naturalized epistemologist in this way. The modest epistemologist suggests that some set or combination of factual properties gives rise to the epistemic properties, but there is no way to reduce the epistemic properties to the factual properties. There are no scientific laws identifying the two kinds of properties. Again, we might use the analogy of being a good person. The modest position suggests that certain combinations of natural properties exist, and if you find these combinations, then you have found a good person. But don't expect, the modest position urges, to find scientific laws that identify "being good" with some set of natural properties. It is not, however, as though "being good" is some sort of unique, nonnatural property. The property of being good comes about because of certain factual properties; knowing what these natural properties are helps us understand something about "being good." Similarly, the modest naturalized epistemologist holds that we learn something about what it is to be good when we know something about the associated natural properties. Unlike the Quinean, we cannot simply settle for science, however. Notice that Goldman, for example, allows that there is still an indispensable role for traditional epistemological theorizing. If we are to have a complete picture of our epistemic endeavors, we must look to both scientific and traditional epistemological methods.

The traditionalist, however, resists even this modest naturalist enterprise. Keith Lehrer, for example, insists that "supervenience fails" because there are no facts about an agent that explain why the agent is in fact trustworthy in what she accepts.[32] Similarly, Richard Fumerton claims that justification arises because of a complex of acts of acquaintance, where acquaintance is an unanalyzable relation.[33] Apart from these specific theories, the traditionalist generally claims that agents have certain properties—for example, being actually trustworthy or being acquainted with certain other objects or properties—that are necessary for understanding epistemic properties. The problem, the traditionalist claims, is that these properties cannot be explained by appealing to natural properties. They are, as Fumerton suggests, *sui generis*. Again, consider the analogy with the property of being good. The traditionalist says that the property of being good is not something that can be understood by talking about factual properties. In fact, the traditionalist suggests, it would be a mistake to think that we can find such natural properties. There are no interesting natural facts always associated with being a good person. Evaluative properties, including epistemic properties, are at most contingently connected with factual or natural properties. As Lehrer describes it, there are no sets of facts about the agent necessitating that the person have the relevant property.[34] Similarly, the traditional epistemologist, in rejecting supervenience, holds that no interesting natural facts are always associated with epistemic properties—for example, being justified in believing. According to traditionalists, we do not get a better picture of our epistemic activities by trying to discover the natural properties underlying epistemic properties.

(As noted previously, terminology can get somewhat complicated here. For example, Robert Audi, who in many ways develops a traditional theory, accepts a kind of supervenience. He accepts that his view is *conceptually naturalistic;* he allows that an analysis of justification may involve concepts that refer only to natural or factual properties. Our aim here, however, is to contrast the three positions with respect to the connection between epistemic and natural properties.[35])

There are, of course, difficulties with each of these positions. The Quinean and modest naturalized epistemologists face similar obstacles. Because epistemic properties are doubtless complex, higher-order properties, the associated factual properties are likely to be extremely complicated. Consider, for example, Goldman's claim that a belief is justified if and only if the belief is the result of reliable process and is not "trumped" by other reliable processes the agent might have used. Now, spelling out the factual properties associated with the latter clause is likely to be rather complicated. Consider, for example, the attempt to find the factual properties associated with "is a piece of money." Paul Teller argues that this economic property is unlikely to supervene on a unique, specifiable set of natural properties.[36] Economic contexts are at once too broad and too diverse. Particular economic properties will always be associated with some natural or factual properties. But, according to Teller, we should not expect that there will be any physical characteristics always associated with "is a piece of money." Teller suggests that supervenience ultimately may amount to little more than the injunction that laws of nature not be violated. A similar problem besets naturalized epistemology. It may be that an indefinite number of natural properties are associated with our preferred epistemic properties. Now, this is not to say that we cannot develop some sense of the variety of natural properties, but we would want to see or know what connects these properties other than that they are relevant to epistemic properties. We would want to know that there is some unity to the kind or type of natural properties.

Of course, the traditionalist also owes us some further explanation. We would like the traditionalist to explain to us what kind of thing epistemic properties are. The traditionalist might be urging that we adopt a kind of dualism of natural properties and epistemic properties. Thus, we would find, if the traditionalist is right, at least two different kinds of properties in the world, natural properties and epistemic properties, or more generally, evaluative properties. This sort of position is not unknown; there are "property dualists" in other areas, such as philosophy of mind. Two persistent questions confronting such dualisms, however, concern the source of such properties and their relation to natural properties. Again, this is not to suggest that the traditional approach lacks promise. It is merely to point out at least one of the issues confronting the traditionalist.

Despite the complexity of these issues, there is a clear value in raising the issue of naturalized epistemology. Of course, one of the aims of epistemological theory is to try to identify the conditions for justification and knowledge. But it is also important to understand how our epistemic endeavors relate to other human endeavors. We want to know whether we can understand our epistemic activities within a generally naturalistic outlook or whether the attempt to understand our epistemic endeavors forces us to look at humans in a quite different way.

Key Concepts

Autonomy of
   epistemology

Modest naturalized
   epistemology

Naturalism

Quinean naturalized
   epistemology

Reduction

Supervenience

Review Questions

1. What are three features of traditional epistemology that are important for understanding naturalized epistemology?

2. What is *first philosophy*? Why does Quine reject it?

3. Can Quine answer the critic's worries about retaining the normative character of epistemology? What is Quine's response to skeptical doubts? Do you think this is a satisfactory response?

4. Why is the concept of supervenience important for naturalized epistemology?

5. Choose an example of an evaluative property (other than those mentioned in the text). Describe what you think the Quinean, the modest, and the traditional positions would be with respect to this property. Which of these accounts do you think gives the best explanation of the property? Why?

For Further Study

The locus classicus of naturalized epistemology is W. V. O. Quine's "Epistemology Naturalized," in *Ontological Relativity and Other Essays* (New York: Columbia University Press, 1969), pp. 69–90. It is reprinted in Hilary Kornblith, ed., *Naturalizing Epistemology* (Cambridge, MA: MIT Press, 1985), pp. 1–29. A less programmatic account of Quinean naturalized epistemology is Quine's *Roots of Reference* (LaSalle, IL: Open Court, 1986). Roger Gibson's *Enlightened Empiricism* (Tampa: University of Florida Press, 1988) is a sustained interpretation and defense of Quine's views; see esp. Chaps. 1–3).

There are three excellent overviews of naturalized epistemology: Philip Kitcher's "The Naturalists Return," *Philosophical Review* 101 (1992): 53–114; James Maffie's "Recent Work on Naturalized Epistemology," *American Philosophical Quarterly* 27 (1990): 281–293; Hilary Kornblith's "Introduction: What Is Naturalistic Epistemology?" in *Naturalizing Epistemology*. These essays provide different accounts of the conceptual motivations of naturalized epistemology, but each highlights important aspects of naturalized epistemology and contains analyses of important arguments. Maffie's bibliography is invaluable. Peter French et al., eds., *Midwest Studies,* Vol. 24 (Notre Dame, IN: University of Notre Dame Press, 1994) contains a number of essays examining naturalized epistemology; some of the essays defend naturalized epistemology while some are critical. Laurence BonJour's essay in this collection, "Against Naturalized Epistemology," pp. 283–300, argues that naturalized epistemology cannot give up the idea of a priori justification.

Jaegwon Kim critiques Quine's position but advocates what we have called a modest naturalized epistemology in "What Is 'Naturalized Epistemology'?" in James Tomberlin, ed., *Philosophical Perspectives, 2, Epistemology* (Atascadero, CA: Ridgeview, 1988), pp. 381–405. Alvin Goldman presents a somewhat more detailed view in *Epistemology and Cognition* (Cambridge, MA: Harvard University Press, 1985), especially the Introduction and Part I.

Larry Laudan develops a naturalistic epistemology that defends a pragmatic and naturalistic view of cognitive value and knowledge in *Science and Values* (Berkeley: University of California Press, 1982).

Jaegwon Kim has worked extensively on the notion of supervenience; see, for example, *Supervenience and the Mind* (New York: Cambridge University Press, 1993) and "Concepts of Supervenience," *Philosophy and Phenomenological Research* 65 (1984): 257–270. The *Southern Journal of Philosophy* 22, Supplement (1983), is devoted to the topic of supervenience. Keith Lehrer's critique of supervenience is located in *Self-Trust: A Study of Reason, Knowledge, and Autonomy* (Oxford: Oxford University Press, 1997), Chap. 3.

Robert Almeder's "On Naturalizing Epistemology," *American Philosophical Quarterly* 27 (1990): 263–279, provides a survey of various arguments against the naturalistic project. A wider range of studies is found in Richard Wagner and Steven Warner, eds., *Naturalism: A Critical Appraisal* (Notre Dame, IN: University of Notre Dame Press, 1993). Richard Fumerton is critical of naturalized epistemology and externalism in *Metaepistemology and Skepticism* (Lanham, MD: Rowman & Littlefield, 1995). A still important critical appraisal of naturalized epistemology is Hilary Putnam's "Why Reason Can't Be Naturalized," in *Realism and Reason* (Cambridge: Cambridge University Press, 1983), pp. 229–247.

The leading proponent of the Strong Programme is David Bloor. His "Sociology of Knowledge" and "Strong Programme," in Jonathan Dancy and Ernest Sosa, eds., *A Companion to Epistemology* (Oxford: Basil Blackwell, 1992), pp. 483–487 and 494, respectively, are convenient introductions. See also Bloor's *Knowledge and Social Imagery,* 2nd ed. (Chicago: University of Chicago Press, 1991). An accessible critique is in Robert Klee, *Introduction to the Philosophy of Science: Cutting Nature at Its Seams* (New York: Oxford University Press, 1997), Chap. 8.

Nicholas Rescher, ed., *Evolution, Cognition and Realism* (Lanham, MD: University Press of America, 1990), is a useful collection for evolutionary epistemology. Donald Campbell's "Evolutionary Epistemology," in Paul Schilpp, ed., *The Philosophy of Karl Popper* (LaSalle, IL: Open Court, 1974), pp. 413–463, is one of the earliest and most influential works in the field. See also M. Ruse, *Taking Darwin Seriously* (Oxford: Basil Blackwell, 1986). A recent work that considers many of these, as well as other issues, is Edward Stein, *Without Good Reason: The Rationality Debate in Philosophy and Cognitive Science* (Oxford: Clarendon Press, 1997).

Notes

1. Robert M. Hazen and James Trefil, *Science Matters* (New York: Doubleday, 1991), p. 227.
2. See Roderick Chisholm, *Theory of Knowledge,* 2nd ed. (Englewood Cliffs, NJ: Prentice-Hall, 1977), p. 16.
3. A. C. Danto's "Naturalism," in Paul Edwards, ed., *Encyclopedia of Philosophy* (New York: Macmillan, 1967), is an accessible introduction to some of the principal tenets often associated with naturalism.
4. W. V. O. Quine, "Things and Their Place in Theories," in *Theories and Things* (Cambridge, MA: Belknap Press, 1981), p. 22.
5. Ernest Sosa, *Knowledge in Perspective* (Cambridge: Cambridge University Press, 1991), p. 153.
6. Philip Kitcher, "The Naturalists Return," *Philosophical Review* 101 (1992): 53–114, and James Maffie, "Recent Work on Naturalized Epistemology," *American Philosophical Quarterly* 27 (1990): 281–293, contain extended discussions of the historical and conceptual origins of naturalized epistemology. Kitcher views the move to naturalistic epistemology as a move from a psychologistic epistemology to an epistemology in which psychology is now viewed as relevant to epistemological theorizing. Quine's "Epistemology Naturalized" is reprinted in Hilary Kornblith, ed., *Naturalizing Epistemology* (Cambridge, MA: MIT Press, 1985), pp. 1–29.
7. As we noted in Chapter Four, however, most foundationalists do not accept this strong form of foundationalism.
8. Quine, "Epistemology Naturalized," p. 21.
9. Quine, "Epistemology Naturalized," pp. 23–24.
10. Jaegwon Kim, "What Is 'Naturalized Epistemology'?" in James Tomberlin, ed., *Philosophical Perspectives, 2, Epistemology* (Atascadero, CA: Ridgeview, 1988), pp. 381–405, especially Sect. 4.
11. Quine, "Epistemology Naturalized," p. 19.
12. W. V. O. Quine, "Natural Kinds," in Kornblith, ed., *Naturalizing Epistemology,* pp. 31–47.
13. W. V. O. Quine, *Roots of Reference* (LaSalle, IL: Open Court, 1974), p. 3.
14. W. V. O. Quine, "The Nature of Natural Knowledge," in Samuel Guttenplan, ed., *Mind and Language* (Oxford: Oxford University Press, 1975), pp. 67–68.
15. W. V. O. Quine, "Reply to Morton White," in L. E. Hahn and P. A. Schilpp, eds., *The Philosophy of W. V. O. Quine* (LaSalle, IL: Open Court, 1986), p. 665.
16. W. V. O. Quine, *The Pursuit of Truth* (Cambridge, MA: Harvard University Press, 1990), p. 20.
17. Quine, "The Nature of Natural Knowledge," p. 70.
18. Quine, "The Nature of Natural Knowledge," p. 70. See also "Natural Kinds," pp. 38–39, where Quine claims that he is not moved by protests that he uses induction to justify induction, because he has adopted the naturalistic perspective. That is, Quine thinks that inductive methods are part of the methodology of science, and he is thus free to utilize any of those methods, as is any naturalized epistemologist.
19. Kornblith, *Naturalizing Epistemology,* pp. 4–5.
20. Steven Stich, "Could Man Be an Irrational Animal?" in Kornblith, ed., *Naturalizing Epistemology,* pp. 257–258. See also Stich's *The Fragmentation of Reason* (Cambridge, MA: MIT Press, 1990), Chap. 3.
21. Stich, *The Fragmentation of Reason,* p. 62.
22. Quine, "Natural Kinds," p. 39.
23. Kim, "What Is 'Naturalized Epistemology'?" pp. 392–394.
24. Kim, "What Is 'Naturalized Epistemology'?" p. 394.
25. Kim, "What Is 'Naturalized Epistemology'?" p. 399.
26. Alvin Goldman, *Epistemology and Cognition* (Cambridge, MA: Harvard University Press, 1985), p. 59.
27. Goldman, *Epistemology and Cognition,* p. 36.
28. Goldman, *Epistemology and Cognition,* p. 66.
29. Goldman, *Epistemology and Cognition,* p. 23.

30. Goldman, at the very least, seems less suspicious of the notion of analyticity (p. 38), and analytic truths might be good candidates for truths knowable a priori. He apparently concedes that some very simple logical truths might be knowable independently of *any* perceptual experience (p. 302). His doubts about the extent of the a priorist program seem to arise from his taking a priori knowledge to be knowledge obtained without any reliance on perceptual experience. This is an extremely strong claim, one that would not be shared by many defenders of the notion of a priori knowledge.

31. See, for example, Richard Fumerton, *Metaepistemology and Skepticism* (Lanham, MD: Rowman & Littlefield, 1995), p. 66.

32. Keith Lehrer, *Self-Trust: A Study of Reason, Knowledge and Autonomy* (Oxford: Clarendon Press, 1997), p. 72.

33. Fumerton, *Metaepistemology and Skepticism,* pp. 73–75. We should be careful here. Although Fumerton insists that epistemic properties are not reducible, he does suggest that animals can be acquainted with various things. "Being acquainted with" then looks like a natural, perhaps psychological, property, even though it cannot be analyzed further. In this interpretation, Fumerton would hold a kind of supervenience view. But we will, in what follows, interpret him as a traditionalist.

34. Lehrer, *Self-Trust,* pp. 72–73.

35. See, for example, Robert Audi, *The Structure of Justification* (Cambridge: Cambridge University Press, 1993), Chap. 10.

36. Paul Teller, "Comments on Kim's Paper," *The Southern Journal of Philosophy* 22, Supplement (1983): 57–61. Teller is particularly concerned with the notion of strong supervenience.

CHAPTER EIGHT

A Priori Knowledge

But though all our knowledge begins with experience,
it does not follow that it all arises out of experience.
IMMANUEL KANT, *CRITIQUE OF PURE REASON*

Many of our beliefs are tied to the varying features of the world around us. Yet we also seem to have beliefs that we know independently of what we learn, directly or indirectly, from our experience of the world. That $\sqrt{16} = 4$ or that a brother is a male sibling are propositions we know to be true. Neither the truth of these propositions nor our knowledge of them seems to depend on our experience. I did not, for example, commission a statistics class to do a survey of randomly chosen brothers and then check to see if each is also a male sibling. On the contrary, I know that anytime one finds a brother, one has indeed found a male sibling. That's just what it is to be a brother. Similarly, there does not seem to be any sensory experience I might have that would lead me to think that the square root of 16 was anything other than 4.

There is a long tradition in philosophy that claims that some of our knowledge is *a priori*. Very roughly, a proposition is known a priori if we know it independently of our experiences. **A posteriori knowledge** requires the evidence of, or depends on, our senses. That there is orange juice in the glass or that rainbows are caused by the refraction of light are known propositions because we have certain kinds of complicated experience. Historically, reason, and not the senses, is thought to be the source of a priori knowledge. This chapter examines the concept of a priori knowledge, the idea that we have some knowledge independently of experience.

In addition to the distinction between a priori and a posteriori, two other pairs of concepts play a significant role in theories of a priori knowledge. The first pair to be considered is that of necessary and contingent propositions. Theories of a priori knowledge sometimes claim that any proposition known a priori is a necessary proposition. The second pair to be considered, the semantic distinction between synthetic and analytic propositions, frames one of the central, and more controversial, issues with theories of a priori knowledge. This distinction between synthetic and analytic propositions raises the issue of whether we have knowledge of synthetic a priori propositions.

These three pairs of concepts thus frame the questions that guide the discussions to follow. First, we address the notion of independence from experience. Next, we introduce the distinction between necessary and contingent, and we consider an argument for the claim that any proposition known a priori must be a necessary proposition. Then we turn our attention to the traditional theory. We also introduce Kant's distinction between synthetic and analytic propositions. Kant's view serves as a departure point for much recent discussion of a priori knowledge, and we discuss these issues in the last sections of the chapter.

THE A PRIORI AND NECESSITY

An Epistemological Distinction: A Priori and A Posteriori

A theory of a priori knowledge must explain the source of a priori justification. The distinction between a priori and a posteriori knowledge is fundamentally an epistemological distinction regarding the way in which knowledge is obtained, or more precisely, the source of the justification for the belief. A belief counts as an instance of a priori knowledge only if it is justified a priori. Our understanding of a priori knowledge thus depends on our understanding of what it is for a belief to be justified a priori. In turn, we need to know how we could have a reason for thinking a belief is true, specifically, a reason that does not rely on experience.

We can take matters a bit more slowly here. The justification of a belief about the world—say, that there is orange juice in the glass—requires empirical evidence. Such justification requires, among other things, that we have some particular kind of experience or input from our senses. To be justified in believing that "Sam has brown eyes" requires that, at some point, some person have a distinctive visual experience of the color of Sam's limpid eyes. My belief that I can make a rainbow with a garden hose on a cloudless California day is justified by virtue of other beliefs, which depend in some way on experience. These other beliefs provide a reason for the truth of my belief about the simple magic of a garden hose, just as the visual experience is held to provide a reason for the truth of the belief about the color of Sam's eyes. Theories of a priori knowledge, however, claim that the a priori justification of beliefs is independent of a person's having certain kinds of experience or empirical beliefs. The reason for holding to the truth of the proposition "All bachelors are unmarried males" is not provided by a person's seeing a bachelor, noting the color of his eyes or the absence of a ring, or testing for the presence of certain chromosomes. Empirical evidence does not provide me with a reason for thinking that it is true that all bachelors are unmarried males. My reason for thinking that it is true that all bachelors are unmarried does not arise from chromosome tests, observation of bachelors, or any other bit of empirical evidence.

In this sense, my reason for thinking that the proposition is true is *independent* of my experience. More to the point, I have an *a priori justification* for the belief that all bachelors are unmarried males if that justification does not depend, even indirectly, on some sort of sensory evidence or experience. Thus far, notice, the characterization of a priori justification is *negative;* we have only seen what does *not* a priori justify a belief.

It could be objected that I was taught the meaning of "bachelor." For me to know that a bachelor is unmarried, I must have initially acquired this information by means of the senses—either I was told it or I read it, for example. However I came by this information, I must have had *some experience.* Similarly, my believing that the square root of 16 is none other than 4 seems to have its source in some experience—for example, my reading an arithmetic book. Thus, one might object that I lack an a priori justification for such propositions precisely because the justification depends on my having the original experiences, which enabled me to acquire the concepts. Pursuing this objection, one might urge that a priori justification must also be independent of processes such as remembering. We would not want to count as a priori justified my belief that the orange juice is in the refrigerator simply because I remember it as opposed to looking in the refrigerator.

In response, theories of the a priori concede that experience is often the source of our possession of various concepts. We acquire the concepts "brother" or "bachelor" or "square root" as a result of some experience. Once we master or understand the concept, however, our justification for certain propositions is independent of any particular type or sequence of experiences. For example, I may acquire the concept of red by being shown red books, red blocks, red clocks, or little red roosters. My mastery of the concept depends on this and other learning experiences. However, my belief that red is a color is not *justified* by these experiences. The reason for the truth of my belief that red is a color is not that someone, somewhere, sometime said to me, "Now, this apple is red," nor is it to be found in any subsequent set of experiences. Rather, the reason for the truth of my belief, the *justification* of my belief, lies elsewhere. Indeed, it seems possible that I could justifiably believe that red is a color even though I never came across any actual red thing. The reason for the truth of the belief is not to be found in the experiences that generated the concept.

The second part of the objection, that memory or perhaps other mental processes must also be excluded, is more problematic. We might notice that such objections arise, in part, because the characterization of a priori justification is thus far only *negative*—a priori justification comes about without the aid of the senses or memory. A possible response to this objection is to suggest that a proposition is a priori justified if it would be justified regardless of the type or sequence of sensory experiences we might have. The justificatory status of the proposition would remain unchanged whatever information about the world we might come to possess as a result of our sensory experiences. My belief that the orange juice is in the freezer would not be justified a priori, because I have that memory as a result of some earlier sensory experience. However, if the details of my experience are irrelevant to my understanding or mastery of a concept, then those details will be irrelevant to the a priori justification of a certain type of proposition. It does not matter who taught me the meaning of "bachelor," or whether I remember Sam is a bachelor, or whether I someday attend Sam's wedding. My belief that all bachelors are unmarried is justified a priori whether I witness Sam's bachelor party, his wedding, or his divorce, or *none of these*, so long as I understand the concepts.

We can now suggest a revision of the notion of **a priori knowledge.** A proposition is known a priori if, once the relevant concepts are acquired, the justification for the proposition is independent of or does not derive from any particular type of experience a person might have. Alternatively, a person has a priori knowledge if the person could have had the same justification even if the person had quite different experiences.[1] Again, thus far, the characterization of a priori knowledge and justification is negative. We know what types of experience are *not* involved in the a priori justification of a proposition. A cautious guess, however, about the positive nature of a priori justification might focus on our understanding or mastery of the concepts. Indeed, this is the focus of the traditional theory, outlined in the next section.

Despite the gaps, our picture of a priori knowledge is a bit more complete. The course of our cognitive endeavors includes the acquisition of concepts and the formation of related beliefs. Typically, we have reasons for thinking our beliefs are true, and some of these reasons are dependent on the content of our experiences. My reason for thinking the belief that this apple is red is true is based on certain experiences I have. My justification comes from the world affecting me in some definite way. But not all of our beliefs are like this. At least some of our beliefs seem to have a different kind of reason for their truth, one that has nothing to do with our having this or that type of experience. Your concept of square was acquired at your teacher's knee. But the truth of your belief that all squares are rectangles is not determined by any past experiences you have had with squares, whether ancient or recent, whether pedagogical or geometric; nor is it determined by any future type of experience. If you have a justification for believing that all squares are also rectangles, then that justification is a priori.

As noted, the distinction between a priori and a posteriori knowledge is an epistemological one, concerned with the type of justification one might have for a particular belief. The epistemological distinction, however, might be thought to overlap with a metaphysical distinction between necessary and contingent.

A Metaphysical Distinction: Necessary and Contingent Propositions

Many theories of a priori knowledge claim that propositions known a priori have the further, distinctive property of being *necessary*. Now, this is not simply an accidental connection between a proposition's a priori character and its necessity; rather, it is part of the nature of a priori knowledge. By contrast, propositions known a posteriori are *contingent* propositions. The remainder of this section elaborates the distinction between necessary and contingent and presents an argument for the claim that propositions known a priori are also necessary.

The distinction between necessary and contingent is metaphysical, not epistemological, because it concerns the properties certain things have, not how we know or come to justifiably believe that those things possess those properties. In this case, the "items" or "things" are propositions, and the properties are those of being necessary or contingent. Whether a proposition is necessary or contingent is sometimes referred to as the *modal status* of the proposition.

Quite simply, a proposition is **necessary** if its truth value could not be other than it is; a proposition is **contingent** if it might have had a truth value different from the one it in fact has. A few examples should help clarify this. Let's begin with contingent propositions. Gold was discovered in California in 1849. Now, as a matter of fact, this proposition is true. Out there in the world, not too far from me, is the town of Coloma, where some 148 years ago, James Marshall discovered gold. It is not too difficult to imagine, however, that this proposition might have been false. We can imagine Marshall slipping off a ladder and knocking himself out just moments before he was to peer anxiously at a glittering lump, the untimely accident thus delaying the discovery until 1850. Similarly, although it is actually true that the glass on the table contains orange juice, it might have contained tea, or it might have contained nothing at all, or there might have been no glass whatsoever, owing to my lack of thirst. These propositions are contingent. Their truth value *depends on* what is actually happening in the world. Their truth or falsity depends on the states of affairs, on the way the world is.

Necessary propositions, however, do not depend on the way the world is or might be. The truth value of necessary propositions could not be otherwise. The proposition that $\sqrt{16} = 4$ is *independent* of the particular antics in the world around us. The propositions that red is a color or that brothers are male siblings are true, regardless of whether apples are only green or whether Cain was his brother's keeper. Similarly, there are necessarily false propositions. It is false, and necessarily so, that $3 + 9 = 13$, no matter how many different kinds of object one puts in groups of three and groups of nine.

It is not difficult to see why one might think that propositions that are known a priori are also necessary. Suppose a certain proposition is known a priori. This implies that its justification is independent of any particular set of experiences one might have. That is, our observations of particular features of the world will not provide any reason for thinking that the proposition is true. What happens in the world is simply irrelevant to the justification of the proposition. If the course of experience will not provide any reason for thinking the proposition is true, then the truth value of the proposition apparently is independent of the course of world events. (Notice that if the truth value was dependent on the way the world is, then seemingly our sensory experiences could provide us with a reason for thinking the proposition is true.) But if the truth value of the proposition is independent in this way, then the proposition is necessary, for no matter what happens in the world, the truth value of the proposition could not be otherwise. This, of course, is precisely what it means to say that a proposition is necessary. So, any proposition known a priori is a necessary proposition.

Two comments about this argument are in order. First, one might wonder whether the converse of the conclusion is true. Is it true that if a proposition is necessary, then it is at least knowable a priori? Notice that the question suggests only that necessary propositions are *knowable,* not that they are actually known a priori. Some necessary propositions—for example, logical or mathematical propositions—may be so complex that their justification might exceed our present cognitive abilities. The following might then be suggested: If a proposition is necessary and knowable, then it is knowable *only* a priori. The intuitive argument for this proceeds along the same lines as the previous argument. Briefly, because the truth of the proposition is independent of actual events in or features of the world, then these events would seem to provide little reason for our believing the proposition to be true. Kant holds, as explained in the next section, that our recognition of the necessity of a proposition is sufficient to indicate that the proposition is known a priori.

The second comment is that both these arguments have recently been questioned. First, some have argued that there are contingent a priori propositions. ("A priori propositions" is but an abbreviation for the more exact "propositions known a priori" or "propositions justified a priori.") Second, some have argued that there are necessary propositions that are known a posteriori. These arguments will be considered later in the chapter. For the moment, we will take a closer look at theories of a priori knowledge.

HISTORICAL THEORIES OF THE A PRIORI

It might be appropriate to begin this section by briefly outlining the motives that led to so many philosophers defending, in one form or another, the claim that some of our knowledge is a priori. Plato, for example, in both the *Meno* and the *Phaedo,* claims that some of our knowledge is independent of this or that particular experience and that we cannot explain how we could have such knowledge by appeal to mere experience. Particular experiences, such as being questioned in an appropriate, if annoying, Socratic fashion or comparing the length of two sticks, may trigger that knowledge. But the knowledge itself arises from ideas we have prior to experience; experience simply leads us to *recall* the ideas that were dormant within us. Plato thus argues that we have some *innate* ideas. But one need not be committed to the existence of innate ideas to hold that we have a priori knowledge. Two interrelated reasons might be offered for holding that some knowledge must be a priori.

Beliefs based on sensory experiences alone might be thought to be insufficiently trustworthy. We have seen that Descartes, in some respects, holds this view; many have attributed something like this view to Plato. If one holds this sort of view, then our knowledge might be thought to depend on something other than experience. Again, however, one can hold that we have a priori knowledge without also holding that our sensory experiences are untrustworthy. Philosophers as diverse as Aristotle, Bonaventure, Aquinas, Leibniz, and Kant claim that our senses provide us with knowledge but that we also have a priori knowledge. The source of a priori knowledge is found in our reasoning capacities. More importantly, it is this higher-order cognitive ability that leads us to certain truths, which are discernible independently of the senses. At least some of these truths, knowable a priori, inform us of significant features of the world we inhabit. Descartes, for example, holds that there are two distinct substances, mind and body. This claim is not obviously knowable simply on the basis of what experience teaches. Similarly, the claims that all events have a cause (Kant) or that this is the best of all possible worlds (Leibniz) seem to exceed what we learn from our sensory experience. The justification, if there is any, for these types of claim seems best understood as a priori, as independent of our senses. Thus, it is plausible to think that very general metaphysical claims about the nature and structure of the world can be claimed as knowledge only if one accepts some version of a priori knowledge. This view, that we can have knowledge about very general features of the world, seems to be a fundamental motive for holding that we have a priori knowledge. This view also proves to be controversial. Indeed, the logical positivists of the early twentieth century targeted just these sorts of metaphysical claim. And as we will see, a principal weapon in their attack is a claim about the extent of our a priori knowledge.

The remainder of this section is divided into two parts. The first outlines the traditional theory; the second is devoted to Kant's contribution on the topic of a priori knowledge. The traditional theory is distinguished by its answers to the questions of the nature of the process of a priori justification and the connection between the a priori and the necessary.

The Traditional Theory of A Priori Knowledge

The traditional theory, as Roderick Chisholm dubs it, is a rough approximation of views held by many philosophers, especially prior to the late eighteenth century.[2] Chisholm describes the core contention of the traditional theory as follows:

> Once we have acquired some concepts (once we know, with respect to certain attributes, just *what* it is for something to have those attributes), we will also be in a position to know just *what* it is for a proposition or state of affairs to be necessary—to be necessarily such that it is true or necessarily such that it obtains. Then, by contemplating or reflecting upon certain propositions or states of affairs, we will be able to see that *they* are necessary.[3]

According to the traditional view, there are truths, knowable a priori, about properties, numbers, or states of affairs.[4] We can recognize that certain propositions are necessarily true because we understand the concepts contained in those propositions. An understanding of the term "brother" suffices for understanding that it is necessarily true that all brothers are male siblings. It is impossible for there to be something that is both a brother and not a male. Further, the recognition that a proposition is necessary does not derive from any sensory experience. More to the point, our recognizing the necessity of a proposition derives from our capacity to reason. It is reason alone that enables us to grasp the necessity of propositions such as "All bachelors are unmarried males" or "Red is a color." Philosophers as diverse as St. Augustine and Bertrand Russell seem to hold something like this.[5] We can grasp the necessity of a proposition simply by virtue of our "contemplating" or "reflecting" on the relevant propositions or states of affairs. Thus, in the traditional view, our recognition of the necessity of a proposition underlies the a priori justification of a belief. Indeed, I am a priori justified in believing that red is a color only to the extent that I grasp or see that this proposition is necessary. Described in this way, the traditional view holds that (a) any a priori justified proposition must be a necessary proposition, and (b) "grasping" or "seeing" that a proposition is necessary is enough to provide a person with an a priori justification for the proposition. The source of a priori justification lies in the purely reason-based seeing of the necessity of a proposition. Again, the use of the metaphor of the mind *seeing* the necessity is frequent; the metaphor can be found in St. Augustine, Russell, and Duns Scotus.[6]

One might reasonably hold that simpler propositions—for example, that red is a color or that bachelors are unmarried—are recognized as necessary. But one might also wonder whether the traditional view is restricted to only such simple propositions. Reflection on the truth that " 'not both Sara and Sam went to the store' is logically equivalent to 'either Sara did not go or Sam did not go to the store' " sometimes leaves one gasping rather than grasping. One possibility for extending our cursory sketch of the traditional theory can be found in elements of Leibniz's view.

Leibniz claims that the principle of contradiction provides a way to distinguish between propositions knowable by reason alone and those that could be known only with the aid of the senses. Although Leibniz does not make use of the terminology of a priori justification, certain propositions, which he calls *truths of reason*, clearly are knowable a priori, and thus are justifiable a priori. But, if our knowledge of certain propositions depends on our senses, then those propositions are *truths of fact*. The former, Leibniz claims, are necessary; the latter, contingent.[7] Leibniz claims that the principle of contradiction will enable us to identify all and only the truths of reason. The rationale is not difficult to see. Because truths of reason are necessary, they cannot be otherwise. The falsity of such propositions is impossible. Thus, the denial of truths of reason yields *impossible propositions* or *self-contradictions*. Moreover, self-contradictory propositions are recognizable by reason alone. Once we understand a proposition, we can determine, by reflection, whether the denial of that proposition is self-contradictory. In a letter he wrote to Queen Sophia Charlotte, Leibniz calls this reflective capacity the *natural light*, a power born within each of us.[8] Our reflective capacity is an innate capacity, natural to each of us.

Leibniz realizes that it is not always obvious whether a proposition is necessary. There are some necessary propositions whose denial is not obviously self-contradictory. Leibniz's resolution of this problem has two features. First, Leibniz claims that identity statements—for example, "Bachelors are bachelors" and "Rational animals are animals"—are the basic form of necessary propositions. Second, Leibniz holds that any necessary proposition can always be translated into an equivalent identity statement. For example, the proposition that red is a color can be translated into the equivalent proposition "The color red is a color." But the denial of this proposition, that the color red is not a color, is, on reflection, evidently self-contradictory. Consequently, we see that "Red is a color" is necessary and a truth of reason. Our belief that red is a color thus is justified a priori and is an instance of a priori knowledge.

Leibniz's view is plausibly classified as an instance of the traditional theory. Our knowledge of truths of reason is dependent on our grasp of, or our seeing the necessity of, such truths. Leibniz's appeal to both the principle of contradiction and the necessity of identity statements enables him to explain how we can come to recognize the necessity of truths of reason. In a sense, any rational person can see that certain propositions are necessary. A subtlety of Leibniz's view, however, can be brought out by brief consideration of a possible objection.

Suppose we want to know whether, in Leibniz's theory, a certain proposition is a truth of reason or a truth of fact. In the *Monadology*, for

The Principle of Contradiction

The Principle of Contradiction asserts that a proposition cannot be both true and false at the same time. (For this reason, the principle is usually called the principle of *non*-contradiction.) Propositions that violate the principle are said to be self-contradictory. For example, it would be self-contradictory to assert that Sam is a husband but is not married. We would be tempted to say that a person who asserted such a proposition did not *understand* the concept of "husband." Perhaps a more familiar case of an apparent violation of the principle is "Having your cake and eating it, too." In standard propositional logic, the principle is equivalent to the Law of Excluded Middle, which states that every proposition is either true or false. The Principle of Contradiction has a long history in philosophy, dating back to Aristotle, who argued that adhering to a version of the principle is a necessary condition of meaningful thought and communication. Along with the Principle of Identity, which says that A is A, the Principle of Contradiction, and the Law of Excluded Middle are sometimes referred to as the "Three Laws of Thought."

example, Leibniz claims that a simple substance neither has a natural beginning nor can be destroyed.[9] It is not immediately obvious how the proposition might be reduced to an identity statement. Suppose we are given the further information that only compound substances have natural beginnings, because only things with parts can have natural beginnings. Suppose as well that this enables us to complete the translation of our original statement into an identity statement. Might we not wonder whether the translated statement was indeed equivalent to the original? Think of the last time you stopped at a convenience store for directions and were given a list of turns, traffic lights, and street names. As you got back in the car, were you confident that you were to go south on I-15 and turn west on I-8, or that you were to go eight miles south on I-15 and then turn west? Or recall the curious anxiety you feel after carefully following directions to your destination and having one of your companions ask, "Is this it?"

Leibniz and traditional theorists assure us that our genuine understanding of a proposition is coextensive with our recognizing its necessity. But suppose we follow directions carefully, arrive at the reduced identity statement for "Simple substances have no natural beginning," and anxiously wonder, "Is this it? Is this the identity version of 'Simple substances . . . '?" Which of the following should we conclude—that the statement is not necessary, that we did not genuinely understand it, or that the reduction was carried out incorrectly, or a combination of these?

Now, one could respond that the traditional theory was never meant to provide a criterion for determining *in advance* which statements are a priori knowable. The theory merely identifies the conditions of a priori knowledge by means of the pair of conditionals "If you grasp the necessity of a proposition, then you know it a priori" and "If you know the proposition a priori, then you grasp the necessity of that proposition." In short, Leibniz's theory might tell us what conditions must be satisfied in order to have a priori knowledge, but the theory might not always enable us tell which are propositions are knowable a priori. It is worth noting, however, that the tight link between necessity and the a priori is disputed, as we will see shortly.

One related feature of Leibniz's theory bears notice. One might wonder whether Leibniz has any reason for thinking that identity statements are necessary, or equivalently, that their denials are self-contradictory. One commentator suggests that Leibniz thinks that the principle of contradiction is *epistemologically indispensable.*[10] To assert a contradiction is to say nothing, or worse, to speak nonsense. Were we to countenance believing explicit contradictions, it would render our thinking and our belief system empty of content and significance. Acceptance of the principle of contradiction is a necessary condition of our reasoning. One advantage of this sort of view is that it seems to provide an independent criterion for a priori knowledge. Roughly, a proposition is a priori knowable if either it is a necessary condition of reasoning or it is derived from such a proposition. Whether Leibniz is actually committed to this view, it bears some resemblance to a very recent view espoused by Hilary Putnam, who claims that a proposition is justifiable a priori if it is *rationally unrevisable.*[11] It is, however, a very special type of proposition that Putnam has in mind: those that are essential to our conception of rationality. Putnam suggests that each of us knows a priori that not all of our beliefs are both true and false. To claim otherwise is to give up our view of how we think and reason, or, as Putnam says, "to have no notion of rationality."[12] If accepting the denial of a proposition would undermine the rationality of our system of thought and belief, then the proposition is justifiable a priori. In Putnam's view, it is our conception of rationality that legitimizes certain propositions as knowable a priori.

This potential affinity between Putnam and Leibniz suggests an interesting extension of the role for the *content* of a priori knowledge. On the one hand, propositions knowable a priori may be simple identity statements. On the other hand, some a priori knowable propositions might describe the requisite conditions for our knowledge of the world. Such propositions describe the nature of our experience of the world. Kant is committed to the idea that there are such propositions and that they are knowable a priori.

Kant and the Synthetic A Priori

Immanuel Kant's (1724–1804) view of a priori knowledge is motivated in part by Hume's negative thesis about the scope of our knowledge. Hume claims that we have knowledge of but two types of propositions: either (a) propositions that merely report what we learn from experience or (b) those that describe what we know of the relations between ideas. The latter is the full extent of our a priori knowledge. The scope of our a priori knowledge, according to Hume, is restricted to the necessary connections between concepts.[13] Typical of the propositions known a priori are mathematical propositions or, more generally, definitional propositions, such as "2 + 2 = 4" or "All bachelors are unmarried males." These propositions are necessary, according to Hume. The source of their necessity lies in our understanding. Specifically, we recognize that the denial of such propositions is inconceivable.[14] Unfortunately, necessary propositions are also wholly uninformative about the world. We are thus confined either to what experience explicitly teaches us or to tracing the connections between our concepts. Left out of this sketch of the meager reaches of human knowledge are propositions of two sorts—those that we would now describe as scientific laws and those that describe very general features of the world, such as "All changes to objects are caused." This latter proposition is neither a report of our experience nor a mere definitional rendering of the term "cause." Indeed, not only the concept of causation but, equally, concepts such as those of substance and the self are not suitable objects of human knowledge, because propositions containing these concepts possess neither the appropriate empirical or conceptual credentials. Thus, Hume argues, famously or infamously, our alleged knowledge of an enduring self cannot be justified on either empirical grounds or by appeals to what we mean by "self." Definition is silent, and experience shows us but a sequence of distinct impressions. Metaphysically, we are all quite shallow.[15] Hume insists that this type of argument can be repeated many times for any proposition that goes beyond the limits of experience or definition. This is not a happy result, especially if one is inclined to think that there is a structure to our experience and its causes, a describable, predictable, knowable structure.

Kant's deep conviction manifests itself in his claim that there are **synthetic a priori propositions,** which are indeed knowable by us. To the pair of distinctions a priori/a posteriori and necessary/contingent, Kant adds a third. **Analytic propositions** (judgments) are those in which the predicate concept is contained in the concept of the subject. **Synthetic propositions** (judgments) are those in which the predicate concept is not contained in the concept of the subject.[16] The notion of containment is, of course, a metaphor, but Kant's intent is at least understandable. Analytic propositions do not give us any new information. Either they are wholly redundant, as in "A rose is a rose," or the predicate merely spells out or explicates the concept in the subject of the proposition. The predicates in "Sisters are female siblings" or "Red is a color" do not add anything new to the subject concepts; they simply set out features, properties, or characteristics of the subject concept. Analytic propositions are thus definitional in nature, although the predicate may provide only a partial definition. Like Leibniz and Hume before him, Kant holds that the essential feature of an analytic judgment is that its denial is self-contradictory.

Synthetic propositions give us new information. The predicate concept provides us with information that cannot be discerned simply by analyzing or spelling out the subject concept. If Sara judges that the frost has killed the acacia tree, the predicate tells us something new. It is not an essential property of frost that it kills any acacia tree, much less this one. Notice that any a posteriori proposition is synthetic. Experience gives us new information: that the acacia tree is dead, that the apple is red, or that Sara's sister works for Apple. The new information cannot be had by mere inspection of the subject. Moreover, such propositions are obviously contingent; after all, the acacia tree might have been saved, and Apple might not be. On this much, Kant and Hume agree: There are synthetic *a posteriori* propositions, which are one and all contingent.

Their agreement extends still further. Analytic propositions, because they merely recount the definitional connections between concepts, are a priori and necessary. Indeed, Kant holds that necessity is an essential characteristic of a priori propositions. Of course, this leads to Hume's and Kant's joint rejection of analytic a posteriori propositions. By definition, analytic judgments do not depend on the course of one's experience. This harmony is summarized in the following three claims:

1. There are synthetic a posteriori judgments, and these are contingent.
2. There are analytic a priori judgments, and these are necessary.
3. There are no analytic a posteriori judgments.

The harmony disappears, however, with respect to synthetic *a priori* judgments. Interestingly, Kant thinks that mathematical judgments are synthetic a priori. He claims that reflecting on the concepts of 5, 7, and addition will not reveal the concept of 12. More importantly, he holds that certain propositions that describe conditions necessary for experience, such as that every event has a cause, are synthetic and knowable a priori. Two matters are of importance at this point.

	A Posteriori	*A Priori*
Analytic	Neither	Hume and Kant
Synthetic	Hume and Kant	Kant

First, it is worth briefly outlining the problematic character of synthetic *a priori* judgments. Synthetic judgments give us new information. More precisely, the information contained in the predicate goes beyond the information that can be obtained through simple analysis of the subject. A priori judgments, by contrast, are independent of experience. Moreover, a judgment is knowledge only if, among other things, it is justified. That is, we must have some reason for thinking that the judgment (belief) is true. Now, what reason might we have for thinking that a synthetic a priori judgment is true? The reason cannot come from an appeal to the meanings of the concepts. Because the judgments are synthetic, the information exceeds that which is revealed by analyzing the meaning of the concepts. Nor can we appeal to experience, for the judgments are a priori. But if we cannot appeal to meaning or experience, where will we find a reason for thinking synthetic a priori judgments are true? Matters are still worse. Kant holds that a priori judgments, whether synthetic or analytic, are necessary. Thus, if we are said to know synthetic a priori propositions, then we must find a reason *that they cannot be otherwise,* and this reason cannot be drawn from our understanding of the concepts or from experience. Where could we find such a reason? If neither the meaning of the terms nor experience provide us with the requisite justification for synthetic a priori judgments, there seems to be no other source for their justification.

The second matter, Kant's defense of our knowledge of synthetic a priori judgments, is a bit more complex. Kant thinks that there are necessary conditions for us to have any knowledge or experience. Synthetic a priori judgments describe these necessary conditions. Now, his intention is to point out something more general and fundamental than simply saying that knowledge is justified true belief. His aim is to identify the conditions that make it possible for us to have justified true belief—indeed, that make it possible for us to have the kind of experience that would lead to our having beliefs at all.

Reflecting on ordinary experience reveals that there are requisite "background conditions," claims Kant. Recall an earlier example, the proposition that the frost killed the acacia tree. There is nothing at all unusual about this sort of judgment. We make use of this type of judgment all the time—that is, we claim that one event caused another. When mom asks who left the ice cream out and let it melt, and Sara insists that Sam did it, Sara is attributing a causal role to Sam. Similarly, when Sara leaves her computer to get an apple, she is generally unworried about the computer's continuing existence while she is out of the room. Things remain the same unless there is some cause of their changing. "It didn't just get up and walk out by itself!" is a familiar response to your sibling's disingenuous claim not to have touched some now-missing item while you were out of the room. The point of the examples is to illustrate the ubiquity of the notions of causality and the general stability of objects, as these notions are reflected in our beliefs about our experience. Everywhere in our experience we find causal connections among relatively enduring, three-dimensional objects.

Actually, it is a bit misleading to say we "find" causal connections or relatively enduring objects. It is a bit closer to Kant's view, perhaps, to say that we put them there. Kant thinks our cognitive makeup is such that we *must* experience objects as enduring or causally connected. Experience does not give us the concept of causality. Rather, experiencing objects as causally related is a precondition of any experience. Similarly, the idea of an enduring self is not to be found in the simple introspection of a series of impressions. Rather, an enduring self is the precondition of the recognition of a *series* at all. Hume could not have had the impression of a whole apple, followed by the impression of an apple with one bite missing, followed by the impression of an apple with two bites missing, . . . , followed by the impression of a ragged-edge apple core unless there was an enduring self that connected the discrete impressions.

Kant's rationale for the existence of synthetic a priori judgments may now be a bit more accessible. He holds that reason can reveal to us the concepts that structure or shape our experience. (He calls these concepts "categories.") The concepts are innate, or part of our cognitive makeup. We thus come to understand the nature of these concepts by means of reason, and independently of experience. Our understanding of these concepts is thus a priori. But from these concepts, we learn something new—specifically, something about the nature of our experience. We learn, for example, that the causal properties of the lighted match are not merely features of our past experience, but that we will find those causal properties in evidence in our future encounters with lighted matches. Thus, propositions containing these special concepts are synthetic. They are also necessary. Appropriate reflection reveals to us that, given that we are the kinds of beings we are, *any* experience we might have must be governed or structured by these concepts. We cannot be the kinds of cognitive beings we are and still experience things other than as causally connected, relatively enduring, three-dimensional objects. Things *cannot* be otherwise. Whether we experience the ice cream melting or the acacia dying, we experience the world around us *as* a world of causes.

At least, things cannot be otherwise *for us*. It is then a somewhat different kind of necessity that attaches to synthetic a priori judgments. It is certainly not the sort of logical necessity underwritten by the principle of contradiction, nor is it obviously a kind of physical necessity. The laws of nature seem indifferent to the precise character of our cognitive nature. The necessity seems to have its source in the design and function of beings like us. Very informally, if you want a being to have a certain kind of knowledge of a certain kind of world, then you had better give that being certain cognitive tools, among them structuring concepts such as cause, necessity, substance, and self. Such beings will, predictably, have certain kinds of experience and not others, but that is the price of having this kind of being. Nonhuman beings might experience things in a quite different way.

While these last remarks are a bit more speculative, perhaps the general outline of Kant's account of a priori knowledge is clearer. Like his predecessors, Kant holds that we can have a priori knowledge of the relations between concepts. Though necessary, analytic judgments, like the identities underlying Leibniz's truths of reason, are rather uninformative. It is precisely their uninformative character that accounts for their a priori status. The explication of "sister" in "All sisters are female siblings" requires no appeal to experience. Our recognition of the necessity of this and similar propositions comes from our understanding, our grasp of the concepts involved.

Kant's distinctive contribution is his claim that we are justified in believing certain propositions, which are synthetic *and* a priori. Our justification derives from our recognizing, by means of reason alone, that certain concepts are necessary for us to have any experience at all. The concepts are not derived from experience, but they inform our experience. The proposition that all events are caused is synthetic a priori. But this proposition, along with other synthetic a priori propositions, describes universal features of our experience. Our experience could not be otherwise; we are bound to experience in the manner described by such propositions. In this sense, synthetic a priori propositions are necessary.

Kant's distinction between analytic and synthetic, and his consequent classification of judgments as analytic a priori, synthetic a posteriori, and synthetic a priori frames much subsequent debate over a priori knowledge. It is Kant's contention that we have synthetic a priori knowledge that proves most controversial. This contention might be pressed in three ways. We have already had a hint of one possibility. One might worry whether such judgments are indeed necessary, even if we allow that the necessity distinctive of synthetic a priori judgments differs from the necessity characteristic of analytic propositions. One might argue that it is a mistake to see our cognitive makeup as the source of the necessity, that the necessity rather lies in the nature of objects and their properties.[17] More recent theories of the a priori turn on two further issues: The intimate connection alleged between necessity and the a priori is subject to doubt, as is the distinction between the synthetic and analytic. These two issues are the principal focus of the next section.

CONTEMPORARY VIEWS OF THE A PRIORI

It is a distinctive feature of the traditional view that propositions known a priori are necessary. We are a priori justified in believing a proposition if we *see* that it is necessary or that it could not be otherwise. We are able to see the necessity of propositions by means of the capacity of reason; we grasp the necessity without the aid of our senses. Indeed, there is a sense in which our seeing the necessity is constitutive of our understanding certain types of propositions. The traditional view, however, leaves us to wonder about the nature of this grasping. Leibniz's appeal to the principle of contradiction extends the traditional view. Necessary propositions are but variants of some identity statement. In his view, we see the necessity of a proposition when we see that it is the denial of some identity statement. And the denials of identity statements are patently contradictory. To the objection that Leibniz's reliance on the principle of contradiction merely shifts the "grasping" of the traditional view onto our grasping the impossibility of a contradiction, we might reply that at least Leibniz has pushed matters about as far back as they can be; he has identified a basic cognitive ability. Forswearing violations of the principle of contradiction is a condition of our continued ability to reason. Kant introduces a further refinement. The class of propositions known a priori is subdivided into analytic and synthetic propositions. With this new distinction comes the explicit claim that we can know a priori something other than the truths of mathematics or analytical connections between concepts. There are propositions knowable a priori that are characteristic, if not of the world, at least of our experience of the world. To his empiricist claim that all knowledge begins with experience, Kant adds the counterpoint anti-empiricist claim that synthetic a priori truths are knowable independently of the particular experiences we have. The empiricism reflected in much of twentieth-century philosophy is ill disposed toward synthetic a priori knowledge.

Linguistic Accounts of the A Priori

While Kant's characterization of analytic propositions as those in which the predicate is contained in the subject is somewhat metaphorical, it is still suggestive. The containment metaphor might be reinterpreted as a claim about meaning. Instead of referring to one concept containing another, we might instead think of one term as part of the meaning of another. We can then determine which propositions are analytic by analyzing the meaning of the constituent terms. The appeal to meaning as a basis for a theory of the a priori came to prominence in mid-century. A. J. Ayer (1919–1989) is one of the principal proponents of this view, which we will call the **linguistic theory of the a priori,** or *linguisticism.* In this view, the a priori and necessary character of a proposition is a function of meaning.

Like Hume, Ayer holds that our knowledge is but one of two types. We know propositions that are in principle confirmable (or disconfirmable) by some course of our experience.[18] It is experience that ultimately shows us the truth or falsity of these propositions. Because experience is the source of justification for these propositions, they are synthetic a posteriori. Ayer is also concerned to show that we do have knowledge of the truths of mathematics and logic, and he holds such truths to be analytic propositions. However, a principle motive for the linguistic theory is the rejection of rationalism and the idea that we can have synthetic a priori knowledge. Ayer is explicit about this motivation:

> For the fundamental tenet of rationalism is that thought is an independent source of knowledge . . . And the ground for this view is simply that the only necessary truths about the world which are known to us are known through thought and not through experience. So that if we can show either that the truths in question are not necessary or that they are not "truths about the world," we shall be taking away the support on which rationalism rests.[19]

Ayer claims that a proposition is analytic if it is true *solely* by virtue of the meaning of its constituent terms.[20] Like Hume, Ayer claims that the necessity of analytic propositions stems from the principle of contradiction. It would be contradictory to assert that Sam is both a bachelor and happily married. With Leibniz, we saw that the contradictory character of a proposition is found in the fact that it denies an identity statement. Linguisticism, however, ties the contradictory character of a proposition to *meaning*—specifically, to the *rules of language.* Thus, Ayer claims that

> the principles of logic and mathematics are true universally simply because we never allow them to be anything else. And the reason for this is that we cannot abandon them without contradicting ourselves, *without sinning against the rules which govern the use of language,* and so making our utterances self-stultifying.[21]

The necessity of a proposition derives from linguistic rules, which govern the proper uses of words and sentences. To assert that Sam is a happily married bachelor is at best to fail to understand the meaning of "bachelor." At worst, it is to traffic in incoherence.

On the surface, the linguistic view seems manageable. Ayer thinks that the linguistic view captures the important aspects of the Kantian view without, as Ayer sees it, the defect of committing to synthetic a priori truths. Nonetheless, there are troubling aspects to the linguistic theory.

As noted, Ayer claims that a proposition is analytic if it is true solely by virtue of the meaning of its terms. But he also describes analytic propositions as those *we can tell* are true without resorting to any actual or possible observation.[22] Now, this is unfortunate. The two formulations are not obviously equivalent, and the first, and more frequent, formulation opens the door to the central criticisms of the linguistic theory. The linguistic theory insists that the truth of any a priori proposition depends solely on its meaning. Consequently, advocates of linguisticism claim that a priori sentences are devoid of any factual content. It follows that there are no propositions knowable a priori that give us information about the world. They then reject the rationalist's claim that reason is a source of knowledge about the world.

Linguisticism thus divides in two the contents of our knowledge. On the one hand, our knowledge of the world is limited to what our senses might provide, whether directly or indirectly. On the other hand, we might come to know a priori propositions of a certain kind, but the truth of these a priori knowable propositions is solely a function of meaning. Taken together, these two claims about the types of propositions we know imply that we can have no a priori knowledge of the world. The claim that our linguistic decisions might determine the *truth* of a proposition is, however, at least as controversial as the claim that there are no synthetic a priori truths.

A fundamental objection to the linguistic theory of the a priori is that meaning alone does not account for the truth of any sentence or proposition, including analytic sentences. No sentence is true *solely* by virtue of the meaning of its terms. The truth of "All bachelors are unmarried" depends not just on the terms in the sentence, but also on the properties possessed by any bachelor, namely, that any such being is also unmarried.[23] There may be some plausibility to the claim that we are *a priori justified* if we can tell whether a sentence is true solely by inspecting the meaning of the terms. This is perhaps the linguistic analogue of claiming that we are a priori justified when we understand the concepts involved and *grasp* the necessity of the proposition. But it is quite another matter to claim that a sentence is true solely by virtue of the meanings of the terms. In some metaphorical sense, we may decide to use the word "bachelor" to pick out a certain kind of object and the word "unmarried" to pick out a certain kind of property. Doing so, however, does not imply that truth is solely a function of meaning. The truth of a sentence depends on whether the sentence represents the world accurately. That is, the truth of any sentence depends, at least in part, on the way the world is. *But meaning does not determine the way the world is,* and truth of a sentence is a function of the way the world is.[24] The sentence "Sara is Sam's sister" is true if the person named by "Sara" is, in fact, the daughter of Sam's parents. Further, "All sisters are female siblings" is *true* if and only if, for any sister we happen across, that person is also female and not an only child. (Notice this is not a comment about how we *know* that all sisters are female siblings. It is a comment about what makes such a sentence *true.*) Linguisticism's account of analytic sentences is a mistaken account of the truth of such sentences. Even if we choose, in some sense, the meaning of our words, we do not thereby make truth solely a function of meaning.

The Traditional, the Linguistic, and the Truth

Although there are some complicated issues involved, we can try to trace them in a simpler way. We have the following as an approximate view of a priori knowledge: Roughly, we are a priori justified in believing a proposition if our justification does not depend on any particular experience or set of experiences. On what does the justification depend? A common type of answer seems to be that we understand the concepts in the proposition. Notice that, so far, we have said nothing about what makes a proposition true; so far, there is no place for linguistic theory. Return to the "common" answer. We might now ask, "Ok, just what is it that we understand?" The answer is that we understand that there is a *necessary* connection between the concepts. A crude gloss of this "necessary connection" is that wherever you find one, you will find the other. But these concepts refer to certain properties. So, if you find something to which the concept "sister" truly applies, then you've found something to which the concept "female" truly applies. This means that whenever you find the *property* "sister," you have found the *property* "female." You might be tempted to drop talk of concepts altogether and simply claim that whenever you find a bachelor, you've found something unmarried; find red, and you've found a color.

You will be forgiven if you find this power of reason somewhat amazing. By virtue of your understanding that the concepts of red and color are about certain properties in the world, your justification for believing that red is a color does not depend on your having any particular experience of red. So, *because of your understanding, you know in advance of any particular experience* that wherever you find red, you have found a color. Another way to put the "necessary connection" idea is that it is always true that wherever you find red, you have found a color. Moreover, it *must* be true that finding a red thing is also finding a colored thing; there's nothing accidental or lucky about the connection between the property of red and the property of color. The common type of answer, which is, of course, the traditional theory, thus connects the a priori with necessity. If you understand the concept of red, then you grasp that wherever you find a little bit of red, then it must be that you will also find a dab of color. Thus, by virtue of our understanding the concept of red, we grasp a certain fact about the world: Anything red is colored. In the traditional view, this is not a very deep fact. Nonetheless, it is a feature of the world, and it is this feature that underlies the truth of the proposition that red is a color. Once you have caught on to the trick, you can recount a great many such facts: Magenta is a color, chartreuse is a color, fuchsia is a color, and so on.

It is perhaps a bit clearer why linguisticism resists these aspects of the traditional view. The traditional theory claims that understanding or reason, not the senses, is the source of at least some, perhaps uninteresting, knowledge about the world. In the hands of philosophers like Descartes, Leibniz, and Kant, this doctrine of the a priori explains our knowledge of more interesting facts about the world—for example, God is not a deceiver, this is the best of all possible worlds, and space is independent of our perception. As we saw in the quote from Ayer, the linguistic theory sought to undermine the legitimacy of any such claims. The obstacle for the linguistic theory was finding an explanation for sentences such as "2 + 2 = 4," "Either P or not P," and "All bachelors are unmarried." Linguisticism could tolerate the idea that we could know the truth of such sentences by reason alone, so long as we were not acquiring any knowledge of the world. This means that analytic propositions could not be about the world in any way; they must be devoid of factual content. If analytic propositions are independent of the world, then clearly the world can play no part in the truth of such propositions. What, then, is the source of the truth of the propositions? The answer apparently has to be *meaning*, because there is not much left to play the required role. It is then an easy, if not predictable, move to the claim that analytic propositions are those that are true solely by virtue of their meaning. Moreover, the advocate of linguisticism cannot simply abandon the account. To do so is to countenance the thought that reason might give us knowledge of the world, even if it is not very new or interesting knowledge.

We might summarize matters in the following way: The traditional view is not exactly forthcoming about what it is to *grasp* or to *see* that a proposition is necessarily true. This is certainly a defect of that view, although we do perhaps have some sense of what it is for a proposition not to violate the Principle of Contradiction. Linguisticism's attempt to replace the traditional account with an account based on meaning leaves us with some puzzling questions about the truth of analytic propositions. But if so, then linguisticism's rejection of synthetic a priori propositions also might be thought to be in doubt.

Quinean Reservations

The linguistic theory of the a priori resists the idea that reason is a source of knowledge about the world by distinguishing between those statements that are purely factual and those that are purely linguistic. The former are synthetic statements, and the latter analytic. In the hands of proponents of linguisticism, the analytic/synthetic distinction becomes a distinction between what the world contributes to our knowledge by means of the senses and what the mind contributes by means of our linguistic decisions. Although one might have doubts regarding the linguistic account of the a priori, one might still think that the distinction between analytic and synthetic could be made clear. W. V. O. Quine challenges the tenability of the distinction in a watershed article, "Two Dogmas of Empiricism."[25] He claims that the difference between analytic and synthetic statements is at most a difference in degree, and not a difference in kind. According to Quine, the analytic/synthetic distinction can be maintained only if we can find an adequate explanation of what it is for a proposition to be analytic. The failure to find an adequate explanation leads to the conviction that we have a difference in degree only.

The basic thought behind Quine's argument is that any explanation of "analytic statement" inevitably appeals to one of a set of notions that, along with "analytic statement," are interdefinable. Attempted explanations are consequently circular, according to Quine, and must be rejected. Quine takes linguisticism's definition of analytic proposition as his departure point.

The linguistic account of the analytic takes the notion of meaning as primary. If, however, a statement is analytic if it is true by virtue of the meanings of its terms, it is natural to reinterpret this as sameness of meaning of the terms. Consider the commonsense explanation of why it is true that all bachelors are unmarried males: The subject and the predicate *mean* the same thing. Indeed, untutored intuition might even hold that *meaning the same thing* explains the necessity of analytic propositions. It might be held that *meaning the same thing* is the twentieth-century analogue of Kant's metaphor of containment: "bachelor" contains "unmarried male" because "bachelor" means the same thing as "unmarried male." When two expressions or terms mean the same thing, we say they are *synonymous*. The task of explaining the notion of analytic proposition now becomes the task of explaining the synonymy of two expressions.

The heart of Quine's argument, which we will be unable to follow in all its technical details, is that any account of the synonymy of two terms ineluctably leads us back to the notion of an analytic proposition. Our explanation is thus hopelessly circular. But we can still give an intuitive sketch of Quine's argument. Consider two terms that are undeniably synonymous: "sister" and "female sibling." How might we explain what it is for these two expressions to be synonymous? We might start with something like the claim that anytime you use one term, you can use the other without changing the truth value of the sentence. For example, "Sara is Sam's female sibling" is unusual, but it communicates the very same thought as "Sara is Sam's sister." This approach is at least intuitively appealing. Yet Quine worries that there are two drawbacks to this manner of explaining synonymy.

First, Quine suggests, the reason we might be able to interchange the two expressions might have nothing to do with the *meaning* of the expressions. Remember that our goal here is simply to identify those sentences that are true solely by virtue of their meanings. There appear to be counterexamples to the interchangeability approach, according to Quine. "Creature with a heart" and "creature with a kidney" are two expressions that obviously differ in meaning. Yet, due to certain biological contingencies, everything that is true of one is true of the other. Thus, we can interchange two terms without changing the truth value of the sentences, but the terms clearly are not synonymous.

Quine's second worry is perhaps more substantial. Roughly, Quine claims the following: This is what is really meant when it is claimed that two expressions, call them A and B, have the same meaning. When you take the two expressions and plug them into a sentence of the form "All ——— are ———," you get a necessary truth. So, A and B have the same meaning if and only if "All A are B" is a necessary truth. "Sister" and "female sibling" are synonymous if and only if "All sisters are female siblings" is necessary. But, according to linguistic theory, necessary truths are simply the analytic propositions. Consequently, we have this tightly knit circle. A sentence is analytic if its terms have the same meaning, or are synonymous. Those terms are synonymous if the appropriate sentence (All ——— are ———) is a necessary truth. But, again, linguistic theory states that necessary truths are the analytic propositions. So, to know which terms are synonymous, you already have to know what an analytic proposition is. But this is precisely what we set out to explain! Moreover, Quine claims that we will not be able to fix this problem by appealing to more formal or technical systems. Thus, we cannot give a satisfactory account of the notion of analytic proposition. That there is a distinction between analytic and synthetic propositions is one dogma of empiricism that must be rejected, according to Quine.

Because we are unable to distinguish between the analytic and the synthetic sentences, we are unable to identify those sentences that are true solely by virtue of the world and those sentence that are true solely by virtue of the meanings *we* assign to the terms. Metaphorically, *any* sentence then has a little bit of us and a little bit of the world mixed into it. Now, Quine claims that this leads to the conclusion that no sentence, *by itself,* is confirmed or disconfirmed by experience. In more familiar terms, no belief is ever justified simply by appeal to a particular experience. My visual experience of the glass and its contents is relevant to *all* my beliefs, not just the belief that there is tea in the glass. Quine calls this view *holism,* although it may justifiably remind you of coherentism. Quine thus rejects the second "dogma of empiricism," which claims that certain beliefs can be directly justified by appeal to experience. Regardless of the final verdict, there is some reason to think that for a period of time Quine's "Two Dogmas of Empiricism" helped to swing the pendulum away from foundationalism and toward holism and coherentism.

Challengers to dogmas often meet with resistance, and Quine was no exception. H. P. Grice and P. F. Strawson were among the first to respond to Quine.[26] They suggest that Quine's requirements for distinguishing the analytic from the synthetic are too stringent. There are other groups of terms that are similarly interrelated—for example, "morally wrong," "blameworthy," and "breaks moral rules." Grice and Strawson claim that simply because we cannot explain one of these terms without reliance on the others does not imply that we should be suspicious of these notions. Moreover, the mere fact that we are unable to draw a clear line between two concepts does not imply the absence of a legitimate distinction. Quine might concede these points but continue to insist that their relevance to the analytic/synthetic distinction is limited. Advocates of the linguistic theory of the a priori clearly intend to draw a clear distinction between analytic and synthetic statements. In particular, they claim that analytic propositions are empty of factual content.

Perhaps somewhat more promising is the suggestion by Grice and Strawson that there is something disingenuous in Quine's claim that we do not have an independent idea of synonymy. Quine would then seem committed to the somewhat extreme thesis that there is no genuine distinction between "means the same as" and "does not mean the same as."[27] We may not be able to draw this latter distinction precisely, but clearly we could not easily do without it. There is nothing unusual about insisting that one's words have not been given a fair rendering. More importantly, the claim that a new sentence "does (or does not) mean the same as" one's original sentence plays an important role in many of our ordinary cognitive endeavors. Rejecting this distinction seems implausible. So, if rejecting the analytic/synthetic distinction has this unhappy consequence, perhaps we ought to rethink Quine's reservations regarding the notion of analytic proposition.

Necessity and the A Priori

Common to all the views considered thus far is the assumption of a connection between the a priori and the necessary. Indeed, the connection was not seriously doubted until the last two decades. Recall that early in the chapter, we briefly scouted the argument that if a proposition is knowable a priori, then it is necessary, as well as the argument for the converse, that if a proposition is necessary, then it must be known a priori. Recently, various examples have been suggested that attempt to cast doubt on these assumptions.

Consider first the claim that any proposition knowable a priori must be necessary.[28] Now, imagine a slight variation of Descartes's "I think, therefore I am." If I reflect on the general fact that I have various experiences that give rise to a range of beliefs, I have a reason for thinking that I exist. As long as I am aware that I have beliefs, then I have a justification for thinking that I exist. Notice that my belief that I exist is independent of any particular experience. No particular experience, whether the experience of a glass of tea, the ringing of a phone, or the scent of jasmine on an evening breeze, is necessary for my acquiring the concept of my existence. Any set of experiences will do. Because my believing that I exist is independent of particular experiences, the justification is a priori. It is, however, surely a contingent fact that I exist. I am quite confident that there is no necessity that I exist, any more than any mortal's existence is necessary. Consequently, we have an example of a contingent belief that is a priori justified.

It might seem that some sleight of hand is at work here. It might be tempting to object that while I do not need *particular* experiences, my justification for my belief that I exist clearly depends on my having some experience or other. So, one might urge that this is not a genuine case of a contingent proposition that is justified a priori. Recall, however, that theories of the a priori acknowledge that experience may be necessary for my *acquisition* of certain concepts. I require experience to learn the concept of bachelor. Similarly, I acquire the concept "my existence" as a result of my experiences. Once I acquire the concept, however, my justification for believing that I exist is independent of the particular course of my experiences. My justification for the belief is thus a priori. In an attenuated sense, it was Descartes's recognition of the *cogito* as independent of any particular experiences that permitted him to frustrate the evil demon. And like Descartes, we can claim that it is trivial to say that if I believe I exist, this belief is true. Hence, I have a priori knowledge of a contingent proposition.

It is also argued that there are examples of propositions that are necessary, but nonetheless we know them a posteriori. Such examples depend on the plausible and traditional assumption that identity statements are necessary. Leibniz, recall, holds identity claims to be paradigmatic instances of necessary propositions. Once it is granted that identity statements are necessary, it is then argued that we learn of or come to know these identity statements as a result of experience or empirical investigation. Take a rather simple example, that water is H_2O.[29] For a substance to be water, it *must* have this particular chemical composition, and anything that has this composition is in fact water. It is necessary that anything that is water is also H_2O; it could not be otherwise. But this is the mark of a necessary proposition. Clearly, however, our knowledge of this identity statement is based on empirical investigation. Science provides us with numerous examples of similar identity statements—for example, that a given element has a certain atomic weight. Our reason for believing such statements, however, clearly derives from experience. Our knowing that water is H_2O is evidently an instance of a posteriori knowledge. But then we would seem to have a posteriori knowledge of at least some necessary statements.

A central aspect of the traditional theory of the a priori is the alleged link between the a priori and the necessary. There is an intuitive argument for this link. As sketched early in the chapter, the argument suggests that the necessity of a proposition indicates that the course of experience could not provide us with any reason for thinking the proposition is true. Similarly, if experience provides no reason for thinking that a proposition is true, then the truth of the proposition would seem to be unaffected by the course of experience, and thus is necessary. The previous examples clearly run counter to this argument, but we might wonder where the argument goes wrong.

Closer inspection of the argument reveals a gap between premises and conclusion. Consider, for example, the necessary proposition that water is H_2O. Because the proposition is necessary, it cannot be otherwise; we will never find an instance of water that is not also an instance of H_2O. In turn, we might understand this as claiming that experience will never give us evidence for the claim that there is a bit of water somewhere that is not also H_2O. But notice what this does *not* imply. It does not imply that experience could never provide us with a reason for believing that water is H_2O. To claim that water is H_2O is only knowable a priori, we need to know that experience cannot be the source of our justification. The necessity of the proposition does not preclude experience as the source of our justification, however.

We find a similar gap in the argument that our a priori knowledge implies the necessity of the proposition. To have a priori knowledge implies that the reason for believing the proposition does not depend on a particular type of experience. From this, according to the traditional view, it is inferred that the proposition must be necessary. That is, the proposition refers to or describes states of the world that could not be otherwise. But it is argued that this is too hasty. The traditional view fails to distinguish between two ways in which the truth value of a proposition might be "indifferent" to the particular features or events in the world of which we might have a priori knowledge. That bachelors are unmarried is necessarily true. There is no way the course of events in the world might have occurred or might occur in the future that would render the proposition false. However, there are propositions whose truth values are fixed by the course of events in the world and our experience of them. Once the truth value is fixed, that truth value is unaffected by the course of events in the world. Clearly, such propositions are contingent, but we depend on our experience only to provide us with the relevant concepts. My existence and my believing that I exist are contingent facts; Mom might never have met Dad. But given that they did, given that other events transpired a certain way, including my acquiring the concept of my existence, there is now a *fixed* truth value for my belief that I exist. No future course of events can alter the truth of my belief that I exist. Nor is any particular experience required for my *justifiably* believing that I exist. I thus have an a priori justification for the contingent belief that I exist.

Cases in which we "fix the referent" of a concept are also held to provide instances of a priori knowledge. We might, for example, fix the referent of the concept "kilogram" by pointing to a certain mass and claiming that this mass is one kilogram.[30] This clump of matter will, from now on, be the standard for what it is to be a kilogram. Fixing the referent, or saying what the concept is about, does two things: (a) It provides the experience by which we acquire the concept of kilogram, and (b) it stipulates that no matter what else happens in the world, this clump is one kilogram. Experience may be required for you to know that the brick that fell on your foot weighs one kilogram, but no further experience is required for you to know that "This clump is one kilogram." In these sorts of case, the particular experience by which you acquire the requisite concepts also provides you with the requisite *experience-independent* justification for your believing the proposition.

If the examples just considered, and the arguments that underlie them, are correct, the link between the a priori and the necessary will be broken. If the arguments are correct, then there are truths about particular, contingent facts that are knowable a priori, and there are necessary identity statements that are knowable a posteriori.[31] We still have one further issue to consider: whether there are general propositions, which are knowable a priori, about the world or the nature of our experience. That is, we still might wonder whether there are synthetic propositions that are necessary and knowable a priori.

No Experience Required: Synthetic A Priori Propositions

Can we have a priori knowledge of facts about the world, or our experience of it, that is not grounded solely in our understanding certain concepts? Our investigation thus far does not rule out an affirmative answer. The linguistic theory of the a priori fails to establish conclusively that any proposition known a priori must be analytic. That is, it need not be the case that any a priori knowledge must have its source in our understanding the relevant concepts. Moreover, the immediately preceding discussion suggests that at least some features of our experience, albeit some quite specific features, are knowable a priori. Consequently, it is still an open question whether we might have a priori knowledge of synthetic propositions.

We might first remind ourselves of the type of proposition at issue. Kant's metaphorical understanding of synthetic propositions consisted in claiming that the predicate concept was not contained in the concept that was the subject of the proposition. The intuitive idea is that the predicate of a synthetic proposition gives us more information than that which is given by the subject. We could not know this additional information simply by understanding the subject concept. In other words, our reason for believing the proposition to be true could not have come simply from our knowledge of the constituent concepts. In the ordinary case, the source of our justification is experience. That the dog is asleep is a synthetic proposition. No understanding of the concept of dog will reveal the dog's watchfulness or state of slumber. Moreover, our justification for believing that there is a sleeping dog is experience of some sort—I see the sleeping pup, or I am told of his slumbering state, or I infer it from other synthetic propositions.

By definition, the justifications of synthetic a priori propositions do not depend on experience. There are then two initial questions: What kinds of proposition might be synthetic a priori? and, If neither experience nor our understanding of the concepts is the source of the justification for such propositions, what is?

Exclusive propositions are often held to be synthetic a priori. For example, that dogs are not giraffes or that nothing is red and green all over are examples of exclusive propositions. Why are such propositions thought to be synthetic? It is claimed that our understanding of the constituent concepts does not include all of the properties that are not contained in the concept. I might understand the concept of dog to refer to creatures normally having four legs and a keen sense of smell and occasionally giving a bark, but my grasp of the concept does not include all properties that dogs do not possess. Understanding the concept of dog implies that I possess a certain prototype or model of what it is to be a dog, not that I possess a model that indicates all the things dogs are not.

It is somewhat unfortunate that advocates of the synthetic a priori are more apt to explain why these propositions are synthetic than why they are knowable a priori.[32] Perhaps understandably, they have focused on arguments that purport to show that any synthetic a priori proposition really is a disguised analytic proposition. Consequently, less attention is given to the claim that we know such propositions a priori. Thus, it is sometimes *claimed* that we *simply see* the truth of propositions such as "Dogs are not giraffes." But we had best be careful about claiming that we simply see the truth of certain synthetic propositions.

A standard example of a synthetic a priori proposition is that nothing can be red and green all over, or equivalently, that being red excludes being green. There is some indication, however, that this proposition might not be true. C. L. Hardin cites an experiment in which subjects reported seeing a reddish-green.[33] Although the findings are disputed, Hardin notes that it is a matter for *experiment*. That is, whether it is true that something may be red and green all over depends on our experience. This is not to suggest that there are no synthetic a priori propositions. Rather, it suggests that we might still wish for an account that does not rely on our simply seeing that a proposition is true.

A plausible rationale for the a priori character of such propositions could be had, however, if there is an experience-independent reason for believing that such propositions are true. Consider all the things that dogs are not. Is it plausible that you require experience to be justified in believing such things? That dogs are not cats, that they are not giraffes, that they are not swallows returning to Capistrano—is experience required to justify these beliefs? It certainly would not seem so. But a potentially more revealing explanation might be something like the following: Given your understanding of the concept of dog, you are able to infer, perhaps implicitly, that being a dog precludes a thing from having certain other characteristics. This, of course, departs from the traditional theory's view that our seeing the truth is immediate or noninferential.[34] Nonetheless, the basis of such an inference might be something like the principle that no thing can have both its essential properties and properties that would exclude its having essential properties. You then recognize that having a certain property—being a giraffe, say—would make the dog something other than what it is. Your grasp of this principle enables you to *extend* your knowledge beyond what you know when you understand the concept of a dog. If an explanation along these lines is plausible, then it would explain not only the a priori character of exclusive propositions but also the necessity of such propositions. The necessity derives from the principle that underlies the inference.

Where does this leave us with respect to the propositions Kant found so interesting? There are propositions that are descriptive of very general features of our experience—for example, that not every statement is both true and false or that every event has a cause. Assuming that such propositions are synthetic, it is also plausible to hold that our justification for believing them does not derive from experience. Rather, reason tells us that the essential character of our experience depends on the truth of such propositions. We would not be experiencing, *thinking* beings were it not for the truth of certain synthetic a priori propositions. These propositions are then necessarily true, because their falsity is incompatible with our being the kinds of beings we are. This goes beyond the claim of rational unrevisability or epistemological indispensability. This line of thinking is not simply claiming that the truth of these propositions depends on our acceptance of them. It claims that certain essential facts about us and our relation to the world underlie our experience and knowledge of the world. That we can know these facts is perhaps remarkable enough. More remarkable still is the thought that we can know them and that there is *no experience required.*

Key Concepts

A posteriori knowledge

A priori knowledge

Analytic and synthetic propositions

Contingent and necessary propositions

Linguistic theory of the a priori

Synthetic a priori proposition

Review Questions

1. What is the traditional view's explanation of the connection between the a priori and the necessary? What are the criticisms of this explanation?

2. What is Leibniz's explanation of the necessity of truths of reason?

3. How does Kant distinguish between synthetic and analytic propositions? Why does Kant think we have a priori knowledge of synthetic a priori propositions? Do you think he is right that certain propositions describe the necessary conditions of our thought?

4. How does the linguistic theory of the a priori attempt to reject the traditional view's claim that reason provides us with knowledge of the world? What is the central criticism of this view?

5. Sketch Quine's argument against the analytic/synthetic distinction. Do you think Grice and Strawson give an adequate response to Quine? Explain.

6. Why are exclusive propositions thought to be an instance of synthetic a priori knowledge? Do you agree? Why or why not?

For Further Study

Two accessible accounts of the traditional view of the a priori are found in Roderick Chisholm, *Theory of Knowledge,* 2nd ed. (Englewood Cliffs, NJ: Prentice-Hall, 1977), Chap. 3, and Robert

Audi, *Belief, Justification, and Knowledge* (Belmont, CA: Wadsworth, 1988), Chap. 4. Two other essays provide a concise account of the relevant issues; see Albert Casullo, "A Priori/A Posteriori," and "A Priori Knowledge," both in Jonathan Dancy and Ernest Sosa, eds., *A Companion to Epistemology* (Oxford: Basil Blackwell, 1992), pp. 1–3 and 3–8, respectively.

Throughout Leibniz's work are remarks on this topic, but Frederick Copleston, S.J., provides a detailed account in *A History of Western Philosophy*, Vol. 4 (Garden City, NY: Doubleday, 1963), Chap. 16. Kant's view is contained in *Critique of Pure Reason* (New York: St. Martin's Press, 1965). Relevant aspects of Hume's view can be found in *A Treatise of Human Nature*, 2nd ed. (Oxford: Oxford University Press, 1978), especially Bk. I. Russell's view is most concisely stated in *The Problems of Philosophy* (New York: Oxford University Press, 1959), Chaps. 8 and 10.

A. J. Ayer presents his version of linguisticism in *Language, Truth and Logic*, 2nd ed. (New York: Dover, 1952). Perhaps the most famous criticism of the analytic/synthetic distinction, and hence of the a priori/a posteriori distinction, is contained in Quine's "Two Dogmas of Empiricism." This essay is widely reprinted but can be found in his *From a Logical Point of View*, 2nd ed. (New York: Harper, 1961), pp. 20–46. H. P. Grice's and P. F. Strawson's response, "In Defense of a Dogma," is reprinted in James F. Harris and Richard H. Severens, eds., *Analyticity* (Chicago: Quadrangle Books, 1970), pp. 56–74. The introductory essay of this anthology is also a very readable and excellent introduction to the issues circa 1970, including summaries of Kant's and Hume's positions. Saul Kripke's *Naming and Necessity* (Cambridge, MA: Harvard University Press, 1980) introduces some technical terminology but is accessible to the interested reader. As noted previously, Kripke challenges the traditional view that there is a link between the a priori and the necessary. In two essays, Philip Kitcher also challenges the traditional view and presents a view of a priori knowledge that he thinks is generally compatible with the reliabilist account of knowledge. "Apriority and Necessity" is reprinted in Paul K. Moser, ed., *A Priori Knowledge* (Oxford: Oxford University Press, 1987), pp. 190–207. "A Priori Knowledge" is reprinted in Hilary Kornblith, ed., *Naturalizing Epistemology* (Cambridge, MA: MIT Press, 1987), pp. 129–145. *A Priori Knowledge* contains several useful essays, including Moser's introduction, which also presents the major issues of the a priori knowledge debate. Moser distinguishes several different accounts of a priori knowledge.

Notes

1. The alternative formulation is a slight variation of the version in Philip Kitcher's "Apriority and Necessity," in Paul K. Moser, ed., *A Priori Knowledge* (Oxford: Oxford University Press, 1987), pp. 190–191.

2. Chisholm outlines this view in *Theory of Knowledge*, 2nd ed. (Englewood Cliffs, NJ: Prentice-Hall, 1977). It is reprinted as "Truths of Reason" in Moser, ed., *A Priori Knowledge*, pp. 112–144.

3. Chisolm, *Theory of Knowledge*, p. 40.

4. Chisolm, *Theory of Knowledge*, p. 34.

5. For St. Augustine's view, see. F. C. Copleston, *A History of Medieval Philosophy* (New York: Harper & Row, 1974), pp. 33–34. Russell's view is succinctly formulated in *The Problems of Philosophy* (New York: Oxford, 1959), especially Chaps. 8 and 10.

6. Copleston, *A History*, pp. 33–34, and Russell, *The Problems of Philosophy*, Chaps. 8 and 10. Duns Scotus's view is briefly described in Copleston, *A History*, pp. 216–217.

7. Gottfried Leibniz, *Monadology*, 33. Reprinted in Leroy E. Loemeker, ed., *Philosophical Papers and Letters* (Dordrecht: D. Reidel, 1969), p. 646.

8. Loemeker, ed., *Philosophical Papers and Letters*, pp. 550–551.

9. Loemeker, ed., *Philosophical Papers and Letters*, p. 641.

10. Margaret D. Wilson, "On Leibniz's Explication of 'Necessary Truth,'" in Harry G. Frankfurt, ed., *Leibniz: A Collection of Critical Essays* (Garden City, NY: Anchor, 1972), pp. 401–419.

11. Hilary Putnam, "Analyticity and Apriority," in Moser, ed., *A Priori Knowledge,* 85–111.

12. Putnam, "Analyticity and Apriority," p. 101.

13. See, for example, David Hume, *A Treatise on Human Nature* (Oxford: Clarendon Press, 1978), Bk. III, I, Sect. I.

14. Hume, *A Treatise on Human Nature,* Bk. I, III, Sects. III and XIV.

15. Hume, *A Treatise on Human Nature,* Bk. I, IV, Sect. VI.

16. Immanuel Kant, *Critique of Pure Reason,* trans. Norman Kemp Smith (New York: St. Martin's Press, 1965), B 10, p. 48. Kant considers analytic or synthetic judgments rather than propositions. This difference will not affect the exposition to follow.

17. Russell offers this sort of objection in *The Problems of Philosophy,* Chap. 8.

18. See A. J. Ayer, *Language, Truth and Logic,* 2nd ed. (New York: Dover, 1952), pp. 5–26.

19. Ayer, *Language, Truth and Logic,* p. 73.

20. Ayer, *Language, Truth and Logic,* p. 16, and Chap. 4.

21. Ayer, *Language, Truth and Logic,* p. 77; emphasis added.

22. Ayer, *Language, Truth and Logic,* pp. 78–79.

23. Chisholm offers this type of objection in *Theory of Knowledge,* p. 54. In "Truth by Convention," and "Carnap and Logical Truth," in *The Ways of Paradox* (Cambridge, MA: Harvard University Press, 1976), pp. 77–106 and 107–132, Quine argues against linguisticism's view of logical truth.

24. This objection does presume at least a kind of the correspondence theory of truth. However, many advocates of linguisticism accepted a version of the correspondence theory.

25. The article is widely reprinted; it appears in W. V. O. Quine, *From a Logical Point of View,* 2nd ed. (New York: Harper, 1961), pp. 20–46.

26. Quine, "In Defense of a Dogma," reprinted in James F. Harris, Jr. and Richard H. Severens, eds., *Analyticity* (Chicago: Quandrangle Books, 1970), pp. 56–74.

27. W. V. O. Quine, "In Defense of a Dogma," pp. 60–61.

28. Saul Kripke's challenges to the traditional theory in *Naming and Necessity* (Cambridge, MA: Harvard University Press, 1980) are perhaps best known. Relevant portions are reprinted in Moser, ed., *A Priori Knowledge,* pp. 145–160. The example here is from Kitcher, "Apriority and Necessity," pp. 194–196. The arguments in the text concerning the connection between the a priori and necessity rely on Kitcher's article.

29. Kripke considers these sorts of identity statement in *Naming and Necessity,* Lect. III.

30. Kripke's example in *Naming and Necessity,* Lect. I, is that of the standard meter bar.

31. Needless to say, Kripke's and Putnam's examples have been disputed, but these arguments are more complicated than we can consider here. Representative criticisms can be found in Albert Casullo, "Kripke on the A Priori and the Necessary," in Moser, ed., *A Priori Knowledge,* and Leonard Linsky, *Names and Descriptions* (Chicago: University of Chicago Press, 1977). For criticism of Putnam's view, see Avrum Stroll, "What Water Is: Or Back to Thales," in Peter A. French, et al., *Midwest Studies in Philosophy* (Notre Dame, IN: University of Notre Dame Press, 1989), pp. 258–274.

32. See, for example, Chisholm, *Theory of Knowledge,* and Robert Audi, *Belief, Justification, and Knowledge* (Belmont, CA: Wadsworth, 1988), Chap. 4.

33. C. L. Hardin, *Color for Philosophers* (Indianapolis, IN: Hackett, 1986), pp. 121–126.

34. Chisholm, *Theory of Knowledge,* pp. 40–46.

CHAPTER NINE

Perception

For most of us, our fundamental contact with the world is by means of perception. The use of our five senses—touch, taste, smell, sound, and sight— is the way we come to have our most basic information about the world. You look up from what you are reading, notice the shape and size and color of the furniture in the room, hear your roommate in the kitchen, and feel the cushion behind you slipping out of place.

Your senses convey to you information about objects and their properties. Doubtless, most of us could tell a rather simple story about how this information is conveyed. Take, for example, seeing the green glass on the table. Light strikes the glass; at least some of that light bounces off the glass, jj striking our retinas; and that light (or energy) is somehow transformed and moved along various passageways in the brain, until finally we have the visual image of the glass. Some of us undoubtedly could give a similar sort of story for the other senses.

Certain assumptions in this simple story are the focus of much of this chapter. First, we take it that there are physical objects. Two of the central characteristics that we assign to physical objects is that they are independent of us and that they are publicly accessible. Even if no one were looking at the glass, the glass would still be there. Further, any normally sighted person could see that the glass was there. A related characteristic, one that is especially important for this chapter, is that the qualities we sense are in the object. The simple story has it that if we see a green glass, then that's merely because the glass is, all by itself, even if no one were looking at it, *green*. If the glass were not green—if, say, it was red—then we would see a red glass and not a green one. Already implicit in what has been said so far is the idea that the object, in this case, the glass, is the cause or source of our consequent visual image, of our seeing what we see. Take the glass away, and we wouldn't see it. Or put a book in its place, and we would see a book.

All this is unremarkable and, according to some, very difficult to hold onto after a little further reflection. In this chapter, we will look at this simple story in more detail; that is, we will examine the philosophy of perception. Actually, this is a bit misleading, for following a long tradition, we will look primarily at but one of our senses, that of sight or vision.

We are concerned with two kinds of problems, one metaphysical, the other explicitly epistemological. It turns out that the metaphysical problem bears on the epistemological problem, so we cannot ignore the former entirely. Indeed, arguably, while worries about perception began in an epistemological setting, the standard way of dealing with such worries is by making some substantive claims about the *nature,* or the metaphysical aspects, of perception. To see these issues more precisely, we initially do two things. First, we put the simple story in a bit more sophisticated terminological guise. Second, we look at a family of arguments designed to show that the simple story cannot possibly be right.

THE SIMPLE STORY: NAÏVE REALISM

The simple story has it that what we immediately perceive are physical objects and their properties. Put differently, to say that we perceive (see) an object is to say that we are immediately aware of that object. But what does it mean to say that we "immediately perceive" or are "immediately aware of" physical objects?

Perhaps this can be best explained by a couple of examples. Suppose, as you finish cleaning the kitchen one evening, you note a single piece of pie, which you promise yourself will later make a nice snack. You return a couple of hours later to find only a smattering of crumbs and infer that your roommate has forsaken her diet. Now, you did not actually witness the pie eating, but you are confident that she is the guilty party. Or consider showing a photograph of a sibling and yourself to one of your friends. Clearly, your friend does not actually see your sibling; what she sees is a picture, or a representation, of that person.

In both examples, there is an intermediary of sorts—the crumbs in the first case and the picture in the second. We become aware of the actual thing by first being aware of something else. Thus, to say that we immediately perceive or are immediately aware of physical objects is to say that we do not first perceive something else (or are aware of something else) and then conclude or infer that there are physical objects. You might be wondering what it is that could possibly come between us and the objects we perceive, but we will come to that in a subsequent section.

A second feature of naïve realism, briefly noted previously, is that the properties we sense are located in the object. These properties are things such as color, scent, taste, shape, and size. Such properties are sometimes referred to as the *sensible qualities* of the object. Were no one around to see or smell them, roses would still be red and fragrant.

Again, this might seem unremarkable to you. Just where else would the sensible qualities be if not in the object? Think for a moment of taking a picture with a flash camera. Until recently, with the introduction of more sophisticated cameras on the market, taking a picture of someone sometimes resulted in a phenomenon known as "red-eye." But no one, upon looking at the picture, thought, "My Grandma, what red eyes you have!" Quite the contrary, we understood that the red glint in the eyes of the subject was but an artifact of the picture-taking process. But naïve realism is committed to the claim that sensible properties are not artifacts of the perceptual process; they really are features of the objects we perceive. To put this in the current vernacular, what you see is what you get.

Thus far, we have identified two features of naïve realism: (a) The direct objects of perception, what we immediately perceive or are aware of, are physical objects, and (b) the sensible qualities inhere in or belong to the objects themselves. These features we may refer to as the metaphysical aspects of perception. That is, they concern the *nature* of the object of perception. But there is another feature of this view that is more explicitly concerned with the epistemology of perception.

The epistemological aspect of naïve realism is that on many occasions, if you see a red rose, then you are immediately justified in believing that there is a red rose. More generally, this epistemological feature is that on many occasions, seeing an object as having a certain property is in and of itself sufficient evidence for your believing that there is such an object with that property.

Two quick explanatory points. First, the reason for the qualifier "on many occasions" is that there are clearly conditions under which seeing something may not yield sufficient justification. You may be too far away, the lighting may not be good, or there may be something wrong with your eyes. So, we might say that under *normal conditions,* if you see an object, then you are immediately justified in believing that there is such an object. Second, the force of "immediate" in "immediate justification" is to indicate that you do not need any further evidence; seeing the object is enough to justify your consequent belief.

Naïve realism is thus the view that under normal conditions, we directly perceive publicly accessible, independently existing physical objects. Similarly, the sensible qualities of the objects are genuine qualities of the object, quite independent of our perceiving them. Further, under normal conditions, to perceive an object or to perceive it as having a certain property is to be immediately justified in believing that there is such an object. Although naïve realism is sometimes distinguished from *direct realism,* for our purposes, we consider the two terms to be interchangeable.

NAÏVE REALISM—AN ILLUSION?

A few years ago when NASA sent one of its first spacecraft to take pictures of the surface of Mars, scientists, administrators, and computer programmers were undoubtedly a bit bemused and embarrassed to see the first close-up, computer-generated pictures of the planet. Red dust sometimes mixes in the planet's atmosphere, making it seem as though the sky is red. Certain programmers had innocently and *naïvely* assumed that things on Mars *looked* the same way they did on earth—that the sky looks blue. Upon discovering the mistake, they summarily changed the program, and Mars was restored to its natural features.

There is a kind of naïve realism at work in this little anecdote, and it seems easy enough to rescue the simple story by pleading abnormal conditions. But there is a family of arguments, known as the **arguments from illusion,** which are designed to undermine the naïve realist view. Specifically, these arguments seek to undermine the claim that we can straightforwardly assign sensible qualities as belonging to the objects themselves. Moreover, such arguments lead to views that hold that we do not directly perceive physical things. Rather, the direct objects of perception are something quite different from the normal roses, glasses, tables, and chairs. As a consequence, it turns out that our justification for our normal perceptual beliefs is quite *indirect.*

Arguments from Illusion

Underlying arguments from illusion in particular and arguments against naïve realism in general is a principle that Howard Robinson calls the Phenomenal Principle:

> If there sensibly appears to a subject to be something which possesses a particular sensible quality then there is something of which the subject is aware which does possess that sensible quality.[1]

The aim of arguments from illusion is to show that naïve realism must be mistaken in its claim that our perceptual experience is directly of properties that are intrinsic to the object.

To illustrate the principle, George Berkeley (1685–1753) suggests that you first put one hand in cold water and the other in hot, and then put both hands in lukewarm water. You will have two different sensations. The water will seem hot on the hand that was previously in cold water and decidedly cool on the hand that was in the hot water. Now, clearly, the water cannot be both cold and hot. That is, the sensible qualities of hot and cold cannot both belong to the water at the same time. Hence, these sensible qualities must be located somewhere other than in the object. But according to the Phenomenal Principle, we must consequently be aware of something that has the sensible qualities.

Initially, one might think that naïve realism can be saved by appealing to normal conditions and that Berkeley's case is not one in which conditions are normal. Yet critics of the view have more ordinary cases in mind. Bertrand Russell, for example, drew attention to the fact that one and the same object might yield very different appearances. Looked at from one perspective, a table might appear rectangular, from another somewhat diamond shaped, and from still another as some sort of irregular quadrilateral. From certain angles the table may appear brown, and from others white.[2]

Examples such as this are designed to show one thing: Sensible properties cannot be straightforwardly attributed as intrinsic properties of the object. Contrary properties, much less contradictory properties, cannot be in the same object in the same respect at the same time. Think again of the table. As we move around the table, it appears to have different shapes, and perhaps even different colors. Now, we certainly don't want to say that the table *itself* is changing. But that seems to be what we must say, so the argument goes, if we want to continue to hold that sensible properties belong to the object. The idea that the object is changing is thought to be untenable, especially insofar as it conflicts with naïve realism. The only other option seems to be that not all the sensible properties, even under normal conditions, can be said to belong to the object. This type of example is an instance of the causal version of the argument from illusion.[3] This version asks us to note the physical and physiological conditions necessary for perception to take place.

Most of us are somewhat aware of the basic facts of perception. Light waves of different lengths, corresponding to what we identify as particular colors, strike objects. Depending on the physical makeup of the object, some waves are absorbed and some are deflected. Those that are deflected sometimes strike our retinas, and after certain physiological processes take place, we see our familiar colors—red, indigo, magenta, lime green. Change the physical or the physiological conditions, and you would see *different* colors. Standing on the surface of a different planet, you might see a different-color sky because different lengths of light waves get through that planet's atmosphere. Or imagine that our physiological makeup were different than it is. Suppose that our eyes could not detect light waves at the longer end of the spectrum. Certain objects might then not only look different to us but not appear to us at all.

Against this simple background, think for a moment about what this causal version of the argument from illusion seems to imply. All that we have done in either supposition (changing our surroundings or changing our physiological makeup) is to change something *external* to the object. In one case, we imagined changing the light waves that struck objects; in the other, we imagined changing the way in which we detected the light waves. No changes were imagined to the object itself, yet there would be a different sensible property. Again, the Phenomenal Principle requires that if the sensible properties are not in the object, then the agent must be aware of *something* that possesses those properties. But if it is not the object that possesses the properties, then it seems as though it must be something in us, something in the mind, that possesses the relevant properties. This seems to lead to the idea that what we are directly aware of in perception is not the object, but something else. So, perception is indirect.

The naïve realist might raise two types of objection. First, it might be held that there are "standard conditions" in which one can reasonably claim that the sensible properties are in the object. Particular colors, for example, are typically thought to provide a plausible case. But "standard conditions" are often quite different from "normal conditions." For example, color scientists often make use of viewing tubes that screen out the normal effect of surrounding colors.[4]

Second, and more importantly, it is argued that there are no physical properties of objects with which determinate colors could be identified.[5] Suppose we try to identify colors with specific lengths of light wave. It turns out that different color sensations can be produced by a single length of light wave, and the same sensation can be produced by different lengths. A second option is to attempt to identify colors with the reflectance properties of surfaces. But not all instances of seeing colors are instances of seeing surfaces.

Another approach to these arguments is to resist the Phenomenal Principle. We cannot pursue this issue in great detail, but we can at least sketch the line of debate. Suppose I look at a quarter from a certain perspective and it appears to me elliptical. According to the Phenomenal Principle, there is something that has this property, even though the quarter does not. It might be held that this conclusion is not obvious, for two reasons. First, one can deny that simply because there appears to be a certain kind of property, then something must have that property. Imagine, for example, that my students tell me I seem happy. It is not obvious that because I appear to them to be happy, there must be something that is, in fact, happy. One might think that we are still owed an explanation of why an object seems to have a certain property. This leads to our second reason. In the last section in the chapter, we consider the adverbial theory, which construes something seeming to have a certain property as a *way* of experiencing or perceiving. Thus, there is no need to claim that there is, in fact, something that possesses the apparent property.

An advocate of the Phenomenal Principle might claim that the objection fails to account for the nature of our actual perceptual experience. We may indeed have perceptual experiences that do not actually correspond to the object. Nonetheless, obviously our experiences seem to have a certain content to them, which cannot simply be dismissed. Thus, when I look at the table from a certain angle, I have a particular mental content that might be described as seeing something trapezoidal. Any adequate theory of perception, one might urge, must account for this feature of my experience. What we require, then, is some explanation for the type of mental content that I have. There is a *fact* about my experience; the experience has a certain content. But seemingly, we cannot explain this fact by a kind of conceptual analysis. Instead, we seem to need some sort of causal explanation of why I seem to see something trapezoidal. Now, the fact that I have this content does not seem to be explicable by referring to the analysis of particular concepts—for example, the concept of an object apparently having a certain property. The challenge, according to the advocate of the Phenomenal Principle, is to explain the *facts* of our perceptual experience, facts that the naïve realist must explain.[6] Whether these arguments on behalf of the Phenomenal Principal are successful, the critic of naïve realism insists that additional arguments show that not all sensible properties are in the object. It is to these that we now turn.

Further Arguments Against Naïve Realism

Appealing to science to determine whether sensible properties are intrinsic to objects is virtually unavoidable. It is not clear that science supports the naïve realist. When we canvas the list of physical properties, we do not find many of our familiar sensible properties. Ions may have a certain valence, electrons a charge, and protons a gravitational mass. But they are not colored, they do not taste sweet or sour, and they are not cool or warm.

Now, this is not to deny that the various physical properties, when appropriately configured under the right conditions, produce in us sensations of red or sweet. But it does suggest that properties such as red and sweet are not causally active in the production of our sensory experience. Combinations of other properties are undoubtedly the source of these sensations, but these are not the properties naïve realism wishes to defend.[7] As we will see, something very much like this argument seems to be at work in Locke.

It is worth briefly mentioning one further argument, if only because philosophers of very different camps grant it some plausibility.[8] The *time lag* argument can be summarized as follows: If naïve realism is true, then we are immediately aware of physical objects. However, we have perceptual experiences of objects after they have ceased to exist. So, the content of our experience exists although the object no longer exists. So, at least on some occasions, the content of our perceptual experience is not the physical object.

On the surface, it is hard to see how the naïve realist might object. The first claim is merely a central tenet of naïve realism. The second is an empirical truth. The light from the sun, for example, takes about eight minutes to reach us. This means that there are times, during a sunset, when the sun is not where it appears to be. And the third claim is but a consequence of the first two. This seems to lead to the unavoidable conclusion that the object of our perceptual experience is not the physical object that causes our experience.

The naïve realist might claim that this argument involves two different senses of "immediately aware." The first premise of the argument understands "immediately aware" as the absence of any intermediate object. The second premise, however, construes "immediately aware" as the absence of any delay in time. Thus, the argument seems to equivocate on these two senses of "immediately aware."[9] The advocate of the time lag argument might claim that there is a connection between the two senses.

We might understand this response in the following way. When I look at the sun setting, just above the far edge of the Pacific Ocean, I have an occurrent mental content—the setting sun just above edge of the horizon. But this content cannot be identical with the sun itself, because the sun is no longer there. So, I am not directly perceiving the sun. Now, it is true that my occurrent mental content is an *effect* of the sun. This concession, however, is compatible with a general opposition to naïve realism.

So far, we have been considering two aspects of the naïve realist view, the claim that sensible properties are in the objects and the claim that we are directly aware of physical objects. The arguments of this section have attempted to undermine the naïve realist view. To the extent that they have been successful, it might have occurred to you to wonder, If these sensible properties are not in the objects, just where are they? And when I look across my table at a lamp or a book or a computer screen, if I'm not seeing those objects themselves, just what am I seeing?

THE WORLD OF SENSE DATA

An Intuitive Approach

Close your eyes for a moment and try to imagine as vividly as you can looking across a valley toward snow-covered mountains. Imagine the vivid greens of the countryside, perhaps the red-tile roofs of buildings, the blues of the sky, and the white, snow-covered peaks in the background; perhaps you can even imagine feeling a certain coolness on your skin. Obviously, you aren't perceiving anything; you are merely imagining. But what you are imagining is something very much like these sensible properties we have been discussing. When you open your eyes, don't think about the objects you see or feel or the events you hear. Focus instead only on the sensations, on the colors, the sounds, the felt qualities. In the early twentieth-century, these sensations were called *sense data*. A little more explicitly, sense data have sometimes been defined as what we are immediately or directly aware of in the perceptual process. To give perhaps a better idea of what is meant by the term, here is how Bertrand Russell characterized it in 1912:

Let us give the name of 'sense-data' to the things that are immediately known in sensation: such things as colours, sounds, smells, hardnesses, roughnesses, and so on. We shall give the name 'sensation' to the experience of being immediately aware of these things. Thus, whenever we see a colour, we have a sensation of the colour, but the colour itself is a sense-datum, not a sensation. The colour is that of which we are immediately aware and the awareness itself is a sensation.[10]

Like Russell, various philosophers have emphasized the *experiential* aspect of the perceptual process. They refer to sensible properties or qualities as features of experience. But unlike the naïve realist, such philosophers have not wanted to make initially any claims about whether these features are also in the objects. This experiential aspect of perceiving is our *sensory field,* our visual field, tactile field, auditory field, and so on. The identifiable, discriminable features of our sensory field are sense data. When I look at the red book lying on the table, my visual field is comprised of a red rectangular patch surrounded by some irregularly shaped gray, black, and brown patches. Each of these *discriminable* parts of my visual field is a sense datum. More importantly, sense data are the content of perceptual experience.

Now, if you think you have some workable idea of what sense data are, refer back to Russell's quote.[11] Notice that sense data are what we discover in *sensation.* Sensation is simply the process of being aware of our sense data, or what is sometimes described as our *sensing sense data.* We do not say that we perceive sense data, for reasons that will become apparent in a moment. Further, Russell holds that in sensation, we are immediately aware of sense data. That is, on this account, we do not sense *objects.*

Russell distinguishes between sensation, construed as the activity of sensing, and its object, sense data. The term "sensation" is, however, often used interchangeably with the term "sense data." In what follows, merely for expository convenience, we will follow this practice and use "sensation" to denote a mental state. Where we need to refer to the activity of sensation, we will do so explicitly.

The Causal-Hallucination Argument

Some hold that an argument that combines certain claims about causes with hallucinations is a persuasive argument against naïve realism.[12] Obviously, an agent conceivably could have a hallucinatory experience that, to the agent, was indistinguishable from a genuine perceptual experience. Moreover, the *internal* cause of this hallucinatory experience could be the same as the *internal* cause of the genuine perceptual experience. Certain brain processes would be the proximal cause of both experiences. Now,

Blindsight?

One of the interesting and controversial issues in recent work on perception is the phenomenon of "blindsight." Subjects who are blind in one area of their visual field are presented with a certain stimulus, typically a simple drawing such as an X or a O, in the blind portion of their visual field. Now, the subjects do not claim to be able to "see" the stimulus. However, when they are questioned by the experimenter, they can identify reliably the type of visual stimulus. Some interpret this to indicate that they have beliefs—perceptual beliefs—even though they do not have the corresponding sensations. A similar sort of phenomenon is reported in some individuals with split brains; these individuals report seeing despite the fact that they report having nothing like the visual sensations we would expect them to have in normal seeing. As noted, the interpretation of these cases is extremely controversial. But some have suggested that they lend support to the idea that sensations or sensory experiences are not necessary for the acquisition of perceptual beliefs. (See "For Further Study.")

given the principle "same cause, same effect," whatever happens in the one case must happen in the other. The effect in both cases is to produce a certain qualitatively identical content. Clearly, however, in the hallucinatory case, the agent cannot be aware of some external object. The agent must therefore be aware of some other object; call it a sense datum. But because the effect in both cases must be the same, it follows that even in the genuine perceptual case, there must be something other than the external object of which the agent is aware. That something is, again, a sense datum.

The conclusion of this argument is that we are not immediately aware of external objects in perception, but we are immediately aware of mental contents—*sense data.*

Some Common Features

Theories that invoke sense data are varied, but some features seem constant among them. First, such theories typically divide the perceptual process into two parts. The first part of the process, at least logically (and in some views, temporally) is sensation. In sensation, we encounter sense data. The second part of the process we might call perception proper. It is here that we can be said to perceive objects. How exactly such perception occurs, and in exactly what it consists, varies. Sense data theories construe perception to be dependent on our first having sense data: Perception depends on sensation.

A second aspect of such theories is that sense data are typically counted, though not uncontroversially, as *mental objects*. Sense data are thus mind-dependent. Were there no minds, there would be no sense data.

One further aspect that can be mentioned here concerns the distinction between sensation, or having of sense data, and perception, or identifying objects. Some hold that there is a distinction between the experience or sensation, *which is unconceptualized*, and the consequent classification or categorization of the experience into certain types or kinds. Thus, perception might be viewed as the conceptualization of our sense data.

To illustrate this, suppose there is a red book on my table. In sensation, in the experience itself, all I have is a red, rectangular patch surrounded by various other shaped colored patches. I haven't yet categorized or classified these sense data as being books, tables, computer printers, cardboard boxes, or gifts from admirers. All I have at the level of sensation are the discriminable sense data. Only when I draw on the concepts or ideas that I have learned and begin to identify the red patch as a book, the gray patch as a printer, the white patch as a gift, and so on, do I get objects. According to this line of thinking, perception is the conceptualization of our sensory experience.

You should bear in mind that sense data theories are a diverse lot. The aspects we have noted may not precisely describe each of those theories. But these features are in many ways typical.

Two questions will serve to introduce our next sections. First, just what is the connection between sense data and the properties the objects actually possess? Second, can this connection tell us anything about what we are justified in believing about the world around us? If all we ever *immediately* get in perception are these mind-dependent experiences, how do we ever *justifiably* get from in here, in the mind, to out there, in the world? Or, more dramatically, do we get back to our physical objects as we ordinarily think of them?

REPRESENTATIVE REALISM

Representative realism is the view that sense data somehow represent the objects and that these objects are causally involved in our production of the sense data. Our perception of objects is thus indirect. Because it is a causal view, it is also known as the *causal representative theory*.

We begin with a version of representative realism rooted in the work of John Locke (1632–1704).[13] Our primary interest here is to present the broad outlines of a general view, that of representative realism, so we will use Locke as a kind of departure point. Later, we will see how Locke's view might be generalized to give us a more contemporary version of representative realism.

Primary and Secondary Qualities

Three brief quotes from Locke's *Essay Concerning Human Understanding* will serve to get us started. The first quote presents us with Locke's official doctrine concerning the use of two important terms:

> Whatsoever the mind perceives in itself or is the immediate object of perception, thought or understanding, that I call idea; and the power to produce any idea in our mind, I call quality of the subject wherein the power is.[14]

Locke claims that the immediate objects of perception are *ideas,* not objects or their properties. Thus, if we are to be able to perceive objects, such perception will clearly have to be indirect. Although Locke did not use the terminology we have been using, sense data clearly would count as ideas in Locke's view. Second, notice that Locke seems to make a causal connection between the objects and the consequent ideas. Specifically, the power of an object to produce in us—to cause in us—these ideas, Locke calls *quality.* A quality, for Locke, is the power of an object to produce certain ideas in us. It turns out that these qualities are of two kinds:

> The ideas of primary qualities of bodies are resemblances of them, and their patterns do really exist in the bodies themselves; but the ideas produced in us by these secondary qualities have no resemblance of them at all.[15]

Interestingly, the primary qualities—solidity (impenetrability), extension (size), figure (shape), motion or rest, and number—are just the sort that could be treated by a quantitative science. Locke regards primary qualities as inseparable from the objects. Whatever change an object undergoes, Locke thinks it will still have these properties. So, an object's particular shape (figure) may change, but there is no shapeless object, nor is there an object that is neither at rest nor in motion. Moreover, notice that Locke thinks that our ideas of these qualities are "resemblances" of those qualities themselves.

This last point is important. Locke seems to think that at least some of our ideas represent the actual qualities of an object. It is easy to see how one can be tempted to interpret this as a kind of pictorial representation. The important point for our purposes is that ideas of primary qualities tell us something about properties that are actually in the object. When I see a round penny, roundness is a feature of the penny itself. It will be of interest to us later how it is that Locke thinks he can justifiably claim this.

Our ideas of secondary qualities—colors, tastes, scents, sounds—do not resemble the objects themselves. In fact, Locke claims that secondary qualities are "nothing in the objects themselves but powers to produce various sensations in us by their primary qualities."[16]

Objects, then, have two types of quality, some of which, under the right sorts of circumstances, cause us to have certain sensations that actually resemble the object. On the one hand, these are primary qualities; when we have ideas of these, we know what the object is like in itself. On the other hand, the primary qualities of an object can "combine" in certain ways to produce in us other sensations or ideas, sensations that in no way resemble the object. Just as the pain that is produced when we cut ourselves in no way resembles the knife, so the fragrance of the rose in no way resembles the actual makeup of the rose.

We can perhaps get some understanding of what Locke has in mind here by again thinking of our rudimentary understanding of current physics and chemistry. When we catch the scent of the rose, what has happened? Certain molecules of the rose "broke off," mixed with the molecules of air, struck our sensory surfaces, and set off a physiological process, which results in our sensation, the scent of the rose. Yet the scent itself bears no obvious resemblance to the molecular structure that is the impetus for our sensation. Indeed, Locke supposed that the sensations are produced in us because certain "insensible particles" emanate from objects and subsequently strike our sensory organs, thus setting off the physiological processes.

If these first two passages give us some tolerable hold of Locke's view of these matters so far, then the next brief quote presents the difficult task:

> It is evident the mind knows not things immediately, but only by the intervention of the ideas it has of them. Our knowledge therefore, is real, only so far as there is conformity between our ideas and the reality of things. But what shall be here the criterion? How shall the mind, when it perceives nothing but its own ideas, know they agree with things themselves?[17]

The first sentence of this passage is a clear statement of indirect, representative realism. And the previous two passages have made it clear that this representative realism is a causal view. But Locke himself recognizes the most difficult task such a representative view must face: Why think that these ideas give us any knowledge of the objects of which they are supposed to be ideas? Why are we not locked forever only in the web of our own ideas or, as some have characterized it, behind a veil of perception?

A Lockean Response or No Way Out?

Locke thought that there was reason to ascribe the causal source of at least some of our ideas to external objects. Our ideas, our sensations, of primary and secondary qualities seemed to be *contravolitional*. That is, they seemed to be imposed on us against our will, unlike some of our other ideas, which apparently could be summoned at will, at least on some occasions.

Once having the notion of an external object as the causal source of ideas, Locke thought that we could make sense of the further supposition that these ideas, in some way, "conform" or "agree" with the objects. In an important chapter in the *Essay,* Locke remarks that our ideas are "fitted" in such a way that we can distinguish or ascertain certain features of the objects that we may "take . . . for our necessities . . ."[18] In fact, Locke specifically mentions sensations such as whiteness and bitterness and suggests that they may be held to "conform" to the objects productive of them as much as may be expected.

It is not easy to see what Locke has in mind here. But he apparently thinks that we may reasonably infer, and thus may be said to know, that there is some quality or combination of qualities in the object corresponding to our ideas. That is, the fact that on one occasion we may have the idea of red and on another blue can be explained by different qualities of objects producing these different effects. In other words, Locke supposes that different sensations are causally connected to different features of an object.

This supposition of Locke's is not entirely without merit. Imagine my talking to some friends and occasionally sipping coffee. If at one time I taste the coffee and it tastes "normal," but a few minutes later I detect a noticeable sweetness that was not there before, I might reasonably conclude that something has changed about the coffee. This fairly simple inference can be thought to be at work in Locke—for distinct sensations there are associated distinct features of the object.

So far, so good. Lockean representative realism has brought us to this point: We have ideas or sensations that we may suppose are produced by the action of external objects. Differences among the sensations may be accounted for by holding that such differences are due to distinct features of external objects. It also seems fairly clear that Locke ultimately wanted to explain our ideas of secondary qualities as due to the features of the object that he had designated as primary qualities.

The problem, however, may be obvious to you by now. If, as Locke stipulates, we always and only directly perceive our ideas, then we can never directly perceive the conformity or resemblance that Locke insists is there between our ideas and the objects. How could we possibly justify such an inference or supposition? Our only access is to our own ideas. But the claim about resemblance or conformity is *a claim about a relationship that is external to our ideas.* We know what it is to conduct independent checks; if I want to check the spelling of this text, my handy spell-checker is but a keystroke away. Or, if I wonder about the veracity of a television news report, I can check another channel or a respected newspaper. In each of these cases, doing an independent check is a matter of getting *outside* the original framework and checking from an *external* perspective. But according to Locke I am forever confined to the internal framework of my own ideas. Once we confine ourselves to only what's inside our heads, there is no way to get outside.

We might pause for a moment to examine our options at this point. Locke is committed to *concept empiricism,* the view that all concepts are acquired from our sensory experience. Moreover, Locke holds that our sensory experiences are caused by mind-independent objects and that our concepts refer to those mind-independent objects. Now, given the commitment to concept empiricism, one might wonder how we could come to form the concept of mind-independent objects, much less have justified beliefs about these objects. It seems that we must have independent access to these mind-independent objects and to the causal connections between those objects and our sensations. But it is not immediately evident that this is the only means for solving Locke's problem. We might reject, for example, the idea that in order to know that A causes B, we must have direct access to A. Indeed, we see in the following section that we need not accept this sort of principle.[19]

Recall that we are interested in answers to two questions: We want to know something about the nature of the objects of our perception, *and* we want to know what sort of justification we have for our perceptual beliefs. To the first, Locke gives an answer that we can make some sense of and that has tempted many. We are directly aware of only our own sensations. Further, Locke gives us at least the outline of how we might view physical objects as the source of those sensations, as what the sensations are sensations of. The problem, however, is that we are left without any justification for the claim that we are at least indirectly perceiving physical objects.

Science to the Rescue?

Despite the difficulties of Locke's representative realism, the framework has not been abandoned. There are some who think that the merits of representative realism outweigh its defects. Contemporary representative realists hold that scientific theory can help to fill out the causal story outlined by Locke. Ordinary physical objects are not directly encountered in perception. Rather, they are inferred from our sensations and the theoretical framework that explains those sensations.[20]

Let's remind ourselves of a method of inference frequently used. Throughout the history of science, to explain an observed phenomenon, scientists have postulated the existence of other *unobserved* phenomena that had certain properties and thus would explain the observed effects. Molecules, atoms, electrons, subatomic particles, and a range of other phenomena that we now routinely invoke were but hypotheses to explain observed events. Contemporary particle physicists, for example, do not observe directly subatomic particles. Rather, they infer the existence of such particles from tracks left in bubble chambers. Invoking these unobservable entities—unlike once postulated entities, such as caloric, phlogiston, or the aether—allows us to predict consistently over a wide range of circumstances what other sorts of phenomena we might observe. The invocation of these unobserved entities permitted us to recognize a certain regularity where previously there had been too many questions.

Could we use something like this method of inference to overcome the difficulty encountered in Locke's version of representative realism? Think about what might be required to accomplish this. Suppose we could use some of our sense data or sensations, Locke's ideas, as a basis for constructing hypotheses about the nature of external objects. If these hypotheses could be confirmed in some way, then we would be able to justify some sort of inference regarding external objects. Well, how might such a view proceed?

Recall that when we introduced primary qualities, we noted that they were precisely the sort that were of interest to the then emerging physical sciences. The significant feature of these qualities was, and *is,* that they could be quantified in very precise ways. Moreover, these quantifications, these formulas, these *laws* permitted us to make predictions about other ideas that we might subsequently come to have.

Now, the archimidean point around which such laws turned was the "supposition" of external objects. But this was a supposition that could now be tested—if only in a roundabout sort of way. It was a hypothesis that we now had some way of confirming. As science performed its task, it would tell us what sorts of ideas or sensations we should expect if physical objects were the sort of thing we thought they were. Science would inform us of what we should come to expect from our complex ideas of objects. If we then discovered that, in fact, we had the experiences predicted, we would have some reason for our supposition of external objects.

The story is, as you are aware, much more complicated than this. But as we've noted previously, our rudimentary knowledge of some of the sciences—physics, optics, and the like—gives us just such a story of our perception of physical objects. Physical objects are disruptions of light waves that result in our having certain kinds of sensation. Interestingly, something like what Locke surmised turns out to be correct according to this story. Different kinds of sensations are correlated with different kinds of objects. I see a red book instead of a blue book precisely because the red book disrupts light waves in a way different from a blue book. I taste a certain sweetness when eating chocolate but a certain tartness when biting a lemon because of a difference in the kind of object. The difference in each case is also due to the structure of my sensory apparatus, but this is as much a part of the story as the inferred structure of the objects.

The details of the outline may vary from case to case, but the general form is discernible. Consider a passage from a recent book on perception:

> Well, suppose we seem to see a table. How do we get to the table? The first
> step in bridging the relevant epistemic gap seems to involve referring that

sensation [seeming to see a table] to an external cause. But if my earlier arguments were correct, belief in the table's existence involves far more than belief in the existence of a cause of that sensation. Rather it involves belief in the existence of something occupying a place in a complex nomological network, something that underlies and explains not a sensation in isolation but complex connections between possible sensations.[21]

Several of the points we have been making about representative realism are apparent here. In the first instance, perception gives us a sensation, the "seeming to see a table." And, quite obviously, an important epistemological gap must be bridged *before* we can justifiably claim we see a table. Just how is this to be done? By invoking a belief—a hypothesis—about a complex nomological network, a network of laws that enable us to make predictions about the way in which all our various sensations, as well as possible sensations, are connected. External objects like tables are inferred from our experiences and the theory that explains them. In this sense, our familiar objects turn out to be *epistemological posits* that are not all that much different philosophically from other kinds of epistemological posits like molecules, neutrons, and magnetic fields. All are underwritten by belief in a vast, very complicated causal story.

A Little Summary

We can set out more succinctly the main features of this revised version of representative realism.

1. The direct objects of perception are our own sensations.
2. We can classify or categorize our sensations and observe the regular connections that obtain among them.
3. Such regular connections can be initially attributed, at least in part, to external objects.
4. Subsequent investigation (noting still other sensations) leads to the development of a causal story that explains why the external objects produce the sensations that they do.
5. On the basis of the account in item 4, we are justified in concluding that we indirectly perceive external objects and that they have at least some of the properties we attribute to them.

To put the matter rather baldly, if we *assume* that external objects are somehow implicated by our sensations, and if we attribute to those objects certain kinds of features or properties, then we get a story that allows us to claim that our assumption of external objects was, after all, a justified assumption.

Some Reactions to Representative Realism

Representative realism obviously conflicts with our commonsense intuitions on at least one important count. Our commonsense view, as reflected in naïve realism, holds that we directly perceive at least some external objects. This, however, is precisely what is denied by indirect realism. This conflict between the naïve and the representative realist does not tell us which view to count as more adequate. But it does lead us to consider some other matters.

In particular, as we have seen, representative realism holds that we are fundamentally in contact only with our own sensory states. It is as though, somehow, we initially (and *only*) view our sensations and from these private viewings construct the world of objects and properties with which we are most familiar. But one may reasonably wonder whether this is the correct description of our perceptual activities. It might seem that awareness of our own sensory states is subsequent to and derivative of our awareness of objects. We first perceive objects and then abstract away from such perception to arrive at a notion of the content of our sensory states (sense data, appearances, Lockean ideas, and so on).[22]

One response, which has been made on behalf of the representative realist, is that while our perceptual experience is only of sensations, our perceptual *knowledge* is direct and concerns objects. According to this view, perceptual experience is nonpropositional. Perceptual knowledge, however, is about the external objects and is a noninferential result of our perceptual experience.[23]

We have also considered the sense in which the representative realist can argue for the existence of a mind-independent world. Now, one might concede that we do have confirmation of a mind-independent world but still wonder whether we have *sufficient* confirmation to be justified in believing that there is such a world. Notice, for example, that the skeptic might suggest that we are also confirming the hypothesis that there is a demon that makes it seem as if there is a world of independent objects.[24]

This sort of defense of representative realism does raise a further question. The attempt to avoid the difficulties encountered by Locke leads, as we saw, to explicit reliance on science. Yet there seems to be a difference between the kind of objects our scientific theories invoke and our more normal sort of object. We were interested in the philosophy of perception because we wanted to know the status of perceptual claims about *familiar* objects, such as "I see my computer" and "I see that the stapler is over there." But are these the sort of objects that our scientific theorizing legitimates? Is science concerned with computers, staplers, oranges, cups, desks, tables, red sweaters as opposed to indigo sweaters, and sweet as opposed to tart apples? Are there complex *nomological* systems, complex law-governed systems that refer to or invoke tables, as suggested by the passage in the previous section? Are there laws for cups and computers, sweaters and staplers?

One might suggest that the *real* world of Locke is a world of empty geometric shapes that somehow are solid. Similarly, the world of contemporary physics seems to be a world of spaces, some a little less busy than others. The scientific world seems to eliminate the properties that *fill up* so much of our familiar world. As I look across the canyon outside my window, I see expanses of shades of green, brown, red, and blue; I hear the sounds of cars and pedestrians; I catch the scent of the late spring bloom. But the science that saves Locke and his kin replaces qualities that fill our world with largely empty spaces, filled only with certain forces.

The difficulty seems to be this: Representative realism threatened to leave us without knowledge of anything more than our own experiences. We were rescued from this skepticism by a kind of scientific theorizing. But the world that was restored seems very much unlike our familiar world. And we might like to know what happened to it. Can science restore *that* world? Can the representative realist tell us how to do this?

There is, of course, a more drastic option. Keep the world that we experience, but deny the existence of a mind-independent world that is allegedly the object of scientific scrutiny. This option is the focus of the next section.

PHENOMENALISM

Moved by the difficulties of both naïve and representative realism, some philosophers have thought that the only viable theory of perception is a view that denies that we should think of perception as involving mind-independent objects at all. Rather, physical objects are identified in some way with our sensations. This view is known as **phenomenalism**. Phenomenalism is actually a family of views. But common to all phenomenalists is the claim that all we are ever directly aware of are our own sensations and that the only sense that can be given to our experience of physical objects is that provided by our own sensations.

Phenomenalists are classified in a variety of different ways, and terminology can differ. For our purposes, we will adopt the following: One version of phenomenalism identifies physical objects with our sensations and thus holds that it makes no sense to think of physical objects existing independently of minds. This we will call *factual phenomenalism*. A second version of phenomenalism holds that talk of external, physical objects is but a kind of abbreviation or shorthand way of talking about sense data. This view we will refer to as *linguistic* or *analytic phenomenalism*. Unlike factual phenomenalists, linguistic phenomenalists need not deny the mind-independence of physical objects. Rather, linguistic phenomenalists are making a claim about the *meaning* of our talk about physical objects. Interestingly, elements of both these views can be seen in George Berkeley's writing, along with a dose of theistic phenomenalism. As we did with Locke, we use Berkeley's view as a departure point for consideration of phenomenalism.

Berkeley's Factual Phenomenalism

Why might anyone be tempted by factual phenomenalism? If we describe any arbitrarily selected physical object, we are likely to cite its sensible properties. This is our principal cognitive grasp of the notion of a physical object—its sensible properties. Peel away these properties, and we are left with something that looks a lot like, well, nothing. But if we identify a physical object with its sensible properties, then just as sensible properties depend on some mind or other, so does the physical object. Thus, a physical object could be held to exist only to the extent that it was an idea (or complex of ideas) in the mind of some perceiver. There is then no sense that can be made of the idea that an object might exist wholly independently of its being perceived.

However, neither Berkeley nor phenomenalists in general deny the *reality* of what we normally refer to as physical objects. My computer is real, just as is the chair in which you sit while you read this. What Berkeley denies is that we can make sense of the claim that some object might exist wholly independently of its being perceived. In particular, Berkeley argues that when we talk about a physical object existing, we can only mean something quite specific:

> And it seems no less evident that the various sensations or ideas imprinted on the sense . . . cannot exist otherwise than in a mind perceiving them. . . . The table I write on, I say, exists, that is, I see and feel it; and if I were out of my study I might perceive it, or that some other spirit actually does perceive it. . . . Their *esse* is *percipi,* nor is it possible that they should have any existence out of the minds or thinking things which perceive them.[25]

In an attenuated sense, in Berkeley's view, we do in fact directly perceive objects because they are nothing more than complexes of ideas, and we directly perceive these ideas. In the representative realist's view, our only contact with objects is via the intermediaries of our sensations. In this respect, at least, Berkeley thought and could plausibly argue that his view was more in line with the views of the ordinary person who thought we could directly perceive objects. Indeed, Berkeley insists that he only denies the existence of mind-independent matter that is the source of the sensible qualities of objects and is forever beyond our cognitive grasp.

Berkeley's factual phenomenalism clearly puts him at odds with the commonsense view, however. Although he does not deny the existence of physical objects, he clearly denies that these could exist independently of being perceived. In Berkeley's view, physical objects are simply complexes of sensible qualities, or in more modern terminology, sense data. Yet the commonsense view holds mind-independence to be a necessary feature of external, physical objects.

There is in Berkeley more than a hint of the linguistic version of phenomenalism. By focusing on what we mean by the "existence of objects," he is suggesting how terms for physical objects can be interpreted as referring only to our sensations.

Linguistic Phenomenalism

Linguistic phenomenalism is centrally a view about the meaning of terms employed in our accounts of perception. The central tenet of analytic phenomenalism is that our talking about material or physical objects is nothing more than a shorthand way of talking about our sequences of sensations. Terms or words that refer to physical objects are consequently parasitic, or dependent on descriptions of our sensory states. To describe linguistic phenomenalism is simultaneously to describe what is its most daunting task. It will be worth pursuing the matter somewhat intuitively to see what is at issue here.

Suppose I am a phenomenalist of this analytic variety. I am thus committed to the claim that my speaking of physical objects is merely a kind of linguistic shorthand. But what does this really mean? It seems to mean at least this: Any time I refer to an object, such as a table or a glass, I could, in fact, simply describe the succession of sensory states I had during a certain span of time. Moreover, this succession of sensory states is all that there is to my talking about, say, the glass on the table.

Clearly, however, I do not talk only about objects that I am currently sensing or perceiving. I sometimes refer to objects that are nowhere in my current visual field. Thus, I might inform you that there is a clean coffee cup in the cupboard, which you are free to use. Recall that Berkeley construed such talk to be about what you would experience, what you would sense were you to open the cupboard and reach for a coffee cup. So, on least some occasions, reference to physical objects is nothing more than saying what I *would* experience or sense *if I were* to do certain things.

Linguistic phenomenalism is thus committed to the claim that certain *equivalences* can be provided. For each statement containing reference to physical objects, there is another statement, equivalent in meaning to the original, that makes reference only to certain sensations that I would have. It is not quite clear, however, that this task can be accomplished.

Is Linguistic Phenomenalism Plausible?

First, let us outline still more precisely the constraints under which the phenomenalist is operating. The phenomenalist cannot smuggle in references to physical objects in reducing statments about physical objects to sensory statements. Thus, if we want an example of the equivalent statement for "I see a table," the phenomenalist cannot be permitted simply to say that this means "I seem to see a tablelike object." This is to abandon the phenomenalist project. Rather, the sort of equivalent statements we expect are "I am having a brown, rectangular-shaped sensory experience." This constraint noted, let us begin with the claim that sentences referring to physical objects can be reconstrued as sentences containing only references to sensations.

I see the glass on the table. To how many sensory experiences is this simple perceptual claim equivalent? There would seem to be an indefinite number of sensory states that I might have with just these two simple objects. As the lighting changes in the room, as I approach the table from a different angle, I will have different sensory states. While certain facts about perception might limit some of the different sensory experiences I might have, there are still a large number that can be associated with just the glass and the table. Few have tried to give anything more than one or two of the possible sequences of sensory states.

The situation may be worse than this. Physical object statements do not obviously entail that I will have the associated sensations. Roderick Chisholm offers the example of "There is really a door in front of me." Presumably, this sentence implies that if I had certain kinds of visual experiences, then I would have certain kinds of tactile experiences (if I saw my hand reaching for the doorknob, I would then have the feeling of touching the doorknob). But this "prediction" need not actually come about. As Chisholm points out, I may be the victim of certain delusions such that when I have certain visual sensations, my tactile sensations are somehow blocked or altered.[26]

Still another objection is that no sensory experience statements imply statements asserting the *existence* of physical object statements. I could have experiences of a rectangular, brown, hard patch; I could have all the experiences the phenomenalist associates with a table, *and the table might still not exist*. Yet to say that I see a table implies that there is a table there. As an analogy, consider the still fairly new technology associated with virtual reality. I could have all the experiences associated with seeing a table. This does not, however, entail the existence of table, unlike my ordinary claim to see a table.

It is important to specify precisely what this latter objection shows. A linguistic phenomenalist may hold that there are mind-independent physical

Linguistic Phenomenalism and the Skeptic

Linguistic phenomenalism was a popular theory among some epistemologists in the early and middle twentieth century. It is not difficult to see why. Suppose for a moment that one accepts the skeptic's challenge of showing how, on the basis of our sensory experiences, we could arrive at our more familiar and scientific beliefs about the world. These beliefs typically involve reference to physical objects and their properties. Linguistic pehnomenalism promises that reference to physical objects is nothing more than reference to a, perhaps complicated, set of sensory states. We could "rationally reconstruct" our claims about the physical world by providing the linguistic equivalents of such claims. Thus, we would have sufficient evidence for our beliefs about the world because such beliefs are simply shorthand ways of talking about our sensory states. Indeed, as Berkeley claimed, one advantage of his phenomenalistic view is that it avoids the skepticism engendered by representative realism. Of course, the difficulty lies in showing that rational reconstruction is possible, a task few currently seem willing to undertake.

objects. Indeed this was the position of many linguistic phenomenalists through the first half of the twentieth century. Now, the current objection would be an objection to this sort of phenomenalism. Yet, if one holds a view similar to Berkeley's, it is not clear that this objection carries much force. All there is to an object existing is that it be perceivable, according to Berkeley. Nonetheless, these objections show that linguistic phenomenalism faces a daunting task.

Berkeley Again

Berkeley himself anticipated many of the very criticisms frequently raised against factual phenomenalism.[27] Here we have but space to consider a few.

One might urge that in the factual phenomenalist view, reality appears all too dreamlike. Berkeley responds that reality is distinguished from dreams in the same way we normally distinguish fact from fiction—by the stability and orderliness of those complexes of ideas we call *real*. Indeed, it is this stability and orderliness that science studies. In doing so, science presents us with laws or regularities that enable us to predict that one type of sequence of sensations will most likely be followed by another type. Thus, Berkeley identifies the causal relations among objects as just this regular succession of types of sequences of sensations. Second, and more importantly, fire does not cause pain, nor does my pounding on the table cause noise. The fire and the pounding are merely signs, signs of the pain and the noise to follow. Interestingly, these signs and that which they signify are authored—caused—by God.

This leads, however, to perhaps the deepest problem for factual phenomenalism. In Berkeley's view, there are no unperceived objects or complexes of ideas; God perceives all. Yet suppose one wishes to dispense with this theistic phenomenalism. How might the factual phenomenalist explain unperceived objects or properties? How might the phenomenalist explain the existence of dinosaurs?

Berkeley asked a somewhat similar question. What sense, he asked, might be given to the question that the earth rotates?[28] (The earth's rotation was widely agreed on in Berkeley's day, but obviously no one had ever perceived its rotation.) Berkeley suggests that were one transported to a certain place in the heavens, one would have the perceptual experience of the earth rotating. Now, this seems a plausible response. However, it is argued that the difficulty the phenomenalist faces is specifying the "somewhere" to which we must be transported to have the requisite experiences. The difficulty lies in providing this specification *without* appealing to external, mind-independent features of the world.[29]

The committed phenomenalist might insist, however, that the references to objective places are not necessary. Such an argument would require that a phenomenalist account be given of unoccupied and unperceived places. If this sort of account is feasible, then factual phenomenalism may be more plausible than is sometimes supposed.

REVIVING DIRECT REALISM

The latter part of the twentieth century has seen attempts to move away from reliance on internal mental states as the direct objects of perception and to recapture the core insights of naïve realism, but without its defects. We will consider two kinds of theories. The first is the adverbial theory.

Adverbial Theory

Representative realism focuses on the thought that our perceptual contact with objects is through the intermediary of sensations. This intermediary is invoked to deal with the problems thought to beset naïve realism. We have seen, however, that this intermediary brings with it its own special problems. If we could retain the primacy of the sensory experience without relying on an intermediary, perhaps we could arrive at a theory that recaptured the intuitive appeal of naïve realism while avoiding its difficulties. Such is the aim of the adverbial theory.

Adverbial theory attempts to recapture the idea that we see or perceive objects directly; it attempts to avoid perceptual intermediaries. But it also wants to retain the idea that our sensory experience plays a key and basic role in our seeing or perceiving objects. The fundamental thought of the adverbial theory is this: We see objects by experiencing them in a certain way. Sensations are not objects of awareness, but rather ways of being aware of physical objects. Thus, adverbial theory is both a direct realism and a causal theory.

A simple example will help illustrate. I sit with my keyboard across my lap, half-reclining, feet on the desk, and I see a blue book on the desk. Like most books, this book has a generally rectangular shape. But because of my particular perspective at the moment, the shape of the book seems to me rather trapezoidal. That is, the kind of visual experience I am having is in part characterized by its trapezoidal nature. I am seeing the book, but the *way* in which this rectangular book appears to me is a trapezoidal way. Similarly, another part of the way in which I am currently visually experiencing the book is in a somewhat Columbia-bluish way.

We can see from this example that sensations are not mental objects, but the ways the mind reacts to visual stimuli. But this naturally leads to a question that prompted indirect theories of perception in the first place: How does the adverbialist diagnose those cases of illusion that motivated indirect theories in the first place? Recall Macbeth's hallucination of the dagger. He believes he sees a dagger, but there is nothing in front of him, so he is clearly not seeing a dagger. But his sensory experience is just what it would be if there were a dagger in front of him. The adverbialist might suggest that in such a case, Macbeth is indeed having a kind of sensory experience, but he is not having a *visual* experience.[30]

The previous example of the blue book leads to what many have considered to be a decisive criticism of adverbial theory. The *many-property problem* suggests that the adverbialist cannot distinguish two different complex sensory experiences of similar properties. Suppose I see a blue book and a red ball. In the adverbial account, I am sensing bluely, rectangularly, redly, and squarely. But this seems no different than what would be said about my seeing a red book and a blue ball.

A response to this criticism has yet to be fully worked out. One suggestion is that some sensory experiences contain others as components. This implies that there is a certain structure to our experiences, that there are parts to our sensory experiences. Now, this may be plausible. But if so, it does not seem that this structure is explained by *adverbial theory*. We need to know how to identify these constituent parts, and advocates of adverbial theory have yet to supply this explanation.[31]

The Doxastic View

Recent developments in the philosophy of mind have led to a quite different sort of view of perception. Instead of viewing the perceptual process as primarily producing sensations or sensory experiences, some now claim that the point of perception is to convey information. In particular, perception generates beliefs, mental states with contents. Seeing is believing. Sensations or sensory experiences are only secondary, and perhaps inessential. Thus, doxastic views emphasize the doxastic and informational character of perception and deemphasize the experiential (sensory) character.[32]

One cautionary remark: Doxastic views are not denying that our senses are the mechanism by which information about the world is conveyed to us. What they deny is that the experiential features of this process are essential to the information delivery function of perception. But then, in this view, just how should we think of the perceptual process?

The doxastic view holds that various physical processes transmit information to our sensory organs. This information is then transmitted through and processed by the various neurological channels that make up our perceptual processes. Having processed the causally transmitted information, the agent subsequently comes to have a perceptual belief. Moreover, such perceptual beliefs often are accompanied by sensory qualities. But, importantly, unlike the representative realist, the doxastic theorist holds that the experiential character of these sensory qualities does not determine the content of our perceptual beliefs. Michael Tye has recently argued that instead we can fully characterize the sensory aspects of perception by means of representational content.[33]

This is both a direct realist and causal view. It is causal because it holds that perception is a process that transforms physical information into mental information, or beliefs. It is a direct realist view because it holds that we are perceiving objects directly, and they actually have many of the properties we perceive them to have.

Perhaps the one thing that has struck critics as odd is the idea that the character of our sensory experiences somehow derives from the informational aspects of our perceptual beliefs. That is, critics claim that we obviously might have sensory experiences, that we might see things, without having perceptual beliefs about those experiences. As I sit in front of my computer, I am seeing a great deal; there is a richness of detail to my *sensory experience* that is not obviously included in any perceptual beliefs that I have. The extreme version of this objection is that I could have sensory experiences without having any perceptual beliefs at all.

The strategy of the doxastic theorist is to try to show that the relevant features of the perceptual process are in some way represented in the beliefs of the agent. Notice that this strategy requires not only that the apparent non-belief-like character and richness of our sensory experience be explained but also that some account be given of the nature of illusions. In response, doxastic theorists, for example, suggest that more of our sensory experience is represented in our beliefs than is assumed. They have also suggested that illusions might be handled by appealing to certain physiological facts together with the idea that certain other beliefs may prevent the agent from acquiring a belief she would have acquired otherwise.[34]

As a way of concluding this chapter, we might note why this sort of response has not appeased critics. As we already noted, the doxastic view can be considered an incomplete account of the nature of our perceptual experience. Perception seems to occur by means of our sensory experiences, and these do not seem to be readily construed as beliefs. One might also claim that arguments from illusion seem to indicate the existence of a mental content that is the proper object of perceptual awareness.

Yet to the extent that we are thus driven from a naïve realism, and given the number of difficulties subsequently encountered, it might be worth revisiting the issue of whether a direct realism can be suitably revived.

Key Concepts

Adverbial theory
Arguments from illusion
Naïve realism

Phenomenalism
Representative realism

Review Questions

1. Why are arguments from illusion thought to undermine naïve realism?
2. What are the essential features of representative realism? Is the representative realist justified in claiming that there are mind-independent objects? Explain.
3. What is Locke's distinction between primary and secondary qualities? Why is this distinction important for Locke?
4. What is the difference between linguistic and factual phenomenalism? How does Berkeley explain the objection that there seem to be objects or properties that we suppose exist, even though they are unperceived? Does the factual phenomenalist have a way of explaining this without invoking the notion of God?
5. Which of the theories of perception do you think is the best or strongest theory? Why?

For Further Study

A defense of a version of naïve realism can be found in James Cornman, *Perception, Common Sense, and Science* (New Haven, CT: Yale University Press, 1975); Cornman considers other theories of perception as well. Bertrand Russell's *The Problems of Philosophy* (London: Oxford

University Press, 1959) is a very accessible introduction to arguments from illusion and the notion of sense data.

D. L. C. Maclahlan's *The Philosophy of Perception* (Englewood Cliffs, NJ: Prentice-Hall, 1989) defends a representative realist approach, as does Richard Fumerton's *Metaphysical and Epistemological Problems of Perception* (Lincoln: University of Nebraska Press, 1985).

I. C. Tipton, ed., *Locke on Human Understanding* (Oxford: Oxford University Press, 1977), contains a number of essays about Locke's theory of perception, including Tipton's introductory essay. J. L. Mackie's *Problems from Locke* (Oxford: Clarendon Press, 1976) provides a closely argued account of Locke's view. George Berkeley's *A Treatise Concerning the Principles of Human Knowledge* (Indianapolis, IN: Bobbs-Merrill, 1965) is very readable.

Two contemporary defenses of phenomenalism are Howard Robinson, *Perception* (London: Routledge, 1994), and Georges Dicker, *Perceptual Knowledge* (Boston: Reidel, 1980).

Two classic works on perception are H. H. Price, *Perception* (London: Methuen, 1932), and Roderick Chisholm, *Perceiving* (Ithaca; NY: Cornell University Press, 1957). Chisholm's is one of the first statements of the adverbial theory. Also of interest is C. L. Hardin's *Color for Philosophers* (Indianapolis, IN: Hackett, 1986).

The central work on blindsight is Larry Weiskrantz, *Blindsight* (Oxford: Oxford University Press, 1986.) For a discussion of blindsight, split brain, and other cases, see Norton Nelkin, "How Sensations Get Their Names," *Philosophical Studies* 51 (1987): 325–339.

Notes

1. Howard Robinson, *Perception* (London: Routledge, 1994), p. 32.

2. Bertrand Russell, *The Problems of Philosophy* (London: Oxford University Press, 1959), Chap. 1.

3. See H. H. Price *Perception* (London: Methuen, 1932), Chap. II.

4. See, for example, C. L Hardin, *Color for Philosophers* (Indianapolis, IN: Hackett, 1986).

5. Hardin, *Color for Philosophers,* especially Chap. 2.

6. See Robinson, *Perception,* for a much fuller discussion of these issues.

7. Here, I have combined two arguments from Robinson, *Perception*, Chap. 3—the argument from secondary qualities and the argument from science.

8. See, for example, Robinson, *Perception*; James Cornman, *Perception, Common Sense, and Science,* (New Haven, CT: Yale University Press, 1975); and D. L. C. Maclahlan, *The Philosophy of Perception,* (Englewood Cliffs, NJ: Prentice-Hall, 1989).

9. Again, my thanks to an anonymous reader.

10. Russell, *The Problems of Philosophy,* p. 12.

11. It turns out to be a not so simple matter to define the term *sense datum.* Note that we cannot say that sense data are parts of our sensory field unless we have some other account of *sensory field* that does not amount to merely saying that it is a collection of sense data. Similarly, there are difficulties with saying that sense data are what are immediately given in experience or sensation unless, again, we have some independent characterization of these terms that does not rely on either the notion of sense data (or the notion of physical object).

12. See Robinson, *Perception,* Chap. 6, and Richard Fumerton, *Metaphysical and Epistemological Problems of Perception* (Lincoln: University of Nebraska Press, 1985), Chap. 3.

13. Of late, there is significant controversy about whether Locke is a representative realist. A very good, balanced summary of the controversy is I. C. Tipton's "Introduction," in I. C. Tipton, ed., *Locke on Human Understanding* (Oxford: Oxford University Press, 1977), pp. 1–18.

14. John Locke, *An Essay Concerning Human Understanding* (Oxford: Clarendon Press, 1975), Bk. II, Chap. 8, Sect. 8.

15. Locke, *An Essay,* Bk. II, Chap. 8, Sect. 15.

16. Locke, *An Essay,* Bk. II, Chap. 8, Sect. 10.

17. Locke, *An Essay,* Bk. IV, Chap. 4, Sect. 3.

18. Locke, *An Essay,* Bk. IV, Chap. 4.

19. An extended discussion of these issues can be found in J. L. Mackie, *Problems from Locke* (Oxford: Clarendon Press, 1976), Chap. 2, especially Sects. 5–7.

20. A very recent and accessible account is found in Maclahlan, *The Philosophy of Perception,* Chap. 10. See also the discussion in Mackie, *Problems from Locke,* Chap. 2.

21. Fumerton, *Metaphysical and Epistemological Problems,* p. 176.

22. See, for example, John Heil, *Perception and Cognition* (Berkeley: University of California Press), p. 70.

23. Robert Meyers suggests this response in *The Likelihood of Knowledge* (Dordrecht: Kluwer Academic Publishers, 1988), Chap. 6.

24. This line of argument was suggested by an anonymous reader.

25. George Berkeley, *A Treatise Concerning the Principles of Human Knowledge* (Indianapolis, IN: Bobbs Merrill, 1965), I, p. 3.

26. Roderick Chisholm, *Perceiving* (Ithaca, NY: Cornell University Press, 1957), Appendix. While we cannot go into the matter here, Fumerton has argued (in *Metaphysical and Epistemological Problems,* Chap. 5) that the linguistic phenomenalist can reply to this argument, making use of the same methods that the representative realist must use. In the end, however, Fumerton claims that in attempting to explain the existence of objects that are not perceived, linguistic phenomenalism collapses into representative realism.

27. See Berkeley, *A Treatise,* I, 34–67.

28. Berkeley, *A Treatise,* I, 58.

29. See Fumerton, *Metaphysical and Epistemological Problems,* Chap. 5. Fumerton considers the linguistic phenomenalist, but it seems that the factual phenomenalist must face the same problem.

30. See, for example, Robert Audi, *Belief, Justification, and Knowledge* (Belmont, CA: Wadsworth, 1988), Chap. 1.

31. Michael Tye has developed the adverbial theory at length and defended it against various objections. See his "The Adverbial Approach to Visual Experience," *Philosophical Review* 93 (1984): 195–226, and *The Metaphysics of Mind* (Cambridge: Cambridge University Press, 1989). Roderick Chisholm also defends an adverbial view; see *Perceiving.*

32. This view should be distinguished from the view developed by Fred Dretske in *Knowledge and the Flow of Information* (Cambridge, MA: MIT Press, 1981), especially Chap. 6.

33. See Michael Tye, "Visual Qualia and Visual Content," in Tim Crane, ed., *The Contents of Experience* (Cambridge: Cambridge University Press, 1992), pp. 158–176. In Tim Crane's "Introduction," the doxastic theory is outlined. What is here referred to as the doxastic theory, Crane calls the informational theory of perception.

34. See, for example, D. M. Armstrong, in Jonathan Dancy, ed., "Perception and Belief," *Perceptual Knowledge,* (Oxford: Oxford University Press, 1988), Chap. VII, and Jack Crumley, "Appearances Can Be Deceiving," *Philosophical Studies* 64 (1991): 233–251. John Heil, "Perceptual Experience," in Brian McLaughlin, ed., *Dretske and His Critics* (Oxford: Basil Blackwell, 1991), pp. 1–16, also seems to be advocating something like the doxastic view.

Glossary

acceptance   a functional state that arises when a person reflectively judges that a certain proposition is true, given the epistemic aim of attaining truth and avoiding error.

adverbial theory   a direct realist view of perception that holds that perception is a way of experiencing objects.

analytic and synthetic propositions   a proposition is analytic if its denial is self-contradictory; alternatively, analytic propositions are true by virtue of their constituent concepts. The truth of synthetic propositions cannot be determined on the basis of the constituent concepts alone. See *synthetic a priori proposition.*

animal and reflective knowledge   animal knowledge is our immediate and direct cognitive response to the environment. Reflective knowledge requires that we understand the source of the belief and its connection to our other beliefs.

a posteriori knowledge   a proposition is known a posteriori if the justification for the proposition depends on experience.

a priori knowledge   a proposition that is known if, once the relevant concepts are acquired, the justification for the proposition is independent of or does not derive from any particular type of experience a person might have.

arguments from illusion   a family of arguments purporting to show that we are not immediately aware of physical objects and that sensible properties are not intrinsic features of the objects. Such arguments are intended to cast doubt on naïve or direct realism.

autonomy of epistemology   a view typical of traditional epistemology that epistemology is independent of the sciences in both subject matter and method.

basic beliefs   beliefs that are self-justified or directly justified. That is, they do not depend on other beliefs for their justification.

causal theories of knowledge   theories that hold that a necessary condition of knowledge is that the belief must be caused in an appropriate way. Goldman holds that such "appropriate" ways are perception, memory, and certain types of inferences.

clairvoyancy objection   an objection to reliabilism that claims that reliability is not a sufficient condition of justification.

cognitive accessibility of reasons   the view that an agent is or can become aware of the reasons for which a belief is held. Theories that require cognitive accessibility as a condition of justification are considered internalist.

coherence theory of justification   a theory that holds that the justification of any belief depends on an agent's other beliefs. Unlike foundationalist theories, such theories hold that there are no basic beliefs.

comparative reasonability   a relation between beliefs or what one accepts; Lehrer's view that one proposition is more reasonable than another, given what else a person accepts.

contingent and necessary propositions   a proposition is necessary if its truth value could not be otherwise. Contingent propositions are those whose truth value might have been otherwise.

Demon Argument Descartes's argument that some beliefs arrived at by reason might be mistaken.

deontological theories of justification internalist theories that require the agent to satisfy certain epistemic obligations. That is, a belief must be epistemically responsible for it to be justified.

doxastic foundationalism a type of foundationalism that holds that basic beliefs are beliefs about appearances or perceptual experiences.

Dream Argument Descartes's argument that our perceptual beliefs may be intrinsically mistaken.

empiricism the view that the justification of our beliefs about the world ultimately derives from sense experience.

evil demon an objection to reliabilism that claims that reliability is not a necessary condition of justification.

externalism the view that the factors relevant to knowledge or justification need not be reflected in an agent's beliefs or cognitive perspective.

foundationalism the view that the justification of our beliefs derives from basic beliefs, which do not depend on other beliefs for their justification.

generality problem an objection to reliable process views that claims that reliabilist views are unable to explain the relevant types of belief-forming processes.

Gettier-type counterexamples examples that purport to show that the traditional analysis of the concept of knowledge is unsatisfactory. Originally, Gettier examples showed that the justification and the truth conditions of the traditional analysis could be satisfied independently of one another.

global or holistic coherence the view that coherence is a property of an entire system of beliefs. BonJour counts coherence as a global property of a system that has the appropriate types of relations among beliefs.

incorrigible beliefs beliefs for which it is impossible to show that the person is mistaken.

indefeasibility theories of knowledge theories that hold that a necessary condition of knowledge is that a person's justification must be such that there are no defeaters of the justification—that is, there are no true propositions such that if they were known by the agent, the agent would no longer be justified.

indubitable beliefs beliefs for which there are no grounds for doubt.

induction a type of argument that purports to show that the conclusion is probably true. Hume was specifically concerned with enumerative induction.

infallible beliefs beliefs that cannot be mistaken, that are not possibly false.

internalism the view that the factors relevant to knowledge or justification are reflected in an agent's beliefs or cognitive processes.

isolation objection the fundamental objection to coherence theories. The claim is that coherence cuts justification off from the world; alternatively, coherence theories cannot explain why our beliefs are likely to be true.

linguistic theory of the a priori the view that the a priori and necessary character of a proposition is to be explained by appeal to the meanings of the terms.

metaepistemology theories about the admissible and appropriate ways of analyzing epistemological concepts.

modest foundationalism   the view that basic beliefs are fallibly justified and that the inferential connection between basic and nonbasic beliefs may be inductive as well as deductive.

modest naturalized epistemology   the view that epistemic properties supervene on natural properties.

naïve realism   the view that under normal conditions, we directly perceive publicly accessible, independently existing physical objects. The sensible qualities of the objects are genuine qualities of the object, quite independent of our perceiving them, and under normal conditions, we are immediately justified in believing that the object is as we perceive it to be. This view is sometimes called *direct realism.*

naturalism   the view that whatever exists is natural and explicable by the natural sciences.

naturalized epistemology   the view that epistemology is continuous with science. See *modest naturalized epistemology* and *Quinean naturalized epistemology.*

necessary and sufficient conditions   A is a necessary condition of B if and only if any time we encounter B we also encounter A; we never find a B without also finding an A. A is a sufficient condition of B if and only if A is enough to bring about B.

necessary propositions   see *contingent and necessary propositions.*

neoclassical foundationalism   the view that basic beliefs are incorrigibly justified but nonbasic beliefs may be fallibly justified.

no-false-premise theories   theories of knowledge that hold that a person's justification must not contain any false, essential premises.

nondoxastic foundationalism   a type of foundationalism that holds that perceptual beliefs, for example, are basic and are justified by nondoxastic perceptual experiences. Generally, basic beliefs are justified by virtue of certain nondoxastic mental states.

phenomenalism   linguistic phenomenalism holds that talk of physical objects is merely an abbreviation for talk of sensations. Factual phenomenalism holds that there are only sensations, whether actual or possible; there are no mind-independent objects.

positive and negative coherentism   positive coherence theories hold that an agent's other beliefs must provide some positive reason for a belief. Negative coherence theories hold that an absence of undermining reasons is sufficient for justification.

Quinean naturalized epistemology   the view that epistemic properties are reducible to natural properties, that there are laws identifying epistemic and natural properties.

rationalism   the view that the justification of at least some of our beliefs about the world depends not on sense experience, but on reason. Rationalists sometimes hold that such beliefs are innate.

realism   the view that the world is mind-independent; the facts—the way the world actually is—do not depend on our beliefs.

reduction   the idea that a property or object can be identified with some other property or object without loss of explanatory power.

Regress Argument   an argument that claims that beliefs are justified only if there is adequate evidence for them. If other beliefs serve as evidence, these must also be justified. Foundationalists often count the Regress Argument as motivating foundationalism.

relational view of coherence   a theory that holds that coherence is a relation between beliefs. See *comparative reasonability*.

reliabilism   the view that a belief is justified or an instance of knowledge only if there is a reliable connection between the belief and truth.

reliable indicator theories   theories of knowledge or justified belief that hold that a belief is an instance of knowledge, or is justified, if the belief is a reliable indication of some fact or state of affairs.

reliable process theories   theories of justified belief that hold that a belief is an instance of knowledge, or is justified, if the belief is a result of a reliable belief-forming process.

representative realism   the view that sense data somehow represent the objects and that these objects are causally involved in the production in us of the sense data. This view is sometimes called *indirect realism*.

strong foundationalism   the view that basic beliefs are infallibly justified and that the inferential connection between basic and nonbasic beliefs is deductive. Neoclassical foundationalism, a variant of strong foundationalism, does not require a deductive connection between basic and nonbasic beliefs.

supervenience   a relation between properties. A property A supervenes on a property B if and only if anything that has the property B has the property A.

synthetic a priori proposition   a proposition that is necessary and known a priori, but whose truth does not depend on its constituent concepts. Exclusive propositions, mathematical propositions, and some propositions held to describe the conditions of experience are cited as examples of synthetic a priori propositions.

traditional analysis of knowledge   the view that knowledge consists of justified true belief.

virtue epistemology   the view that justification or knowledge arises as a result of certain intellectual traits; beliefs are epistemically praiseworthy only if they exhibit or manifest intellectual virtue.

Bibliography

Almeder, Robert. "On Naturalizing Epistemology." *American Philosophical Quarterly*, 27 (1990):263–279.

Almeder, Robert. *Blind Realism*. Lanham, MD: Rowman & Littlefield, 1992.

Alston, William. "An Internalist Externalism." In Alston, *Epistemic Justification*. Ithaca, NY: Cornell University Press, 1989, pp. 227–245.

Alston, William. "Concepts of Epistemic Justification." In Alston, *Epistemic Justification*. Ithaca, NY: Cornell University Press, 1989, pp. 81–114.

Alston, William. "What's Wrong with Immediate Knowledge?" In Alston *Epistemic Justification*. Ithaca, NY: Cornell University Press, 1989, pp. 57–78.

Alston, William. *Epistemic Justification*. Ithaca, NY: Cornell University Press, 1989.

Armstrong, D. M. *Belief, Truth and Knowledge*. London: Cambridge University Press, 1973.

Armstrong, D. M. "Perception and Belief." In Jonathan Dancy, ed., *Perceptual Knowledge*. Oxford: Oxford University Press, 1988, Chap. 7.

Audi, Robert. "Causalist Internalism." In Audi, *The Structure of Justification*. New York: Cambridge University Press, 1993, pp. 336–349.

Audi, Robert. "Justification, Truth, and Reliability." In Audi, *The Structure of Justification*. New York: Cambridge University Press, 1993, pp. 299–321.

Audi, Robert. *Belief, Justification, and Knowledge*. Belmont, CA: Wadsworth, 1988.

Audi, Robert. *The Structure of Justification*. New York: Cambridge University Press, 1993.

Ayer, A. J. *Language, Truth and Logic*, 2nd ed. New York: Dover, 1952.

Ayer, A. J. *The Problem of Knowledge*. Harmondsworth, England: Penguin Books, 1956.

Beauchamp, Tom L., and Alexander Rosenberg. *Hume and the Problem of Causation*. New York: Oxford University Press, 1981.

Bender, John, ed. *The Current State of Coherence Theory*. Dordrecht: Kluwer Academic Publishers, 1989.

Bender, John. "Coherence, Justification, and Knowledge: The Current Debate." In Bender, ed., *The Current State of Coherence Theory*. Dordrecht: Kluwer Academic Publishers, 1989, pp. 1–14.

Berkeley, George. *A Treatise Concerning the Principles of Human Knowledge*. Indianapolis, IN: Bobbs-Merrill, 1965.

Bloor, David. "Sociology of Knowledge." In Jonathan Dancy and Ernest Sosa, eds., *A Companion to Epistemology*. Oxford: Basil Blackwell, 1992, pp. 483–487

Bloor, David. "Strong Programme." In Jonathan Dancy and Ernest Sosa, eds., *A Companion to Epistemology*. Oxford: Basil Blackwell, 1992, p. 494.

Bloor, David. *Knowledge and Social Imagery*, 2nd ed. Chicago: University of Chicago Press, 1991.

Bogdan, Radu J. "Hume and the Problem of Local Induction." In Bogdan, ed., *Local Induction*. Dordrecht: D. Reidel, 1976, pp. 217–234.

Bogdan, Radu J., ed. *Local Induction*. Dordrecht: D. Reidel, 1976.

BonJour, Laurence. "Against Naturalized Epistemology." In Peter French et al., eds., *Midwest Studies in Philosophy*, Vol. XIX. Notre Dame, IN: University of Notre Dame Press, 1989, pp. 283–300.

BonJour, Laurence. "Externalist Theories of Empirical Knowledge." In Peter French et al., eds., *Midwest Studies in Philosophy*, Vol. V. Minneapolis: University of Minnesota Press, 1980, pp. 53–73.

BonJour, Laurence. "Replies and Clarifications." In John Bender, ed., *The Current State of Coherence Theory*. Dordrecht: Kluwer Academic Publishers, 1989, pp. 276–292.

BonJour, Laurence. *The Structure of Empirical Knowledge*. Cambridge, MA: Harvard University Press, 1985.

Campbell, Donald. "Evolutionary Epistemology." In Paul Schilpp, ed., *The Philosophy of Karl Popper*. LaSalle, IL: Open Court, 1974, pp. 413–463.

Casullo, Albert. "A Priori/A Posteriori." In Jonathan Dancy and Ernest Sosa, eds., *A Companion to Epistemology*. Oxford: Basil Blackwell, 1992, pp. 1–3.

Casullo, Albert. "A Priori Knowledge." In Jonathan Dancy and Ernest Sosa, eds., *A Companion to Epistemology*. Oxford: Basil Blackwell, 1992, pp. 3–8.

Casullo, Albert. "Kripke on the A Priori and the Necessary." In Paul Moser, ed., *A Priori Knowledge*. Oxford: Oxford University Press, 1987.

Chisholm, Roderick. *The Foundations of Knowing*. Minneapolis: University of Minnesota Press, 1982.

Chisholm, Roderick. *Theory of Knowledge*, 2nd ed. Englewood Cliffs, NJ: Prentice-Hall, 1977.

Clark, Thompson. "The Legacy of Skepticism." *Journal of Philosophy* (1972).

Cohen, Stewart. "Justification and Truth." *Philosophical Studies* 46 (1984):279–295.

Conee, Earl. "The Basic Nature of Epistemic Justification." *Monist* 71 (1988):389–404.

Conee, Earl. "Why Solve the Gettier Problem." In Paul Moser, ed., *Empirical Knowledge*. Oxford: Oxford University Press, 1987, pp. 261–265.

Copleston, S.J., Frederick. *A History of Western Philosophy*, Vol. 4. Garden City, NY: Doubleday, 1963.

Cornman, James. *Perception, Common Sense, Science*. New Haven, CT: Yale University Press, 1975.

Crumley, Jack. "Appearances Can Be Deceiving." *Philosophical Studies* 64 (1991):233–251.

Curley, E. M. *Descartes Against the Sceptics*. Cambridge, MA: Harvard University Press, 1978.

Dancy, Jonathan, and Ernest Sosa, eds. *A Companion to Epistemology*. Oxford: Basil Blackwell, 1992.

Dancy, Jonathan, ed. *Perceptual Knowledge*. Oxford: Oxford University Press, 1988.

Danto, A. C. "Naturalism." In Paul Edwards, ed., *Encyclopedia of Philosophy*. New York: Macmillan, 1967.

Davidson, Donald. "A Coherence Theory of Truth and Knowledge." In E. LePore, ed., *Truth and Interpretation*. Oxford: Basil Blackwell, 1985, pp. 307–319.

Davidson, Donald. "Empirical Content." In E. LePore, *Truth and Interpretation.* Oxford: Basil Blackwell, 1985, pp. 307–332.

Day, Timothy Joseph. "Circularity, Non-linear Justification, and Holistic Coherentism." In John Bender, ed., *The Current State of Coherence Theory.* Dordrecht: Kluwer Academic Publishers, 1989, pp. 134–141.

Descartes, René. *Meditations.* Reprinted in *The Philosophical Works of Descartes,* Vol. I. Trans. Elizabeth Haldane and G. R. T. Ross. Cambridge: Cambridge University Press, 1968, pp. 131–199.

Dicker, Georges. *Perceptual Knowledge.* Dordrecht: Kluwer Academic Publishing, 1980.

Dretske, Fred. *Knowledge and the Flow of Information.* Cambridge, MA: MIT Press, 1981.

Dretske, Fred. *Seeing and Knowing.* London: Routledge & Kegan Paul, 1969.

Everitt, Nicholas, and Alec Fisher. *Modern Epistemology: An Introduction.* New York: McGraw-Hill, 1995.

Fales, Evan. *A Defense of the Given.* Lanham, MD: Rowman & Littlefield, 1996.

Feldman, Richard, and Earl Conee. "Evidentialism." *Philosophical Studies* 48 (1985):15–34.

Feldman, Richard. "An Alleged Defect in Gettier Counterexamples." In Paul Moser, ed., *Empirical Knowledge,* 2nd ed. Lanham, MD: Rowman & Littlefield, 1996, pp. 241–243.

Feldman, Richard. "Epistemic Obligation." In James Tomberlin, ed., *Philosophical Perspectives, 2, Epistemology.* Atascadero, CA: Ridgeview Press, 1988, pp. 240–256.

Feldman, Richard. "Reliability and Justification." *Monist* 68 (1985):159–174.

Foley, Richard. "What's Wrong with Reliabilism?" *Monist* 68 (1985):188–202.

Foley, Richard. *Working Without a Net.* Oxford: Oxford University Press, 1993.

Frankfurt, Harry G. *Demons, Dreamers, and Madmen.* Indianapolis, IN: Bobbs-Merrill, 1970.

Frankfurt, Harry G., ed. *Leibniz: A Collection of Critical Essays.* Garden City, NY: Anchor, 1972.

French, Peter, et al., eds. *Midwest Studies in Philosophy,* Vol. V. Minneapolis: University of Minnesota Press, 1980.

French, Peter, et al., eds. *Midwest Studies in Philosophy,* Vol. XIII. Notre Dame: University of Notre Dame Press, 1989.

French, Peter, et al., eds. *Midwest Studies in Philosophy,* Vol. XIX. Notre Dame: University of Notre Dame Press, 1994.

Fumerton, Richard. *Metaepistemology and Skepticism.* Lanham, MD: Rowman & Littlefield, 1995.

Fumerton, Richard. *Metaphysical and Epistemological Problems of Perception.* Lincoln: University of Nebraska Press, 1985.

Gibson, Roger. *Enlightened Empiricism.* Tampa: University of Florida Press, 1988.

Goldman, Alan. *Empirical Knowledge.* Berkeley: University of California Press, 1988.

Goldman, Alvin "What Is Justified Belief?" In Hilary Kornblith, ed., *Naturalizing Epistemology,* Cambridge, MA: MIT Press, 1987, pp. 91–113.

Goldman, Alvin. "A Causal Theory of Knowing." In Michael D. Roth and Leon Galis, eds., *Knowing: Essays on the Analysis of Knowledge.* New York: Random House, 1970, pp. 67–87.

Goldman, Alvin. "Discrimination and Perceptual Knowledge." *Journal of Philosophy* 73 (1976):771–779.

Goldman, Alvin. "Epistemic Folkways and Scientific Epistemology." In Paul Moser, ed., *Empirical Knowledge,* 2nd ed. Lanham, MD: Rowman & Littlefield, 1996, pp. 423–446.

Goldman, Alvin. "Reliabilism." In Jonathan Dancy and Ernest Sosa, eds., *A Companion to Epistemology.* Oxford: Basil Blackwell, 1992, pp. 433–436.

Goldman, Alvin. "Strong and Weak Justification." In James Tomberlin, ed., *Philosophical Perspectives, 2, Epistemology.* Atascadero, CA: Ridgeview Press, 1988, p. 62.

Goldman, Alvin. *Epistemology and Cognition.* Cambridge, MA: Harvard University Press, 1986.

Gosling, J .C. B. *Plato: The Arguments of the Philosophers.* London: Routledge & Kegan Paul, 1973.

Grice, H. P., and P. F. Strawson. "In Defense of a Dogma." In James F. Harris and Richard H. Severens, eds., *Analyticity.* Chicago: Quadrangle Books, 1970, pp. 56–74.

Haack, Susan. *Evidence and Inquiry: Towards Reconstruction in Epistemology.* Oxford: Basil Blackwell, 1993.

Hamlyn, D. W. *The Theory of Knowledge.* London: Macmillan, 1970.

Hardin, C. L. *Color for Philosophers.* Indianapolis, IN: Hackett, 1986.

Harman, Gilbert. *Thought.* Princeton, NJ: Princeton University Press, 1973.

Harris, James F., and Richard H. Severens, eds. *Analyticity.* Chicago: Quadrangle Books, 1970.

Harrison, Jonathan. "Does Knowing Imply Believing?" In Michael D. Roth and Leon Galis, eds., *Knowing: Essays on the Analysis of Knowledge.* New York: Random House, 1970, pp. 155–170.

Hazen, Robert M., and James Trefil. *Science Matters.* New York: Doubleday, 1991.

Heil, John. "Perceptual Experience." In Brian McLaughlin, ed., *Dretske and His Critics.* Oxford: Basil Blackwell, 1991, pp.1–16.

Holland, John H., et al., *Induction.* Cambridge, MA: MIT Press, 1986.

Hookway, Christopher. *Skepticism.* London: Routledge & Kegan Paul, 1990.

Horgan, Terence, ed. "Supervenience." *Southern Journal of Philosophy,* 22, Supplement (1983).

Horwich, Paul. "Theories of Truth." In Jonathan Dancy and Ernest Sosa, eds., *A Companion to Epistemology.* Oxford: Basil Blackwell, 1992.

Hume, David. *An Enquiry Concerning Human Understanding,* 3rd ed. Ed. L. A. Selby-Bigge, rev. by P. H. Nidditch. Oxford: Clarendon Press, 1975.

Hume, David. *A Treatise of Human Nature,* 2nd ed. Ed. L. A. Selby-Bigge, rev. by P. H. Nidditch. Oxford: Clarendon Press, 1978.

Jackson, Frank. "Knowledge of the External World." In G. H. R. Parkinson, ed., *The Handbook of Western Philosophy.* New York: Macmillan, 1988, pp. 140–158.

Johnson, Oliver. "The Standard Definition." In Peter French, et al., eds., *Midwest Studies in Philosophy*, Vol. V. pp. 113–126 .

Kant, Immanuel. *Critique of Pure Reason.* Trans. Norman Kemp Smith. New York: St. Martin's Press, 1965.

Kaplan, Mark. "It's Not What You Know That Counts." *Journal of Philosophy* 82 (1985):350–363.

Kemp-Smith, Norman. *The Philosophy of David Hume.* London: Macmillan, 1941.

Kim, Jaegwon. "What Is 'Naturalized Epistemology'?" In James Tomberlin, ed., *Philosophical Perspectives, 2, Epistemology.* Atascadero, CA: Ridgeview Press, 1988, pp. 381–405.

Kim, Jaegwon. *Supervenience and the Mind.* New York: Cambridge University Press, 1993.

Kim, Jaegwon. "Concepts of Supervenience." *Philosophy and Phenomenological Research* 65 (1984):257–270.

Kitcher, Philip. "A Priori Knowledge." In Hilary Kornblith, ed., *Naturalizing Epistemology.* Cambridge, MA: MIT Press, 1987, pp. 129–145.

Kitcher, Philip. "Analyticity and Apriority." In Paul Moser, ed., *A Priori Knowledge.* Oxford: Oxford University Press, 1987, pp. 85–111.

Kitcher, Philip. "Apriority and Necessity." In Paul Moser, ed., *A Priori Knowledge.* Oxford: Oxford University Press, 1987, pp. 190–207.

Kitcher, Philip. "The Naturalists Return." *Philosophical Review* 101 (1992):53–114.

Klee, Robert. *Introduction to the Philosophy of Science: Cutting Nature at Its Seams.* New York: Oxford University Press, 1997.

Koriat, Asher. "How Do We Know That We Know? The Accessibility Model of the Feeling of Knowing." *Psychological Review* 100 (1993):609–639.

Kornblith, Hilary, ed. *Naturalizing Epistemology.* Cambridge, MA: MIT Press, 1987.

Kornblith, Hilary. "How Internal Can You Get?" *Synthese* 73 (1988):27–41.

Kornblith, Hilary. "Introduction: What Is Naturalistic Epistemology?" In Kornblith, ed., *Naturalizing Epistemology.* Cambridge, MA: MIT Press, 1987, pp. 1–13.

Kornblith, Hilary. "Justified Belief and Epistemically Responsible Action." *Philosophical Review* 92 (1983):33–48.

Kornblith, Hilary. "Naturalism: Both Metaphysical and Epistemological." In Peter A. French, et al., eds., *Midwest Studies in Philosophy*, Vol. XIX. Notre Dame, IN: Notre Dame University Press, 1994, pp. 39–52.

Kornblith, Hilary. "The Unattainability of Coherence." In John Bender, ed., *The Current State of Coherence Theory.* Dordrecht: Kluwer Academic Publishers, 1989, pp. 207–214.

Kripke, Saul. *Naming and Necessity.* Cambridge, MA: Harvard University Press, 1980.

Laudan, Larry. *Science and Values.* Berkeley: University of California Press, 1982.

Lehrer, Keith. "Knowledge, Truth, and Evidence." In Michael D. Roth and Leon Galis, eds., *Knowing: Essays on the Analysis of Knowledge.* New York: Random House, 1990, pp. 55–66.

Lehrer, Keith. "Reply to My Critics." In John Bender, ed., *The Current State of Coherence Theory.* Dordrecht: Kluwer Academic Publishers, 1989.

Lehrer, Keith. *Knowledge*. Oxford: Oxford University Press, 1974.

Lehrer, Keith. *Self-Trust: A Study of Reason, Knowledge, and Autonomy*. Oxford: Oxford University Press, 1997.

Lehrer, Keith. *Theory of Knowledge*. Boulder, CO: Westview Press, 1990.

Leibniz, Gottfried. *Monadology*. Reprinted in Leroy E. Loemaker, ed., *Philosophical Papers and Letters*. Dordrecht: D. Reidel, 1969.

LePore, Ernest, ed. *Truth and Interpretation: Perspectives on the Philosophy of Donald Davidson*. Oxford: Basil Blackwell, 1985.

Linsky, Leonard. *Names and Descriptions*. Chicago: University of Chicago Press, 1977.

Locke, John. *An Essay Concerning Human Understanding*. Oxford: Clarendon Press, 1975.

Luper-Foy, Steven, ed. *The Possibility of Knowledge*. Totowa, NJ: Rowman & Littlefield, 1987.

Luper-Foy, Steven. "The Reliabilist Theory of Rational Belief." *Monist* 68 (1985).

Lyons, William. *The Disappearance of Introspection*. Cambridge, MA: MIT Press, 1986.

Maclahlan, D. L. C. *The Philosophy of Perception*. Englewood Cliffs, NJ: Prentice-Hall, 1989.

Maffie, James. "Recent Work on Naturalized Epistemology." *American Philosophical Quarterly* 27 (1990):281–293.

Mandler, George. "Memory: Conscious and Unconscious" In P. R. Soloman, et al., eds., *Memory: Interdisciplinary Approaches*. New York: Springer-Verlag, 1989, pp. 84–106.

McGrew, Timothy, J. *The Foundations of Knowledge*. Lanham, MD: Littlefield Adams, 1995.

Meyers, Robert G. *The Likelihood of Knowledge*. Dordrecht: Kluwer Academic Publishers, 1988.

Moser, Paul, ed. *A Priori Knowledge*. Oxford: Oxford University Press, 1987.

Moser, Paul, ed. *Empirical Knowledge*, 2nd ed. Lanham, MD: Rowman & Littlefield, 1996.

Norton Nelkin, "How Sensations Get Their Names." *Philosophical Studies* 51 (1987):325–339.

Pappas, George, and Marshall Swain, eds., *Essays on Knowledge and Justification*. Ithaca, NY: Cornell University Press, 1978.

Parkinson, G. H. R., ed. *The Handbook of Western Philosophy*. New York: Macmillan, 1988.

Penelhum, Terence, and J. J. MacIntosh, eds., *The First Critique: Reflections on Kant's Critique of Pure Reason*. Belmont, CA: Wadsworth, 1969.

Pollock, John. *Contemporary Theories of Knowledge*. Totowa: Rowan & Littlefield, 1986.

Popkin, Richard H. *The History of Skepticism from Erasmus to Spinoza*. Berkeley and Los Angeles: University of California Press, 1979.

Putnam, Hilary. "Why Reason Can't Be Naturalized?" In Putnam, *Realism and Reason: Philosophical Papers*, Vol. 3. Cambridge: Cambridge University Press, 1983, pp. 229–247.

Putnam, Hilary. *Realism and Reason: Philosophical Papers*, Vol. 3. Cambridge: Cambridge University Press, 1983.

Putnam, Hilary. *Reason, Truth and History*. Cambridge: Cambridge University Press, 1981.

Quine, W. V. O. "Carnap and Logical Truth." In Quine, *The Ways of Paradox*. Cambridge, MA: Harvard University Press, 1976, pp. 107–132.

Quine, W. V. O. "Epistemology Naturalized." In Hilary Kornblith, ed., *Naturalizing Epistemology*. Cambridge, MA: MIT Press, 1987, pp. 1–29.

Quine, W. V. O. "Natural Kinds." In Hilary Kornblith, ed., *Naturalizing Epistemology*. Cambridge, MA: MIT Press, 1987, pp. 31–47.

Quine, W. V. O. "Reply to Morton White." In L. E. Hahn and P. A. Schilpp, eds., *The Philosophy of W. V. O. Quine*. LaSalle, IL: Open Court, 1986, p. 665.

Quine, W. V. O. "The Nature of Natural Knowledge." In Samuel Guttenplan, ed., *Mind and Language*. Oxford: Oxford University Press, 1975, pp. 67–81.

Quine, W. V. O. "Things and Their Place in Theories." In Quine, *Theories and Things*. Cambridge, MA: Belknap Press, 1981, p. 22.

Quine, W. V. O. "Truth by Convention." In Quine, *The Ways of Paradox*. Cambridge, MA: Harvard University Press, 1976, pp. 77–106.

Quine, W. V. O. "Two Dogmas of Empiricism." In Quine, *From a Logical Point of View*, 2nd ed. New York: Harper, 1961, pp. 20–46.

Quine, W. V. O. *From a Logical Point of View*, 2nd ed. New York: Harper, 1961.

Quine, W. V. O. *Roots of Reference*. LaSalle, IL: Open Court, 1986.

Quine, W. V. O. *The Pursuit of Truth*. Cambridge, MA: Harvard University Press, 1990.

Quine, W. V. O. *The Ways of Paradox*. Cambridge, MA: Harvard University Press, 1976.

Radford, Colin. "Knowledge by Examples." In Michael D. Roth and Leon Galis, eds., *Knowing: Essays on the Analysis of Knowledge*. New York: Random House, 1970, pp. 171–185.

Rescher, Nicholas, ed. *Evolution, Cognition and Realism*. Lanham, MD: University Press of America, 1990.

Robinson, Howard. *Perception*. London: Routledge, 1994.

Rorty, Richard. "World Well Lost." In Rorty, *Consequences of Pragmatism*. Minneapolis: University of Minnesota Press, 1982, pp. 3–18.

Roth, Michael D., and Leon Galis, eds., *Knowing: Essays on the Analysis of Knowledge*. New York: Random House, 1970.

Ruse, M. *Taking Darwin Seriously*. Oxford: Basil Blackwell, 1986.

Russell, Bertrand. *The Problems of Philosophy*. London: Oxford University Press, 1959. (Originally published 1912.)

Schilpp, Paul, ed. *The Philosophy of Karl Popper*. LaSalle, IL: Open Court, 1974.

Schmitt, Frederick F. *Truth: A Primer*. Boulder, CO: Westview Press, 1995.

Schmitt, Frederick F. "Justification as Reliable Indication or Reliable Process?" *Philosophical Studies* 40 (1981):409–417.

Schmitt, Frederick F. *Knowledge and Belief*. London: Routledge, 1990.

Shope, Robert K. *The Analysis of Knowing: A Decade of Research*. Princeton, NJ: Princeton University Press, 1983.

Soloman, P. R., et al., eds. *Memory: Interdisciplinary Approaches.* New York: Springer-Verlag, 1989.

Sosa, Ernest. "Methodology and Apt Belief." In Sosa, *Knowledge in Perspective.* Cambridge: Cambridge University Press, 1991, pp. 245–246.

Sosa, Ernest. *Knowledge in Perspective.* Cambridge: Cambridge University Press, 1991.

Stein, Edward. *Without Good Reason: The Rationality Debate in Philosophy and Cognitive Science.* Oxford: Clarendon Press, 1997.

Stich, Stephen. "Could Man Be an Irrational Animal?" In Hilary Kornblith, ed., *Naturalizing Epistemology.* Cambridge, MA: MIT Press, 1987, pp. 257–258.

Stich, Stephen. *The Fragmentation of Reason.* Cambridge, MA: MIT Press, 1990.

Strawson, P. F. *Introduction to Logical Theory.* London: Methuen, 1952.

Strawson, P. F. *Skepticism and Naturalism: Some Varieties.* New York: Columbia University Press, 1983.

Stroll, Avrum. "What Water Is: Or Back to Thales." In Peter A. French, et al., eds., *Midwest Studies in Philosophy*, Vol. XIII. Notre Dame: University of Notre Dame Press, 1989, pp. 258–274.

Stroud, Barry. "Transcendental Arguments." In Terence Penelhum and J. J. MacIntosh, eds., *The First Critique: Reflections on Kant's Critique of Pure Reason.* Belmont, CA: Wadsworth, 1969, pp. 54–69.

Stroud, Barry. *Hume.* London: Routledge & Kegan Paul, 1977.

Stroud, Barry. *The Philosophical Significance of Skepticism.* Oxford: Clarendon Press, 1984.

Swain, Marshall. *Reasons and Knowledge.* Ithaca, NY: Cornell University Press, 1981.

Swain, Marshall. "Epistemic Defeasibility." In George Pappas and Marshall Swain, eds., *Essays on Knowledge and Justification.* Ithaca, NY: Cornell University Press, 1978, pp. 160–183.

Taylor, A. E. *Plato, the Man and His Work.* London: Methuen, 1926.

Teller, Paul. "Comments on Kim's Paper." *The Southern Journal of Philosophy* 22, Supplement (1983):57–61.

Thagard, Paul. *Conceptual Revolutions.* Princeton, NJ: Princeton University Press, 1992.

Tomberlin, James, ed. *Philosophical Perspectives, 2, Epistemology.* Atascadero, CA: Ridgeview Press, 1988.

van Cleve, James. "Epistemic Supervenience and the Circle of Belief." *Monist* 68 (1985):90–104.

Wagner, Richard, and Steven Warner, eds. *Naturalism: A Critical Appraisal.* Notre Dame, IN: University of Notre Dame Press, 1993.

Weiskrantz, Larry. *Blindsight.* Oxford: Oxford University Press, 1986.

White, Nicholas. *Plato on Knowledge and Reality.* Indianapolis, IN: Hackett, 1976.

Williams, Michael. *Unnatural Doubts.* Oxford: Blackwell, 1991.

Wilson, Margaret D. "On Leibniz's Explication of 'Necessary Truth.' " In Harry G. Frankfurt, ed., *Leibniz: A Collection of Critical Essays.* Garden City, NY: Anchor, 1972, pp. 401–419.

Wilson, Margaret D. *Descartes.* London: Routledge & Kegan Paul, 1978.

Wright, J. P. *The Sceptical Realism of David Hume.* Minneapolis: University of Minnesota Press, 1983.

Zagzebski, Linda. *Virtues of the Mind: An Inquiry into the Nature of Virtue and the Ethical Foundations of Knowledge.* New York: Cambridge University Press, 1996.

Index